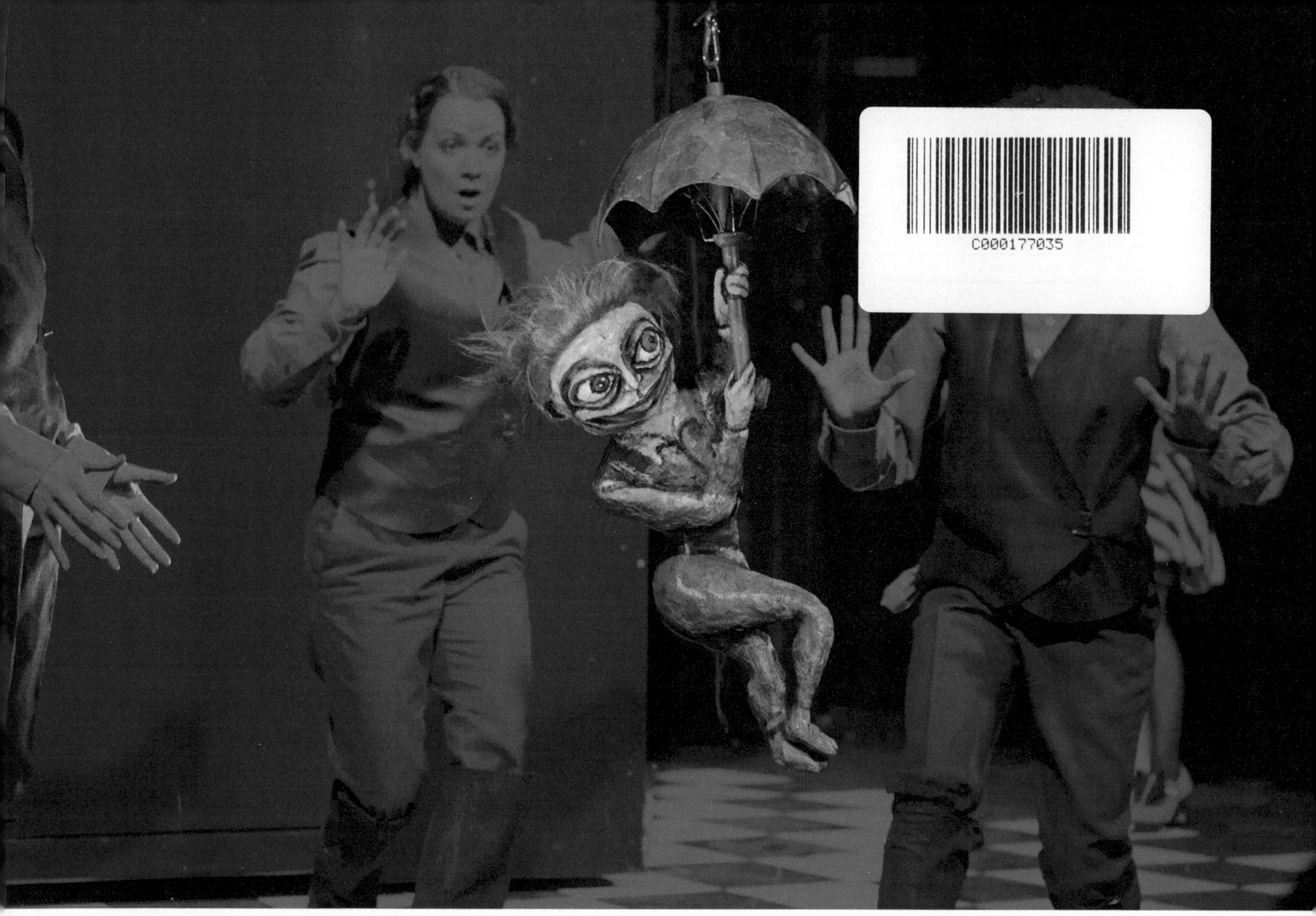

C000177035

AQA GCSE Drama

Revised Edition

Published in 2021 by Illuminate Publishing Limited, an imprint of Hodder Education, an Hachette UK Company, Carmelite House, 50 Victoria Embankment, London EC4Y 0DZ

Orders: Please visit www.illuminatepublishing.com or email sales@illuminatepublishing.com

British Library Cataloguing-in-Publication Data

A catalogue record for this book is available from the British Library.

ISBN 978-1-912820-50-4

Printed by: Ashford Colour Press, UK

08.22

The publishers' policy is to use papers that are natural, renewable and recyclable products made from wood grown in sustainable forests. The logging and manufacturing processes are expected to conform to the environmental regulations of the country of origin.

Editor: Roanne Charles, abc Editorial
Design and layout: emc design ltd
Cover design: Nigel Harriss
Cover photograph: Paul Fox

Text acknowledgements

p10: Extract from ***A View from the Bridge***, Copyright © A VIEW FROM THE BRIDGE, Arthur Miller, 1983, 1985, 1988, used by permission of The Wylie Agency (UK) Limited; Extracts from ***The Crucible***, Copyright © THE CRUCIBLE, Arthur Miller, 1952, 1953, used by permission of The Wylie Agency (UK) Limited. p190: Extract from 'Review of Denise Gough in ***People, Places & Things***' by Susannah Clapp, 6 September 2015, ***The Observer***, Copyright © Guardian News & Media Ltd 2020. p190: Extract from 'Review of Chiwetel Ejiofor in First Night: ***Othello***, Donmar Warehouse, London' by Paul Taylor, 4 December 2007, ***The Independent***, © Paul Taylor / The Independent. p190: Extract from 'Review of Daniel Radcliffe in ***Equus***' by Charles Spencer, 28 February 2007, ***The Telegraph***, © Charles Spencer / Telegraph Media Group Limited 2007. p209: ***'What if?'*** by Lemn Sissay, reprinted by kind permission of Canongate Books, © Lemn Sissay, 2016. p240: Extract from ***Citizenship*** by Mark Ravenhill, © Mark Ravenhill, 2006, 2015, Methuen Drama, an imprint of Bloomsbury Publishing Plc. pp241 and 263: Extracts from ***The Trial*** by Steven Berkoff, © Steven Berkoff 1981, originally published by Amber Lane Press Ltd. pp257 and 267: Extracts from ***Kindertransport*** by Diane Samuels, © 1995, 1996, 2008 Diane Samuels, reproduced with permission from Nick Hern Books: www.nickernbooks.co.uk. p271: Extract from 'The Golden Goose' from ***Collected Grimm Tales*** by Carol Ann Duffy. Published by Faber & Faber. Copyright © Carol Ann Duffy. Reproduced by permission of the author c/o Rogers, Coleridge & White Ltd., 20 Powis Mews, London W11 1JN.

Other extracts in this book are taken from:

A Raisin in the Sun by Lorraine Hansberry, Plume
Around the World in 80 Days by Jules Verne, adapted by Laura Eason, Nick Hern Modern Plays
A Taste of Honey by Shelagh Delaney, Methuen Drama
Blood Brothers by Willy Russell, Methuen Modern Classics
Macbeth by William Shakespeare, Oxford School Shakespeare
Noughts & Crosses by Malorie Blackman, adapted by Dominic Cooke, Nick Hern Modern Plays
Romeo and Juliet by William Shakespeare, Palgrave Macmillan
Tastes of Honey by Selina Todd, Chatto & Windus
The Crucible by Arthur Miller – A Bristol Old Vic Production Directed by Tom Morris – Education Pack
The Importance of Being Earnest by Oscar Wilde, Penguin Plays
The Play of George Orwell's Animal Farm, adapted by Peter Hall, Heinemann
Things I Know to be True by Andrew Bovell, Nick Hern Modern Plays
Things I Know to be True by Andrew Bovell: A Comprehensive Guide for students (aged 14+), teachers & arts educationalists, Written by Scott Graham, with contributions from the creative team, Compiled by Frantic Assembly.

This textbook has been approved by AQA for use with our qualification. This means that we have checked that it broadly covers the specification and we are satisfied with the overall quality. Full details or our approval process can be found on our website.

We approve textbooks because we know how important it is for teachers and students to have the right resources to support their teaching and learning. Please note, however, that the publisher is ultimately responsible for the editorial control and quality of this book.

Please note that when teaching the AQA GCSE Drama (8261) course, you must refer to AQA's specification as your definitive source of information. While this book has been written to match the specification, it cannot provide complete coverage of every aspect of the course.

A wide range of other useful resources can be found on the relevant subject pages of our website: www.aqa.org.uk

CONTENTS

Acknowledgements

The author would like to thank the following theatre makers for their generous help in the preparation of this book: Jonathan Brody, Jordan Castle, Peter Forbes, Kerry Frampton, Nikki Gunson, Alex Harland, Mark Hutchinson, Gavin Maze, Baker Mukasa, Max Perryment, Tim Shortall, Alice Smith and Zőe Wilson. Thanks also to Rachel Izen for her introductions to two of our theatre makers.

Image acknowledgements

pp10, **11**, **99** (top) and **141** (top) public domain; **p14** (top) © Joan Marcus, (bottom) Jan Versweyveld; **p18** (top) © Simon Mayew, (bottom) Zoë Wilson; **pp20–24**, **45**, **67** (top), **118**, **137**, **138**, **195** (top) and **261** emc Design Ltd; **p29** (bottom) courtesy Pearson Scott Foresman; **p30** (centre) INTERFOTO / Alamy Stock Photo; **p32** (centre) Stephen Dorey / Alamy Stock Photo, (bottom) Alamy Classic Image / Alamy Stock photo; **p33** (bottom) Creative Commons; **pp50**, **57** (right) and **161** (bottom) Trinity Mirror / Mirrorpix / Alamy Stock Photo; **p56** Heritage Image Partnership Ltd / Alamy Stock Photo; **p57** (left) © Van Dyke; **p72** William Robinson / Alamy Stock Photo; **p76** (Crewdson) dpa picture alliance archive / Alamy Stock Photo; **p83** (centre) Columbia / AA Film Archive / Alamy Stock Photo, (top right) Moviestore Collection Ltd / Alamy Stock Photo; **p88** Michael Brosilow, Manuel Harlan; **p95** Alphonse de Neuville and Léon Benett; **p97** United Artists; **p98** (bottom) Chronicle / Alamy Stock Photo, Granger Historical Picture Archive / Alamy Stock Photo; **p99** (left) United States Library of Congress's Prints and Photographs division, (bottom right) Image Professionals GmbH / Alamy Stock Photo; **p100** Walker Art Library / Alamy Stock Photo, Amoret Tanner / Alamy Stock Photo; **p102** (top) Chronicle / Alamy Stock Photo; **pp105** and **111** (bottom) Andrew Billington; **p111** (top) Robert Day; **p117** Manuel Harlan / Circus 1903; **pp122** and **187** (bottom) © Brinkhoff Mögenburg; **pp126** and **153** (bottom) Geraint Lewis / Alamy Stock Photo; **p134** (bottom) © Alice Philipson; **p140** (top) 20th Century Fox / PictureLux / The Hollywood Archive / Alamy Stock Photo, (bottom) BHE Films / Photo 12 / Alamy Stock Photo; **p142** Jacopo Bassano / Kimbell Art Museum, Giovanni Battista Moroni / Liechenstein Museum, Giovanni Battista Moroni / National Gallery; **p146** Matt Kizer; **p147** Echo Lake Entertainment / Swarovski Entertainment; **p153** (top) Bavarian State Library; **p154** John Gilbert / Dalziel Brothers; **p158** Lebrecht Music & Arts / Alamy Stock Photo; **p161** (top) PA Images / Alamy Stock Photo; **p162** Peter Barritt / Alamy Stock Photo; **p163** (top) David Colbran / Alamy Stock Photo, (bottom left and centre) Allan Cash Picture Library / Alamy Stock Photo, (bottom right) Tony Henshaw / Alamy Stock Photo; **pp164** (left) and **176** (bottom) Russ Rowland; **p164** (right) Buttrick; **p166** Brenda Kean / Alamy Stock Photo; **p170** BFI; **pp176** (top) and **178** Marc Brenner; **p176** (bottom) Russ Rowland; **pp185** and **223** (bottom) © Greg Veit; **p187** (top) © Alastair Muir; **pp188** (top three), **192**, **195** (bottom three), **216**, **217** (top), **231**, **247** (bottom), **254** (bottom), **257**, **263** and **269** (top) © Paul Fox; **p201** Vibrant Pictures / Alamy Stock Photo; **pp204**, **208**, **210**, **217** (bottom), **221**, **222**, **227**, **232**, **234** and **241** Splendid Productions; **p209** Chris Bull / Alamy Stock Photo; **p211** (top) dpa picture alliance / Alamy Stock Photo; **p212** (top) Slumdog Millionaire, dir. Danny Boyle [DVD], 2008, Celador Films, Channel 4 and Twentieth Century Fox; (bottom) © Yinka Shonibare / Victoria and Albert Museum; **p214** Chronicle / Alamy Stock Photo, Jeffrey Blackler / Alamy Stock Photo; **p223** (top and centre) © Brian Roberts; **p238** Nir Alon / Alamy Stock Photo; **p244** Cedarville University; **pp247** (top) and **248–250** © Clare Park; **pp252**, **254** (centre) and **255** Gavin Maze; **pp256**, **258** and **259** © Dan Court; **p262** © Tim Shortall; **p267** Pinterest; **p269** (bottom) © Sharronwallace.com; **pp270–272** Nikki Gunson.

All other images: **Shutterstock**:
pp5 and **6** Pavel L Photo and Video; **pp15** and **229** Meilun; **p16** (middle) Khakimullin Aleksandr, (bottom) aerogondo2; **p17** NY Studio; **pp28**, **29** (top), **30** (bottom left), **33** (top), **83** (left), **145** and **213** Everett Collection; **p30** (top left) Chris Peterson, (top right) littleny, (bottom right) patrimonio designs ltd; **p32** (top) Morphart Creation; **p48** (top to bottom) (top three) Monkey Business Images, Joana Lopes, stockyimages, Dragon Images, Ashwin, Kdonmuang; **p51** Shaun Jeffers; **p52** (top two) chrisdorney, (third) Jason Wells, (bottom) kenny1; **p54** kenny1, seehooteatrepeat / Shutterstock.com; **p55** V.Kuntsman; **p60** Aratemida-psy, Marbury; **p70** (bottom) Fer Gregory; **p73** Luzhbin Aleks; **p74** amophoto_au; **p75** CMYK, gmstockstudio, Serban Bogdan; **p76** (top) Anthony Cottrell, (right) Markus J, Elena Elisseeva, Sam Wordley, amophoto_au, bmphotographer; **p78** LIGHTITUP; **p80** jackmazur; **p82** Mladen Mitrinovic, Clara/Shutterstock.com; **p83** (bottom) Elzbieta Krzysztof / Shutterstock.com; **p96** Joyce Nelson / Shutterstock.com; **p98** (top) Marusya Chaika; **p102** (bottom) PinkyWinky; **p104** Rod Zadeh, Lois GoBe; **p113** Tukaram.Karve / Shutterstock.com; **p114** Roman Tiraspolsky; **p115** (bottom) Jim Byrne Scotland; **p134** (top) Oleksandr Berezko; **p139** Giambattista Lazazzera / Shutterstock.com; **p140** (centre) Muzhik; **p141** (bottom) Alberto Masnovo, Dmitriy Feldman svarshik / Shutterstock.com, Love Lego; **p156** rawf8; **p157** (top) Damiano Buffo / Shutterstock.com; **p167** (left and centre) Gaianami Design, (right) Hannahs Treasures; **p168** ingenium, Mark Yuill; **p179** (top) JasminkaM; **p183** aerogondo2; **p188** (bottom) ostill, Darrin Henry, pathdoc, Ozgur Coskun; **p211** (bottom) Inga Nielsen; **p224** Norman Chan, fotogestoeber, Guzel Studio, Dmitry Kolmankov, passion artist, pavila; **pp225** and **266** Rawpixel.com; **p236** fizkes; **p251** ID1974, Elnur; **p253** FrameAngel, StudioADFX, Epitavi; **p254** (top) Andrii Zhezhera; **p273** Kdonmuang.

INTRODUCTION TO GCSE DRAMA

How to get the most out of Drama

Drama is an exciting subject that uses your knowledge, talent and imagination. Throughout the course there will be opportunities to act, devise, design, review and analyse. It is a creative subject that will give you the chance to employ a wide variety of skills and test your abilities. You may explore an idea or interpretation, try it out practically and then evaluate how well it worked. You will learn not only from your teacher, but also from your fellow students, as you work together to achieve a devised or scripted production. It is an active course where you will not only be up and doing, but also one where you must be able to reflect on your work and the work of others.

At the beginning of the course, you will probably not feel equally confident in all of these areas – very few people do. You will have the chance to learn and grow in these skills, however. At times, you may make choices in order to play to your strengths. For example, you may choose to perform or design for Component 2 Devising Drama and Component 3 Texts in Practice. However, do be open to trying new skills – you may discover talents you didn't know you had.

Understanding

By reading and through practical tasks, you will become familiar with several plays. You will study a set play for Component 1, Section B and will work practically on a contrasting play for Component 3. You will also view and analyse a production of a third play for Component 1, Section C. This will expose you to different periods or types of dramatic literature and you will learn how theatre is created.

Creativity

One of the pleasures of Drama is that you have the opportunity to express your own ideas, thoughts and interpretations. In Drama there can be many different 'right' answers.

Responsibility

Drama requires self-discipline. You need to be an active, trustworthy group member. You will need to be on time, meet deadlines and fulfil your responsibilities.

Making connections

Although the course is divided into three components, there is a great deal of crossover between the skills in each one. When you review a professional actor's performance, this can aid your understanding and development of your own acting. When you notice a technique used in a set text, you may want to recreate that in your devising. Build on the skills you are learning to enrich your work in each component.

▲ *The choice of colour and fabric is an important element of costume design.*

Course outline and how you will be assessed

COMPONENT 1 UNDERSTANDING DRAMA (WRITTEN EXAMINATION)	COMPONENT 2 DEVISING DRAMA (PRACTICAL AND DEVISING LOG)	COMPONENT 3 TEXTS IN PRACTICE (PRACTICAL)
What is assessed	**What is assessed**	**What is assessed**
• Knowledge and understanding of drama and theatre • Study of one set play from a choice of seven • Analysis and evaluation of the work of live theatre makers.	• Process of creating devised drama • Performance of devised drama (students may contribute as performer or designer) • Analysis and evaluation of own work.	Performance of two extracts from one play (students may contribute as performer or designer). Free choice of play but it must contrast with the set play chosen for Component 1.
How it is assessed	**How it is assessed**	**How it is assessed**
Written exam: • 1 hour and 45 minutes • Open book (clean book, no annotations in it). 80 marks in total. 40% of GCSE. This component is marked by AQA examiners. • Section A: Theatre roles and terminology: multiple choice (4 marks) • Section B: Study of a set play: four questions on a given extract from the set play chosen (44 marks) • Section C: Live theatre production: one question (from a choice) on the work of theatre makers in a single live theatre production (32 marks).	• Devising log (60 marks) • Devised performance (20 marks). 80 marks in total. 40% of GCSE. This component is marked by teachers and moderated by AQA.	• Performance of Extract 1 (20 marks) • Performance of Extract 2 (20 marks). 40 marks in total. 20% of GCSE. This component is marked by a visiting AQA examiner.

TIP

It is very possible that you will not study the components in the order given above. However, keep looking for opportunities to apply the learning gained in one component to another.

Actors rehearsing in a proscenium theatre

How to get the best out of this book

The book is arranged to cover each of the assessed components of the course:

- Component 1 Understanding Drama (divided into three sections)
- Component 2 Devising Drama
- Component 3 Texts in Practice.

This book isn't designed to be read from cover to cover, but for you to use the sections which apply to the texts you are studying or the skills you are developing. In order to help you get the most from it, we have created some special features:

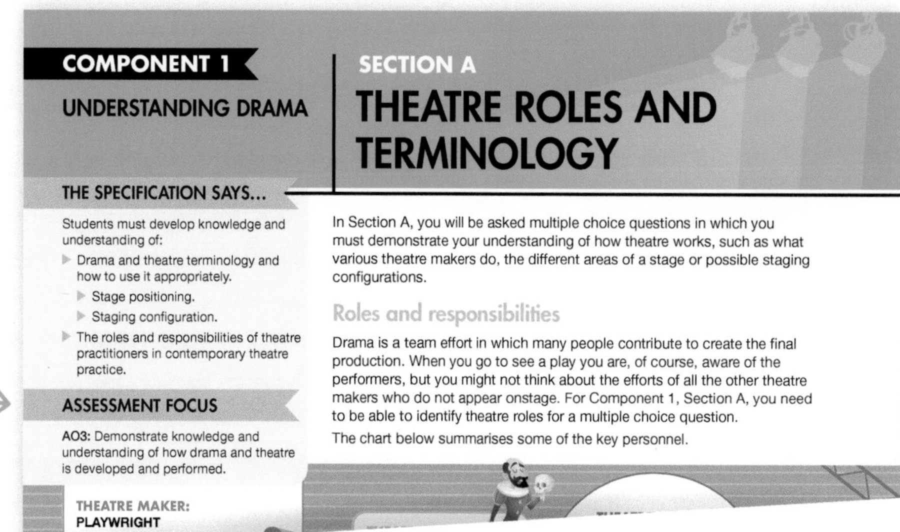

COMPONENT 1

UNDERSTANDING DRAMA

SECTION A

THEATRE ROLES AND TERMINOLOGY

THE SPECIFICATION SAYS...

Students must develop knowledge and understanding of:

- Drama and theatre terminology and how to use it appropriately.
  - Stage positioning.
  - Staging configuration.
- The roles and responsibilities of theatre practitioners in contemporary theatre practice.

ASSESSMENT FOCUS

AO3: Demonstrate knowledge and understanding of how drama and theatre is developed and performed.

THEATRE MAKER:
PLAYWRIGHT

In Section A, you will be asked multiple choice questions in which you must demonstrate your understanding of how theatre works, such as what various theatre makers do, the different areas of a stage or possible staging configurations.

Roles and responsibilities

Drama is a team effort in which many people contribute to create the final production. When you go to see a play you are, of course, aware of the performers, but you might not think about the efforts of all the other theatre makers who do not appear onstage. For Component 1, Section A, you need to be able to identify theatre roles for a multiple choice question.

The chart below summarises some of the key personnel.

ASSESSMENT FOCUS: these panels will remind you of the assessment objectives that underpin the specification itself and how they are covered in each section.

PRACTICE QUESTIONS: there are examples of practice questions so that you can become familiar with the type of questions you will be asked and can practise answering.

SAMPLE RESPONSES: these are samples of a typical student's work Some of them have comments to indicate how the responses demonstrate various skills.

SET PLAY 4: *Around the World in 80 Days* by Jules Verne, adapted by Laura Eason 4

In Question 2, you will discuss in detail how you would perform a particular line as a given character. For example (in Act 1, Scene 1):

> You are performing the role of **James**.
> Describe how you would use your vocal and physical skills to perform the line below and explain the effects that you want to create.
> James: Terribly sorry, sir. *(Knowing he's done for.)* I expect that's it for me, then. Shall I place an advertisement for a new man before I go?

In this scene, the audience will see the clock-like precision of Fogg and James's relationship. Throughout, as James, I will have an upright posture and a calm, unemotional manner, deferring to Fogg in every matter. 1 On this line, I know I have let Fogg down. I will drop my gaze, slightly bow and softly say 'Terribly sorry sir.' There will then be a sight pause as the severity of my error sinks in. 2 My voice, which has previously been an imitation of an upper-class one, will slightly slip back to my natural voice when I say, with a hint of a Cockney accent, 'I expect that's it for me, then.' 3 I will turn away to go, then turn back and offer to place an advertisement with a matter-of-fact tone. Throughout my facial expression is blank, matching the lack of emotion of Fogg. 4 The comedy of this exchange is that such a little matter could lead to my being fired and how both of us accept this as natural. The audience will see how comically particular Fogg is and how even someone as precise as James can't always meet his high standards. 5

1 Understanding of character and context of line; mentions 'posture'

2 Notes use of pause as well as detailed physical skills

3 Highlights vocal skills

4 Describes physical skills (movement, facial expression) and vocal skills (tone), and justifies them

5 Notes effect on audience

THEATRE MAKER ADVICE:

these are excerpts from interviews with professional theatre makers, such as designers and performers. They provide up-to-date insights into the practical aspects of theatre and offer ways of improving your own work.

During rehearsals

Jordan Castle, understudy and musical theatre performer

I am currently the understudy for two roles in the musical *Cats*. As an understudy you get a lot less rehearsal time than if you were actually playing the part, which can be difficult because you don't get the same one-to-one time with the director to explore the character. In rehearsals, I pay attention to everything the actors I am covering do, and make notes. I know I will need to add some of my own interpretation because we are very different people. But it is important to learn all the blocking and not to change that. Luckily I was well-prepared, because I did end up going on and performing each role with very little actual rehearsal.

KEY TERMS:

Director: the person responsible for the overall production of a play, including the performances and overseeing the designers

During performance

During a performance of *Richard III* that I was stage managing, there

Zoë Wilson,

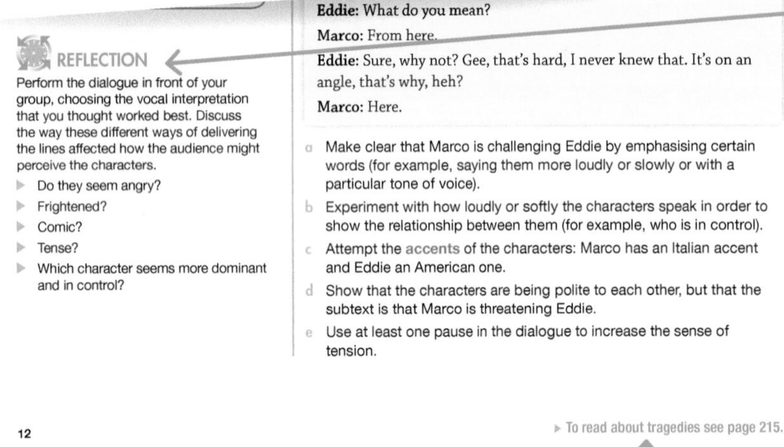

Eddie: What do you mean?

Marco: From here.

Eddie: Sure, why not? Gee, that's hard, I never knew that. It's on an angle, that's why, heh?

Marco: Here.

REFLECTION

Perform the dialogue in front of your group, choosing the vocal interpretation that you thought worked best. Discuss the way these different ways of delivering the lines affected how the audience might perceive the characters.

- Do they seem angry?
- Frightened?
- Comic?
- Tense?
- Which character seems more dominant and in control?

a Make clear that Marco is challenging Eddie by emphasising certain words (for example, saying them more loudly or slowly or with a particular tone of voice).
b Experiment with how loudly or softly the characters speak in order to show the relationship between them (for example, who is in control).
c Attempt the accents of the characters: Marco has an Italian accent and Eddie an American one.
d Show that the characters are being polite to each other, but that the subtext is that Marco is threatening Eddie.
e Use at least one pause in the dialogue to increase the sense of tension.

12

▸ To read about tragedies see page 215.

REFLECTION:

at the end of some tasks, there will be guidance for thinking about what you have learned and how that learning can be applied to your assessment tasks.

LOOK HERE:

these notices point out other pages of the book where you may find further information on a topic. For example, when revising sound design for Component 1, you may be directed to look at the sound design advice and technical terms in Component 3.

CHALLENGE

Research furniture from the time. Based on your research, draw sketches of key furniture items, such as the Lyons' dining table or Mrs Johnstone's kitchen table, which you believe would be appropriate for your design. Explain how they could be used in a scene.

TIP

Consider how you will accomplish the quick scene changes. For example, how will you move on Mrs Johnstone's kitchen set and then remove it? Will you use trucks? Casters on the furniture? Fly the set pieces in? Have actors carry or push the set pieces on/off?

KEY TERMS:

Truck: a platform on wheels upon which scenery can be mounted and moved.

Fly: raising and lowering scenery or other items onto the stage using a system of ropes and pulleys.

WHOSE HOME? Lyons – middle class, private home

FEATURES

1 If there is a street sign outside the house, what might the street name be?
2 What are the main colours used?
3 What materials are the walls made of? (Brick? Stone? Wood? Concrete?)
4 What condition are the walls in? Are there any special features that make the home seem prosperous? (Columns? Steps?, Balcony? Window boxes?)
5 What are the size, shape and colour of the doors and windows?
6 Are there any external features such as a garden, pathway or plants?
7 In what period do you think the home was originally built?

54

CHALLENGES:

exercises to really stretch and extend your drama skills.

TIPS:

guidance to help you with your assessments and to avoid common errors.

KEY TERMS:

definitions of terms to help you understand how drama works and express your ideas fluently. There is also a glossary at the back of the book to remind you of the definitions.

Learning how to work with performance texts and dramatic works

The GCSE Drama specification is set out as follows:

- There are seven set plays – you will read ONE of them.
- Component 1 Section C – you will study another play and watch a performance of it.

You may read all or some of the play that you see for Component 1, Section C. Your knowledge of plays may influence your devising in Component 2 when you will be creating your own dramatic work. So it is important that you are aware of how to read a performance text and learn the correct terminology for discussing it.

THE SPECIFICATION SAYS...

You must develop knowledge and understanding of characteristics of performance texts and dramatic works.

COMMON FEATURES OF A PLAY

Genre: a category of drama, such as historical drama or musical.

Dialogue: what the characters say.

Monologue: a long speech spoken by one character.

Performance style: the way in which something is performed. A realistic performance has a believable or life-like performance style, or a comedy might feature multi-role or physical comedy as its performance style.

Plot: the main events of the play presented in a particular sequence by the playwright.

P L O T

Character: a person or other being (such as a talking animal) in a play, novel or film.

Character list: a list of the characters that appear in the play. Some lists include a short description of the characters, such as their age or occupation.

Resolution: the end of the plot when the problems of the play are resolved.

Dramatic climax: the moment of greatest dramatic **tension** in a play.

Stage directions: descriptions of aspects of the play not conveyed by the actors' speeches. These may include a description of what the set or characters look like, and the actions of the characters and how certain lines of dialogue are spoken. It may also note pauses, silences or beats to indicate when characters are not speaking.

EXIT STAGE LEFT

KEY TERM:

Tension: a sense of anticipation or anxiety.

Moving from 'page to stage'

Throughout the course you will have chances to study scripts and then to think about how a script could be moved from the page to the stage. One way is by considering how your interpretation of it could be realised by performance and design choices. Over the next few pages there are examples of exploring a sample script, *A View from the Bridge*, which will introduce you to some of the skills and terminology that will be useful throughout the course.

▲ *Playwright Arthur Miller (1915–2005)*

Sample exploration of a play

Beyond identifying the different features of a script, you must also learn to **analyse** its meaning, **genre**, **characterisation** and **style**. Read the excerpt below from the end of Act 1 of the modern **tragedy** *A View from the Bridge* (1955) by the American **playwright** Arthur Miller. This scene is considered the climax of the play's first act.

Earlier in the play, Eddie, a middle-aged American dockworker, and his wife, Beatrice, have agreed to allow two of Beatrice's cousins, the young Rodolpho and Marco, to live with them. The cousins have arrived from Italy without work papers. Rodolpho has begun to date Eddie's niece, Catherine, much to Eddie's annoyance. Right before this scene, Eddie has tried to show that he is the most powerful person in his home by hitting Rodolpho while pretending to give him a boxing lesson. Shortly afterwards, Rodolpho and Eddie's niece, Catherine, begin to dance. Marco approaches Eddie.

[Rodolpho *takes her in his arms. They dance.* Eddie *in thought sits in his chair, and* Marco *takes a chair, places it in front of* Eddie*, and looks down at it.* Beatrice *and* Eddie *watch him.*] 1

Marco: Can you lift this chair? 2

Eddie: What do you mean?

Marco: From here. [*He gets on one knee with one hand behind his back, and grasps the bottom of one of the chair legs but does not raise it.*] 3

Eddie: Sure, why not? [*He comes to the chair, kneels, grasps the leg, raises the chair one inch, but it leans over to the floor.*] Gee, that's hard, I never knew that. [*He tries again, and again fails.*] It's on an angle, that's why, heh? 4

Marco: Here.

[*He kneels, grasps, and with strain slowly raises the chair higher and higher, getting to his feet now.* Rodolpho *and* Catherine *have stopped dancing as* Marco *raises the chair over his head.*

Marco *is face to face with* Eddie*, a strained tension gripping his eyes and jaw, his neck stiff, the chair raised like a weapon over* Eddie's *head – and he transforms what might appear like a glare of warning into a smile of triumph, and* Eddie *grin vanishes as he absorbs his look.*] 5

KEY TERMS:

Analyse: to examine something, perhaps by looking at the different elements of it, and to explain it.

Genre: a category or type of music, art or literature, usually with distinctive features.

Characterisation: how the qualities of a character are conveyed, typically through description, dialogue and actions.

Style: the way in which something is written or performed, such as the use of realistic dialogue or choreographed movement.

Tragedy: a play involving the downfall of its lead character leading to an unhappy ending.

Playwright: responsible for the writing of the script of the play. This includes the dialogue and stage directions.

TASK 1

After reading the excerpt from the play, refer to the numbered sections and answer the related question in your notebook.

1. What **motivations** might be revealed by this stage direction? For example, is Marco just pleasantly passing the time or is he confronting Eddie?
2. What might be the **subtext** of Marco's line? What is he thinking and feeling? How might his voice, body language or facial expression show his thoughts and feelings?
3. How do these stage directions create tension? If the stage directions are performed slowly or quickly do you think they would create more or less tension?
4. What do we learn about the character of Eddie from this dialogue? How might Eddie's facial expression, tone of voice or use of eye contact show how he feels?
5. How does this stage direction suggest **conflict** between Eddie and Marco?

KEY TERMS:

Motivations: what a character wants or needs in a scene. For example, 'I need to escape' or 'I want you to admire me'. These are sometimes called 'objectives'.

Subtext: the unspoken meaning, feelings and thoughts 'beneath' the lines, which may be shown in the characters' body language, tone of voice and facial expressions, for example, although not explicitly stated in the text.

Conflict: when two or more characters' desires are in opposition (external conflict) or when a character experiences opposing emotions (internal conflict).

WRITTEN BY
ARTHUR MILLER
DIRECTED BY
PATRICK WALSH
A VIEW FROM THE BRIDGE
ALL TICKETS £10
A VIEW FROM THE BRIDGE 23-26 Nov 2016

▲ *Although written and first performed in the 1950s,* A View from the Bridge *is frequently revived.*

TIP

As you study plays, look for the characters' motivations and how subtexts might be revealed through the characters' actions. When thinking as a performer, consider how you can explore these elements of the character and play.

THE SPECIFICATION SAYS...

Performers' vocal interpretation of character such as accent, volume, pitch, timing, pace, intonation, phrasing, emotional range and delivery of lines.

Performers' physical interpretation of character such as build, age, height, facial features, movement, postures, gesture and facial expression.

Introduction to performance skills

Throughout the course, you will be exploring how you might perform certain characters or evaluating how others have performed them. When performing or writing about performance you will often focus on:

- vocal skills
- physical skills.

In addition, you will learn about:

- characterisation
- interaction between characters (how they react to each other)
- use of the performance space (how they are positioned in or move around the space).

You will need to think about the effects that are being created:

- Do you want the audience to feel tense and anxious about the situation your character is in?
- Do you want them to sympathise with your character?
- Do you want them to laugh at your character?

To begin working on characterisation, you might consider the character's background, their motivations and their relationship to the other characters in the play.

Vocal skills

Using only the dialogue from the scene from *A View from the Bridge*, explore different vocal choices a performer might make.

KEY TERM:

Accent: a way of pronouncing words that is associated with a particular country, region or social class. This includes foreign accents, such as American or German.

TASK 2

Working in pairs, speak this dialogue from *A View from the Bridge* in the different ways suggested below:

Marco: Can you lift this chair?

Eddie: What do you mean?

Marco: From here.

Eddie: Sure, why not? Gee, that's hard, I never knew that. It's on an angle, that's why, heh?

Marco: Here.

a Make clear that Marco is challenging Eddie by emphasising certain words (for example, saying them more loudly or slowly or with a particular tone of voice).

b Experiment with how loudly or softly the characters speak in order to show the relationship between them (for example, who is in control).

c Attempt the **accents** of the characters: Marco has an Italian accent and Eddie an American one.

d Show that the characters are being polite to each other, but that the subtext is that Marco is threatening Eddie.

e Use at least one pause in the dialogue to increase the sense of tension.

REFLECTION

Perform the dialogue in front of your group, choosing the vocal interpretation that you thought worked best. Discuss the way these different ways of delivering the lines affected how the audience might perceive the characters.

- Do they seem angry?
- Frightened?
- Comic?
- Tense?
- Which character seems more dominant and in control?

▶ To read about tragedies see page 215.

Physical skills

One of the main ways actors create their characters is through their use of posture, gesture and facial expression.

- Both Eddie and Marco are used to physical labour – how might that affect the way they move?
- Eddie is older than Marco – how might that be shown in his posture?
- Marco is a guest in Eddie's apartment – will that change how he behaves in Eddie's living room?

Working with a partner and using the same scene as before, try Task 3.

TASK 3

a Many people **interpret** this scene as showing a transfer of power from Eddie to Marco. Create two **still images**, one showing their relationship at the beginning of the scene and the second showing their relationship at the end. Either take a photograph of these images or quickly sketch them and label them, showing how you used physical skills to show what is happening in the scene.

b Perform the scene trying the following:

i Create one clear gesture for each character that they use at a significant moment.

ii Choose when the characters maintain eye contact and when they look away.

iii Choose when the characters should move during the scene and how close or far away they are from each other at key points.

iv Choose one moment for each character when their facial expression changes.

KEY TERMS:

Interpret: to make choices about a play. There may be many possible interpretations.

Still image: a frozen moment showing the facial expressions and physical positions, including posture and gesture, of one or more characters.

REFLECTION

Discuss if any of the choices you made for Task 3 revealed physical choices that you could use in an actual performance. Are there any sections of the dialogue where changing levels or moving towards or away from each other seem to help convey the action of the scene?

Introduction to design skills

Throughout the components there are opportunities to explore design specialisms that include:

- lighting design
- sound design
- set design
- costume design
- puppet design.

Designers use their skills to create an element of the production that helps to contribute to the meaning of the play. One aspect they may consider when creating their designs is the **context** of the play, such as where and when it takes place.

The context of *A View from the Bridge* is New York in the 1950s. However, a designer may choose to interpret that context in different ways.

KEY TERMS:

Designer: person responsible for an aspect of the production, such as lighting, costumes, set, sound or puppets.

Context: the circumstances of the setting of a play, such as the location, period of time or conventions.

TIP

Throughout all the components of the course, you will have opportunities to explore how plays and their designs may be interpreted. Whatever your interpretation, it is important to explain why you have made your design choices.

TIP

Be aware if a question is asking you to refer to the context or not. In Section B, there will be one design question that asks you to refer specifically to the context. However, other design questions allow you to update, change or reinterpret the context.

KEY TERMS:

Naturalistic: life-like, realistic, believable.

Abstract: not realistic or life-like, but instead using colours, shapes, textures, sounds and other means to achieve an effect.

Stylised: non-realistic, done in a particular manner, perhaps emphasising one element.

Minimalistic: simple; using few elements; stripped back.

Symbolic: using something that represents something else. Examples of symbolic design might be characters dressed in white to symbolise their purity or a set resembling a boxing ring to symbolise the conflict between the characters.

Costumes: what the characters wear onstage.

Sets: items put onstage such as furniture or **backdrops** to create the world of the play; sometimes called scenery. There may also be **props**, which are objects used onstage.

Backdrop: A large painted cloth that serves as scenery, often at the back of the stage.

Props: small items that actors can carry onstage.

TIP

These two designs are very different, but both productions were successful. This shows that there is no single correct way of interpreting a play. If you were designing the set or costumes, you might make very different choices.

For example, they may choose to research that period of time and location to recreate the furniture, fabrics and music associated with them. Many **naturalistic** productions do this in order to create a believable world for the characters to inhabit. On the other hand, a designer may make more **abstract** or **stylised** choices where they do not attempt to create a realistic version of the world, but instead make choices which might be **minimalistic** or **symbolic**. Some productions may ignore the original context and choose another context, for example by updating the production to a different time or changing the location.

Below are production photographs showing the **set** and **costumes** of two different productions of *A View from the Bridge*.

From a Broadway production, 2010, starring Liev Schrieber, sets by John Lee Beatty, costumes by Jane Greenwood

Young Vic production, starring Mark Strong, design and lighting by Jan Versweyveld, and costumes by An D'Huys, 2014

TASK 4

a What differences do you see between the costumes in the two productions? Note the choice of fabrics, colours, the fit or shape of the clothes, the footwear, and the hair and make-up.

b What differences do you see between the sets in the two productions? Note the furniture, walls, colours and flooring.

c Re-read the script extract on page 10. Which of the costume and set designs most closely matches your ideas about the design of the play? Why?

The tasks above are just an introduction to some of the skills, terminology and ideas that you will be developing over the different components of the course. Throughout your course, consider the different ways that plays can be interpreted.

WHAT HAVE I LEARNED?

HOW WILL I BE ASSESSED?

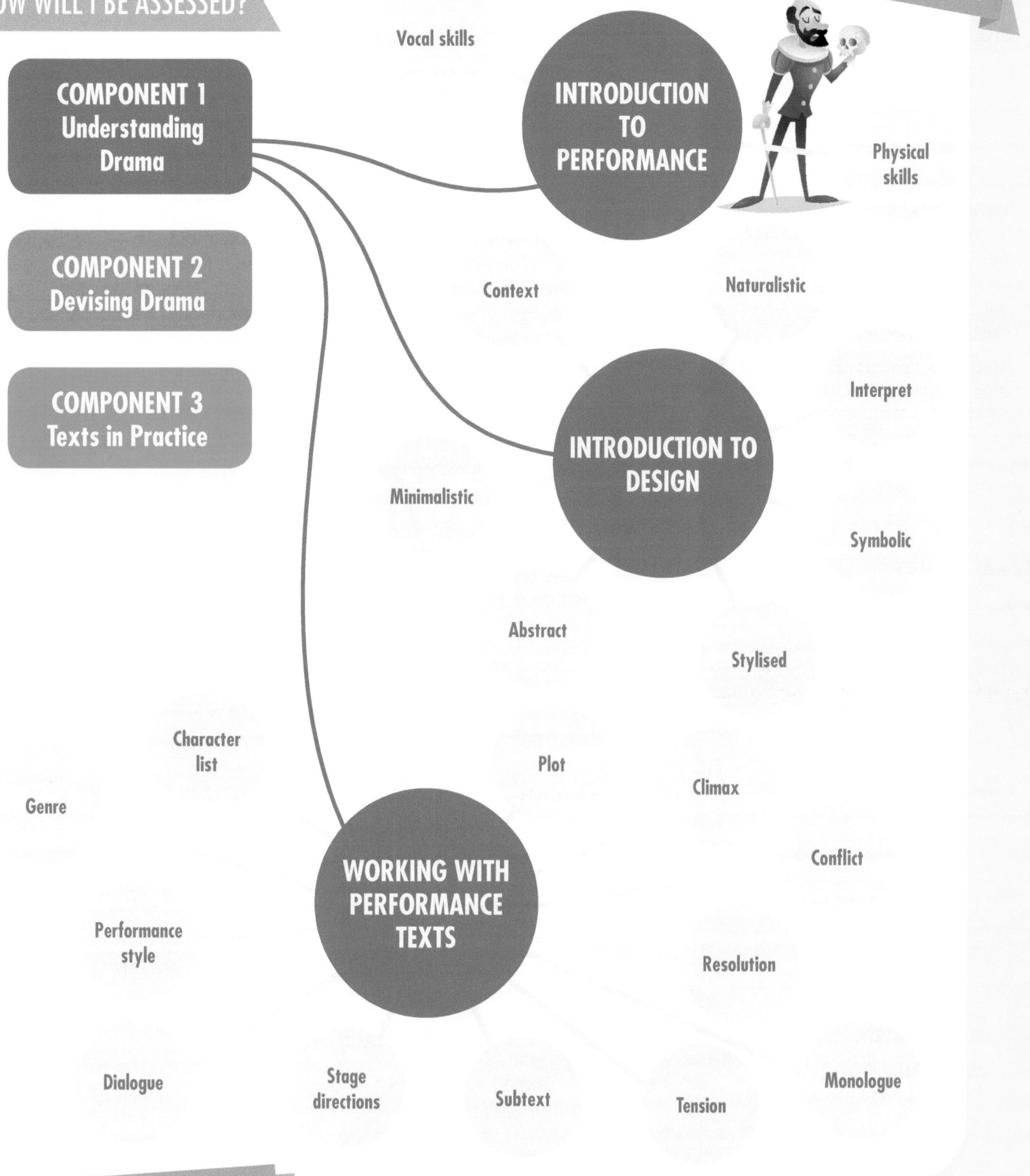

COMPONENT 1
Understanding Drama

COMPONENT 2
Devising Drama

COMPONENT 3
Texts in Practice

INTRODUCTION TO PERFORMANCE

- Vocal skills
- Physical skills

INTRODUCTION TO DESIGN

- Context
- Naturalistic
- Interpret
- Minimalistic
- Symbolic
- Abstract
- Stylised

WORKING WITH PERFORMANCE TEXTS

- Character list
- Plot
- Climax
- Genre
- Conflict
- Performance style
- Resolution
- Dialogue
- Stage directions
- Subtext
- Tension
- Monologue

CHECK YOUR LEARNING

If you are uncertain of the meaning of any of the terms above, go back and revise.

Use the downloadable version of this summary as your own checklist of what you have learned: Samples & Downloads at www.illuminatepublishing.com.

SECTION A

THEATRE ROLES AND TERMINOLOGY

THE SPECIFICATION SAYS...

Students must develop knowledge and understanding of:

- Drama and theatre terminology and how to use it appropriately.
  - Stage positioning.
  - Staging configuration.
- The roles and responsibilities of theatre practitioners in contemporary theatre practice.

ASSESSMENT FOCUS

AO3: Demonstrate knowledge and understanding of how drama and theatre is developed and performed.

In Section A, you will be asked multiple choice questions in which you must demonstrate your understanding of how theatre works, such as what various theatre makers do, the different areas of a stage or possible staging configurations.

Roles and responsibilities

Drama is a team effort in which many people contribute to create the final production. When you go to see a play you are, of course, aware of the performers, but you might not think about the efforts of all the other theatre makers who do not appear onstage. For Component 1, Section A, you need to be able to identify theatre roles for a multiple choice question.

The chart below summarises some of the key personnel.

THEATRE MAKER:
PLAYWRIGHT

WHAT THEY DO:
Write the script of the play, including the dialogue and stage directions.

THEATRE MAKER:
PERFORMER

WHAT THEY DO:
Appear in a production, for example by acting, dancing or singing. They create a performance or assume a role onstage in front of an audience.

THEATRE MAKER:
LIGHTING DESIGNER

WHAT THEY DO:
Design the lighting states and effects that will be used in a performance. They understand the technical capabilities of the theatre and create a lighting plot.

THEATRE MAKER:
UNDERSTUDY

WHAT THEY DO:
Learn a part, including lines and movements, so they are able to take over a role for someone if needed when there is a planned or unexpected absence.

THEATRE MAKER:
SOUND DESIGNER

WHAT THEY DO:
Design the sound required for the performance, which may include music and sound effects. They consider if amplification, such as the use of microphones, is needed, and create a sound plot.

THEATRE MAKER:
COSTUME DESIGNER

WHAT THEY DO:
Design what the actors wear onstage. They make sure that costumes are appropriate for the style and period of the piece and ensure the costumes fit the actors.

THEATRE MAKER:
SET DESIGNER

WHAT THEY DO:
Create the set of the play and the set dressing (objects placed on the stage). They provide sketches and other design materials before overseeing the construction of the set.

THEATRE MAKER:
STAGE MANAGER

WHAT THEY DO:
Run the backstage elements of the play and supervising the backstage crew. They organise the rehearsal schedule and keep lists of props and other technical needs. They create a prompt book and call the cues for the performance.

When theatre makers undertake their responsibilities

It is useful to see in context when professional theatre makers undertake their responsibilities and to read what some professional theatre makers do before rehearsals, during rehearsals and during performances.

THE SPECIFICATION SAYS...

Knowledge and understanding should cover:

- The activities each may undertake on a day-to-day basis.
- The aspects of the rehearsal/performance process each is accountable for (their contribution to the whole production being a success).

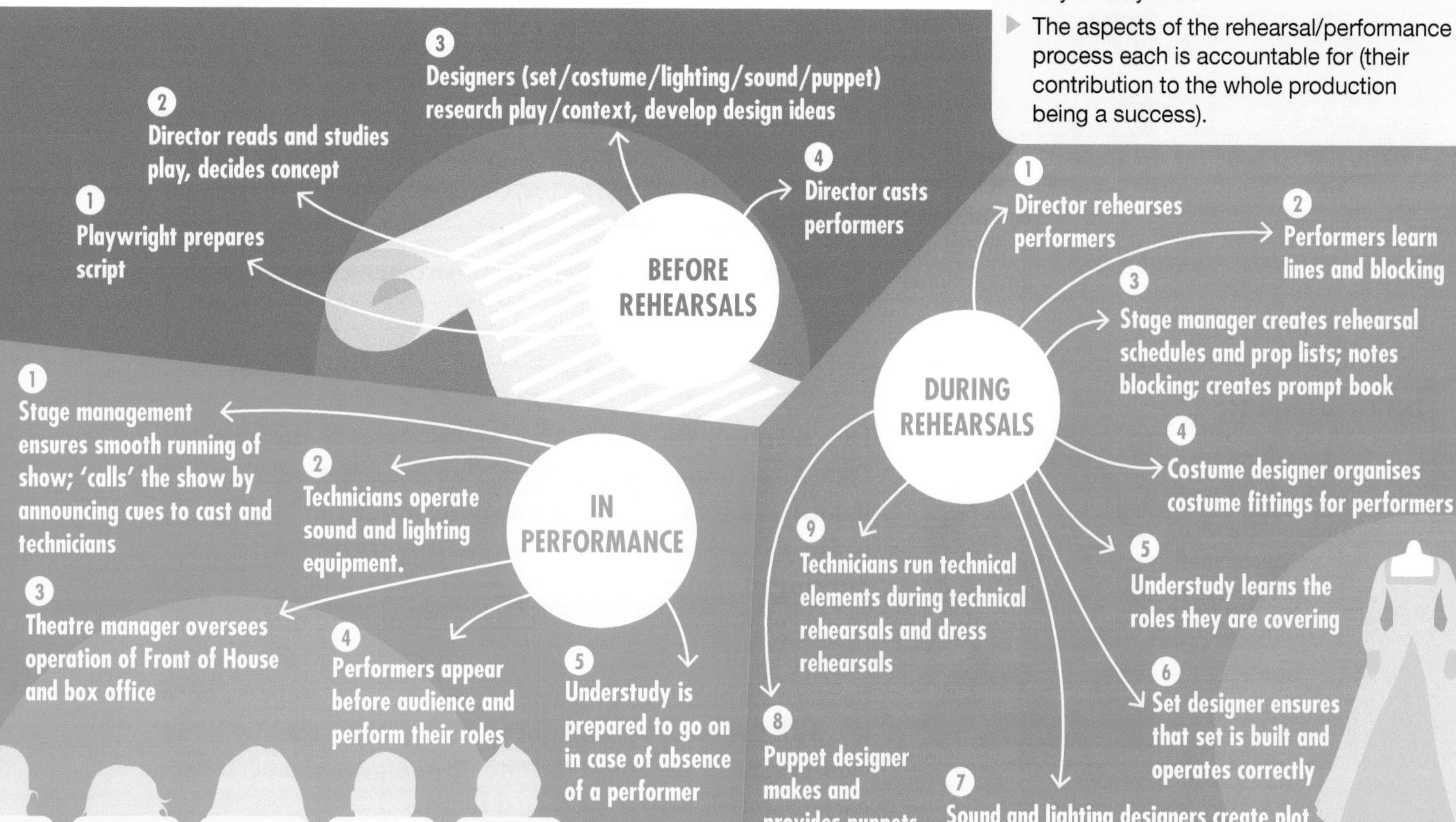

THEATRE MAKER:
PUPPET DESIGNER

WHAT THEY DO:
Design the puppets for a production, taking into account the style of puppets and how they will be operated.

THEATRE MAKER:
TECHNICIAN

WHAT THEY DO:
Operate the technical equipment, such as the lighting and sound boards, during the performance.

THEATRE MAKER:
DIRECTOR

WHAT THEY DO:
Oversee the creative aspects of the production. They develop a 'concept' or central unifying idea for the production. They liaise with designers, rehearse the actors and ensure that all technical elements of the play are ready. They give 'notes' to the actors to help improve their performances and agree the blocking (or movements) of the actors.

THEATRE MAKER:
THEATRE MANAGER

WHAT THEY DO:
Run the theatre building, including overseeing the Front of House staff (ushers) and the box office staff who sell tickets.

TIP

Some productions do not begin with a finished script but are created collaboratively during rehearsals. This is called devising, which you will learn more about in Component 2.

BOX OFFICE

THEATRE MAKER ADVICE

Before rehearsals

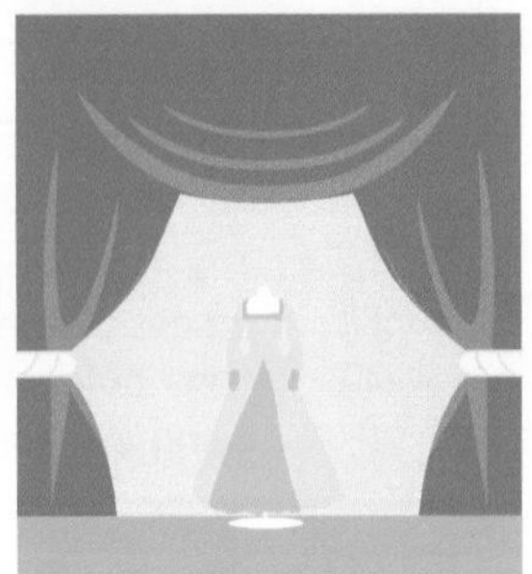

Tim Shortall, West End costume and set designer

What I ideally aim for upon very first reading the script is purely an overall direct personal response to it, much as you would have when reading a book.

Then I'll read it again, but this time looking specifically at the likely physical/design requirements of each scene. These may be literally stated in the script or be in some way evident from the scenes. This is most probably at such an early stage in the proceedings that I have not yet discussed anything with the director, or heard their views and intended approach.

That discussion can then of course often change my whole view of the script.

During rehearsals

Jordan Castle, understudy and musical theatre performer

I am currently the understudy for two roles in the musical *Cats*. As an understudy you get a lot less rehearsal time than if you were actually playing the part, which can be difficult because you don't get the same one-to-one time with the director to explore the character. In rehearsals, I pay attention to everything the actors I am covering do, and make notes. I know I will need to add some of my own interpretation because we are very different people. But it is important to learn all the blocking and not to change that. Luckily I was well-prepared, because I did end up going on and performing each role with very little actual rehearsal.

KEY TERMS:

Director: the person responsible for the overall production of a play, including the performances and overseeing the designers.

Covering: learning the words and movements for a part that you do not usually perform.

Blocking: the movements of the actor. These are often written down by the **stage manager** to ensure that they can be repeated. For example, *Jo enters and moves DSL (downstage left).*

Interval: a break in a performance for both the performers and the audience. This often occurs between the first and second acts of plays. Some plays have more than one interval and some run without an interval.

Stage manager: the person responsible for the backstage elements of the production, such as calling cues and checking props.

During performance

Zoë Wilson, stage manager

During a performance of *Richard III* that I was stage managing, there was a table with wheels on one end which gets taken on and off the stage during scene changes. At one point, two actors sit in chairs on top of this table. During one performance, in the first half, one of the wheel's rubber surfacing fell off which made the table slightly wobbly. Although it was only a slight wobble this could cause a risk to the actors in the second half. So in the interval I had to make the decision to take the table offstage with my ASM [assistant stage manager] and call for our construction member and crew backstage to take both wheels off to make the table more stable. I then had to inform the actors of what had happened so they were updated and aware. We ended up getting the table on in good time to end the interval on time.

Stage positioning

In order to discuss theatre, you need to be able to explain quickly and simply where you want something to occur. To do this, imagine that the stage (an end on stage in this instance) has been turned into a grid as below:

TIP

To understand if it is 'right' or 'left', imagine you are an actor standing on the centre of the stage facing the audience. Stage right is to your right and stage left is to your left.

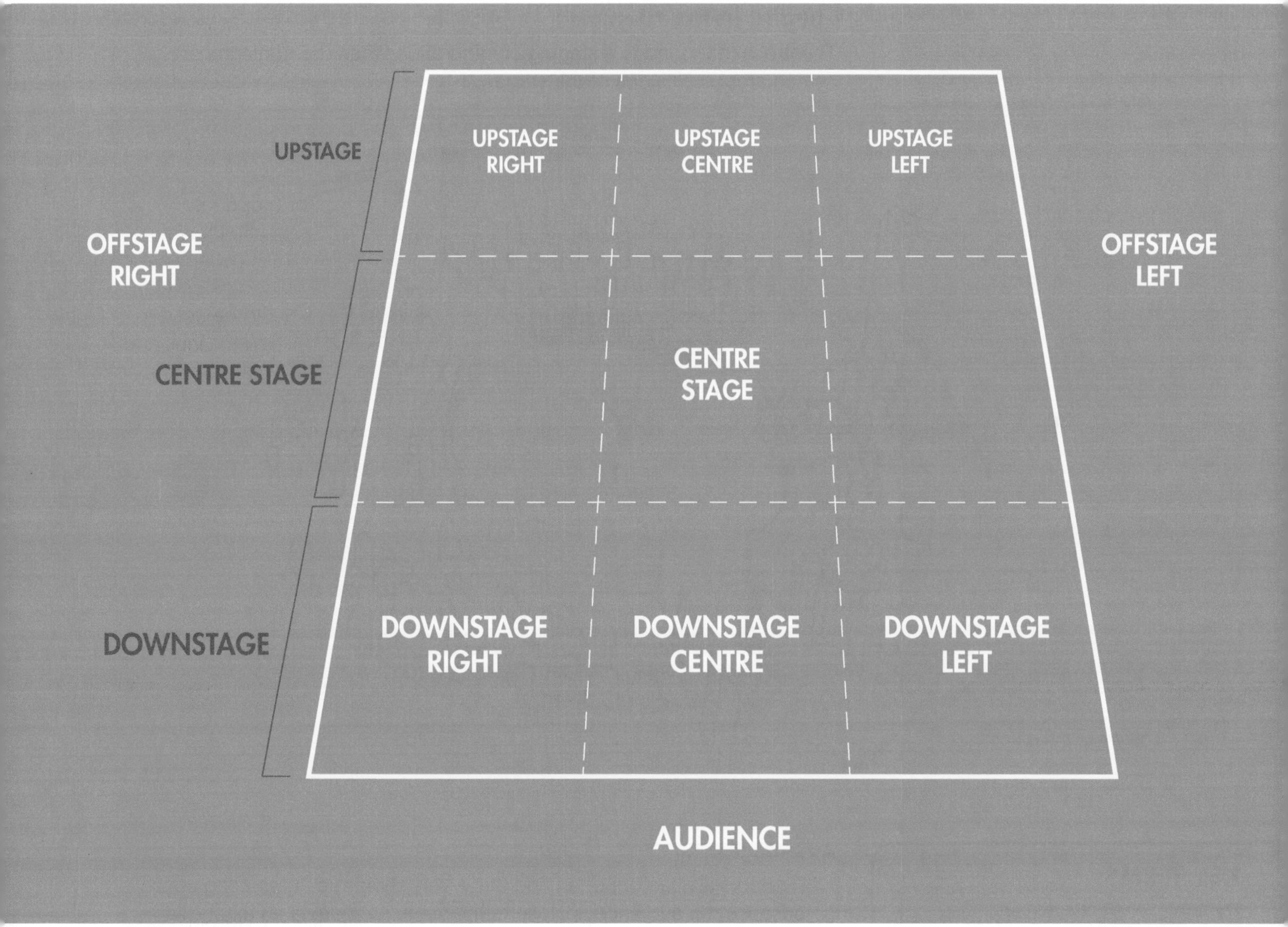

UPSTAGE

CENTRE STAGE

DOWNSTAGE

OFFSTAGE RIGHT

OFFSTAGE LEFT

UPSTAGE RIGHT	UPSTAGE CENTRE	UPSTAGE LEFT
	CENTRE STAGE	
DOWNSTAGE RIGHT	DOWNSTAGE CENTRE	DOWNSTAGE LEFT

AUDIENCE

TASK 1

Copy the stage positioning diagram for an end on stage, above. Then use it to complete the follow directions:

a Mark an X to show where a doorway could be positioned for an entrance upstage left.
b Draw a sofa centre stage.
c Draw a ramp coming from downstage right into the audience.
d Draw a large **projection** screen that will hang upstage centre.

KEY TERM:

Projection: A technique where moving or still images are projected to form a theatrical backdrop.

Staging configurations

KEY TERM:

Staging configuration: the type of stage and audience arrangement.

Although the stage positions shown on the previous page are designed for theatres where the audience sits looking straight on at a rectangular stage, as is typical of end on or proscenium stages, there are many other **staging configurations** that influence how the actors perform and what the audience experiences. Below are examples of different types of stages.

Theatre in the round

Theatre in the round is a staging configuration when the audience are seated around all sides of the stage.

Theatre in the round

KEY TERMS:

Dynamic: energetic, forceful.

Fourth wall: an imaginary wall between the audience and the actors giving the impression that the actors are unaware they are being observed.

Flat: a piece of scenery mounted on a frame, to represent a wall, for example.

Sightline: the audience's view of the stage.

Advantages:

- Directors and actors often find this a very **dynamic**, interesting space because the audience is close to the stage as there is an extended first row.
- The actors enter and exit through the audience, which can make the audience feel more engaged.
- Unlike spaces such as proscenium theatres, there is no easily achieved 'artificial **fourth wall**' separating the audience from the acting area.

Disadvantages:

- Designers cannot use backdrops or **flats** that would obscure the view of the audience.
- Stage furniture has to be chosen carefully so that **sightlines** are not blocked.
- Actors have to be carefully blocked so that no section of the audience misses important pieces of action or facial expressions for too long.

Proscenium arch

Proscenium arch is a common form of theatre, popular for larger theatres or opera houses. The proscenium refers to the frame around the stage, which emphasises that the whole audience is seeing the same stage picture. The area in front of the arch is called an **apron**.

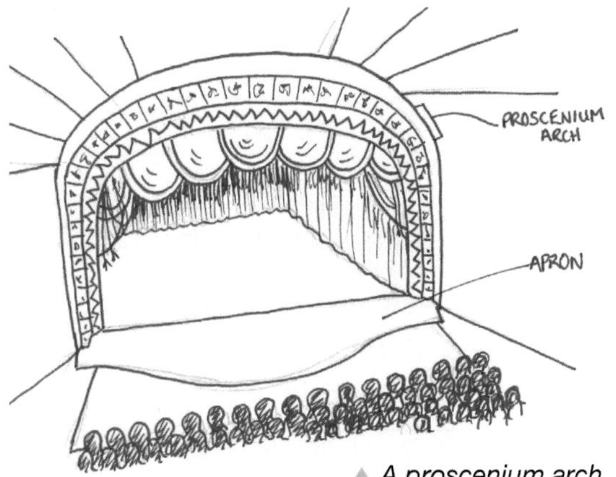

▲ *A proscenium arch*

Advantages:

- Stage pictures are easy to create as the audience look at the stage from roughly the same angle.
- Backdrops and large scenery can be used without blocking sightlines.
- There may be **fly space** and **wing spaces** for storing scenery.
- The frame around the stage adds to the effect of a fourth wall, giving the effect of a self-contained world.

Disadvantages:

- Some audience members may feel distant from the stage.
- The auditorium could seem very formal and rigid.
- **Audience interaction** may be more difficult.

KEY TERMS:

Apron: the area of the stage nearest the audience, which projects in front of the curtain.

Fly space: area above the stage where scenery may be stored and lowered to the stage.

Wing spaces: areas to the side of the stage. This is the area where actors, unseen by the audience, wait to enter and where props and set pieces may be stored.

Audience interaction: involving the audience in the play, for example by bringing them onstage, going into the audience to speak with them or passing them props to hold.

Box set: a set with three complete walls, often used in naturalistic set designs, for example to create a believable room.

Thrust stage

◀ *A thrust stage*

A thrust stage protrudes into the auditorium with the audience on three sides. This is one of the oldest theatre types of stage.

Advantages:

- Combines some of the advantages of proscenium and theatre in the round stages.
- As there is no audience on one side of the stage, backdrops, flats and large scenery can be used.
- The audience may feel closer to the stage as there are three first rows – one on each of the stage's three sides

Disadvantages:

- Sightlines for those on the extreme sides may be limited or obstructed.
- The audience on the right and left sides of the auditorium have each other in their view.
- **Box sets** (where three sides of a room are constructed) cannot be used as this would block views for much of the audience.

CHALLENGE

Greek amphitheatres, with their audience seated around almost half the curved stage, are a type of thrust theatre. Elizabethan theatres are thrust stages and the audience in the lowest level, 'the pit', would stand around three sides of the stage.

Why do you think this has remained such a popular type of theatre configuration?

Traverse

On a traverse stage the acting area is a long, central space with the audience seated on either side facing each other.

Advantages:

- The audience feel very close to the stage as there are two long, front rows.
- They can see the reactions of the other side of the audience who are facing them, which can work well for audience interaction.
- Sometimes, extreme ends of the stage can be used to create extra acting areas.

A traverse stage ▲

Disadvantages:

- Big pieces of scenery, backdrops or set can block sightlines.
- The acting area is long and thin, which can make some blocking challenging.
- Actors must be aware of making themselves visible to both sides of the audience.
- Lighting for traverse stages needs to be arranged carefully to avoid shining lights into the audience's eyes or light spilling onto them unnecessarily.

End on staging

An end on stage is similar to a proscenium stage, as the audience is seated along one end of the stage, directly facing it. It doesn't have the large proscenium frame, however.

Advantages:

- The audience all have a similar view.
- Stage pictures are easy to create.
- Large backdrops or projections may be used.

Disadvantages:

- Audience members in the back rows may feel distant from the stage.
- It doesn't have the 'frame' of the proscenium arch theatre, which can enhance some types of staging.
- It may not have the wing and fly areas typical of proscenium arch theatres.

End on staging ▲

Promenade theatre

To promenade means 'to walk' and promenade theatre is when the audience stand or follow the actors through the performance. This may occur in a conventional theatre space or it may be designed for a site specific show when an unconventional space is used for the production.

> **KEY TERM:**
> **Site specific:** a performance in a location, such as a warehouse or park, which is not a conventional theatre. The space has often been adapted to suit the production.

Promenade theatre ▲

Advantages:

- This is an interactive and exciting type of theatre where the audience may feel very involved.

Disadvantages:

- The audience may find moving around the space difficult or get tired of standing.
- Actors or crew need to be skilled at moving the audience around and controlling their focus.
- There can be health and safety risks.

TASK 2

a Using the excerpt from *A View from the Bridge* on page 10 or another play that you know well, experiment with staging it for all the different configurations: theatre in the round, end on, thrust, traverse, proscenium and promenade. It is important to agree where entrances/exits will be and where you will place any pieces of set furniture.

b Discuss what adjustments you had to make for the different spaces, and decide which you think worked best for the style and content of that particular scene.

TIP

Understanding staging configurations will help you with Component 1, Section A, and will also be useful in Component 1, Sections B and C and Components 2 and 3 when analysing or creating set designs.

PRACTICE QUESTIONS FOR SECTION A

You will answer a number of multiple choice questions.

1 In professional theatre, who is responsible for operating the technical equipment such as lighting during a performance?

- A The theatre manager
- B The stage manger
- C The technician [1 mark]

2 When performing on a thrust stage which of the following is true?

- A You can only perform centre stage.
- B The audience is positioned along three sides of the stage.
- C The audience is encouraged to walk around during the performance. [1 mark]

3 What type of stage is shown in Figure 1 on the right?

- A Proscenium arch
- B Traverse stage
- C Thrust stage [1 mark]

4 With reference to Figure 1 on the right, in what position is the gate?

- A Upstage left
- B Upstage centre
- C Downstage centre [1 mark]

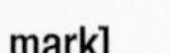

Figure 1

Additional practice for Section A

1 In the professional theatre, if a performer is unable to perform, who should go on in their place to play the role instead?

- A The stage manager
- B The theatre manager
- C The understudy [1 mark]

2 Which of the following staging configurations is best suited for using large, high pieces of set and backdrops?

- A Proscenium
- B Theatre in the round
- C Traverse [1 mark]

3 What type of stage is shown in Figure 2 on the right?

- A Thrust stage
- B Theatre in the round
- C End on stage [1 mark]

4 With reference to Figure 2 on the right, what stage position is the table in?

- A Centre stage
- B Upstage left
- C Downstage right [1 mark]

Figure 2

TIP

Check your work for simple errors. One of the most common is to confuse stage left with stage right.

WHAT HAVE I LEARNED?

ROLES AND RESPONSIBILITIES

WHO DOES WHAT AND WHEN?

- Playwright
- Sound designer
- Costume designer
- Stage manager
- Puppet designer
- Lighting designer
- Understudy
- Theatre manager
- Technician
- Performer
- Director
- Set designer

WHERE DOES THE PERFORMANCE TAKE PLACE?

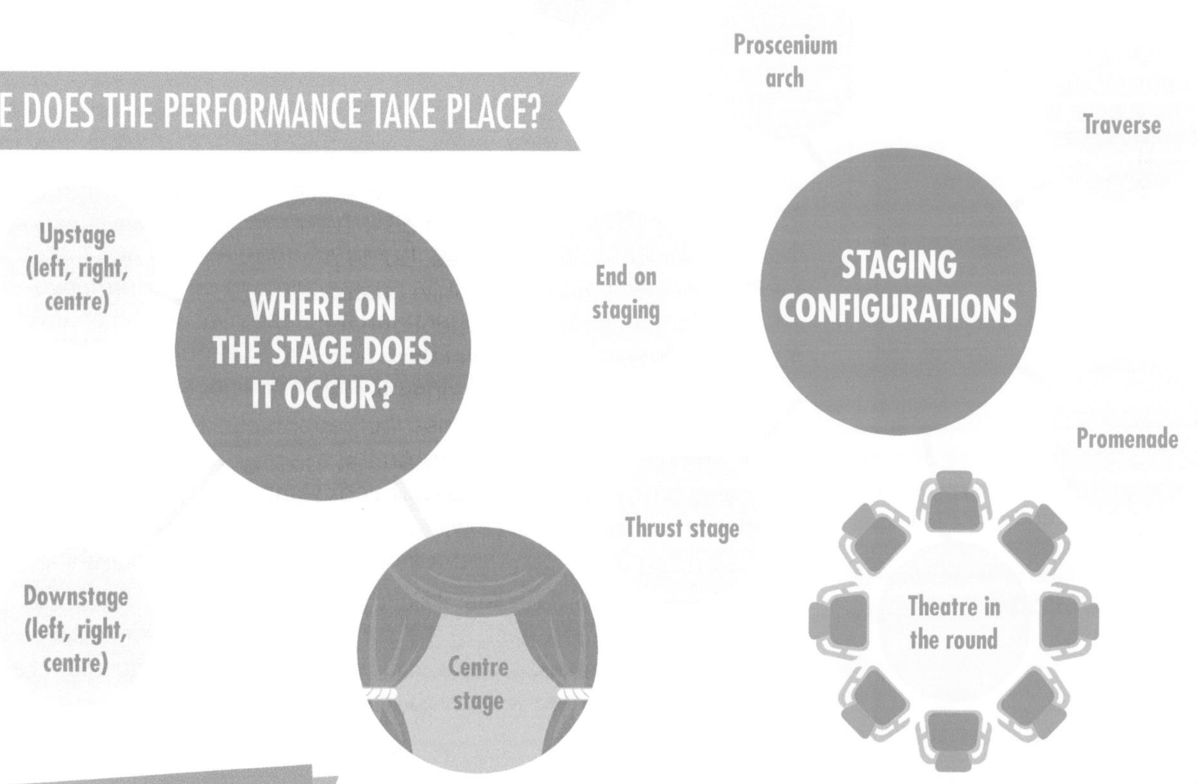

WHERE ON THE STAGE DOES IT OCCUR?

- Upstage (left, right, centre)
- Downstage (left, right, centre)
- Centre stage

STAGING CONFIGURATIONS

- Proscenium arch
- Traverse
- End on staging
- Promenade
- Thrust stage
- Theatre in the round

CHECK YOUR LEARNING

If you are uncertain of the meaning of any of the terms above, go back and revise.

Use the downloadable version of this summary as your own checklist of what you have learned: Samples & Downloads at www.illuminatepublishing.com.

SECTION B
STUDY OF A SET PLAY

THE SPECIFICATION SAYS...

- Students are expected to know and understand the characteristics and context of the whole play they have studied.
- One extract from each set play is printed in the question paper.
- Students answer questions relating to that extract, referring to the whole play as appropriate to the demands of the question.

ASSESSMENT FOCUS

AO3: Demonstrate knowledge and understanding of how drama and theatre is developed and performed.

KEY TERMS:

Kitchen sink drama: a type of realistic drama popular after the Second World War, which depicted the lives of working-class characters. They often showed the difficult domestic situations of the characters and explored important social issues.

Concept: a unifying idea about the production, such as when it is set or how it will be interpreted and performed.

TIP

Build on the knowledge you have gained in your 'page to stage' and Section A work. For example, consider the benefits and disadvantages of the different staging configurations covered in Section A.

TIP

Question 1 will ask you to consider the original context of the play. This means the play's setting or style, not necessarily when it was written. Your design ideas for this question should show how you have used your research in context to inspire your design.

For Component 1 Section B you will study one of seven set plays and be asked questions to demonstrate your understanding of how those plays may be interpreted through acting, staging configurations and design decisions.

The set plays have been chosen to represent a range of theatrical genres:

The Crucible – a historical drama

Blood Brothers – a musical

Things I Know to be True – a suburban drama

Around the World in 80 Days – a comedy

Noughts & Crosses – a teen drama

Romeo and Juliet – a tragedy

A Taste of Honey – a kitchen sink drama

Whichever play you study, you will have the chance to explore how the plays could be performed, staged and designed, and each will offer you the opportunity to show your creativity.

In the examination, you will read an extract from the play and then answer three questions – one focusing on design and two on performance – in order to demonstrate your understanding of the play and its characters, style and context. You will then have a choice of a fourth question where you may choose to focus on either acting or design.

It is important that you think about the play practically. It's not expected that you will mount a complete production of the play, but you should be on your feet trying out your performance ideas or sketching your design **concepts** in order to see if these ideas will work. The best ideas come from a deep understanding of the play. You will need to explain how your choices work in a practical theatre setting.

In the following pages, each of the set texts is analysed for its content, context and performance, and design elements. Sample questions and responses are provided to aid your study.

TIP

There is a strong element of interpretation based on your own insight into the play, so there may be many 'right' answers.

▶ There are additional detailed notes on the practical aspects of the different specialisms in Component 3.

SET PLAY 1: *The Crucible* by Arthur Miller

1

Synopsis

The play opens in a bedroom in the house of **Reverend Parris** in the town of **Salem** in **America**, during **1692.** His daughter, **Betty**, is ill in bed. Various Salem residents, including servant girls and neighbours, as well as **Tituba**, an enslaved person from Barbados, come to enquire how she is. When the servant girls, led by **Abigail**, are left alone with Betty, they discuss how they were discovered, with Tituba, dancing in the woods. **Mary Warren** is afraid they will be called witches.

John Proctor, a neighbour, enters and sends Mary Warren, his servant, home. When he and Abigail are left alone, she asks him for a 'soft word' and he tells her that he is 'done with' that. There is conflict between Parris and Proctor over matters of money, community and religion. **Reverend Hale**, an educated minister from another parish, arrives to treat Betty. Parris describes finding the girls, including Betty and Abigail, dancing in the woods. Abigail is asked if they were calling the Devil. Abigail blames Tituba who, she says, made them drink blood. Tituba claims that the Devil has visited her, accompanied by women of Salem. Abigail cries out that she wants the light of God and begins naming people she saw with the Devil. Betty rises from her bed and joins in the accusations.

Act 2, in the Proctor home, Proctor and his wife, **Elizabeth**, discuss Mary Warren and the upcoming court case. Many people have been put in jail, based on the girls' accusations. Elizabeth wants Proctor to declare Abigail a fraud. They argue over Elizabeth's suspicions. Mary Warren returns and presents Elizabeth with a doll she has made. Mary tells Elizabeth that she was accused in court. Elizabeth asks Proctor to intervene with Abigail, who she believes wants to kill her in order to be with him.

Hale arrives and questions the Proctors' commitment to the Church. Proctor admits a dislike of Reverend Parris. Proctor tells Hale that Abigail said they made up the witchcraft story to avoid punishment for dancing in the woods. **Giles Corey** and **Francis Nurse** arrive to say their wives have been taken by the court. Elizabeth is arrested. The doll Mary Warren gave Elizabeth is to be used as evidence against her. Proctor orders Mary to tell the truth in court.

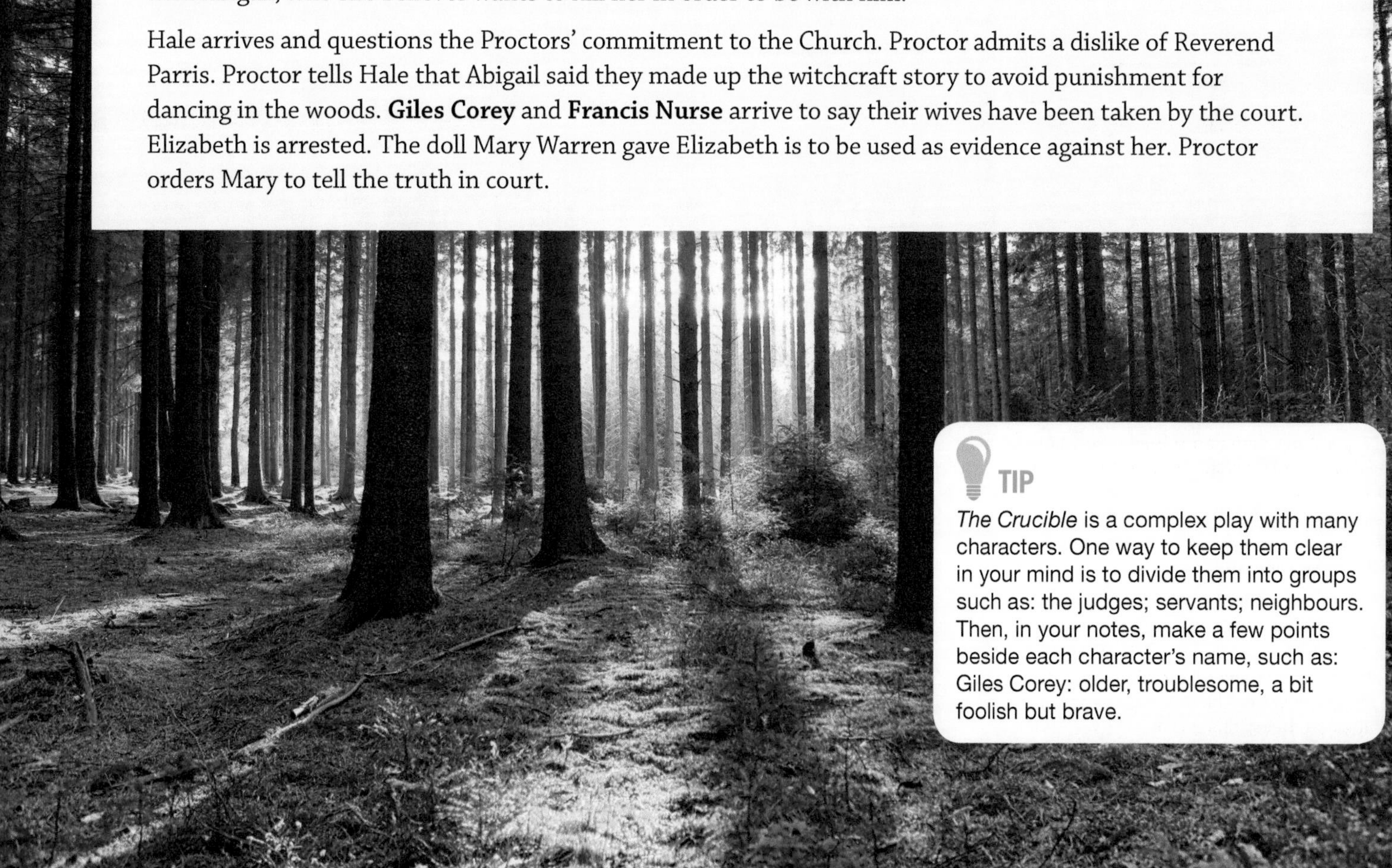

TIP

The Crucible is a complex play with many characters. One way to keep them clear in your mind is to divide them into groups such as: the judges; servants; neighbours. Then, in your notes, make a few points beside each character's name, such as: Giles Corey: older, troublesome, a bit foolish but brave.

Act 3 is in the Salem meeting house where the court is held. Proctor brings Mary before the judges. She tells them the stories were false. The Deputy Governor, **Danforth**, reveals that Elizabeth has told the court that she is pregnant, which could spare her life for at least another year. Proctor presents a statement by neighbours in support of the accused women.

Giles Corey, who states that **Thomas Putnam** is making false accusations of witchcraft for monetary gain, is arrested. Proctor hands the court Mary's deposition. The accusing girls are brought into court which hears Mary's faltering account of their dishonesty. The girls, led by Abigail, claim that Mary is sending an evil spirit or a 'bird' to control them. Proctor calls Abigail a 'whore'. He confesses that he has 'known' Abigail and that is the motivation for her actions. Elizabeth is brought into court and asked if her husband is a 'lecher'. To protect her husband's good name, she says, 'No, sir.' Elizabeth is taken away and the girls begin screaming. Mary turns and accuses Proctor of being the Devil. Proctor is taken to jail.

Act 4 takes place in a cell in the Salem jail. Reverend Parris tells Danforth that his niece, Abigail, stole money from him and has vanished. Parris expresses doubts about executing members of high standing in their community such as Rebecca Nurse and John Proctor. Hale meets with the accused hoping to get them to confess to witchcraft in order to spare their lives. Hale asks Elizabeth to plead with Proctor to confess so he won't be killed.

Proctor is brought in. He asks for Elizabeth's forgiveness. He declares that he wants to live. He is asked to sign a confession. Danforth wants him to name others who he has seen with the Devil. Proctor refuses and declares he cannot sign his name to the false confession, 'Because it is my name!' He kisses a weeping Elizabeth. Rebecca Nurse and Proctor are taken out to be executed, while Hale weeps in prayer.

TASK 1

a After reading the synopsis above, with your group choose ten key plot points and create a still image for each one. Discuss what you think are the most important moments in the play.

b With your group, list some of the challenges in performing and designing a production of the play. You could try to find at least two points for each of the following design areas: sound, costume, lighting and set. You might begin by:
- creating the period setting
- differentiating between the different characters.

Context

SET PLAY 1:
The Crucible
by Arthur Miller
1

The play is set in **Salem, Massachusetts, in 1692** and is based on historic events. The 'witch trials' of this time were among the most famous episodes of Colonial America.

New England, on the east coast of America, had been colonised by people, called Puritans, seeking freedom from the Church of England, in order to practise their particular branch of Christianity. The Puritans were fiercely religious and had strong ideas about appropriate Christian behaviour, which they hoped to practise without interference.

In the community of Salem there were many disputes about legal and religious issues. The Church and local minister were central to the community and the appointment of Reverend Parris, their first ordained minister, was a controversial one, adding to the discontent.

At this time, the roles of women and men were clearly divided. Women were in charge of the home and, in many cases, would have servant girls to help them with their chores.

Child-bearing was an important role for women and it is a source of conflict in the play that Rebecca Nurse has so many surviving children while Mrs Putnam had buried 'all but one' of hers. Women who were pregnant would not be executed, so it is significant when Elizabeth reveals that she is pregnant.

Abigail, who is the orphaned niece of Reverend Parris, was a servant to the Proctors until she was replaced by Mary Warren when Elizabeth learned of Abigail's relationship with her husband. Tituba, a person enslaved by Reverend Parris from Barbados, is treated with suspicion by other characters due to her different background and beliefs. The men in the play are shown in a variety of roles, including farmers, ministers and judges. Money is discussed in some detail, such as Reverend Parris' salary or Giles Corey's various lawsuits. Reverend Hale is an outsider to the community. Miller's description of him as an 'intellectual' or a man of learning, is backed up by his entrance carrying 'a dozen heavy books'. His education is respected by others.

▲ *The Salem witch trials*

▲ *Architecture of the period: a) interior; b) exterior of Judge Corwin's house, known as Witch House, in Salem*

KEY TERM:

Clapboards: wooden boards used to cover the outside of buildings.

Buildings in Salem at this time would usually be simple wooden structures. In Act 2, John Proctor tells how the community 'built the church', which was a '**clapboard** meeting house'. There would be limited decorative adornments inside, with many objects being obviously hand-made by the residents.

Women would dress modestly in long dresses, often with an apron, a shawl and cap. Petticoats or underskirts were worn under skirts for warmth and modesty. When outside, they might wear a hooded cape.

Men would dress differently depending on their occupations. A minister or wealthy man might wear a wide-brimmed hat, a doublet or long waistcoat, breeches (knee-length trousers) and buckled shoes. Outdoor work would require simpler, sturdy clothing, such as woollen breeches, a collarless shirt, a neckcloth (a strip of fabric tied around the neck), hard-wearing boots and a leather or coarsely woven waistcoat. Puritans dressed in plain colours, often earth tones, such as tan or brown, or grey, with white or off-white cuffs and collars. Black was a more expensive dye, so that was used for formal clothes or for wealthier people, such as the judges. Linen and wool were the most popular fabrics.

Men's hair was usually shoulder-length and some wore expensive wigs. Although very young girls might wear their hair down, women would put their hair in a bun, usually tucked under a cap for modesty.

▲ *Costumes of the period* ▶

TASK 2

Look at the images of Puritan clothing on this page and decide which characters in the play might wear costumes that look like them. Make notes in your notebook describing their outfits and why they are suitable for those characters.

Costume, hair and make-up design inspired by context

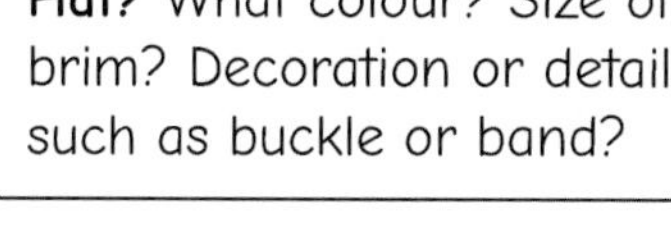

TASK 3

Use your understanding of the play's context and the prompts below to design a costume for **Reverend Hale** for Act 1.

Hair: Long or short? Wig or natural? Colour?

Make-up: Beard or clean-shaven? Pale or dark? Healthy or sickly? Is he careful or careless about his appearance?

Costume: Show that he has travelled and what his role is.
Colour: Black to signify role as minister and relative wealth? Cloak or jacket? Black or contrasting colour?
Fabrics: Wool? Cotton? Felt? Linen? Lace?
Fit and shape: Loose or closely fitted?

Shoes: Boots or shoes? Buckles or plain? New or worn?

Hat? What colour? Size of brim? Decoration or detail, such as buckle or band?

Collar: Collarless, neckcloth or collar? White? Tidy? Messy? Clean? Soiled?

Accessories: Glasses? Belt? Bag? What will demonstrate that he is an educated man?

TIP

When writing about your costume design choices, it is important that you not only describe them, but you also justify your choices. How will your choices show that you have understood the character of Reverend Hale and his place in this Puritan society?

CHALLENGE

Consider the character of Rebecca Nurse and create a costume design for her. It is important to consider: hair, make-up, fabric, fit and shape, and shoes. Rebecca is a much respected member of the community and would observe the expectations of a good Puritan woman. In Act 4, Rebecca is shown imprisoned and then led off to be executed. How might her costume change from Act 1 to Act 4?

Download a printable version from Samples & Downloads at www.illuminatepublishing.com.

Set design inspired by context

Each act of *The Crucible* has a different setting in the context of a Puritan community in the late 17th century. Although it can be interpreted in different ways, typically the play is performed and designed in a naturalistic style when the aim is to make the interpretation as realistic as possible. The first question will ask you to refer specifically to the context. As a designer, you will need to consider how your design will:

- serve the practical needs of the play
- show the period setting
- suggest the appropriate atmosphere.

After choosing your stage configuration, use the following to begin formulating ideas for your set design (the requirements have been started for you, but you may discover additional aspects of the set or props that you wish to include):

ACT 1

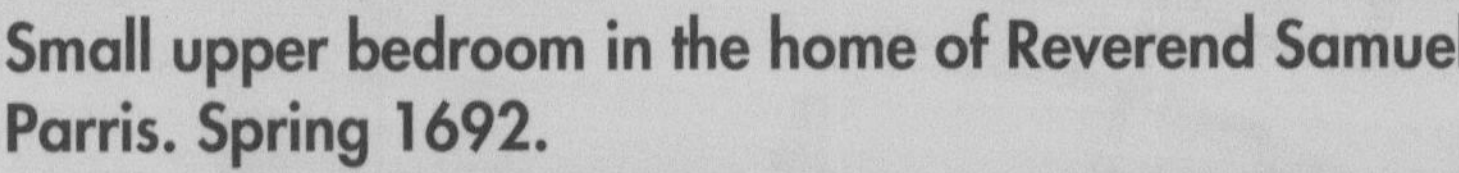

Small upper bedroom in the home of Reverend Samuel Parris. Spring 1692.

REQUIREMENTS OF LOCATION

Window. Candle. Chest. Chair. Table. Door. Bed.

DESIGN CHOICES

1. How will you show that this is a 17th-century building? What specific period features, such as wooden beams or leaded windows, could you use?
2. What choices of materials would you make for the walls and flooring? Wood? Stone? Plaster?
3. What are the main colours in the room?
4. Where would you arrange the furniture? (How central should the bed be, for example? Where will others sit or stand?)
5. What, if anything, can be seen outside the window?

ACT 2

The common room (living room) of Proctor's house. Eight days later.

REQUIREMENTS OF LOCATION

Outside door. Fireplace with pot. Opening leading to stairway. Basin. Table. Chairs. Plates, drinking utensils, cutlery.

DESIGN CHOICES

1. What is the atmosphere in the room? What can we learn about the Proctors from this room?
2. How can the room indicate the period (for example, how cooking and washing were done)?
3. What are the main colours in the room?
4. Where will you place the outside door for maximum effect when characters make their entrances?
5. What is the size of the table and where will you place it onstage?

The Salem meeting house, now serving as the courthouse.

REQUIREMENTS OF LOCATION

High windows. Heavy beams. Two doors leading into the meeting house. Another door leads outside. Two benches. A long meeting table. Stools. One armchair.

DESIGN CHOICES

1. How will the set show the difference in the atmosphere in contrast with the previous two sets?
2. Where will you position the judges' table and the benches to give the impression of a court and the importance of the judges?
3. Where will you position the doors to create dramatic effects, for example when Giles is carried in or the girls enter?
4. Where on the set will the girls claim to see 'the bird'?
5. What are the main colours in the room and what materials will you use for the set?

ACT 4 A cell in the Salem jail. Autumn, 1692.

REQUIREMENTS OF LOCATION

High, barred window. Heavy door. Two benches.

DESIGN CHOICES

1. How will this set demonstrate the different atmosphere in this act in contrast with the previous acts?
2. How can you create a design that makes clear this is a prison, how harsh the conditions are in the 17th century and how difficult it would be to escape? (Think about the door and window, for example.)
3. How can you make it clear that when this act begins it is night-time? How can you use light and shadow to create atmosphere?
4. What materials can you use to emphasise how uncomfortable the jail is?
5. Where will you position the door where Proctor finally exits to emphasise the importance of that moment?

MARTHA CORY AND HER PERSECUTORS.

▲ *Rebecca Nurse's homestead*

TASK 4

You are designing a set for a performance of Act 2 of *The Crucible*. The setting must reflect the context of a Puritan community in the late 17th century. Describe your design ideas for the setting.

You may wish to include:

- How the Proctors' common room reflects the simple beliefs of the Puritan community.
- How the materials used in the set reflect those available in the 17th century and the needs of those living in the house.
- What the set shows about the lives of Elizabeth and John Proctor.

TIP

When considering how you will design your set, it is important to know that you will often not use the actual materials of the time, but create the set out of materials that can be made to look like them. For example, you would probably paint plywood or other lightweight material to create the effect of stones in the jail, or stain a lighter wood to create dark wooden beams in the meeting house.

Writing about your design ideas

Question 1 will always ask you to consider an aspect of design for the play in relation to its context. Below is a student's plan for the following question:

You are designing a costume for Reverend Hale to wear in a performance of this extract from the first act. The costume must reflect the context of *The Crucible*, set in a Puritan community in the late 17th century. Describe your design ideas for the costume.

1 Understanding of character in play:

Reverend Hale is an educated, religious man. (1) His costume must reflect this.

2 Period:

Colours and fabrics: black breeches, white collar, black, long waistcoat. (2) Emphasise his role as a Puritan minister in Colonial America in the 17th century. (3) White linen shirt. Black wool for other items.

3 His relationship to the community:

Enters wearing cloak, shows he has travelled and comes from another community. (4) Wears glasses and carries a leather satchel of books to indicate his studious nature. (5)

4 Character:

His clothing is neat, well-pressed, suggesting a slight vanity. He is clean-shaven, with shoulder-length clean, fair hair. His buckled shoes are well polished showing that he does not do heavy manual or dirty work. (6)

(1) Demonstrates understanding of character

(2) Understand typical clothing of this period

(3) Refers to his role in this context

(4) Understanding of play and what has happened before this scene

(5) Shows understanding of how accessories can help establish character

(6) Considers hair and other period details and what they reveal about character

TIP

It is important to know that there are other interpretations of how Reverend Hale might be costumed.

TIP

It is important that you justify your ideas. Explain why you are making these specific choices; don't just describe what the character will look like. What do we learn about Mary as a young servant and her role in Puritan Salem from your costume choices?

- Understanding of character in play
- Period
- Her relationship to the community
- Character.

TASK 5

Using the plan above as a guide, create your own plan for the character of Mary Warren in answer to the following question:

You are designing a costume for Mary Warren to wear in a performance of this extract from the second act. The costume must reflect the context of *The Crucible*, set in a Puritan community in the late 17th century. Describe your own design ideas for the costume.

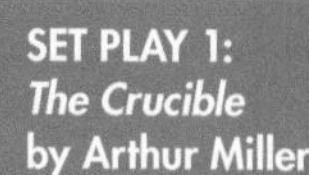

Practical explorations of characters, themes and style

When writing about performing roles in the play, you must demonstrate that you understand the characters and how they interact. You need to use the performance space to show your understanding of the play. Below are two themes from the play that you can explore practically to develop your understanding of the play and its characters.

Reputation

Reputation is an important theme in the play, with consequences for many characters. Proctor loses his reputation as a good Christian man in his community when he confesses to his 'lechery' with Abigail; Mary Warren risks her reputation with the girls by speaking up against them; Abigail lies to protect her own reputation by accusing Tituba and others; in the final act, Proctor chooses his reputation over his life.

TASK 6

a Focus on the character of Proctor. Read the scene with Proctor, Danforth and Hale in Act 4, starting with Danforth's line: 'Mr. Proctor. When the Devil came to you did you see Rebecca Nurse in his company?' and ending with Danforth's 'Why? Do you mean to deny this confession when you are free?'

b With your group create a 'conscience alley' to help Proctor make up his mind. One of you will be Proctor and the rest will form two facing lines. One side of the line must think of reasons why Proctor should sign the confession and the other side should think of reasons why he should not. As 'Proctor' walks down the alley between the two lines, each person shouts out a reason for or against signing the confession. At the end of the alley, 'Proctor' must refuse to sign and say the line 'Because it is my name.'

c Discuss how it felt to hear all the conflicting reasons and how the performer playing Proctor made their decision.

d Everyone in the group should have a turn saying 'Because it is my name'. Write your observations on the following in your notebook:

- projection/volume
- emotion
- pace, pause and timing
- inflection (words said with particular emphasis).

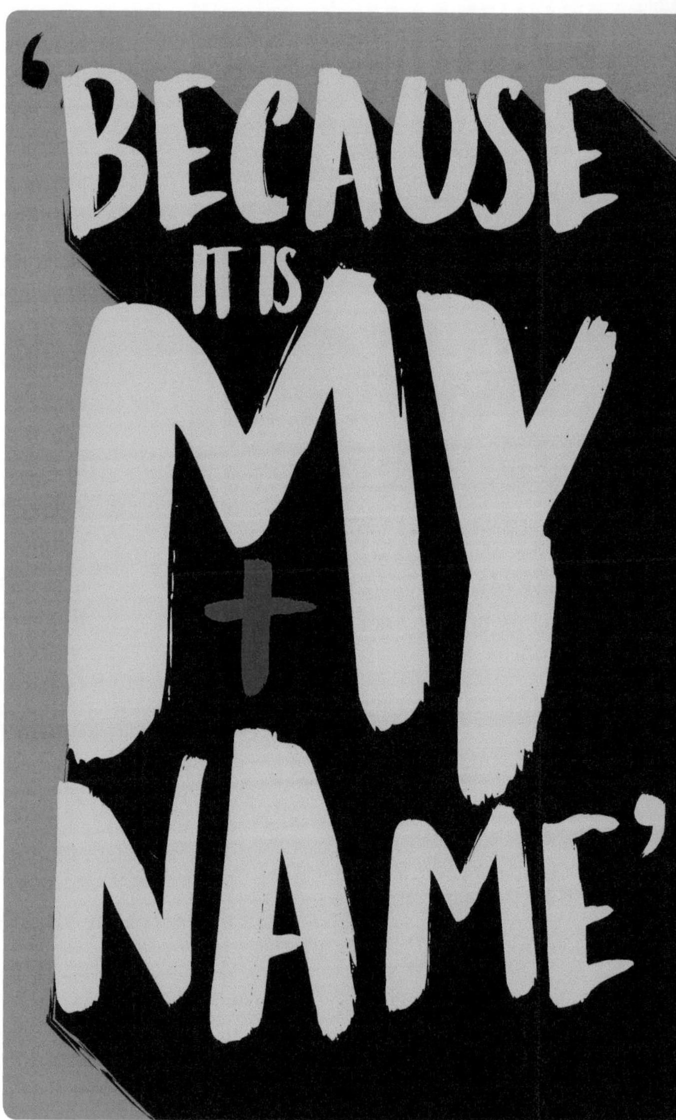

Love

There are several examples of love in the play, most particularly the love between Elizabeth and Proctor.
In Act 2, their relationship is strained and there is a great deal of unspoken tension between them. Beneath their lines, there is a subtext, which is influenced by Proctor's former relationship with Abigail.

KEY TERM:

Repressing: holding back or restraining.

TASK 7

a With a partner, read a section of Act 2 from Proctor's line: 'It's well seasoned' to Elizabeth's line 'I couldn't stop her.'

b Now read the scene again, but thought-track what the characters are really thinking after each line.

Here is an example:

> **Proctor:** It's well seasoned.
>
> **Thought-track:** Only because I put more salt in.
>
> **Elizabeth:** I took great care. She's tender.
>
> **Thought-track:** I'm so happy - I am really trying to please him. Does he mean it though? Is everything all right? Or is he just saying it?

c Now read through the scene a third time, without saying the thought-tracking lines, but keeping them in mind with the way you speak. Do these thoughts create more pauses or awkwardness in the way they speak to each other?

d In the notes you make accompanying your script, jot down any discoveries you have made.

e Now read the scene between Proctor and Elizabeth in Act 4, when they speak frankly of their feelings for each other, starting with Elizabeth's line 'It is not for me to give, John I am' and ending with Elizabeth's line 'It were a cold house I kept!'

f Discuss with your partner the contrasts between how Proctor and Elizabeth speak to each other in this scene compared with the scene in Act 2.

g Again, note down any discoveries you have made.

h Lastly, write a few sentences describing the physical and vocal choices that could be made when performing these scenes and how the love between the characters could be shown.

Here is a sample response:

In Act 4, Elizabeth finally speaks frankly to John about her feelings. Instead of judging him and repressing her feelings, she is emotional and open. (1) Playing her, I would speak harshly when I say 'cold wife' and I would gesture angrily at myself. (2) When I say 'so plain', I would look down, unable to meet John's eyes. (3) However, I would look up at him and take a step closer when I say 'I should say my love.' (4) I think this is the first time Elizabeth has actually said the word 'love' to him and it would be said in a 'trembling way'. (5)

(1) Explains why choices are made
(2) Describes vocal and physical choices
(3) Detail of use of eye contact
(4) Detail of use of eye contact and stage space
(5) Explains why choices are made

TIP

Remember that only clean (unannotated) copies of the script can be taken into the exam.

Interpretation of character

SET PLAY 1:
The Crucible
by Arthur Miller

1

You will need to show how you can interpret a character. This means that you understand the character's motivations and goals and the obstacles they face. Then you must be able to use your vocal and physical skills to portray the character and create particular effects for the audience, such as tension, comedy, surprise, pity or sorrow.

Look below at one interpretation of the character of **Giles Corey** (your interpretation may differ).

FACTS:

Age: *he is an old man, 83*

Job: *farmer, still active*

Interpretation:

PHYSICAL APPEARANCE:

I imagine Corey to be short and, for his age, muscular.

HAIR:

Long, grey, somewhat tangled and not recently washed.

VOICE:

Speaks in a stronger dialect than other characters – 'readin'. He is simple and straightforward with a tendency to repeat himself 'deep, deep'. Low-pitch, gruff, often shouts.

MAKE-UP:

Emphasise his age, with deep grooves on his forehead. Skin is rough from outdoor work.

BODY LANGUAGE:

Solid, rooted to the ground, ready for a fight, often raises his fists. At his age, he may have a slight limp from decades of hard work, but that doesn't slow him down. Possibly hard of hearing, so leans forward to make sure he catches everything.

COSTUME:

Rough, practical clothes. Brown breeches, sturdy plain leather shoes, no buckle. Poorly repaired stockings – he would think it a waste to get new ones. Coarse woollen, brown waistcoat, off-white linen shirt, with some stains.

EFFECT ON AUDIENCE:

Giles Corey is the most comic character in the play and his stubbornness and, early in the play, his willingness to fight should cause some amusement. However, he is also very brave and when the audience hear about his death in Act 4 they should be sad.

Download a printable version from Samples & Downloads at www.illuminatepublishing.com.

TASK 8

Using your own understanding of the characters in the play and how they could be interpreted, create an interpretation on paper, with the following as a guide, of Mary Warren, Rebecca Nurse or Ann Putnam. In this instance, think about total characterisation, which includes facts about the characters and their appearance as well as how they could be interpreted through acting, costume and make-up choices. This will help you to think about all aspects of interpreting the character, even when writing about acting or design.

Download a printable version from Samples & Downloads at www.illuminatepublishing.com.

Performing choices

SET PLAY 1: *The Crucible* by Arthur Miller

1

In Question 2, you will be asked to discuss in detail how you would perform a particular line as a given character. For example:

You are performing the role of Abigail. Describe how you would use your vocal and physical skills to perform the lines below and explain the effects you want to create.

Abigail: And you must. You are no wintry man. I know you, John. I *know* you.

In this scene, Abigail wants to win Proctor's affections again. (1) As Abigail, I would move closer to Proctor on 'And you must.' (2) I would put my hand on his chest on the word 'wintry' and maintain eye contact, (3) making clear that I can see that he is attracted to me. (4) On the word 'wintry' my tone will be sarcastic (5) because I know he is warm-hearted and passionate. On 'I know you John' I will move even closer and put my arms around him. (6) I will speak those words slowly and softly as if to mesmerise him, (7) but also making sure that we cannot be overheard by others. (8) I will emphasise the word 'know' (9) because, in those days, know, in the biblical sense, meant having sexual relations, so my tone will suggest our past. (10) I will speak those words with a breathy, seductive voice, with my face close enough to him that we could kiss. (11) The effect of these choices for these lines will show the power that Abigail wants to have over Proctor. (12)

Annotations: (1) Effect; (2) Physical skills; (3) Physical skills; (4) Effect; (5) Vocal skills; (6) Physical skills; (7) Vocal skills; (8) Effect; (9) Vocal skills; (10) Effect; (11) Vocal and physical skills; (12) Effect

TIP

It is a good idea to write in the first person ('I') so you can fully imagine your own performance of the role. Do more than describe the vocal and physical skills you would use: also think about how your choices will add to the audience's understanding of the play, its characters and their relationships.

TASK 9

Experiment with different ways of using your vocal and physical skills for each of the following lines:

Tituba: Act 1: Oh, how many times he bid me kill you, Mr Parris!

Proctor: Act 2: Oh, Elizabeth, your justice would freeze beer!

Hale: Act 2: Aye. But the Devil is a wily one, you cannot deny it.

Mary: Act 3: Let me go, Mr Proctor, I cannot, I cannot –

Elizabeth: Act 3: She – dissatisfied me. [*Pause.*] And my husband.

Parris: Act 4: Thirty-one pound is gone. I am penniless.

Danforth: Act 4: Why, for the good instruction of the village, Mister; this we shall post upon the church door.

TASK 10

a Make notes in your workbook on:
- vocal skills
- physical skills
- effects achieved.

b Then, using the example answer above as a guide, write an answer to the same question referring to the characters and lines in Task 9.

c Check your work by marking or highlighting:

V for each vocal skill you mention

P for each physical skill

E for an effect on the audience.

Character revision sheet

Below is a partly completed character revision sheet for **Abigail Williams**. Copy the grid and complete it.

Character and importance to the play	Abigail Williams Leader of the girls and the cause of conflict between Elizabeth and John.
What do they want?	Wants to be with John. Wants adventure.
What obstacles do they face?	John rejects her. The Puritan society confines and restricts her.
What are their key scenes?	Act 1: Scene with Parris about being found in the woods. Act 1: Scene with Proctor about their previous relationship. Act 1: Scene with Hale and others accusing Tituba of leading them in witchcraft. Act 3: Scene in court responding to Mary Warren's accusations.

How might they be costumed?	How might their hair and make-up be done?
Draw a simple sketch or write a description of it. Consider: • colours • fabrics • shape and fit • character's personality and status.	Draw a simple sketch or write a description of it. Consider: • style and colour of hair • type of make-up (realistic or fantasy; colours; how it is appropriate for character, setting and period).

How might they use body language? • Posture • Gait (the way they walk) • Facial expression	
How might they use their voice? • Emotional range (angry, sad, happy, irritated, desperate, dominating and so on) • Pitch and volume (low or high; loud or soft) • Accent or other distinctive vocal features	
Choose one important line and analyse how they might say it.	Act 1: 'A wild thing may say wild things.'

TASK 11

Using the grid for guidance, create similar revision sheets for all major characters including: Elizabeth, John Proctor, Hale, Mary Warren, Danforth, Tituba and Parris.

Download a printable version from Samples & Downloads at www.illuminatepublishing.com.

Using the performance space and interaction with others

There are opportunities to explore the space and interaction with others in a number of different ways in the four settings of the play. There are intimate two-person scenes, such as the scenes between Proctor and Elizabeth or Proctor and Abigail, and busy, crowded scenes, like the trial; there are scenes set during the day and others at night; scenes in domestic settings and others in public places. When you are writing about performance space and interaction, make sure that you focus on the effects you wish to achieve, such as tension, surprise, humour, pity or sorrow, and how you will use your skills to achieve them.

TASK 12

Look closely at the entrance of John Proctor in Act 1, starting from '*Enter* John Proctor. *On seeing him,* Mary Warren *leaps in fright*' and ending with Abigail's 'Give me a word, John.'

a Read the scene, taking particular notice of any stage directions.

b Agree what stage configuration you are going to use: end on, theatre in the round, thrust, promenade, proscenium or traverse. Mark where the entrances will be and any pieces of furniture.

c Decide what effects you wish to achieve. To help with this, think about the following issues:

- Proctor's character: Miller describes him as having 'a quiet confidence' and 'an unexpressed, hidden force'. How might this affect the way the performer stands and moves?
- Mary's reaction to him: she is his servant and is frightened of him. Yet when she leaves she tries to 'retain a shred of dignity' and exits slowly. How could the performer make clear what she wants to show the others?
- Abigail's reaction to him: how obvious is her attraction to him? Does she do anything to catch his attention?
- How Mercy reacts to him: what does the stage direction for Mercy ('*both afraid of him and strangely titillated*') mean and how could the performer show this?
- Do John and Abigail behave differently when Mercy and Mary leave the room? How does it add to the tension of the scene that they may be overheard or interrupted at any time?

d How will you use stage space? Try the following:

Proctor's entrance:

- Have Proctor enter and stand in the doorway, slowly observing the other characters.
- Have Proctor enter quickly and stand centre stage, ignoring Abigail.
- Have Proctor enter at a steady pace, stop and see Abigail, briefly make eye contact with her, and then continue walking across the room.

Mary's reaction:

- Have Mary jump up, let out a small shriek, and then hide her face in her hands.
- Have Mary hide behind Abigail, while nervously twisting the end of her apron.
- Have Mary run past John towards the door, avoiding eye contact.

e Continue working through the scene, experimenting with different staging configuration ideas. Then answer the following question:

> You are performing the role of **John Proctor**.
>
> Focus on the lines 'Be you foolish, Mary Warren?' to '… my wife is waitin' with your work.' Explain how you might use the performance space and interact with the actor playing Mary Warren to **create tension** for the audience.

Answering a question about character interpretation

If you choose to answer Question 4, you will need to write about how you would use your acting skills to interpret a character both in the extract provided and in the play as a whole.

An example of this sort of question might be:

TIP

It is important to know that you will have your own interpretation of this character, this is just one example.

> You are performing the role of **Parris**.
>
> Describe how you would use your acting skills to **interpret Parris' character**. Explain why your ideas are appropriate for:
>
> - this extract (Act 1, 'And what shall I say to them' to 'Do you understand that?')
> - the performance of your role in the play as a whole.

Below is a sample student plan for this question.

This extract:

1 Character of Parris and reasons for making acting choices:

Minister, self-important, but also distressed because of daughter and what he has seen of the girls' actions. Wants high status. Suspicious of others.

2 Acting skills: vocal:

Well-spoken. Orders others: 'Sit you down.' Tries to dominate, uses volume and speaks directly and with authority. Speaks more quickly on 'And what shall I say to them?' and more softly so as not to be overheard on 'my daughter and my niece' – he's embarrassed. More emotion on 'This child is desperate' and 'There is a faction ...' – is fearful both for his daughter and his position.

3 Acting skills: physical:

Upright posture. Eye contact with Abigail, willing her to tell the truth. Remains standing when he makes Abigail sit. Towers over her, trying to dominate. Towards end of extract, gestures become more pleading – points towards Betty, wrings his hands anxiously. Moves towards Abigail trying to convince her. Looks over his shoulder, suspicious, anxious, when talking about a 'faction'. Shows his fear.

Rest of play:

1 Character of Parris and reasons for making acting choices:

By end of the play, a broken man who has lost almost everything. His certainty and status are gone. Important that status is established in earlier scenes, so loss of it at the end is felt.

2 Acting skills: vocal:

Act 3: speaks bitterly of Giles Corey and Proctor. Suspicious, complaining. Shocked when Proctor brings in Mary Warren, shouts out. More confident tone when discussing the Bible, takes a condescending, knowing tone. Totally different in Act 4. He is troubled. Speaks quickly, with high emotion, breaks into sobs. Voice ragged, shouts final line.

3 Acting skills: physical:

In Act 4: anxious, nervous energy, quick gestures. Afraid of Proctor. Tries to be kind to Proctor but has to accept his rejection. Bows his head before Proctor. Clear loss of status in his movements at ending.

TASK 13

Using the plan above as a guide, create your own plan in answer to the following question using the headings in the Tip on the left:

> You are performing the role of **Elizabeth**.
>
> Describe how you would use your acting skills to **interpret Elizabeth's character** in Act 2, from Elizabeth's 'Oh, the noose, the noose is up!' to 'John – grant me this.' Explain why your ideas are appropriate for:
>
> - this extract
> - the performance of your role in the play as a whole.

TIP

It is important to include both vocal and physical skills. Highlight key moments when these points can be discussed.

- Character and reasons for making acting choices
- Acting skills: vocal
- Acting skills: physical.

Design choices

If you choose to answer Question 5, you will be thinking as a designer and commenting on one aspect of design. See the question on the right, for example.

You may choose to focus on set design, costume design, lighting design, sound design or puppet design. Whichever you choose, you must explain why your ideas are appropriate to the play as a whole. You might refer to:

- how your design helps to show the action and the nature of the characters
- how your design for the extract is consistent with the design requirements of the rest of the play (Don't, for example, suddenly change mid-scene from a period to a modern setting.)
- how you have used design methods that fit in with the mood of the play
- props, anything that the actors may carry onstage.

The Crucible is usually performed and designed in a naturalistic way, with an emphasis on its period setting. However, some productions use symbolism to emphasise certain themes or choose more minimalistic sets to focus on the acting. A production may introduce a colour, such as red, at certain points to indicate danger. Others show the woods where the girls were dancing in every act to indicate their importance to the plot.

You may choose to use modern techniques such as projections to suggest the New England countryside or to highlight religious imagery. You could use music or sound effects to create the sense of doom in the final act or to underscore the girls' visions of the Devil. You could choose lighting effects to pick out key moments or to emphasise the passing of time.

You are a designer working on **one** aspect of design for this extract.

Describe how you would use your design skills to create effects which **support the action**. Explain why your ideas are appropriate for:

- this extract
- your chosen design skill in the play as a whole.

TIP

Whatever design choices you make, you must make sure that they show your understanding of the play and its needs.

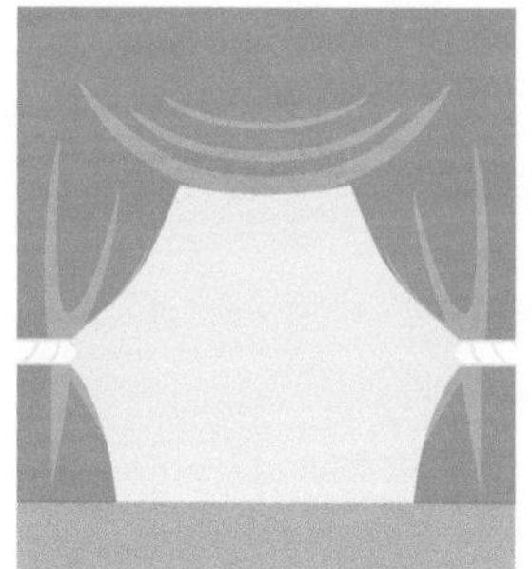

Robert Innes Hopkins, designer

Can you explain your design for *The Crucible*?

As a Puritan community in Massachusetts in the 1600s, the characters in *The Crucible* would have built their own homes and would not have had many possessions. Therefore, everything onstage is very simple, with a handmade feel that uses natural materials such as wood. For the first half, I have the challenge of housing all the actors onstage, even when they are not in the scene. To achieve this, I have made a playing space on a circular disc in the middle of the stage, with benches alongside where the actors will sit and enter and exit the performance space without the use of doorways – eliminating that level of naturalism. It is not designed to be a naturalistic actual space, but we represent the three main settings with unique pieces of set, for example a window or a door to demonstrate a change in environment. (Bristol Old Vic, Education Pack)

Costume design

For costume design, you might consider:

- style, cut and fit of costume
- colour, fabric, decorative features
- condition (worn or new; neat or wrinkled; clean or stained)
- footwear/headgear
- accessories
- status or social role of character
- make-up and hairstyle.

Below is an extract from a sample response based on Abigail in Act 1, in her scene with Proctor.

In this scene, I would have Abigail dressed in clothing typical of the other servant girls: a long, plain, brown woollen dress, white apron, cap and white shawl-like collar. (1) However, I want to show her character through her costume, by emphasising her awareness of her own beauty. (2) Although she is wearing a cap, there will be tendrils of hair escaping from it, creating a softer, more seductive look. (3) Her clothes will be neater and in better condition than the other girls. (4) Her brown leather shoes will be unmarked and shiny. She will wear the modest collar of the others, but it will be more open at the neck, exposing a little more of her chest than the others. (5) Her dress will be closely fitted at the waist, showing her attractive shape. (6) Abigail is a rebel and, although ornamentation would be frowned upon by Puritans, I would have her wear a little decorative object, like a feather, pinned under her collar, to show her willingness to break the rules. (7) In this extract, her costume should demonstrate how she stands out from the other girls and her sensual appeal to John Proctor. (8)

In Act 3, I would remove any of the features from the first act that made her stand out, with her hair tucked neatly into a cap, looking proper, so her testimony would be believed. (9)

(1) Fabric, colours and style consistent with setting and period of the play

(2) Understanding of character and action of the scene

(3) Discusses hairstyle and effect on portrayal of character

(4) Condition of clothing

(5) Costume detail to portray character

(6) Shape and fit of costume

(7) Ornamental detail

(8) How costume helps to convey action of play

(9) How costume would be altered for her role in the rest of the play

TASK 14

Draw a sketch showing Elizabeth's costume, make-up and hair for Act 2. Then create a contrasting sketch of her for Act 4. Label the drawings, showing the differences between the costumes.

TIP

You might want to consider the following about Deputy Governor Danforth when considering his costume: his status and authority; his relative wealth; what we learn about his character.

TASK 15

a Write an answer, as a costume designer, to the following question:

> Focus on Act 3, from '*Enter* Deputy Governor Danforth' to 'Giles [*through helpless sob*]: It is my third wife, sir.'
>
> You are a designer working on **one** aspect of design for this extract.
>
> Describe how you would use your design skills to create effects which **support the action**. Explain why your ideas are appropriate for:
>
> - this extract
> - your chosen design skill in the play as a whole.

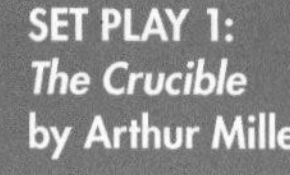

b Check that you have:

- referred to fabric, colours, shape/silhouette, fit, condition
- included headwear and/or footwear, as appropriate
- considered make-up and hairstyle, as appropriate
- explained how the costume helps the action of the extract
- related your design to the rest of the play.

Set design

For the set design, you might consider:

- stage configuration
- if you will use one main set to represent all locations or will have four separate sets
- the scale (how large) your set will be
- if there will be any levels, ramps or stairs
- the entrances/exits
- if there will be backdrops, flats or projections
- the colour palette you will use
- how the materials, textures and shapes will help to create a suitable setting
- which props are needed.

TASK 16

a Imagine that you You have been asked to design the set for Act 4 for the stage configuration of your choice. You need to emphasise the dark, frightening nature of the jail and how trapped the characters are. Create a sketch showing your ideas. The idea below is one of many ways of beginning a set sketch.

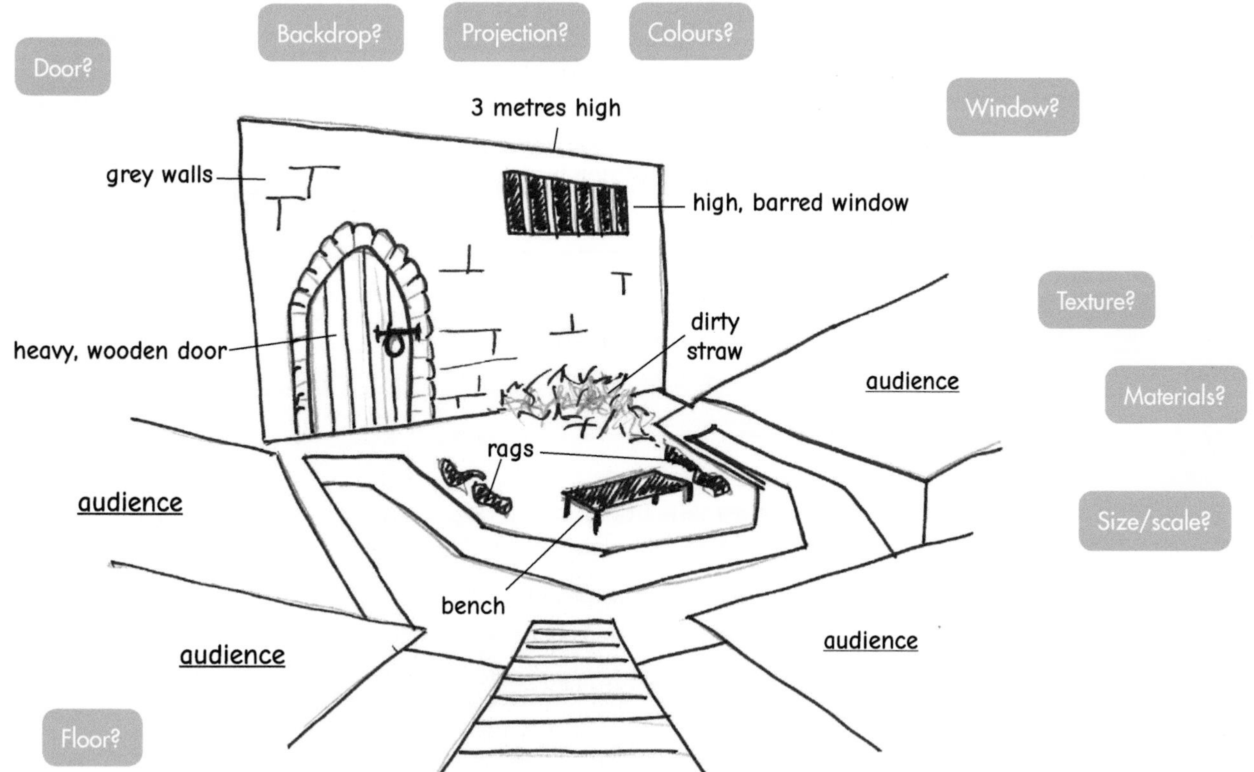

b Draw your sketch showing:
- the colours and textures (rough, smooth, patterned, irregular) you will use
- the materials for the set (or what they will look like, e.g. stone, wood, plaster, metal)
- the scale of the set in relation to the size of the actors
- any levels (stool, benches, platforms)
- where key events like entrances/exits will occur.

Below are three different sample responses about the set in Act 4.

A

As I am working on a thrust stage, I will use only the back wall to show the setting. (1) I will have a projection (2) showing a typical jail cell, (3) with bars on the windows. Everything on the stage will be dark and dirty. It will look very uncomfortable. There will be a stool for characters to sit on.

1. Identifies stage configuration and its limitation in terms of scenery
2. Uses projection
3. Refers to jail cell, but says 'typical', which may be stereotypical and not entirely clear

B

In order to create the feeling of entrapment, (4) I will try to make the thrust space seem much smaller than in the previous acts. To accomplish this I will use piles of boxes and rags along the edges, some of which will be hiding characters like Sarah Good at the beginning of the act. (5) Upstage right there will be a dark-brown, over-sized door, at least three metres tall (6) and will appear to be very heavy to open. This will make clear how hard it would be to escape.

4. Explains how it will help the action of the scene
5. Explains how it will help introduce a character
6. Discusses colour and scale

C

My design will combine both naturalistic and symbolic touches. (7) The walls will have chains and the high, barred windows will let in little light. The back wall upstage will be a very dark grey, appearing to be made of dark, rough stone with a large ragged splash of red, like blood, on it. (8)
The dark, uneven stones represent the frightening prison and the red splash symbolically suggests the frightening death that awaits them. (9) The grey and red colour palette will be used throughout my design. (10) When Proctor exits to his death, the backdrop behind the doorway will be bright red. (11)

7. Shows approach to overall design
8. Discusses colours and texture
9. Explains effect of choices
10. Comments on overall design
11. Shows how design supports the action of the scene

TASK 17

All of the responses above have different strengths. Read through them and decide which one you think best explains their design and why.

TASK 18

Now choose a scene from Act 1, 2 or 3. As a set designer, using the stage configuration of your choice, answer the following question:

> You are a designer working on **one** aspect of design for this extract.
> Describe how you would use your design skills to create effects which **support the action**.
> Explain why your ideas are appropriate for:
> - this extract
> - your chosen design skill in the play as a whole.

Lighting design

When creating your lighting design you might consider how to create:

- time of day and, possibly, season
- atmosphere
- focus to highlight particular moments
- how to help convey the setting, action and characters of a scene (such as a follow spot to focus the audience on a character's journey or backlighting to make them appear mysterious).

Some of your tools are:

- colours
- angles and intensity
- light from onstage sources (lanterns, candles and so on)
- use of shadow and silhouette
- **special effects**
- use of blackouts or fades.

KEY TERM:

Special effects: lighting and sounds that are not 'usual' for the scene or production, such as lighting to recreate headlights or fires and the sounds of thunder or gunfire.

TASK 19

Use the mind maps below to make notes in your notebook on the different lighting demands of Act 1 and Act 4.

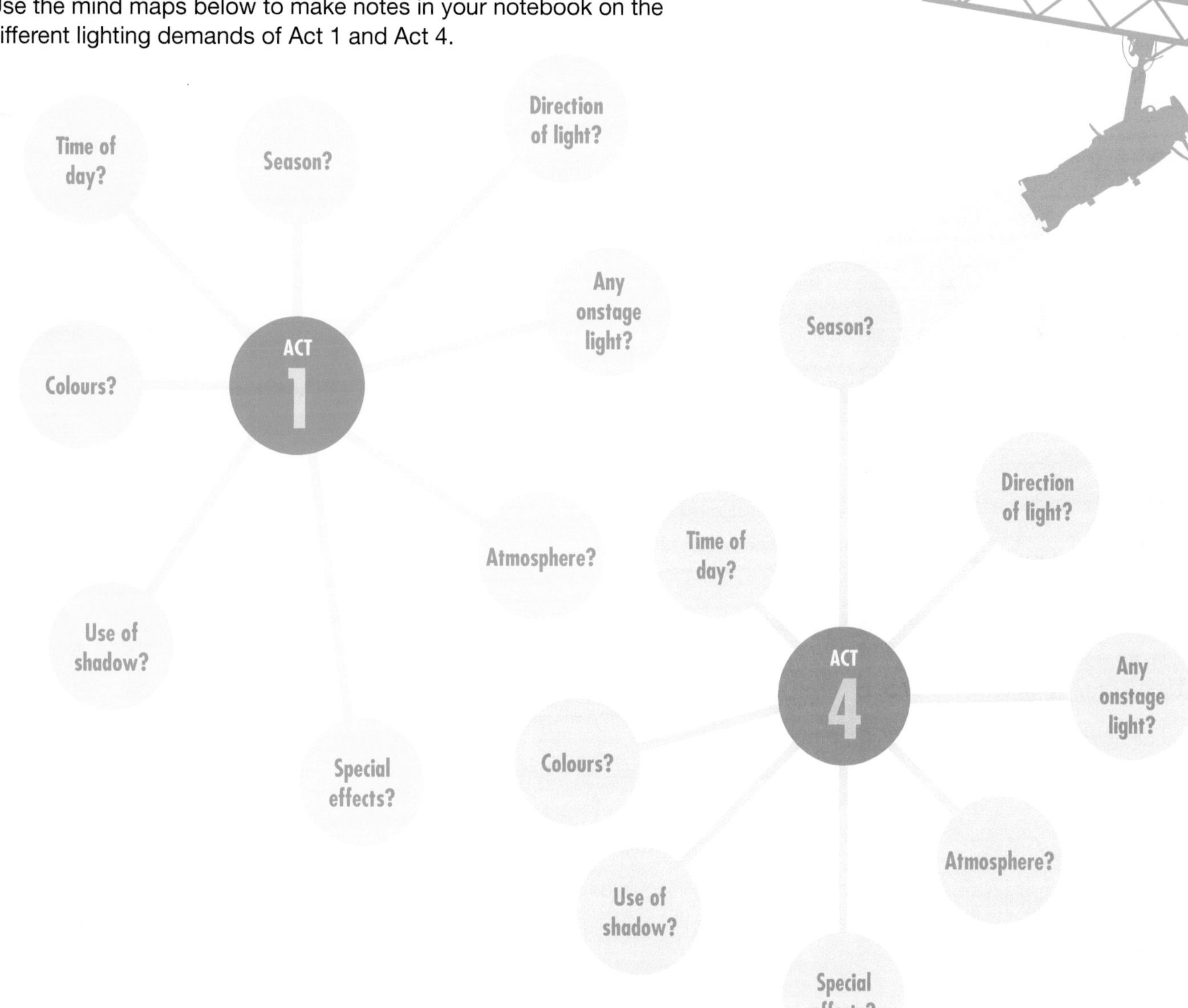

Below are some brief ideas in response to the demands of lighting *The Crucible*.

Technical term (footlights) and notes location

Explains effect

A

In order to capture the eerie quality of the jail, I will use footlights downstage (1). These will cast eerie shadows back onto the faces of the actors and emphasise how tired and desperate they look. (2)

B

I want to show how ordinary Act 1 is in comparison to the others, so I will use soft, slightly yellow light coming in through the bedroom window from a lighting rig in the wings using gels, projecting a light like a lovely spring afternoon.

KEY TERMS:

Footlights: lights placed at the front of the stage at the level of the actor's feet, with their light directed upwards.

Rig: what the lights are positioned on (a lighting rig) or 'to rig the lights' is to set them in position.

C

In Act 3, on the moment when Proctor shouts 'Elizabeth, I have confessed it,' I will use a strobe to create a flash of lightning to indicate that this is a moment when everything goes wrong for the Proctors.

D

In Act 4, I will have the actors using lanterns, while much of the stage will be dark. This means that, at certain moments, when they hold the lanterns close to their faces they will be lit and other times in shadows.

E

At the end of Act 1, I would have the lights slowly dim from the moment the girls begin naming various women as being with the Devil. I want to create the effect that their naming of people will go on a long time, even after the lights are out.

F

In Act 2, I will have a warm orange light on the fireplace, as that is the source of warmth in the household. Outside the door and window, a blue evening spring light will be streaming diagonally into the room.

G

In Act 1, I will have Reverend Hale backlit when he enters the doorway, creating almost a halo around him. I want to give the impression at first that he is a good man of God who is there to help.

H

Act 4 goes from night to morning, so I would have the ghostly, pearly white light, representing moonlight, entering from the barred windows, gradually change to a rosy glow by the end of the play. This light would be shining on Proctor as he exits.

TASK 20

Read the excerpts on this page and highlight any which refer to:

- colours
- angles
- special effects
- onstage lights
- dimming
- blackouts.

Check that you are confident identifying different ways lighting can be used in your response.

Sound design

When creating your sound design for *The Crucible*, you will want to consider how to:

- create atmosphere
- add to the action and emotion of a scene
- contribute to the setting and style of the play
- fulfil practical needs of the script.

Some choices you can make involve:

- live or recorded sound
- volume/amplification (use of microphones)
- naturalistic or symbolic sound
- music.

On the right is a sample of possible sound design ideas for Act 2.

Opening:

Music: recorded period folk song, 'Greensleeves'. Fades. Same song is picked up by actor playing Elizabeth, who sings it live.

Sound: recorded bird song and distant sounds of cattle, projected from upstage speaker.

Singing: live (offstage): actor playing Elizabeth singing 'Greensleeves'.

Sound: live (offstage): children murmuring as being put to bed.

Sound: recorded: outside bird and cattle noises fade to silence.

Sound: live: Proctor's footsteps.

TASK 21

Focus on Act 3, from Abigail's line 'Look out! She's coming down!' and ending with Mary's 'No, I love God.' How could you add extra tension to this scene through your sound design?

Some choices you could make include:

- adding recorded music under the scene
- having performers onstage or offstage playing instruments to highlight certain moments
- adding recorded sound effects such as squealing violins, squawking birds or rushing wind
- experimenting with the volume of the sound (suddenly getting louder or softer)
- adding either live or recorded drumming or other percussive instruments to highlight key moments.

Experiment with different versions of this scene. Then, in your notebook accompanying your script, make notes about which choices you thought were most effective.

2 SET PLAY 2: *Blood Brothers* by Willy Russell

Synopsis

Blood Brothers was **first performed in 1983** and is set in **Liverpool**. The play opens with a **Narrator** warning the audience that **Mrs Johnstone**, a working-class mother, is 'so cruel' because she had twins and gave one away. Mrs Johnstone sings about her husband who, after she had many children, left her for a younger woman.

Mrs Johnstone has a job cleaning for a middle class couple, the **Lyons**, who are unable to have children of their own. When Mrs Johnstone discovers she is pregnant with twins, **Mrs Lyons** convinces her to give one of the twins to her. Mrs Lyons tells the superstitious Mrs Johnstone that if the boys ever learn they are twins they will both die.

At age seven, the twins, **Edward** and **Mickey**, meet and, unaware of their relationship, become best friends and 'blood brothers'. Edward's and Mickey's upbringings are very different. Edward is protected by Mrs Lyons, whereas Mickey spends his days playing in the streets with his friends, including **Linda**. He is bullied by his older brother **Sammy**, who he both admires and fears.

Mrs Lyons convinces Mr Lyons that they should move away. When Edward comes to say goodbye to Mickey, Mrs Johnstone gives him a locket with a photograph of a young Mickey and her in it.

The first act ends with Mrs Johnstone celebrating the news that they are being rehoused to a council estate in the country, which they hope will be a bright new start for them.

Act 2 begins with Mrs Johnstone singing about the joys of their new life, but also suggesting that they have brought their problems with them. In particular, Sammy has begun to get into trouble with the law. Mickey is now a self-conscious 14-year-old. Linda declares her love for him. Meanwhile, Edward is at a nearby private school where he is suspended after a teacher tries to take his locket from him. Mickey and Linda are also suspended for talking back in class. Linda and Mickey go up to a field, but Mickey finds he can't express himself to Linda and she storms off. Edward arrives and the boys resume their friendship.

Mrs Lyons, who is behaving in an increasingly unstable way, confronts Mrs Johnstone. Mrs Lyons lunges at Mrs Johnstone with a knife, but Mrs Johnstone fights her off. Linda, Mickey and Edward have three idyllic summers together, with both boys attracted to Linda, but neither declaring his love. As Edward prepares to go to university, he encourages Mickey finally to ask Linda out.

Mickey gets a job at a factory. Linda becomes pregnant and she and Mickey get married.

When Edward comes back for the Christmas holidays, he discovers an unhappy Mickey who has been laid off from his job. Edward and Mickey argue. Edward declares his love to Linda and she tells him that she's now pregnant and married to Mickey.

Sammy convinces Mickey to take part in a robbery. Sammy kills the petrol station worker and he and Mickey go to jail. When Mickey leaves jail, he is addicted to pills.

Edward is now a Councillor. With Edward's help, Linda arranges to get a new home and a job for Mickey.

Mrs Lyons shows Mickey that Edward and Linda are meeting in secret. Armed with a gun, Mickey goes to the Town Hall where Edward is speaking at a council meeting. Afraid that Mickey is going to kill Edward, Mrs Johnstone tells him, 'He's your brother.' Mickey is enraged, saying, 'I could have been him!' The gun goes off and kills Edward. The police shoot Mickey. Mrs Johnstone is left mourning her two sons.

TIP

Although *Blood Brothers* is a play with musical numbers, you will not be tested on your knowledge of musical theatre techniques, such as singing or choreography. Instead, focus on how characters are created and the plot is developed.

TASK 1

a With your group, create ten still images showing what you think are the most important plot points in the play.

b Then discuss and make a list of what you think are the biggest challenges in performing and designing the musical *Blood Brothers*. You might consider costumes, setting, sound and lighting, and the demands on the actors. For example:

Timescale – showing characters getting older.

Making the ending moving/sad.

Balancing the comic and serious elements.

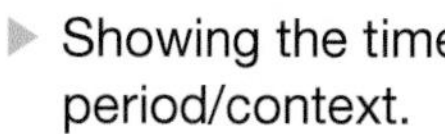

Showing the time period/context.

TIP

When you are asked to reflect on the context of *Blood Brothers* it is the context of Liverpool between the 1960s and the 1980s and its working-class community (as represented by the Johnstones) or the middle class (as represented by the Lyons) that you should discuss.

Context

Willy Russell has set his play in a **working-class community in Liverpool**, his own hometown. Liverpool was for many decades a thriving port city and supported many industries.

The play spans the 1960s to the early 1980s. In the 1960s, Liverpool became internationally famous for its culture, particularly music by popular groups such as the Beatles. However, in the 1970s and early 1980s, Liverpool suffered a great economic decline (which some blamed on the Prime Minister at that time, Margaret Thatcher), which led to many lost jobs. Russell refers to this in the song 'Take a Letter, Miss Jones' when Mr Lyons fires a number of employees as 'an unfortunate sign of the times'. At some points, the unemployment rate was as high as 50 per cent. The recession heightened the differences between the working class and middle and upper classes.

In *Blood Brothers*, Linda and Mickey, like Willy Russell himself, attend a secondary modern, a state school for students who did not pass their 11 plus examination – a test that state school children took to establish their academic potential and future schooling. Edward attends a private boarding school, spending term times at school and returning home for the holidays. Russell highlights the contrasts between the two schools by cutting straight from one to the other, showing the differences between the students and the teachers.

In the first act of the play, the Lyons and the Johnstones are shown to be living close to each other despite their different levels of wealth. At the end of the first act, the Lyons relocate to the countryside with Mrs Lyons hoping that a move away from the Johnstones will mean that Edward will not only avoid learning about his true mother, but also that he will mix with what she believes will be a better class of people.

However, the Johnstones, who have probably been living in a small rented terraced house, are moved out to one of the suburban council estates that were being built, not far from where the Lyons now live and where Edward goes to school. The move away from inner-city areas was a government plan aimed at improving the quality of housing for poorer people, but many residents missed the sense of community and the convenience of their city homes.

TASK 2

a Look at the photographs of houses on this page. Select which ones best represent your idea of:

  i what the Lyons' house might look like

  ii what the Johnstones' house might look like.

b Carefully read the scenes that take place within the Johnstone and Lyons houses.

  i List which props are mentioned in the text.

  ii What additional props could be added to create the context of the homes?

Costume, hair and make-up design inspired by context

SET PLAY 2:
Blood Brothers
by Willy Russell
2

In the beginning of Act 2, the teenage Sammy is 16 and getting into trouble with the police. Although he didn't have much money, like many young men at this time, Sammy's fashion choices were influenced by rock bands, such as the Bay City Rollers, and other well-known figures, such as the footballer George Best. In some working-class communities there was a revival of Teddy Boy clothing, with exaggerated 1950s big jackets, rolled jeans and heavy shoes or boots.

As a designer, how would you costume **Sammy** for the scene in Act 2 when he gets into trouble with the bus conductor? Consider:

- how the costume will reflect his personality
- how the costume will reflect the play's context.

TIP

It is important to explain why you have made your design choices. For example, have you chosen bright colours to suggest he has an outgoing personality, or chosen heavy boots, which might make him seem more dangerous or threatening? Does he take care with his appearance or model himself on people he admires?

Teenage Sammy

Hairstyle: Short? Long? Styled?

Make-up: Clean-shaven or stubble? Clear complexion or spots?

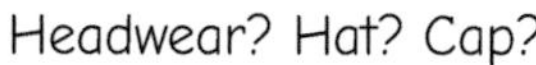

Jacket: Leather? Cotton? Polyester? **Fit:** Loose? Fitted? **Shape:** Long? Short?

Shirt: Plain or patterned? Tucked in or left out? Long sleeves or short sleeves?

Accessories: Watch? Bandana? Belt? Other?

Trousers: Jeans? Chinos? Suit? Corduroy? **Fit:** Loose or tight? Short or long? Rolled or not? **Condition:** Worn or new? Patched?

Footwear: Trainers? Boots? Loafers? **Materials:** Suede? Leather? Cloth?

TASK 3

Now create a costume design for Mrs Johnstone. Think about how the costume can be adapted for when she is working and when she is at home. Will there be costume pieces or accessories, which she adds or removes depending on what she is doing? Take into account her personality and lack of money, as well as the fashions of the time.

Download a printable version from Samples & Downloads at www.illuminatepublishing.com.

Set design inspired by context

The set must be flexible enough to accommodate a number of different locations, while having enough detail to convey the context of the play.

In the first act there is the opportunity to show both the exteriors and interiors of the Johnstones' and Lyons' homes in Liverpool. Often, productions show the two exteriors of the homes at the same time at the beginning of the play, highlighting the contrasts between the two.

TASK 4

Note the differences between the exteriors of the two homes, using the following questions to help you:

WHOSE HOME? Johnstones – working-class, poor, rented, small terraced home

FEATURES

1 If there is a street sign outside the house, what might the street name be?
2 What are the main colours used?
3 What materials are the walls made of? (Brick? Stone? Wood? Concrete?)
4 What condition are the walls in? (Paint peeling? Graffiti? Other signs of wear?)
5 What are the size, shape and colour of the doors and windows?
6 Is there any way of indicating how many children live in the house?
7 In what period do you think the home was originally built?

WHOSE HOME? Lyons – middle class, private home

FEATURES

1 If there is a street sign outside the house, what might the street name be?
2 What are the main colours used?
3 What materials are the walls made of? (Brick? Stone? Wood? Concrete?)
4 What condition are the walls in? Are there any special features that make the home seem prosperous? (Columns? Steps?, Balcony? Window boxes?)
5 What are the size, shape and colour of the doors and windows?
6 Are there any external features such as a garden, pathway or plants?
7 In what period do you think the home was originally built?

TIP

It is important to know that you do not have to create the exterior of the homes in your set at all. However, this is a useful exercise to begin thinking about the differences between the families and their homes.

TIP

When considering how you will design your set, it is important to know that you will rarely use the actual materials of the buildings, but create the set out of materials that have the appearance you want. If you want one of the homes to be built of brick, for example, you would use painted wood or a canvas backdrop to indicate that. If you want an ornate street lamp, you would use a lighter material and paint it to look like metal.

CHALLENGE

Research furniture from the time. Based on your research, draw sketches of key furniture items, such as the Lyons' dining table or Mrs Johnstone's kitchen table, which you believe would be appropriate for your design. Explain how they could be used in a scene.

TIP

Consider how you will accomplish the quick scene changes. For example, how will you move on Mrs Johnstone's kitchen set and then remove it? Will you use **trucks**? Casters on the furniture? **Fly** the set pieces in? Have actors carry or push the set pieces on/off?

KEY TERMS:

Truck: a platform on wheels upon which scenery can be mounted and moved.

Fly: raising and lowering scenery or other items onto the stage using a system of ropes and pulleys.

Writing about your design ideas

Question 1 will ask you to consider an aspect of design for the play in relation to its context. Below is a student's plan for the following question:

TIP

It is important to know that there are many other interpretations of how Mrs Johnstone might be costumed.

You are designing a costume for Mrs Johnstone in a performance of this extract (from 'Hello, Mrs Johnstone' to 'O, I see …' from the first act). The costume must reflect the context of *Blood Brothers*, set in a working-class Liverpudlian community in the late 1960s. Describe your design ideas for the costume.

1 Understanding of the character in the play:

Mrs Johnstone is a working-class, single mother who works as a cleaner to support her family.

2 Period:

Colours and fabrics: 1960s bright prints, inexpensive fabrics, such as polyester and cotton. Knee-length dress as appropriate for the late 1960s.

3 Occupation/role:

She would wear an apron or tabard to protect her clothes. She is a cleaner, so clothes need to be practical and hard-wearing. Her hair would be pulled back so it doesn't get in her way. Her shoes are well-worn flats, which need to be replaced, but she can't afford to yet.

4 Character shown through costume:

She is naturally cheerful and tries to make the best of bad situations, so, even though she doesn't have much money, her dress, though worn, would be neat. The dress might be brighter than the drab tabard over it. She has put on weight since having children, so the fit of her clothes would be shapeless to suggest this. Her simple clothes should contrast with Mrs Lyons' more expensive outfits.

TIP

It is important that you justify your ideas. Explain why you are making these specific choices; don't just describe what they will look like. What do we learn about the Narrator's role in the play and what effect do you want them to have?

- Understanding of the character in the play
- Period
- Occupation/role
- Character shown through costume.

TASK 5

Using the above plan as a guide, create your own plan for the character of the Narrator in answer to the following question:

> You are designing a costume for the Narrator to wear in a performance of this extract from the first act (from the opening 'So did y'hear the story of the Johnstone twins?' to 'How she came to play this part'). The costume must reflect the context of *Blood Brothers*, set in a Liverpudlian community in the late 1960s. Describe your design ideas for the costume.

▲ *Observe the children's facial expressions and body language to inform your own still images.*

KEY TERM:

Proximity: the distance between people or objects; how near or far.

TIP

For comedy, you might look for sudden changes in status; unexpected movements or gestures; a quick pace or use of exaggeration.

CHALLENGE

Now write bullet points in your notebook on the following task, based on the extract in Task 6:

> You are performing the role of **Linda**.
>
> Explain how you might use the performance space and interact with the actors playing the other children to **create comedy** for your audience.

Practical explorations of characters, themes and style

When writing about performing roles in the play, you must demonstrate that you understand the characters and how they interact. You need to use the performance space to show your understanding of the play. Below are two themes from the play that you can explore practically to develop your understanding of it and the characters, and how it can be performed.

Childhood

Throughout the play we see Mickey, Linda and Edward grow from young children into adults. These roles are usually cast with adult actors who have to play the different ages though their use of body language, facial expression and vocalisation. To help you develop ways of performing and interacting, try the exercises in Task 6.

TASK 6

a Start by playing 'It' or 'Tag'. When someone is tagged they have to freeze. Think about how you use your bodies, how much energy you expend, how you avoid getting tagged and what each other's facial expressions are like when playing.

b Play 'Cops and Robbers' by dividing your group into criminals who have got away with a crime and 'cops' who pursue and arrest them. Have one person be 'Sammy', who tells everyone else what their roles are and dictates when the game begins and ends. Discuss what it was like having Sammy as a leader.

c Study photographs of children and note the following about them:

- facial expressions
- **proximity** to each other
- use of levels.

Choose one photograph and create a still image based on it, do your best to capture the children and their proximity to each other. Then create a series of still images showing the relationships between the children. For example, who is the leader? Who wins? How do the others react?

d Now read from the stage directions on page 41 of *Blood Brothers*, '*They all laugh at* Mickey' to Linda's 'I hate them!' How can you use your vocal skills to show the youthfulness of the characters and the comedy in the situation? Try the following:

- Speak with a higher pitch.
- Over-enunciate unfamiliar words.
- Speak energetically and with enthusiasm.
- Exaggerate the characters' Liverpool accents.
- Use a quick pace and sudden pauses.

Put in your notebooks any changes in your voice that are helpful for showing the characters' ages and personalities.

d Create four still images showing the characters' movements during this extract. It is important to include their use of facial expressions and gestures. Take a photograph of the images or quickly sketch and label them.

Mark Hutchinson, actor

Playing Eddie at four different stages is a challenge, costumes obviously help, but I also decided to change my hairstyle three times in the show:

- tidy side parting for 7
- centre parting for Act 2 teenager
- completely gelled back for the scenes when he is a councillor.

Vocally, a brighter, open, slightly higher, but not too high tone, to suggest age and innocence, slightly lower and awkward for teenager, and older, louder and very assured for the councillor.

Physically, I decided, Eddie was a very still child, an only child brought up by strict parents, so very still as a seven-year-old, with very proper posture and a very calm physicality, very different from Mickey and the other children. I play him more physically awkward as a teenager, and then very confident as an adult.

Status

One of the main themes in the play is status. Although Edward and Mickey are twins, they have different opportunities in life because of the families in which they are raised. Willy Russell emphasises this in several scenes by contrasting how the boys are treated by others. For example, the policeman is much harsher with Mrs Johnstone than he is with the Lyons about the boys' misbehaviour; the two schools offer different opportunities; Edward goes to university, while Mickey loses his job at the factory; and, at the end, Edward is a respected Councillor, while Mickey only has a home and a job because of Edward's help.

To explore this theme try Task 7.

TASK 7

a Use any props and costumes you can find and put them either into a pile labelled 'Johnstone' or a pile labelled 'Lyons'. Discuss how you made your choices. For example, were you influenced by the fabrics, style or condition of the item? What do you learn about how we judge people's status by what they wear and what they own?

b Focus on the scene when Edward and Mickey at age seven meet in the first act. Concentrating on your vocal skills, explore how you can contrast their different upbringings. Experiment with the following:

- Use of dialect – would one of the boys have a stronger working-class Liverpool accent?
- Use of volume – would one of the boys speak more softly?
- Use of pace – would the boys speak at different paces? Is one more impulsive and one more thoughtful?
- Enunciation – does one speak with a clearer diction? Does one use more slang?
- Use of inflection or intonation – can comic effects be created through vocal tone or emphasis?

In your notebook, write down any discoveries you make.

c Focus on the policeman scenes in the first act, when he visits Mrs Johnstone and then the Lyons. Create two still images showing the difference in the policeman's attitude towards each family. Either take a picture or draw a sketch for each still image and label how it shows the different status of the families.

Interpretation of character

You will need to show how you can interpret a character. This means that you understand the character's motivations and goals, and the obstacles they face. Then you must be able to use your vocal and physical skills to portray the character and create particular effects for the audience, such as tension, comedy, surprise, pity or sorrow.

Look below at one interpretation of the character of **Linda** as a 14-year-old in the second act, in the scene in the field with Mickey (your interpretation may differ).

FACTS:

Background: a working-class 14-year-old

Job: student, attending a secondary modern

Interpretation:

PHYSICAL APPEARANCE:

I imagine Linda to be active and attractive.

HAIR:

Freshly washed hair, tied up in a high ponytail.

BODY LANGUAGE:

She is physically confident. She pretends she is helpless in the field scene, but it is an act. She stands her ground and can stick up for herself. She looks for any excuse to touch and flirt with Mickey.

MAKE-UP:

Emphasises her fresh-faced youth. 1970s make-up often used pink tones with shiny cheeks, aiming for a healthy, natural look. Peach- or berry-coloured lip gloss. Eyeliner, cream eye shadow and mascara, perhaps applied heavily as make-up is a new skill for her.

VOICE:

Speaks with a working-class Liverpool accent. She speaks loudly as doesn't care who hears her. She sometimes teases Mickey, so has a playful tone and laughs a lot.

COSTUME:

School uniform (white blouse, grey skirt) which she has adjusted to fit her sense of fashion. She has rolled the waistband over to make her skirt very short. Mini-skirts were popular at this time, so she would be imitating people she'd seen in magazines, and would be turning her knee-length skirt into a mini. Her green school tie is knotted and shortened as an act of rebellion. She takes off her grey school jumper and ties it around her waist when trudging up the hill. She is wearing non-school regulation high heels with flesh-coloured tights.

EFFECT ON AUDIENCE:

The audience should see a startling transformation from the tomboyish seven-year-old to this attractive, confident teenager. She is beginning to be aware of her effect on boys, but is still outspoken and protective of Mickey as she was when they were children.

TASK 8

Using your own understanding of the characters in the play, write an interpretation of Edward, Mickey, Mrs Lyons, Mrs Johnstone or the Narrator, using the following headings:

- Age
- Job/Education
- Physical appearance
- Voice
- Body language
- Costume
- Hair
- Make-up.

In this instance, think about total characterisation, which includes facts about the characters and their appearance as well as how they could be interpreted through acting, costume and make-up choices. This will help you to think about all aspects of interpreting the character, even when writing about acting or design.

Performing choices

In Question 2, you will be asked to discuss in detail how you would perform a particular line as a given character. For example:

You are performing the role of Mrs Lyons.

Describe how you would use your vocal and physical skills to perform the line below and explain the effects you want to create.

Mrs Lyons (Act 1): 'Do you go to the same school as Edward?'

In this scene, Mickey has turned up unexpectedly at the Lyons house and Mrs Lyons is immediately suspicious of him. I want to establish that Mrs Lyons is not welcoming to Mickey and wants to discover who he is. (1) Playing Mrs Lyons, I would hold myself very stiffly and formally, making no gestures of welcome to Mickey. (2) I would look down at him and examine him, noting that his clothing and accent are not what I would expect of Edward's friends. (3) I don't have a strong Liverpool accent; instead I speak received pronunciation, which indicates my background and education. My voice is well-modulated, not rude, but I would use a slightly cold tone. (4) I would emphasise the word 'you' as there is a sense of disbelief that Mickey could go to the same school as Edward. (5) I would say Edward's name warmly and protectively, as I think of him as my boy. I would speak slowly and clearly, determined to get an answer. (6) At the end of the line, I would look between the boys, beginning to realise who Mickey is. (7) I would then move closer to Edward, blocking Mickey from him, my facial expression beginning to show my alarm. (8)

Annotations:
1. Effect
2. Physical skills
3. Physical skills
4. Vocal skills
5. Vocal skills
6. Vocal skills and effect
7. Physical skills and effect
8. Physical skills and effect

KEY TERM:

Received pronunciation (RP): a way of speaking which is considered the 'standard' form of English pronunciation. It is not specific to a certain location, but, instead, is associated with education and formal speaking.

TASK 9

Experiment with different ways of using your vocal and physical skills for each of the following lines:

> **Mrs Lyons:** Give one of them to me.
>
> **Mrs Johnstone:** Well, I ... I just ... It's ... couldn't I keep them for a few more days, please, please, they're a pair, they go together.
>
> **Edward:** Well, my mummy doesn't allow me to play down here actually.
>
> **Mr Lyons:** Mummy will read the story, Edward. I've got to go to work for an hour.
>
> **Linda:** Well, he is. An' what do you care if I think another feller's gorgeous, eh?
>
> **Narrator:** And who'd dare tell the lambs in spring, / What fate the later seasons bring?
>
> **Mickey:** You don't understand anything, do ye? I don't wear a hat that I could tilt at the world.

TIP

It is a good idea to write in the first person ('I') so you can fully imagine your own performance of the role. Do more than describe the vocal and physical skills you would use: also think about how your choices will add to the audience's understanding of the play, its characters and their relationships.

TASK 10

a Make notes on the following:
- vocal skills
- physical skills
- effects achieved.

b Then, write an answer to the question on the previous page, referring to each of the characters and lines in Task 9. Use the response on the previous page as a guide.

c Check your work by marking or highlighting:

V for each vocal skill you mention

P for each physical skill

E for an effect on the audience.

Make sure that you have answered this question fully.

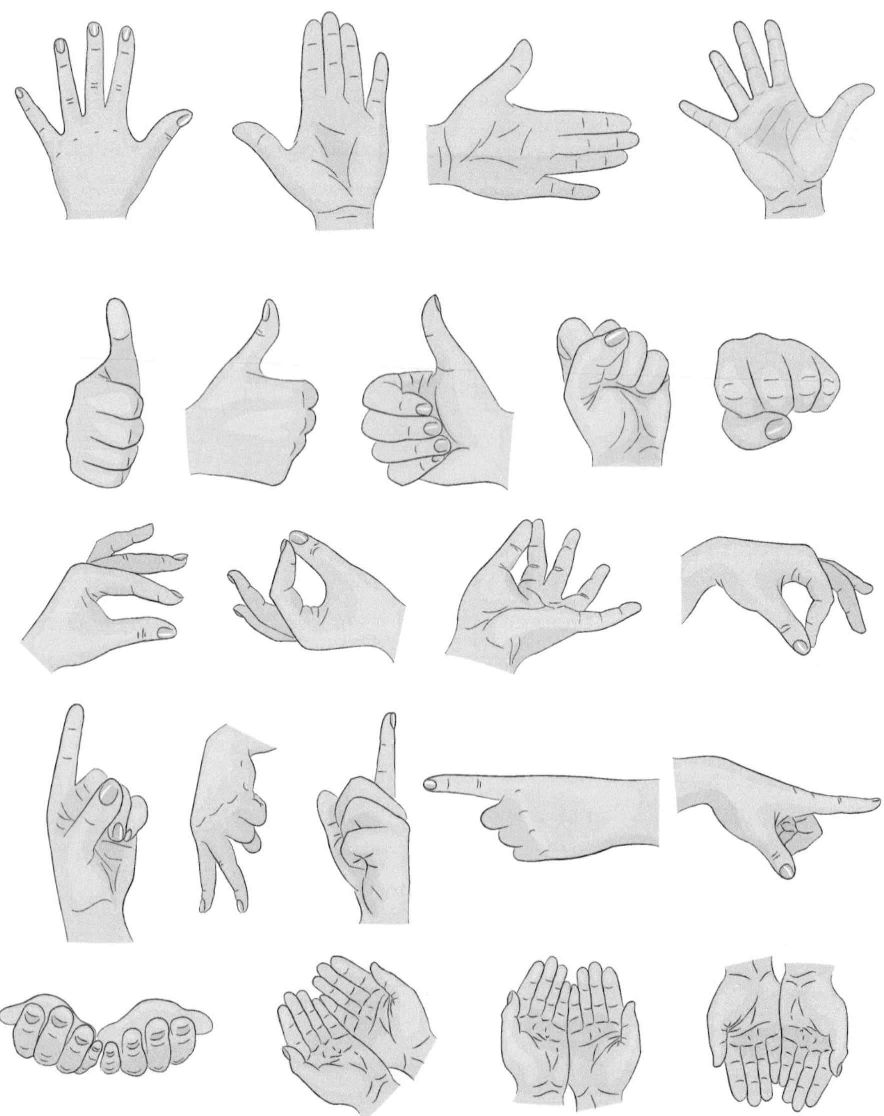

When thinking about physical skills consider your use of gestures.

Character revision sheet

SET PLAY 2:
Blood Brothers
by Willy Russell

2

Below is a partly completed character revision sheet based on **Mrs Lyons**. Copy the grid and complete it.

Character and importance to the play	Mrs Lyons
What do they want?	She wants a baby. She wants a perfect, happy home.
What obstacles do they face?	She and her husband can't have children. Fear that Mrs Johnstone will reclaim Edward.
What are their key scenes?	Act 1: Discovering Mrs Johnstone is pregnant. Act 1: Asking Mrs Johnstone to give a baby to her. Act 1: Coming to collect the baby. Act 1: Fires Mrs Johnstone. Act 1: Mickey comes to their house. Mrs Lyons hits Edward. Act 1: Increasingly paranoid. Suggests they move. Act 1: Move to new home. Act 2: Dancing with Edward. Act 2: Finds Edward's locket. Act 2: Attacks Mrs Johnstone.

How might they be costumed?	How might their hair and make-up be done?
Draw a simple sketch or write a description of it. Consider: • colours • fabrics • shape and fit • character's personality and status.	Draw a simple sketch or write a description of it. Consider: • style and colour of hair • type of make-up (realistic or fantasy; colours; how it is appropriate for character, setting and period).

How might they use body language? • Posture • Gait (the way they walk) • Facial expression	
How might they use their voice? • Emotional range (angry, sad, happy, irritated, desperate, dominating and so on) • Pitch and volume (low or high; loud or soft) • Accent or other distinctive vocal features	
Choose one important line and analyse how they might say it.	Act 2: 'Are you always going to follow me?'

TASK 11

Using the grid for guidance, create similar revision sheets for all major characters including: Mrs Johnstone, the Narrator, Mickey, Edward, Linda and Mr Lyons.

Download a printable version from Samples & Downloads at www.illuminatepublishing.com.

Using the performance space and interaction with others

KEY TERM:

Ensemble: an approach to acting involving everyone working together, rather than singling out 'star' performers. It also refers to a group of actors who play many roles in a play or a chorus.

There are opportunities to explore the space and interaction with others in a number of different ways in the play. There are large **ensemble** scenes and intimate two-person scenes. Some productions may choose to perform the play very naturalistically, while others rely on the conventions of musical theatre, such as group movement or dancing. Many productions combine both naturalistic and stylised acting. Willy Russell also provides additional challenges by having some scenes overlapping or cross-cutting. When you are writing about how you will use the performance space and interaction with others, make sure you focus on the effects you wish to achieve, such as tension, surprise, humour, pity or sorrow, and how you will achieve them.

TASK 12

Focus on the scene between Mickey and Linda in Act 2, which begins: 'Mickey, Mickey, come on, you'll be late …' to Mickey's exit with the pills.

a Read the scene, taking particular notice of any stage directions.

b Agree what stage configuration you are going to use: end on, theatre in the round, thrust, promenade, proscenium or traverse. Mark where the entrances will be and any pieces of furniture.

c Decide what effects you wish to achieve in this scene. To help you do this, answer the following questions about the various issues:

- Mickey's character after leaving prison. How have his mental state and dependency on drugs affected his movement, facial expressions and entire personality?
- Linda's reaction to him. Linda has always loved Mickey and is now his wife. However, he is very changed. How does she look at him? What are her motivations in this scene?
- Use of props. How does he feel about Linda handing him his lunch? How important is it to Mickey that he finds his pills? Where does he look for his pills?
- Turning point. What convinces Linda to give him her bag so he can find his pills?
- Use of subtext. Are there any instances when you believe characters are not saying entirely what they are thinking or feeling? How could that be conveyed?

d How will you use stage space? Try the following:

- Mickey's entrance:
  - Mickey enters quickly, avoids eye contact with Linda. Begins looking immediately for pills around the flat.
  - Mickey enters slowly, with careful movements. He goes to where his pills are usually kept. Freezes momentarily confused when they aren't there.
  - Mickey enters putting on his jacket. His hands are visibly shaking and he struggles to get his jacket on. He pushes aside Linda's hand offering the lunch bag.
- Linda's reaction:
  - Linda follows Mickey around the room, like a mother dealing with an uncooperative toddler.
  - Linda smiles brightly, trying to pretend that everything is all right. She continues to get ready to go out herself, putting on her earrings and chatting casually to him.
  - Linda tries to block him from finding the pills and hides her bag. She clearly feels worried and guilty, finding it hard to meet his eyes.

e Continue working through the scene, experimenting with different staging configuration ideas. When you have finished, answer the following question:

> You are performing the role of **Mickey**.
>
> Focus on the lines 'I didn't sort anythin' out, Linda' to 'Now give me the tablets … I need them.' Explain how you and the actor playing Linda might use the performance space and interact with each other to **create tension** for the audience.

Answering a question about character interpretation

If you choose to answer Question 4, you will need to explain how you would use your acting skills to interpret a character in the extract and in the **play as a whole**. An example might be:

> You are performing the role of **Mrs Johnstone**.
>
> Describe how you would use your acting skills to **interpret Mrs Johnstone's character** in this extract (Act 1, 'Mrs Johnstone: I had it all worked out' to 'Give one to you?'). Explain why your ideas are appropriate for:
>
> - this extract
> - the performance of your role in the play as a whole.

Below is a sample student plan for this question.

This extract:

1 Character of Mrs Johnstone and reasons for acting choices:

Working-class, superstitious, single mother, struggling financially. Worried about managing with two more babies; afraid social services will take her children. Wonders if one of the twins will have a better life with the Lyons.

2 Acting skills: vocal:

Liverpool accent. Informal diction. Mrs Lyons is her boss so I will speak with a respectful tone to her. Tries to please. Anger on the word 'they' about all those officials who want to take children and don't give me the support I need. Emotional on lines like 'kids can't live on love alone'. A shocked pause before saying 'Give one to you?' to show I can't believe what I am hearing.

3 Acting skills: physical:

Heavily pregnant, but still have to work. Movements are automatic as I speak thoughts aloud, I continue to dust. When I clean something low, I struggle a bit getting up again. Touch my belly when I say, 'I'll even love these two ...' to show I am already attached to the babies.

Rest of play:

1 Character of Mrs Johnstone and reasons for acting choices:

She is a warm, relatable person, but haunted by her decision to give up one of her sons. In her two scenes alone with Edward, her love for him is apparent and, in the final scene, she rejects her own superstition in an effort to save him and Mickey.

2 Acting skills: vocal:

In scene with Edward towards the end of Act 1, speak softly and affectionately. Don't want their conversation to be overheard. Comforts him when he's crying, 'Shush, shush'. Laughs on, 'God help the girls when you start dancing.' At the end of the play, voice is loud and desperate: 'Mickey. Don't shoot.'

3 Acting skills: physical:

Physically affectionate with children, hugs and teases them. Always busy, cleaning, cooking, looking after others. Towards end suggest weariness in some movements (slow to rise from chairs, more hesitant) but still strong. Fights off Mrs Lyons and rushes to town council.

TASK 13

Using the above plan as a guide, create your own plan in answer to the the following question:

> You are performing the role of the **Narrator**.
>
> Describe how you would use your acting skills to **interpret the Narrator's character** in Act 2, from their entrance to Edward's line: 'Hey.' Explain why your ideas are appropriate for:
>
> - this extract
> - your chosen design skill in the play as a whole.

TIP

It is important to include both vocal and physical skills. Note key moments when these skills can be discussed.

1 Character of the Narrator and reasons for making acting choices:

2 Acting skills: vocal:

3 Acting skills: physical:

Design choices

If you choose to answer Question 5, you will be thinking as a designer and commenting on one aspect of design. For example:

> You are a designer working on **one** aspect of design for this extract.
>
> Describe how you would use your design skills to create effects which **support the action**. Explain why your ideas are appropriate for:
>
> - this extract
> - your chosen design skill in the play as a whole.

You may choose to focus on set design, costume design, lighting design, sound design or puppet design. Whichever you choose, you must explain why your ideas are appropriate to the play as a whole. You might refer to:

- how your design helps to show the action of the play and the nature of the characters
- how your design for the extract is consistent with the design requirements of the rest of the play (for example, don't suddenly change the style of the production)
- how you have used design methods that fit in with the mood or atmosphere of the play
- props, anything that the actors may carry onstage.

Blood Brothers is usually performed and designed with a combination of naturalistic and stylised musical theatre features. The presence of the Narrator and the use of song tell the audience that this won't be an entirely naturalistic production. There are rapid, fluid transitions from one scene to another. Many productions move various pieces of scenery on and off a basic set. Some productions use scaffolding in the set to provide extra levels, such as a platform from which the Narrator may watch and comment on the action. Some use the ensemble to change the set, which is presented in a minimalistic and symbolic way using just a few key props and set pieces. Others create highly realistic interiors for both the Johnstone and Lyons households in order to highlight the differences in their social classes.

Most productions employ multi-role (Willy Russell even has a joke in the script about the milkman giving up his job to become a gynaecologist), so the costume designer must create costumes that can quickly be changed into in order to indicate the new role an actor is playing.

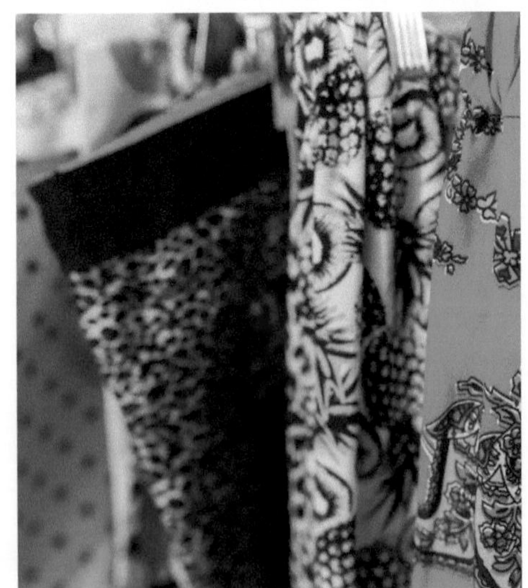

▲ *The choice of fabric, including colour, texture and pattern, is important.*

Music is central to the play, but additional sound effects to create comedy or tension can be added. Lighting effects can be used to pick out key moments or to emphasise the passing of time. Whatever design choices you make, you must make sure that they show your understanding of the play and its needs.

Costume design

For costume design, you might consider:

- style, cut and fit
- colour, fabric, decorative features
- condition (worn or new; neat or wrinkled; clean or stained and so on)
- footwear/headgear
- accessories
- status or social role of character
- make-up and hairstyle.

Below is an extract from a sample response for a question based on Mr Lyons in Act 1, in his scene with Mrs Lyons, beginning 'Oh Richard, Richard.' It describes how a costume designer would use their skills to create effects that support the action of this extract and the rest of the play.

In this scene, I would have Mr Lyons dressed as if he's just come in from work to find his wife once again distressed. (1) He has an important job in manufacturing, so I would dress him in a conservative grey, pin-striped wool suit, with a matching waistcoat and a white shirt and a conservative navy-blue tie. (2) There is nothing particularly fashionable about his clothing, he would blend in with the crowd, but small details, like wearing gold cufflinks and a good watch, would show his relative wealth. (3) I imagine he has just come in from work, so I would have him enter carrying a newspaper and a brown leather briefcase. He wears dark-rimmed spectacles to read, but these will be in his pocket at the beginning of the scene. (4) His shoes are dark, leather and well-shined. Everything about him suggests competence and order, which reinforces why he is so annoyed to find his wife coping so poorly. (5) He would like to be met with a drink, but instead immediately has to begin solving problems. In my interpretation, Mr Lyons is a little older than his wife, so I would use make-up to indicate that his hair is greying at his temples. (6) His appearance in this scene would stress how important his work is to him and how he is not totally comfortable at home. (7)

In the rest of the play, he would wear variations of this outfit for most scenes. When playing with Edward he would take off his jacket. With Miss Jones, he would be at his most formal, wearing his glasses and very neatly presented to show his power and his apparent lack of concern for his employees. (8) One moment of contrast in his outfit might occur towards the end of Act 2, when the family has moved to the country. In order to show how they have changed from city dwellers to country people, I would costume him in a green waxed jacket with a warm plaid flannel lining and black wellington boots. (9) However, for most of the play, he presents authority and his costume must indicate that.

(1) Understanding of the action of the scene

(2) Discusses colour and fabric and effect achieved

(3) Shows how accessories can create effect

(4) Accessory reveals aspect of character

(5) Condition of footwear and effects achieved

(6) Some mention of hair/make-up, although this could be more developed

(7) Insight into the action of the scene

(8) How costume helps to convey the action in the rest of the play

(9) How costume would be altered for his role in the rest of the play

TASK 14

Draw sketches of contrasting costumes, make-up and hair for Mickey and Edward at their first meeting, when they are seven. Label the sketches, showing the differences between the costumes. It is important to consider: fabrics, condition of clothing, colours, shape and fit.

TIP

You might want to consider the following:

- the characters' relative wealth
- their relationship as employer and employee
- what we learn about the character.

TASK 15

a Write an answer to the following question as a costume designer.

> Focus on Act 1, from 'Mrs Lyons: Hello, Mrs Johnstone …' to 'Mrs Lyons: Oh, I see …'
>
> You are a designer working on **one** aspect of this extract.
>
> Describe how you would use your design skills to create effects which **support the action**. Explain why your ideas are appropriate for:
>
> - this extract
> - your chosen design skill in the play as a whole.

b Check that you have:

- referred to fabric, colours, shape/silhouette, fit, condition
- included headwear and/or footwear, as appropriate
- considered make-up and hairstyle, as appropriate
- explained how the costume helps the action of the extract
- related your design to the rest of the play.

Set design

For the set design, you might consider:

- stage configuration
- if you will use one main set to represent all locations or if you will have a number of different sets
- the scale (how large) your set will be
- if there will be any levels, ramps or stairs
- the entrances/exits
- if there will be backdrops, flats or projections
- the colour palette you will use
- how the materials, textures and shapes will help to create a suitable setting
- which props are needed.

TASK 16 CONTINUED ON PAGE 67

You have been asked to design the set for the opening of Act 1 for the stage configuration of your choice. Consider how you will use the set to:

- establish role and importance of the Narrator
- establish the setting of working-class Liverpool in the 1960s
- create interest in Mrs Johnstone's story.

TASK 16 CONTINUED

SET PLAY 2: *Blood Brothers* by Willy Russell

2

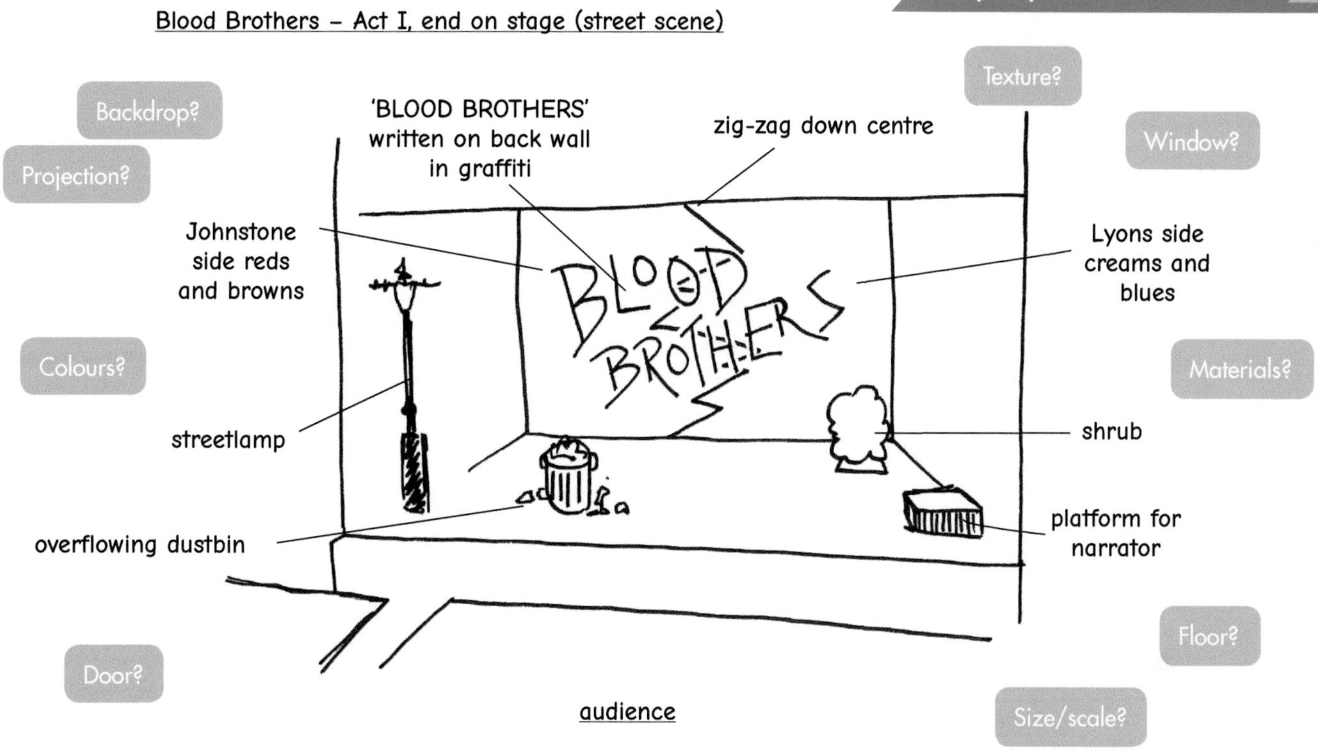

Blood Brothers – Act I, end on stage (street scene)

Backdrop?
Projection?
'BLOOD BROTHERS' written on back wall in graffiti
zig-zag down centre
Texture?
Window?
Johnstone side reds and browns
BLOOD BROTHERS
Lyons side creams and blues
Colours?
Materials?
streetlamp
shrub
overflowing dustbin
platform for narrator
Floor?
Door?
audience
Size/scale?

Draw a sketch showing:

- the colours and textures (rough, smooth, patterned, irregular) you will use
- the materials for the set (or what they will look like, such as stone, wood, plaster, metal)
- the scale of the set in relation to the size of the actors
- any levels (balconies, scaffolding, upper windows, platforms)
- where key events such as entrances/exits will occur.

Below are extracts from three different sample responses about the set at the beginning of Act 1.

A

I am creating an abstract, non-naturalistic setting for the play, so will use large, metal scaffolding. In the upstage centre section of the scaffolding there will be a large screen upon which different images of Liverpool in the 1960s will be projected as the audience walks in and while the overture plays. (1) It will freeze on an image of boy twins and the caption: The Johnstone Twins. Upstage left is a smaller platform about two metres high which can be accessed by ladders. The Narrator will make his first appearance there. (2) Downstage centre, Mrs Johnstone will appear, unaware of the narrator above her. I think this will create suspense and interest for the audience who will wonder about the connection between the two characters and the projected image. (3)

1. Establishes 1970s setting and style of design
2. Discusses scale and how the set will be used
3. Considers effect of design choices

B

I want to highlight the theme of social class, so my initial set will show the exterior of the Lyons' home stage left and the Johnstones' home stage right. 4 Both will use painted canvas. The Lyons' house will be creams and blues, while the Johnstones' house will be painted dark red brick. 5 There will be white columns either side of the front door of the Lyons' home and an overflowing bin in front of the Johnstones', in order to show the difference in their social class. 6

4 Explains intentions of design

5 Explains how homes will contrast

6 Provides details to establish characters

C

I think the Liverpool street is an important aspect of the set, so the first image the audience will see will be painted flats that create a brick wall with graffiti written on it and posters advertising rock groups from the 1960s and 1970s. 7 The stage will be made of a series of ramps that lead up to a central circular acting area. The Narrator will make their first appearance in this highest, most prominent area, appearing in the light of a street lamp, which makes them look mysterious and important. 8 The wall will be mounted on trucks that part to reveal the two contrasting homes. 9

7 Establishes the period

8 Discusses use of levels

9 Explains how the set can be changed to help the action of the play

TASK 17

a All of the responses above have different strengths. Read through them and, with a partner, discuss which design is best at establishing the location, period and mood of the opening.

b Sketch your own ideas about how the play's opening set would look.

TASK 18

You are now going to create a design for the end of Act 1 set using the stage configuration of your choice. At this point, the characters have moved to the country. How can the set design represent this change? Think about:

- entrances/exits and areas for key moments
- use of backdrops, projections or set furniture
- how to create atmosphere
- scale.

TASK 19

Now, writing as a set designer and using the stage configuration of your choice, choose any setting from either Act 1 or Act 2 and answer the following:

> You are a designer working on **one** aspect of design for this extract.
>
> Describe how you would use your design skills to create effects which **support the action**. Explain why your ideas are appropriate for:
>
> - this extract
> - your chosen design skill in the play as a whole.

Lighting design

When creating your lighting design you might consider how to create:

- time of day and, possibly, season
- atmosphere or mood
- highlight particular moments
- how to help convey the setting and action, or enhance the impact of a character (such as a follow spot to focus the audience on a character's journey or backlighting to make them appear mysterious).

Some of your tools are:

- colours
- angles and intensity
- light from onstage sources (lamp-posts, lamps, neon signs)
- use of shadow and silhouette
- special effects
- use of blackouts or fades.

TASK 20

Use the mind map below to make notes in your notebook on the different lighting demands of Act 2, showing the three summers of the teenage Mickey, Edward and Linda, starting with 'There's a few bob in your pocket' and ending with 'Where's Mickey?'

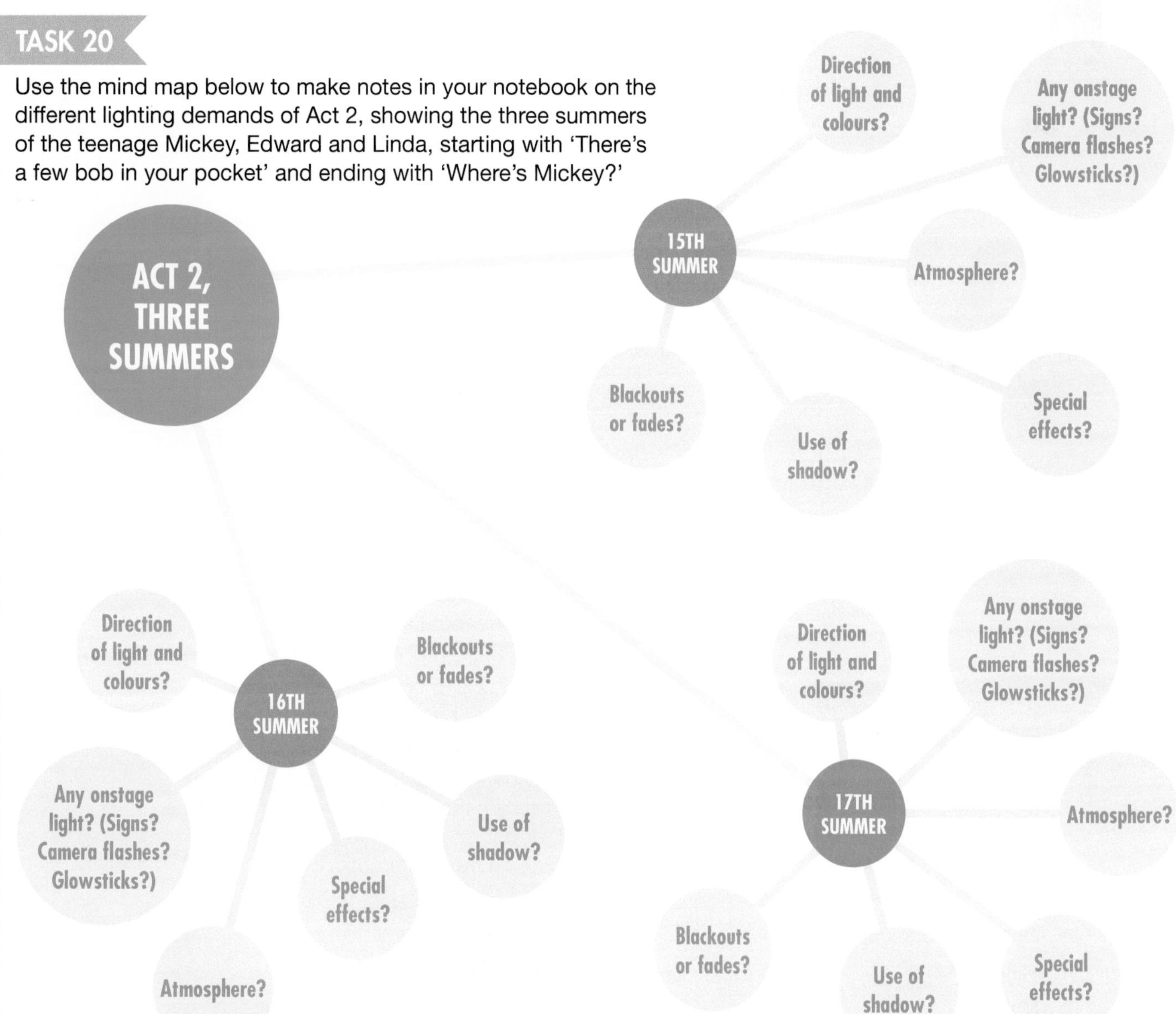

Below are some short excerpts from various responses to the demands of lighting in other scenes from the play *Blood Brothers*.

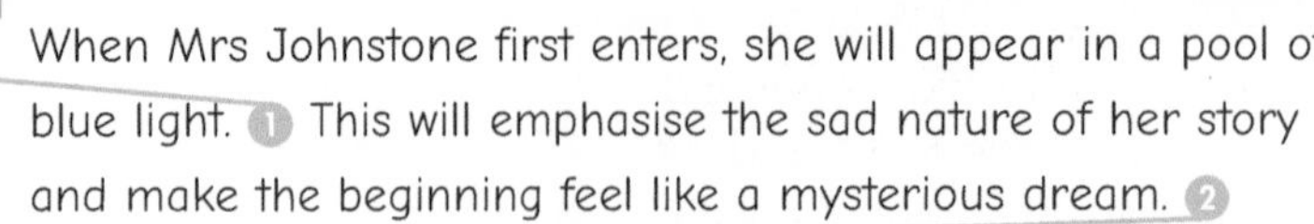

Shape and colour

Reason for choice and effect created

A

When Mrs Johnstone first enters, she will appear in a pool of blue light. (1) This will emphasise the sad nature of her story and make the beginning feel like a mysterious dream. (2)

B

I want the Narrator to appear like a harsh judgemental character. I will use some low-angled lights that will cast shadows on their face, making them appear gaunt and frightening.

C

At the end of the Marilyn Monroe song, I will have the rosy bright light from the profile spots, fade to a cooler, more ordinary daylight, to show the contrast between Mrs Johnstone's dreams and reality.

D

During the Narrator's 'Shoes upon the table' I will have the lighting become more intense and harsh. The Narrator will be lit from the front, casting large looming shadows behind them. On the final 'He's knocking on the door' there will be a brief blackout and, when the lights come back on, the Narrator has disappeared.

E

To indicate Mickey's mental state when he is looking for Edward towards the end of Act 2, I will have flashing red lights, showing his anger. These will be replaced by blue flashing lights when the police appear.

TASK 21

Re-read the responses above and highlight references to:

- colours
- angles
- special effects
- onstage lights
- dimming
- blackouts.

Sound design

Blood Brothers offers many opportunities for sound design, not only because it is a musical, but also because there are moments when tension or a character's psychological state might be emphasised through the use of sound.

Sound design can help to:

establish location

enhance the atmosphere

aid a transition from one scene to another

highlight a particular moment or character

TASK 22

Focus on Act 2, from 'Mrs Lyons *enters and goes to* Mickey' to the Narrator's 'There's a mad man / there's a mad man.'

a Work in a group. Using materials you can find and your own voices, create a **soundscape** to accompany this scene. Consider:
- Volume: when will the sound get louder and when will it be softer?
- Type of sound: will it be gentle and tuneful or harsh and discordant?
- Character and action: will there be different sounds/instruments to accompany certain characters or actions?

b Discuss how you could use either live or recorded sound effects/ music to accomplish the effects that you want.

c Make notes in your workbook to explain your discoveries.

KEY TERM:

Soundscape: a collection of sounds that create a setting or suggest a scene, or a drama technique where performers use their voices (and sometimes other items) to create sounds.

When creating your sound design you should make notes of your ideas, including:

- Live or recorded?
- Produced onstage or offstage?
- Volume/amplification.

Here is an example:

(1) Sammy leaps from the 'bus' (2) and is pursued by two policemen. (3) The 'bus' pulls away (4) leaving Mickey and Linda alone on the pavement. (5)

- (1) Recorded sound of bus
- (2) Recorded sound of screeching stop. Comically loud
- (3) Live sound of police whistles from onstage
- (4) Recorded sound of bus pulling away. Volume decreases as it goes into the distance
- (5) Sudden silence

TASK 23

At the end of Act 1, the Johnstones move from the city to the country. Focusing on the script from Mickey's 'It's like the country, isn't it, Mam?' In your notebook, describe how you would use sound design to show the change in location and mood.

TIP

Remember that only clean (unannotated) copies of the script can be taken into the exam.

3 SET PLAY 3: *Things I Know to be True* by Andrew Bovell

Synopsis

It Begins Like This

In an Australian suburb, **Bob Price**, a former car factory worker in his 60s, stares at a phone, while his four adult children narrate his fears. At the end of the scene, the phone rings and he answers it.

Berlin

Bob's daughter, **Rosie**, is on a train platform in Berlin after travelling alone around Europe for three months. When she video-calls home, she pretends to be having a great time because she doesn't want her family to be disappointed. She describes (to the audience) meeting a beautiful boy, Emmanuel. They spent three days together and, just as she begins to imagine a future with him, he steals from her and disappears. She makes a list of all the things she knows. One of these is that she needs to go home.

Home

Bob's wife, **Fran**, a nurse, reminds him to pick up their grandchildren. Unannounced, Rosie arrives. Fran calls Rosie's siblings to tell them to come over as Rosie is back. Fran guesses that a boy has hurt Rosie. Rosie's married sister, **Pip**, and brothers, **Ben** and **Mark**, arrive. They squabble about family issues: Mark breaking up with his girlfriend and how much Fran helps Ben and Pip. When left alone in the garden with Bob, Rosie says that she fell in love with the wrong guy and that she tried to 'grow up'.

Autumn

Pip reflects on all the important things that have happened in the garden. She remembers seeing her mother cry and bash her head against a tree. Rosie and Fran find her. Pip tells Fran that she is leaving her husband, Steve. Pip remembers a time when she was 14 and baby Rosie was hurt when she should have been looking after her. Fran was so angry she tore out some of Pip's hair. Fran tells Bob that Pip is leaving Steve. Pip says she doesn't love Steve. Fran accuses Pip of having another man. Pip announces she is taking a new job in Vancouver and leaving the children with Steve. Pip and Fran argue. When Fran goes inside, Pip denies to Bob that she has another man. Bob encourages her to grab the new job opportunity with both hands and that he will help with the children. When Pip leaves, Fran tells Bob that Pip was lying, but he says all the children know that a lie to his face would 'kill' him. Fran and Bob embrace for an 'unforgiving moment'.

▲ Hallett Cove, Adelaide

As Autumn Turns
Bob is tending the garden while Rosie and Fran work in the kitchen. Fran encourages Rosie to get a job and suggests nursing. Fran is worried that Bob seems forgetful. She would like to take him on a trip and admits she has a secret stash of money. Fran feels that Bob's world and sense of self-worth have shrunk since he was made redundant. Ben arrives to drop off his laundry. Bob disapproves of Ben's flashy new car. Bob and Ben argue and Ben leaves. Fran tells Bob that he should notice that Ben is doing well for himself. Bob says that by Ben's age he had children and a mortgage. Rosie says that she is planning to move out. In a letter from Pip to Fran, Pip reflects on mother-and-daughter relationships and confesses that she has gone to Vancouver to be with the married man she is having an affair with. When Bob asks her what Pip says, Fran replies, 'It's cold in Vancouver.'

Winter
Fran is smoking in the garden. Mark remembers that when he was younger, he would sit up in a tree and observe his family. The garden was where his mother would sneak a cigarette, usually when she was trying to solve one of the children's problems. Fran tells Bob that Mark is coming over. She wonders if Mark is gay.

Later that night, Mark arrives, soaked by a rainstorm. Fran and Bob fuss over him. Bob jokes that the only thing that would shock them would be if Mark said he had 'decided to become a woman'. In the silence, they realise that a truth has been revealed. Mark is beginning the process of living as a woman. Bob retreats to the garden and Fran says they hadn't seen this coming. Mark says he is moving to Sydney as there is 'no place for me here'. Fran angrily says she wishes she had never had children. Bob tells Mark that he is 'a beautiful man' and that he shouldn't 'mess' with that. Mark says he loves them, but that is too much to ask. Fran tells him to become the person that he needs to be, but she doesn't want to see it, as she will mourn the son she has lost.

Interval
As Winter Turns
Mark packs as he and Rosie discuss the move to Sydney. Mark says he has decided to go by the name Mia. Mia describes the trip to the airport with Rosie and Bob. When they part, Bob weeps. Mia says that her father's grief 'is a price I am prepared to pay' and that, by the time she lands in Sydney, she will be a new person.

Spring
Bob and Fran are dancing while their children watch. Ben describes how, in the daily chaos of their busy household, when a favourite song came on the radio, he would grab Fran to dance. Bob breaks away from the dancing and wonders if life has passed him by. Fran suggests they go away together and that they need to remember 'who we are'.

Home That Night
An agitated Ben arrives looking for his parents. Rosie says they are out celebrating their anniversary. When Fran and Bob return, they suspect Ben has taken drugs. Bob goes to attack Ben, but is stopped. Ben explains that he has stolen some money. Over a period of time, he has taken a large amount of money from his company. He wanted to keep up with people from more affluent backgrounds. Bob again goes to attack him, but Ben hits himself. As Fran and Rosie try to stop him, Ben raises his fist to Fran. Fran says that they will remortgage the house to help Ben pay back the money. When Bob disagrees, she says she will use her secret stash. Bob insists that Ben must tell his employers and go to jail. Bob confronts Fran about her secret money. She also confesses that there was another man who wanted her, but she chose Bob and the family. Bob says he knew she was unhappy and that he was glad Rosie was born as that kept Fran with them. Bob says she can give money to Ben, but she has to give an equal amount to the other children.

Summer
A year after Rosie's return from Europe, she tells her father she is going on a creative writing course in Brisbane. Bob is distressed that she is moving so far away and that all of the children have chosen lives so different from his and Fran's.

Life Goes On
Fran wonders if she drove the children away. Bob says they 'made their own choices'. Fran suggests they tear up the garden and start all over again.

And It Ends Like This
The phone rings and Bob answers it. The children narrate what it is like to receive bad news. Rosie describes Fran's last journey from the hospital when she died in a car accident. In despair, Bob tears up the rose bushes in the garden. Pip, Mia and Ben, dressed in their funeral clothes, tenderly wash and dress Bob. Rosie breaks off from her journey and reflects on the things that she knows, including that the day her mother died her childhood ended. She joins the others and they leave for Fran's funeral.

TASK 1

a Read the synopsis, then work in your group to choose ten important plot points. Create a still image for each. Discuss which moments you think are the most exciting and dramatic.

b Then list some of the performance and design challenges in staging *Things I Know to be True*. It is important to consider: lighting, sound, costume and setting. You might begin by deciding how to:

- create the setting
- portray the different characters
- explore the play's themes
- mark the transitions between the play's scenes.

Context

Things I Know to be True is set in a **contemporary working-class Australian suburb**. This context will influence your understanding of the play and the possibilities for its design.

The play was written by award-winning Australian writer Andrew Bovell, who also co-wrote the screenplay for the popular 1992 film *Strictly Ballroom*. Bovell began working on the script in June 2014. The premiere was in Australia in May 2016.

The play is set in a suburb of Adelaide, South Australia, and deals with many issues recognisable to an Australian audience, from the younger generation's urge to travel abroad to the familiar barbeque 'most Sundays' and the garden being central to family life. However, the original directors also realised that the play addressed universal concerns. For example, many countries suffered under the financial crisis of 2007–08 and the subsequent loss of factory jobs. This had a profound effect on the lives of working- and middle-class families. The tensions between the generations and the rivalries within the family are also widely recognisable themes. Parents around the world have made sacrifices to give their children advantages they did not have themselves only to realise that their children have different hopes and plans. The co-director Scott Graham has written that the play is about 'family, love, loss and dreams that are exposed to be nothing more than that' (*Things I Know to be True Comprehensive Guide*).

The play is set in Hallett Cove. It has a reputation for being a safe, comfortable place to live, popular with families and retired people. Houses here are usually single storey with generous gardens. In the script, Bovell describes the setting as 'not unlike any other working-class suburb… in the Western world'. Bob's dream is that their children will settle down near them and have lives which are 'better versions of us'. Bob left school at 16, never travelled abroad and worked most of his life for the same company. His children have been given more opportunities in terms of education and travel, but, despite their advantages, are dissatisfied. Over the course of the play, three of the four children move away. Mark/Mia relocates to Sydney, 1162 km from Adelaide, Rosie goes to Brisbane, over 2100km by road, and Pip leaves Australia entirely for Canada.

Cars are the main means of transport, which is reflected in the discussions about the best roads to take and whether to call home for a lift or take a taxi. Car manufacturing was once an important industry in Australia, but by 2009, production had drastically reduced and most cars now are foreign imports. Bob is made redundant from his job at a car factory, where part of his final deal was a car at cost 'and a bit more'. He is irritated by Ben buying an expensive European car.

The action of the play takes place over approximately a year, the seasons appearing in most of the section titles. The climate in Adelaide is pleasant most of the year. The Australian summer is December to February. Winter is June to August. As the weather is usually warm, lighter fabrics, such as cotton, are often worn. The stereotype of Australian fashion is very casual, such as shorts and flip-flops, but those working in the city and most other jobs would dress more formally.

▲ *Adelaide, Sydney and Brisbane*

Many Australians enjoy spending time outside. As Pip says, 'This garden is the world' and it has been the site of many key events in the Prices' lives. Mark recalls climbing up the gum tree to hide, while Pip remembers her mother bashing her head against it. Bob also plants roses and spends time clearing away garden debris, such as leaves. Fran would like instead a garden 'full of chaos and mess' with 'vines and creepers, and herbs'.

Geoff Cobham, the designer of the first production, was influenced by *Stop Making Sense*, a 1984 film of a Talking Heads concert, which starts with an almost bare stage, with musicians and design elements added throughout the concert. Another influence were the photographs of Gregory Crewdson, whose intricately staged images of American suburbs turn ordinary places into locations that are eerie and unsettling.

Question 1 in the exam will ask you to describe how a specific design skill could reflect the context of *Things I Know to be True* set in a contemporary working-class suburb of Australia. The following pages explore various design areas and how they could reflect the context of the play.

TASK 2

Study the images on these pages of contemporary Australia. Make notes on how they could influence a design for the play. Consider:

- costumes
- props
- setting and set dressings.

▲ *Gregory Crewdson with a photograph from his series* Beneath the Roses

CHALLENGE

The popular television soap operas *Neighbours* and *Home and Away* are both set in fictional Australian suburbs. Study an episode or stills from one. Note any inspirations for your design or performance.

Costume, hair and make-up design inspired by context

SET PLAY 3: *Things I Know to be True* by Andrew Bovell 3

The contemporary Australian context will influence the style of costumes. The costumes need to suit the characters' ages, occupations and personalities. The older Prices' costumes may suggest their working-class background, more than their children, who have different life experiences. Pip is a working mother with a responsible job in an education department, so she might dress with a certain practical formality. Rosie is a teenager who has been travelling, so her clothes could be colourful and informal.

There are also opportunities for the characters to change costumes, such as the anniversary evening out, the funeral and, significantly, Mark's transition to Mia. The condition of their clothes might also give hints about a character's mental state and priorities, such as when Ben returns home distressed.

TASK 3

Use the play's context and the prompts below to design a costume for one male character and one female character. Consider the character's age, personality and occupation, as well as suitable colours and fabrics.

Hair:
Men: Long or short? Bald? Colour?
Women: Up or down? Colour? Straight, curled or braided? Headbands? Scarves?

Costume:
Men:
Trousers: Fabric? Colour? Fit? Shorts?
Shirt: T-shirt? Business shirt? Colour?
Waistcoat? Jacket? Blazer? Suit?
Pyjamas?
Colours: Bright or dark?
Fabrics: Linen, cotton, silk, knitted?
Women:
Dress? Suit? Trousers?
Blouse? A uniform?
High or low neckline?
Bath robe?
Fabrics: Plain or patterned?
Cotton, linen, knitted, silk?
Condition: Wrinkled or pressed? Faded or new?
Clean or soiled?
Outerwear:
Coat? Jacket? Cardigan?

Make-up:
Pale or dark? Ageing? Lines? Youthful?
Men: Beard, moustache?

Accessories:
Men: Ties? Watch? A suitcase?
Women: Jewellery? Handbag? Travel bag? A lanyard?

Footwear:
Men: Leather shoes? Boots? Trainers? Slip-ons? Sandals? Barefoot?
Women: High or low heel? Boots? Slippers? Sandals? Barefoot?

TIP
When writing about your costume choices, it is important that you show your understanding of the character and the context. For example, you can reflect how the Australian climate and the characters' activities affect their choice of clothing.

TIP
Carefully read the stage directions. They might suggest or specify particular costumes, make-up, hair or accessories. In 'Spring', for example, Fran wears 'a lovely dress… and her hair is down'. In 'And It Ends Like This', Bob is in 'his pyjamas and bare feet'.

Download a printable version from Samples & Downloads at www.illuminatepublishing.com.

TASK 4

a Choose a different character from those in Task 3. Design a costume for them in a key scene. Consider: hair, make-up, fabric, fit, accessories, headwear and shoes.

b Write a paragraph explaining how the costume suggests the character's role in the play and the effect their external presentation will have on the audience.

Set design inspired by context

One of the challenges of designing *Things I Know to be True* is capturing its different settings, seasons and moods. As there are quick changes of location, you will need to think about how you can suggest these without long, impractical scene changes. Consider how your design will:

- serve the practical needs of the play
- show the period and location
- contribute to the atmosphere and purpose of the scene.

In the script, the Price family home is said to contain: 'A family room, a kitchen and patio extension at the back open to a classic Australian backyard. A **Hills Hoist**, a lemon tree, a well-cut lawn, a rose garden, a shed up the back somewhere and an ancient eucalypt towering above'.

KEY TERMS:

Hills Hoist: a brand of rotary clothes line particularly popular in Australia.

Cyclorama: a large piece of stretched fabric upon which lights or images can be projected.

Further specific contextual features which might influence the set include:

- working-class family kitchen
- garden shown through the seasons
- background projections or **cyclorama** to suggest the time of day or season
- contemporary tables and chairs.

The characters frequently move in and out, which suggests that the garden is as much a living space as the house.

TASK 5

The chart on the next page lists some of the main settings of the play. After you have chosen your stage configuration, use it to begin formulating ideas for your set design.

LOCATION: **Interior of the Prices' home**

REQUIREMENTS: It Begins Like This. Home. As Autumn Turns. Winter. Spring. Home That Night. And It Ends Like This

DESIGN CHOICES:

1 What colours and materials would capture a suburban working-class home?
2 What props or set dressings could help to establish the setting and characters in 'Home'?
3 How could you use the stage space to indicate where characters may enter and exit?
4 What props and set dressings would you use to create the kitchen?
5 How would you handle transitions such as 'Spring', which moves from the house to 'the local pub or a dinner/dance at a local Surf Life Saving Club'?

LOCATION: **The Garden**

REQUIREMENTS: Home. Autumn. As Autumn Turns. Winter. Summer. Life Goes On. And It Ends Like This

DESIGN CHOICES:

1 Could particular design features indicate features of the garden and how it changes with the seasons?
2 Would there be any large items in the garden, such as a shed, wheelbarrow, planting beds, tables, chairs, benches or barbeque? Where would they be positioned onstage?
3 Where would Pip be for the beginning of 'Autumn'? What set dressings would you use in this scene?
4 Where would Mark be at the beginning of 'Winter'? Will you use different levels? What set dressings will contribute to this monologue?

LOCATION: **Berlin**

REQUIREMENTS: Berlin

DESIGN CHOICES:

1 How will you suggest that Rosie is in Berlin?
2 Will you use projections, backdrops or set furnishings?
3 Where will Rosie be on the stage at the end of the scene?

LOCATION: **Mark's home / Journey to Airport**

REQUIREMENTS: As Winter Turns

DESIGN CHOICES:

1 What props and stage furnishings could establish Mark's flat?
2 Where will this scene take place on the stage?
3 Will the staging change when he moves to the car? Will the car be presented onstage?
4 Will there be a change when the characters arrive at the airport?

TASK 6

Choose a scene set in the garden. Describe the set and how it fits the play's context. You could include how your set:

- is appropriate for the chosen scene
- reflects the working-class suburban Australian setting
- functions practically in terms of the action and other key moments.

CHALLENGE

Research contemporary Australian photographers such as William Broadhurst and Warren Kirk, whose work focuses on suburban settings. Make a list of how their photographs could inspire your design.

Sound and lighting design inspired by context

Sound and lighting design can be used to suggest the various locations and the contemporary period in a number of ways, including:

- use of contemporary music
- sound effects of cars or aeroplanes
- lighting to suggest different geographical areas, times of day or seasons
- lighting to create moods or to act metaphorically for the play's themes.

Sound

The original production used music by Nils Frahm, a German composer and pianist, throughout the play. His compositions in the play use both traditional and electronic keyboards to create an urgent soundtrack. Music could be used in many other ways, however, such as pop songs to support certain scenes or a musical **motif** or instrument associated with each character. The seasons could be introduced with appropriate musical excerpts. A sound designer might research the music that the older Prices like and decide what tunes they might dance to.

KEY TERM:

Motif: a repeated image, idea or phrase of music.

KEY TERM:

Soundscape: a collection of sounds that create a setting or suggest a scene, or a drama technique where performers use their voices (and sometimes other items) to create sounds.

Research music that is popular in 21st-century Australia. Suggest at least three moments in the play where the use of particular songs would support the play's action.

Sound effects which could aid the creation of the context include:

- **soundscapes** to establish the different locations in Berlin
- an Australian radio programme
- gardening equipment, such as lawn mowers and leaf blowers
- a ringing telephone
- car engines
- aeroplanes
- rain
- birds, insects and other wildlife from South Australia.

TASK 7

The play mentions a Leonard Cohen song, 'Famous Blue Raincoat,' that Fran used to play 'over and over'. Listen to it and make notes on the mood and lyrics and why the song would have been important to Fran.

TASK 8

Another aspect of sound design is knowing when silence is important. With a partner, choose at least three moments in the play that might be enhanced by silence. Discuss the impact silence would have.

Lighting

To help establish the context, you could use lighting which replicates that in a suburban Australian home, such as table and standard lamps. There could also be garden lighting, such as outdoor lanterns or fairy lights. Your lighting design could establish the time of day, season and different locations. For example, would you use different-coloured gels for the scene in Berlin from the ones in Australia? Using gobos and other specialist equipment, it is also possible to create effects such as leaves and trees, clouds, rainfall and architectural features. Think about how lighting could create a sense of movement when characters are travelling in cars or planes.

TASK 9

a Read the play's opening scene in your group. Make notes on possibilities for sound and lighting design.

b Work through the scene, stopping to agree effects that would suit the action and mood of the scene. Consider:
- music
- sound effects
- lighting effects
- transitions.

Practical explorations of characters, themes and style

When writing about performing, you should demonstrate that you understand the play's characters, themes and style. The practical activities below will help you to explore these aspects of the play.

Family

The only characters in the play are the members of the Price family. Their past, relationships and dreams are the heart of the play. Use the following exercises to explore the family dynamics.

TASK 10

Choose five moments from the play when all or most of the characters are onstage. Create a still image for each moment to show the relationships between the characters. Discuss their use of facial expression, **proximity**, gesture and posture.

TASK 11

a Work in a small group. Each member of the group should take on the role of someone in the Price family. Let each character, one by one, sit in the hot seat while the rest of the group asks them about their childhood, when they were most happy, how they feel about their lives, and so on.

b Then, staying in character, two family members should face each other and take turns to say:

- something that they admire about the other character
- something they dislike
- one memory they have of them
- something that they want from them
- a secret they have kept from them.

For example, Rosie might tell Mark:

- why he is her favourite
- how she dislikes it when he doesn't communicate with her
- a childhood memory of him helping her
- the way she would like them to be together in the future and the secret fears she has.

c After each character has been in at least one pair, look at scenes between those characters and see if your discoveries could affect how the scene is acted. If, as in the example above, you have worked on Rosie and Mark, you might then rehearse 'As Winter Turns', using your discoveries to influence how you play the scene.

KEY TERM:

Proximity: the distance between people or objects; how near or far.

Style: realism versus stylisation

The play combines mostly realistic dialogue with opportunities for stylised movement. Scott Graham, one of the co-directors, is one of the founding members of Frantic Assembly, a theatre company known for its adventurous and innovative use of movement and music. Examples from the original productions can be found online, but are not described in the script. You might choose to create a stylised production, or it could be more rooted in naturalism. The movement choices you make should be there to help create the mood of the scene, tell the story and engage the audience.

One technique used by the directors was using photographs as inspiration, such as Mohammed Ali knocking out Sonny Liston to inspire the scene between Bob and Ben. After studying the image, the actors explored how Bob and Ben could move so that Bob would be similarly 'dominant of a prone Ben' (*Things I Know to be True Comprehensive Guide*).

TASK 12

Choose a photograph or painting you have found, or use an image from these two pages, to inspire movement improvisations in one key scene of the play.

TASK 13

a Choose either an extract from a scene or a transition from one scene to the next. Experiment with the movement. Decide what you want the mood of this section to be, such as mysterious, frantic, dangerous, touching or funny. Then try the following:
   - Move in slow motion.
   - Move in double-time.
   - Pick up a prop and pass it from character to character.
   - Experiment with levels, with one person on the ground, one sat and one standing at all times.
   - Find a moment when there is some contact between characters, such as touching hands, leaning on each other or pushing another character.

b Discuss what worked well and what could be developed further.

Characterisation and conflict

Each member of the Price family has a distinct perspective and there is frequent conflict between the characters. One of the challenges for performers is to create a believable family and show why and how they disagree.

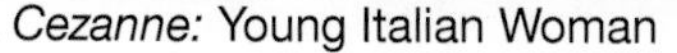

▲ *Cezanne:* Young Italian Woman

▲ Postcards from the Edge

SET PLAY 3:
Things I Know to be True by
Andrew Bovell
3

▲ The Great Santini

▲ *Mathematicians Stefan Banach and Otton Nikodym in discussion*

TASK 14

a Working in a small group, choose a dynamic scene from the play, such as Pip's argument with Fran (pages 30–31), Ben's argument with Bob and Fran (pages 66–67) or Fran and Bob's row (pages 70–71). Have one person 'sculpt' each performer so that they are arranged into a tableau to begin the scene. While the performers are holding this position, the sculptor will point at each one in turn. They should say what their character is thinking and feeling at that moment.

b Now have a new group member sculpt the group into a closing tableau for the extract. See if their thoughts and feelings have changed.

c Then rehearse the full scene, discovering how the characters moved from the first tableau to the last.

TASK 15

a In a group, discuss how conflict can be shown without violence. For example, how can eye contact, volume, proximity and touch indicate conflict without being overtly aggressive?

b Choose an apparently low-key scene, such as the discussion of cars and roads or Ben's laundry/chores and experiment with small, detailed ways the characters can show they are annoyed or disagree. They might turn their back, for example, raise an eyebrow, sigh or laugh sarcastically.

TASK 16

There are a number of important **offstage characters** who are spoken about but never seen.

a In order to understand their effect on the Price family, create a short improvisation about each of the following characters:

- Pip and Steve discussing childcare arrangements
- Mark breaking up with his girlfriend, Taylor
- Ben trying to impress his wealthier workmates.

b Then return to the script and discuss how your understanding of these characters could influence how Pip, Mark or Ben perform scenes where they are mentioned.

TIP

Use film stills or other artworks to inspire the physical aspects of your performance and characterisation.

KEY TERM:

Offstage character: a character who is mentioned in a play, and often influences the action or characters, but is never seen by the audience.

Key characters

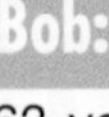

Bob: 63-year-old father; worked in a car assembly plant; keen gardener.

Fran: 57-year-old nurse; Bob's wife and mother to Pip, Mark, Ben and Rosie.

Pip: 34-year-old eldest daughter; married to Steve and mother to two daughters; an education department bureaucrat.

Mark: 32-year-old son; recently broke up with girlfriend; IT specialist; transitions to Mia; Rosie's favourite sibling.

Ben: 28-year-old son; Fran's favourite child; financial services worker; enjoys spending money; has stolen from his company.

Rosie: 19-year-old youngest daughter; returns from unsuccessful trip to Europe; eventually decides to take a creative writing course in Brisbane.

TASK 17

Locate where in the scene 'Home' each character makes their first entrance. Experiment with how they might enter and suggest their relationship with the other characters. Consider what the audience's impression of the character might be.

CHALLENGE

Create a timeline of the key events in the family's life. Include, for example: what year Bob and Fran married and when each child was born; when Bob started at the car factory and when he took redundancy.

TASK 18

a With a partner, choose at least two characters from the list above to study more closely. Discuss your impressions of them.

b Look at the adjectives below and select at least three to describe each character. Explain why you have made those choices:

angry brave sensitive emotional romantic
intelligent calm tempestuous silly unstable loyal
forgetful unimaginative secretive deceptive sad
protective changeable cruel commanding impetuous
unlucky steady sensible passionate powerful
passive cold distant weak strong plotting
peaceful playful moody hopeful self-centred
wise greedy guilty manipulative

SET PLAY 3: *Things I Know to be True* by Andrew Bovell

3

Interpretation of character

You will need to show how you can interpret a character. This means that you understand the character's motivations and goals, and the obstacles they face. In your interpretation, you might decide that a character is, for example, sympathetic, changeable, selfish, passive, intelligent, funny, emotional, heroic, or a combination. Then you must be able to use your vocal and physical skills to portray the character and create particular effects for the audience, such as tension, romance, surprise, anger, comedy, pity or sorrow.

Answer these questions to begin interpreting members of the Price family.

KEY SCENES:

Choose one significant scene for each character.

Bob (for example, upset at the idea of Rosie moving away, pages 76–77)

Fran Mark Rosie

Pip Ben

FACTS:

A family living in South Australia. The father has retired. The mother is still working as a nurse. They own their house, have no debt and help their children in different ways, from providing childcare for Pip's daughters to doing Ben's laundry.

POSSIBLE COSTUME CHOICES:

- How will their costumes indicate their age, occupation and status?
- When and how will their costume change in the play?
- Will they alter their costume onstage, such as adding a cardigan or a jacket, or taking off something like a tie or their shoes?
- Will they have any notable accessories, such as jewellery, spectacles, a handbag or suitcase?

POSSIBLE VOCAL CHOICES:

- What accent/dialect might they use to show their background?
- What changes might they make in volume and tone when they are angry or emotional?
- How might they use diction, pitch, tone or emphasis when making an important point?
- How might they use volume, tone or emphasis when they want someone to agree with them?

TASK 19

Using these prompt questions, write two paragraphs of your interpretation of two contrasting characters in the play.

POSSIBLE PHYSICAL CHOICES:

- How might their posture and body language demonstrate when they want to overpower or convince someone?
- What gestures might they habitually make?
- When and how does the pace or rhythm of their movements change?
- What use of body language, posture, eye contact and gesture might they make when unhappy, frightened or worried?

EFFECT ON AUDIENCE:

- What first impression of this character should the audience have?
- Are there moments when you want the audience to:
  - admire them
  - be amused by them
  - judge this character harshly?

Download a printable version from Samples & Downloads at www.illuminatepublishing.com.

TIP

It is helpful to write in the first person ('I') so you can fully imagine your own performance. Do more than just describe vocal and physical skills: think about how your choices will add to the audience's understanding of the play, its characters and their relationships.

Performing choices

In Question 2, you will discuss in detail how you would perform a particular line as a given character. For example, from 'Berlin':

> You are performing the role of Rosie.
>
> Describe how you would use your vocal and physical skills to perform the line below and explain the effects that you want to create.
>
> Rosie: But I know that at 25 Windarie Avenue, Hallett Cove, things are the same as when I left and they always will be.

In this scene, Rosie has suffered a devastating experience of not only being left by a boy she thought she loved, but also having him steal her belongings. Alone in a foreign city, she is desperate to return home, so, as Rosie, my posture at the beginning of the line is slumped and defeated. (1) I will briefly pause and look down at the ground before I speak because Rosie is at her lowest point. However, as Rosie makes her decision to go home, I will raise my head and, with clear, precise diction, announce my exact address. (2) I will use an Australian accent and make my voice youthfully high-pitched. (3) I will plant my legs in a wide stance and my facial expression is soft, gently smiling as I fondly remember my parents. This is an emotional moment, so my voice will break when I say 'they always will be'. (4) From this, the audience will see that Rosie is young and naïve and finds comfort in the idea of home. (5)

Understanding of character and context of line, mentions 'posture'

Vocal skills (pause and diction) and physical skills (looking down, raises head)

Vocal skills (accent, pitch)

Physical skills (stance, facial expression), vocal skills (breaking voice) and justification

Effect on audience

TIP

You should write about both physical and vocal skills, but you can write about them in combination rather than physical and then vocal, if that helps you to express your ideas clearly.

If you choose to write about Australian dialects, you could explore online examples. Decide what features of the dialect or accent you would emphasise.

TASK 20

a Choose one line from the play spoken by each of these characters:

- Bob
- Mark
- Fran
- Pip
- Ben.

Experiment with different ways of using your vocal and physical skills.

b Answer the following question for each character's line:

Describe how you would use your vocal and physical skills to perform the line and explain the effects that you want to create.

c Check your work by marking or highlighting:

V for each vocal skill you mention

P for each physical skill

E for an effect on the audience.

TIP

In a UK production, the actors used their own British dialects. This emphasised the relevance of the concerns for a UK audience, rather than distancing them with an accent which might be uncomfortable for the actor to maintain.

Character revision sheet

Below is a partly completed character revision sheet.
Copy and complete one for each character.

SET PLAY 3:
Things I Know to be True by
Andrew Bovell

3

Character and importance to the play (for example, position within family and effect on other characters)	
What do they want? (Who do they love? Where do they want to go? What do they think will make them happy?)	
What obstacles do they face? (Who or what keeps them from achieving what they want?)	
What are their key scenes/speeches?	
How might they be costumed?	**How might their hair and make-up by done?**
Draw a simple sketch or write a description Consider: • colours • fabrics • shape and fit • personality, background and status.	Draw a simple sketch or write a description. Consider: • length, colour and style of hair • type of make-up (colours; how it is appropriate for character, setting and period).
How might they use body language? • Posture • Gait • Facial expression	
How might they use their voice? • Emotional range (angry, sad, happy, irritated, desperate, dominating) • Pitch and volume (low or high; loud or soft) • Accent or other distinctive features	
Choose one important line and analyse how they might say it.	

Download a printable version from Samples & Downloads at www.illuminatepublishing.com.

Using the performance space and interaction with others

There are many opportunities to explore the space and interact with characters. You might think about how to establish the changing relationships between the characters and express conflict or affection.

You could reflect on the use of proximity, levels, touch and reactions.

When you are writing about performance space and interaction, make sure that you focus on the effects you want to achieve, such as romance, surprise, tension, pity, excitement or comedy.

TASK 21

Look at the production photos on this page and make notes on the use of performance space and interaction. Consider:

- where on the stage they are positioned
- use of proximity and levels
- gestures
- moments when the characters are touching
- reactions.

TASK 22

a Look closely at 'And It Ends Like This', from 'A telephone is ringing' to 'the roses lie strewn across the lawn'. Note any suggested or specified actions, such as entrances, reactions or exchanges of items.

b Choose a stage configuration. Sketch this and mark where entrances and any pieces of furniture will be.

c Decide the effects you want to achieve in this scene, for example tension, surprise, sorrow or pity.

d How will you use the stage space to help with this? You could try the following interpretations for the beginning of the scene:
- Bob standing centre stage (facing away from the audience), with his children in a wide semi-circle facing him.
- Bob moving in slow motion towards the phone, while his children move in normal time around the stage.
- All the characters moving in slow motion towards the phone.
- Bob standing at one end of the stage while his children pass the phone to him to answer.

e Experiment with different reactions, such as facial expressions, eye contact, gestures and movements:
- What is Bob's expression when he hears the news?
- What gestures, facial expression or movements do the children make when they speak?
- Are there any moments when the children move towards or touch each other?
- How does Bob move when he tears up the rose bushes? Is it slow or quick? Calm or chaotic? How much effort is involved? What is his facial expression like?

f Try different ways of performing the scene then answer the following question:

> You are performing the role of **Bob**.
>
> Focus on Bob. Explain how you might use the performance space and interact with the actors playing Ben, Pip, Mia and Rosie to show the audience **Bob's reaction to Fran's death.**

Answering a question about character interpretation

If you choose to answer Question 4, you will write about how you would use acting skills to interpret a character both in the extract provided and the play as a whole. An example of this sort of question might be:

> You are performing the role of **Rosie**.
>
> Describe how you would use your acting skills to **interpret Rosie's character**. Explain why your ideas are appropriate for:
>
> - this extract
> - the performance of your role in the play as a whole.

TASK 23

a Write a response to the question on the previous page, based on the extract in Task 22.

b Check that you have discussed:
- vocal skills
- physical skills
- the extract
- the rest of the play
- why your ideas are appropriate.

TASK 24

Choose a scene in which Fran is featured. Use the spider diagrams below to prepare a response about her character.

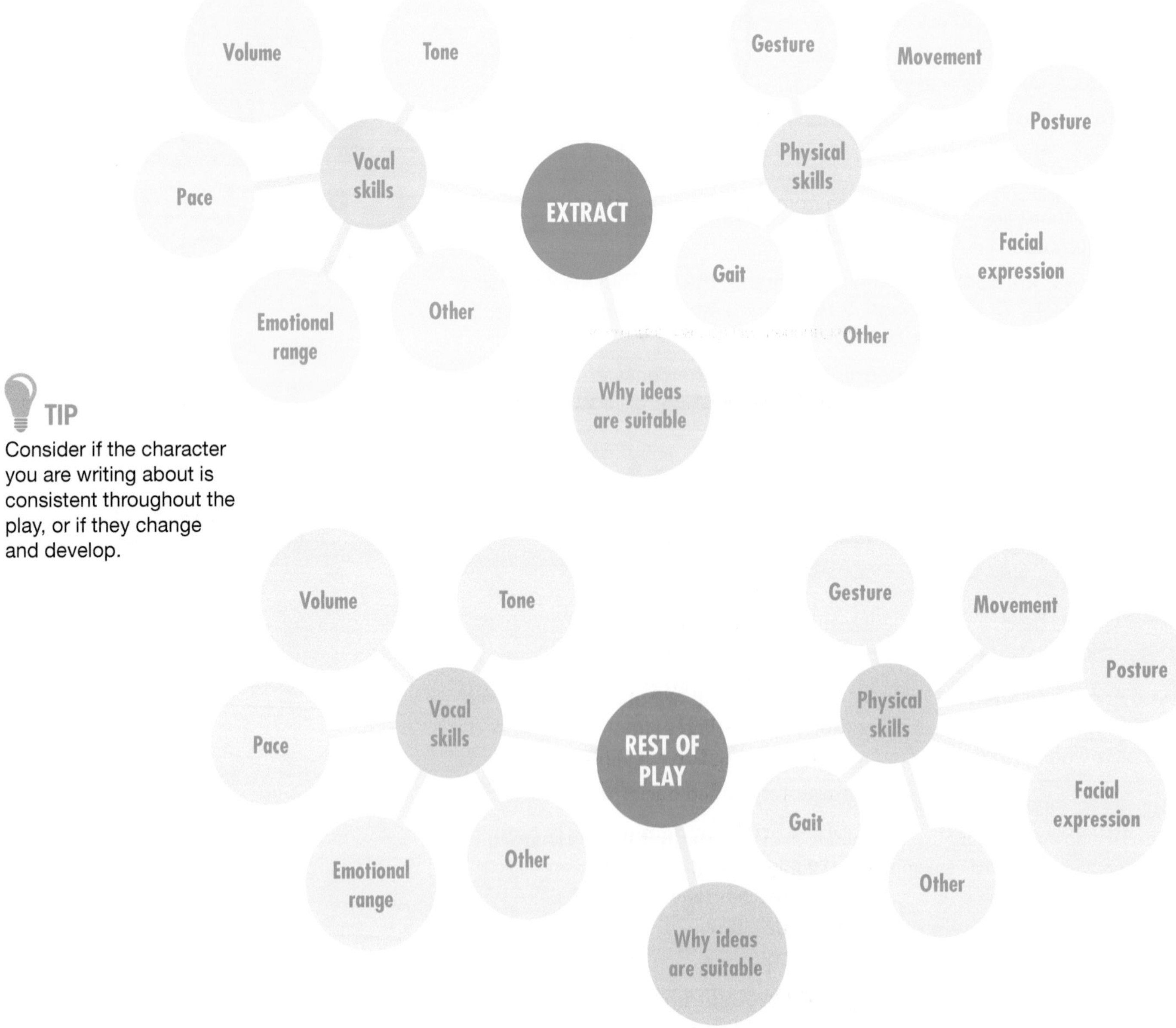

TIP

Consider if the character you are writing about is consistent throughout the play, or if they change and develop.

SET PLAY 3: *Things I Know to be True* by Andrew Bovell 3

Design choices

If you choose to answer Question 5, you will be thinking as a designer and commenting on one aspect of design. For example:

> You are a designer working on **one** aspect of design for this extract.
>
> Describe how you would use your design skills to create effects which **support the action**. Explain why your ideas are appropriate for:
>
> - this extract
> - your chosen design skill in the play as a whole.

You may choose to focus on set, costume, lighting or sound design. Whichever you choose, you must explain why your ideas are appropriate for the whole play. You might describe how:

- your design helps to show the action of the play and the nature of the characters
- your design for the extract is consistent with design requirements for the rest of the play (for example, in style, tone or conventions)
- the technical aspects of your specialism support your design ideas.

Question 1 of the exam will focus on the contemporary period and the Australian suburban location. For Question 5, you may explore this context in naturalistic detail or you may develop a more abstract or symbolic design. Whatever choices you make, you need to demonstrate an understanding of the play and its requirements.

Costume design

For costume design, you might consider:

- style, cut and fit
- colour, fabric, decorative features
- whether realistic or stylised
- condition (worn or new, neat or wrinkled, clean or stained)
- footwear and headwear
- accessories
- status or social role of the character
- make-up and hairstyle.

As costume designer, you will also be responsible for practical choices about fabrics and fit. You could:

- highlight differences between older and younger characters
- associate outfits with particular jobs or locations
- establish the characters' personalities and how they might change during the play
- consider practically how costume changes can be made.

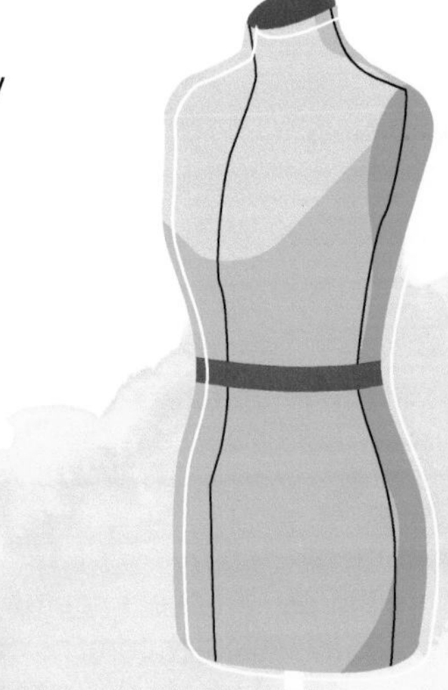

If you concentrate on the Australian setting, you could research the types of clothing worn, such as typical outfits for nurses or young professionals and how choices of colour, accessories, fabric and fit will convey messages about the characters. On the other hand, you may make less naturalistic choices, such as using colours to represent certain characters. Make sure, however, that you still consider how the characters and their positions in the world of your production are shown by their costumes.

TASK 25

a Sketch costume designs for **three** characters.

b Choose **one** of the characters in one scene. Write about their costume for that scene and ideas for the rest of the play.

c Check that you have:

- referred to fabric, colours, shape/silhouette, fit, condition
- included headwear and/or footwear, as appropriate
- considered make-up and hairstyle, if appropriate
- explained how the costume helps the action of the extract
- related your design to the whole play.

Set design

For set design, you might consider:

- staging configuration
- the location and atmosphere of the scene
- if there will be any levels, platforms, ramps or stairs
- entrances and exits
- if there will be backdrops, flats or projections
- whether there will be special effects
- the colour palette you will use
- how materials, textures and shapes can help to create a suitable setting
- what props or set dressings are needed.

One of the challenges is to decide how realistic or artificial/stylised you want your set to be. Alongside this, you need to know how you will incorporate the different settings into this. You could, for example:

- have a composite set, which represents several settings at once, a minimalistic set or set changes where scenery will be brought onstage
- ask the actors to bring on set items or construct or dismantle parts of the set in front of the audience
- use modern technology, such as projections or a revolve
- suggest themes through **theatrical metaphors**, such as colours, symbols or backdrops associated with families, loss or memory.

A set design could perhaps suggest an idealised version of the family which is then dismantled, or the garden could be a symbol of life from birth to death.

KEY TERM:

Theatrical metaphor: when comparisons and symbols are used to suggest meaning. For example, a set design which resembles a head might suggest that all the action is a characters' thoughts or dreams.

TASK 26

Create three set design sketches for scenes in the garden, the living room and Mark's flat. Consider:

- dominant materials, colours and textures
- positioning of important set items or props
- levels
- the atmosphere you want to create
- how the set supports the action of the play.

TASK 27

Look at the sketch below of a traverse stage. Choose a scene from the play which occurs inside the house. Create a set design for it using this configuration.

TASK 28

Choose one significant prop or piece of scenery that appears in the play. Sketch several ideas of how it could be designed. Some important items include:

- the kitchen table
- the rose bushes
- the shed.

Important props include:

- Mark's suitcase
- Rosie's travel bag
- Ben's laundry.

TASK 29

In 'Winter', there is a rainstorm. Think of:

- at least two different ways this effect could be created practically
- where on your set it might occur for maximum effectiveness.

Lighting design

When creating your lighting design, you might consider how to present:

- time of day and season
- mood or atmosphere
- the setting, action and characters of a scene (such as a follow spot to focus the audience on a character's journey or backlighting to make them appear mysterious)
- a focus on a particular moment.

Some of your lighting tools are:

- colours
- angles and intensity
- light from onstage sources (candles, outdoor lanterns, indoor lamps)
- use of shadow and silhouette
- special effects
- transitions, blackouts or fades.

Lighting was very important in the original production. Geoff Cobham, who designed the set and lighting, used lighting to heighten the play's action and make it appear more 'surreal'. He used coloured gels to create atmosphere and hung 131 light bulbs above the set, which he said represented the 'bubble that Bob the father lives in'. (*Things I Know to be True Comprehensive Guide*) There are many other ways, however, that lighting could be used.

The action of the play covers four seasons over a year, with scenes inside and outdoors. The lighting could be naturalistic to represent these locations as closely as possible. The angle of lights might suggest certain times of day, or colours could represent different seasons.

On the other hand, lighting could be more stylised, with certain colours representing memories or spotlights used to follow a character. Conflict between characters could be indicated with special effects such as strobes, backlighting or sudden blackouts.

Your lighting might also change to reflect the differences between more naturalistic scenes and more stylised ones.

TASK 30

Some sample lighting effects a student might want to create are given below. Consider:

- where in the play they might be suitable
- how they could be accomplished technically.

A I want my lighting to suggest the romantic feelings that Bob and Fran still have for each other.

B My lighting, through the use of focused spotlights and coloured gels, will show how lonely Rosie feels in Berlin.

C To depict the changing seasons, I will use high-angled lights with gobos suggesting light filtering through leaves.

D At this point, I will have some of the family members backlit so that we only see their outlines.

E I want the lighting to suggest that each character is in their own world.

F To create an emotional response from the audience, I want the lighting to seem magical and otherworldly.

TASK 31

Choose two contrasting scenes from the play. Write down your ideas of how lighting could help to convey the actions of these scenes and the necessary mood.

Sound design

When creating your sound design for *Things I Know to be True*, you will want to consider how to:

- create atmosphere
- add to the action and emotion of a scene
- contribute to the setting and style of the play
- fulfil the practical needs of the script.

Some choices you can make involve the use of:

- live or recorded sound
- volume/amplification (use of microphones and speakers)
- naturalistic or symbolic sound
- music.

TASK 32

Below are some sound effects which could be used in the play. Identify when they might be used and how they could be created:

- music suitable for dancing
- noises from a nightclub
- sounds or music to increase tension and suspense
- a telephone ringing
- the siren of an ambulance
- a car horn
- thunder and rain
- a leaf blower
- music which suggests the past
- crickets, frogs or other wildlife sound effects.

TASK 33

Consider the different moods in the play, including romantic, violent, tense and sad, and choose pieces of music to underscore at least **four** different moments.

TASK 34

a Identify two contrasting scenes from the play. Describe what effects you want to create for the audience, such as increasing tension and conflict, suggesting love or tenderness, aiding a transition or creating a surprise.

b Write a detailed explanation of how your sound design will create these effects. Consider:
  - when the sound/music will start and end
  - its volume
  - how it will be created (live, recorded, onstage or off)
  - if it will fade in and out or snap on and off
  - what direction the sound will come from (position of speakers, and so on).

TIP

Remember that only clean (unannotated) copies of the script can be taken into the exam.

SET PLAY 4: *Around the World in 80 Days* by Jules Verne, adapted by Laura Eason

4

Synopsis

Act 1, Scene 1: Day 1 'Morning in London, Monday September 30th, 1872'

Phileas Fogg enacts his daily routine of getting up, being given tea and toast by his valet, James, playing cards at the Reform Club and returning home. This is repeated the next two days, but on the third day, Fogg notices that his tea is not at the perfect temperature. James offers to advertise for his replacement. Fogg accepts.

Scene 2: **Jean Passepartout**, a French former circus performer, approaches Fogg and is hired as his new valet. Passepartout is happy that he will now have a quiet life.

Scene 3: The whist players at the club discuss a recent robbery of the Bank of England where a thief escaped with £55,000 and now could be anywhere in the world. Fogg makes a wager for £20,000 with his card-playing friends that he can travel around the world in 80 days.

Scene 4: Fogg returns home and tells Passepartout to prepare for the journey. Fogg packs £20,000 in banknotes. The pair begin their adventure.

Scene 5: They arrive in Italy and Fogg makes plans. They head off by ship to Bombay.

Scene 6: At the British consulate office in Suez, **Inspector Fix** has been sent to find the Bank of England thief. From the description in the newspaper, Fix believes it might be Fogg. Fogg and Passepartout arrive to have their passports stamped by the consul. Fix spots the banknotes in Fogg's bag, confirming his belief that Fogg is the thief. He follows them onto the ship.

Scene 7: When Fogg goes off to play whist with fellow passenger Mr Naidu, Fix invites Passepartout to have a drink and tell him about Fogg.

Scene 8: At the Reform Club, Stuart says that a warrant has gone out for Fogg's arrest for the robbery. The members bet on whether or not Fogg is the thief.

Scene 9: The travellers arrive in Bombay. While Fogg goes to have their passports stamped, Fix takes Passepartout to a temple, where Passepartout is attacked for not removing his shoes. Fix hopes this will delay their leaving Bombay, but Passepartout escapes.

Scene 10: On the train to Calcutta, Mr Naidu and Fogg play cards. The train stops in a forest and the travellers have to disembark because the railway line has not yet been finished.

KEY TERM:

Valet: a gentleman's personal servant who is usually responsible for his clothes and grooming.

Whist: a card came for four players, popular in the 18th and 19th centuries.

▲ *Fogg is offered a wager at the Reform Club in this book illustration by Alphonse de Neuville and Léon Benett.*

KEY TERM:

Suttee: an ancient Hindu custom where a devoted wife was expected to kill herself when her husband died, usually by throwing herself on his funeral pyre.

Funeral pyre: a wooden structure which is set alight to cremate a body.

▲ *A cabin deck on a 19th-century steamship*

Scene 11: Mr Naidu and Fogg negotiate with Miss Singh to allow her elephant to carry them onwards.

Scene 12: As they journey through the forest, the pair come upon a suttee, where a young widow, **Kamana Aouda**, is going to be forced onto a funeral pyre. Fogg saves her and they escape on the elephant. In Allahabad, they say farewell to Miss Singh and the elephant. Fogg offers Mrs Aouda his protection and she agrees to travel with him.

Scene 13: The travellers arrive in Calcutta. Fogg is arrested.

Scene 14: Fogg and Passepartout are put on trial because Passepartout violated the temple by wearing shoes. Fix is pleased they are sentenced to 15 days in prison. Fogg convinces the judge to impose a fine instead. Fix orders a warrant to be sent to Hong Kong for Fogg's arrest.

Scene 15: Mrs Aouda and Fogg have tea on the deck of the boat, where her more romantic and his more 'mathematical' natures are contrasted. Fix pretends to be surprised to see Passepartout onboard.

Scene 16: They arrive in Hong Kong and Fogg sets out to locate Mrs Aouda's cousin.

Scene 17: Fogg returns to the hotel to tell Mrs Aouda that her cousin has moved to Holland. She agrees to join Fogg on his travels to London.

Scene 18: In the Hong Kong consul's office, Fix finally receives the warrant for Fogg's arrest, but it has expired. Passepartout arrives to have their passports stamped. Mr Fix invites him to a tavern to try a local tobacco. Passepartout agrees to a quick visit before they set sail on the *Carnatic*.

Scene 19: Fix and Passepartout sit in an opium den. After trying one pipe, Passepartout passes out. Fix, triumphant, runs out. Passepartout partially revives, remembers the ship they must catch and stumbles out.

Scene 20: The next morning on the docks, Fogg and Mrs Aouda are wondering where Passepartout is. Fix arrives and tells them that their boat sailed last night. Fogg convinces the captain of a smaller ship to take them to Yokohama and invites Fix to join them.

Scene 21: Passepartout is on a different ship. He believes Fix has tricked him and may be working with the Reform Club members who made the wagers. Passepartout realises that he forgot to tell Fogg the ship's departure time had changed.

Act 2

Scene 22: In Yokohama, Batulcar's Acrobatic Troupe warm up and Passepartout demonstrates his acrobatic skills and joins the circus act. When he sees Fogg and Mrs Aouda in the audience, he accidentally causes the tumblers to fall. Passepartout, Mrs Aouda and Fogg run to catch the next ship to America.

Scene 23: On board, Fogg and Mrs Aouda drink tea. Passepartout reminds Fogg of the time and he goes to bed. Mrs Aouda tells Passepartout that his watch is exactly 12 hours behind the local time. Passepartout sees Fix and beats him. Fix explains that he is a police detective seeking to arrest Fogg for the robbery. Passepartout asserts that Fogg is innocent. They agree to work as allies to get Fogg to London quickly.

Scene 24: On a train crossing the American plains, the travellers play cards. Colonel Stamp Proctor criticises Fogg's card playing. As they argue, the train is attacked by bandits and Passepartout is dragged away.

Scene 25: With the help of Colonel Proctor, Fogg sets out to rescue Passepartout.

Scene 26: Fogg and Proctor return to the train platform with Passepartout. Mrs Aouda tells them that the next train is not until tomorrow. Fix arranges that they will travel by sledge to New York.

Scene 27: On the New York Dock, the travellers discover they have just missed their ship. By offering a huge payment, Fogg convinces Captain Speedy to take them on his ship heading for Bordeaux.

Scene 28: Fogg takes over as captain and the ship is redirected to Liverpool. There is a storm and Fogg is informed that there is not enough coal to go full speed. Fogg burns the upper sections of the ship as fuel.

Scene 29: In Liverpool, Fix arrests Fogg. A local policeman explains that the real thief was arrested three days ago. Fogg, Passepartout and Mrs Aouda each punch Fix, who admits he deserves it. They rush to the train station.

Scene 30: Arriving in London, Fogg realises they are moments too late for the deadline.

Scene 31: At home, after spending the day putting his affairs in order, Fogg tells Passepartout he is no longer in any position to keep a valet. Fogg and Mrs Aouda confess how alone each of them is and Mrs Aouda asks if he wouldn't like a devoted companion. Fogg asks Passepartout to arrange for them to be married the next day.

Scene 32: Passepartout realises that, because he had never adjusted his watch, they were one day earlier than he thought.

Scene 33: The Reform Club members wait to see if Fogg will meet the deadline. He arrives at the last possible second.

Scene 34: At the wedding, Passepartout explains how Fogg gained a day and won £20,000. Fogg says to pack their bags as they are all going on a honeymoon. He has 'travelled the world' but not yet 'seen it'.

TASK 1

a After reading the synopsis, work in a group to choose ten key plot points. Create a still image for each. Discuss which moments are the most exciting and dramatic.

b List some of the performance and design challenges of putting *Around the World in 80 Days* on the stage. Consider: lighting, sound, costume, set and puppetry. Think about how to:

- create the period setting
- differentiate between the many characters
- establish the nationalities of the characters and various locations
- transition between the many scenes to show the journey.

▲ *In the 1956 film, Fogg and Mrs Aouda use chopsticks as they cross the South China Sea.*

Jules Verne, 1828–1905

KEY TERM:

Satirical: a humourous way of criticising behaviour by mocking it.

TIP

A popular image of the story is of a hot-air balloon. This comes from the 1956 film, however, and is not part of the journey in Verne's novel or Eason's play. In the play, there is a joke about this when Passepartout suggests a hot-air balloon. Fogg says 'no' and tells the audience, 'There is no balloon in the book.'

Context

Around the World in 80 Days is set in the **late 19th century**, starting in London, then travelling around the world by various means, before returning again to London. The Victorian era (1837–1901) was one of colonial expansion and technological innovation, with the British empire ruling almost a quarter of the world's population. This context will influence your understanding of the play and the possibilities for its design.

The play is based on the popular novel of the same name by French author Jules Verne. It was published in sections in 1872 in the newspaper *Le Temps*, and as a novel in 1873. Verne wrote adventure novels, such as *A Journey to the Centre of the Earth* and *20,000 Leagues Under the Sea*, which, like *Around the World in 80 Days*, involve exciting and difficult journeys. Unlike those two novels, however, *Around the World in 80 Days* is not science fiction, but instead reflects the technical advances in transportation of the time, which made such a trip possible.

These included the opening of the Suez Canal, connecting the Mediterranean and Red seas; the first transcontinental railroad across the United States; and the expansion of railways across India. In the age before air travel, people would depend on trains and steamships for long journeys. As Fogg says, 'rail, steamboat, rail, steamer, rail, steamer, steamer…' Rapid engineering improvements were being made in shipbuilding, and companies were competing to have the quickest and most luxurious ships. The best were often like grand hotels.

Verne was a Frenchman writing about an Englishman, Phileas Fogg, and there are some **satirical** aspects to his portrayal of the English. Fogg is an exaggeration, presented as mechanical in his routine, in contrast to his emotional, adventurous French valet, who says about Fogg that he has seen 'wax figures at Madame Tussaud's more lively than him!' Fogg's routine is an extreme version of that of an upper-class Englishman, with his tea, bath, cards and membership of the Reform Club. This was a social and political men's club in London, which opened in 1836 and had many powerful and influential members. The bet of £20,000 in 1872 would be worth well over £2 million in 2021, demonstrating the wealth of the men involved.

An Englishman enjoys his chota haziree *('little breakfast') in colonial India in 1880.*

Passengers for an American rail locomotive, c1870

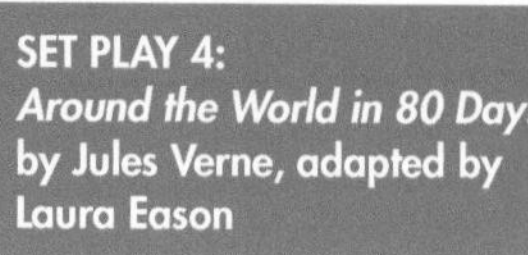

At this time, the main sources of information were printed newspapers, magazines, books, maps and timetables. It is said that Verne was inspired to write the novel after reading travel articles. Thomas Cook began operating his first tourist excursions in the 1840s and organised the first round-the-world tour in 1872–73. It took 222 days, rather than 80. The printed word plays an important role in the play, from Fix's obsession with Fogg based on a newspaper story to Fogg's consulting the *Journal of the Royal Geographical Society* for travel plans, and the passports which must repeatedly be stamped.

On his travels, Fogg displays little interest in learning about other cultures or countries, but instead is intent on proving that his calculations were correct and on winning his bet. He is more concerned with timetables and the best means of transport than seeing the sights. Indeed, when Passepartout does explore the local culture, it almost always lands him in trouble.

Fogg's sense of superiority is one of the driving forces of the play and one which Verne might well have associated with a wealthy Englishman. A Victorian gentleman like Fogg would most likely be convinced that the English were a civilising force. His growing attachment to Mrs Aouda, however, makes him realise his ignorance.

Question 1 in the exam will ask you to describe how a specific design skill could reflect the context of *Around the World in 80 Days* in the late 19th century of the location of the extract. The following pages explore various design areas and how they could reflect the context of the play.

TASK 2

Study the images on these pages of the late 19th century. Make notes on how they could influence a design for one of the locations. Consider:

- costumes
- props
- setting and set dressings.

Valet outfits from 1900

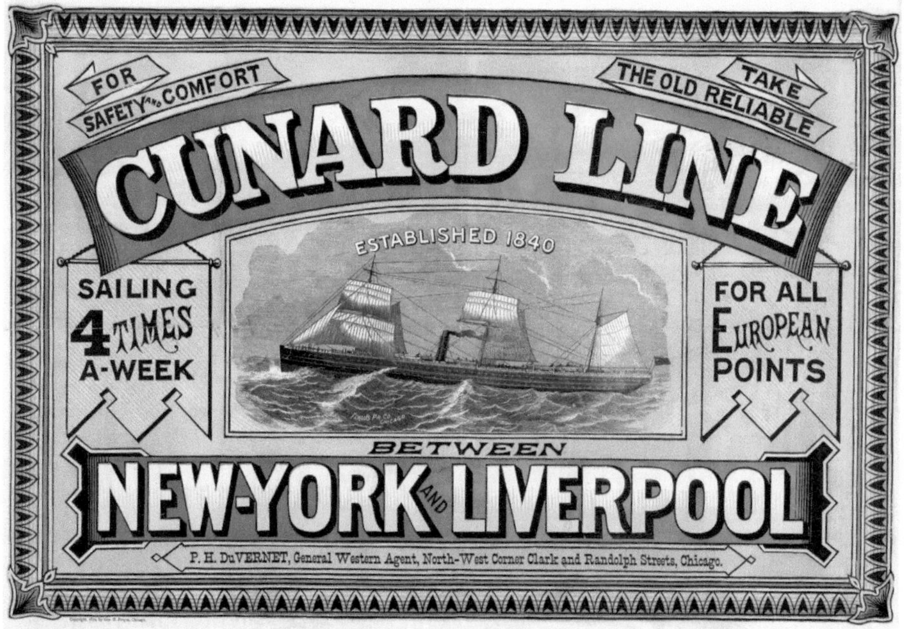

A Cunard line steamship advertising poster from 1875

A lounge in the Carlton Club

KEY TERMS:

Frock coat: a formal knee-length coat.

Morning coat: a single-breasted coat often worn as part of a suit.

Top hat: a high crowned hat with a flat top, associated with formal wear.

Bowler: a black hat with a brim and a rounded top.

Boater: a stiff, flat-topped straw hat with a ribbon band around its crown.

Sari: an Indian garment of wrapped and draped fabric.

Costume, hair and make-up design inspired by context

The late 19th century context of the play will influence the style of costumes. Many characters will be dressed as appropriate for people in England at this time, but as Fogg's journey begins, he encounters people from different nationalities, and their costumes might reflect their culture. A typical Victorian English gentleman might wear tailored trousers, a starched white shirt, a waistcoat and a **frock coat** or **morning coat**. On formal occasions, a **top hat** was necessary; at other times, a **bowler** or, when the weather was warm, a straw **boater** was worn. Typical accessories include ties, pocket watches, gloves and walking sticks.

English women in the Victorian era wore floor-length dresses or skirts, fitted at the waist. A working-class woman might wear an apron or shawl and a simple bonnet.

Locations the travellers visit include Suez, Bombay, Calcutta, Singapore, Hong Kong, Yokohama, the American West and New York. Some of the characters encountered in these locations would wear uniforms required by their jobs, such as ship captains, acrobats, consuls, policemen and conductors, while others may have outfits which reflect their nationality or social role. Miss Singh and Mrs Aouda, for example, may wear **saris** made of Indian print fabrics. Mrs Aouda is said to be wealthy, so the quality of the fabrics and her jewellery could reflect this. Her outfit might also change when she leaves India.

TIP

When writing about costume choices, it is important to show understanding of the character and the context. For example, you can reflect how Englishmen from this period would typically dress, or the types of uniform that would be seen. You should also show knowledge of the fabrics available at the time and how colours and fabrics will deliver a message about the characters.

TASK 3

a Choose a main character from the play. Design a costume for them in a key scene. Consider: hair, make-up, fabric, fit, accessories, headwear and shoes.

b Write a paragraph explaining how the costume suggests the character's role in the play and the effect their external presentation will have on the audience.

TIP

Carefully read the stage directions. They might suggest or include costumes or accessories. In Act 1, Scene 1, for example, Fogg 'gets his hat and walking cane' and 'collects his winnings into a little purse'. Passepartout carries 'two **carpet bags**' in Scene 4. In Scene 20, Mrs Aouda is 'wearing a new dress'. Make a note of these that you find in the script. Consider how they could be designed to suit the character and scene.

KEY TERM:

Carpet bag: hand luggage made of a carpet-like material.

▲ *A 19th-century Hindu prince and members of his family*

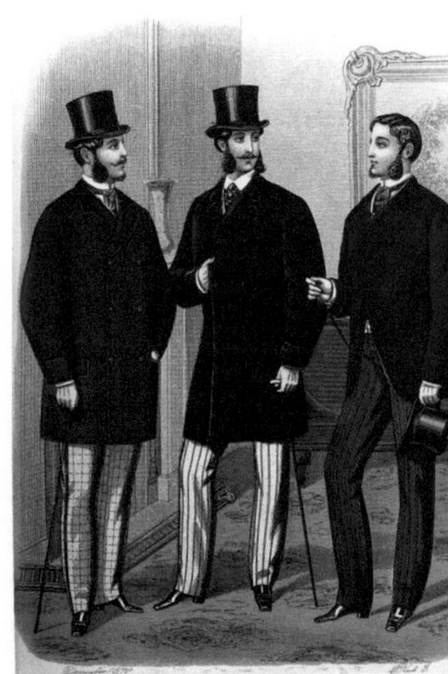

▲ *A plate for a Western fashion magazine from 1870*

TASK 4

SET PLAY 4:
Around the World in 80 Days by Jules Verne, adapted by Laura Eason

4

Use the play's context and the prompts below to design a costume for one male character from the play and one female character. (Choose different characters from those in Task 3.) Consider the character's status, social role and occupation, as well as suitable colours and fabrics.

Hair:
Men: Long or short? Bald? Colour?
Women: Up or down? Colour? Straight, curled or braided?

Outerwear:
Men: Overcoat? Mackintosh?
Women: Cloak? Shawl? Jacket?

Costume:
Men:
Trousers: Plain or patterned?
Shirt: White, coloured or patterned?
Waistcoat?
Jacket? Single or double-breasted?
Colours: Bright or dark?
Fabrics: Wool, linen, cotton, silk?
Ornaments: Gold, silver or black buttons? Badges or stripes?
Women:
Victorian English/European dress or sari?
High or low neckline?
Sleeves: Long or short?
Fabrics: Plain or patterned? Velvet, silk, wool, cotton, linen?

Headwear:
Men: Top hat, bowler, boater, cap, cowboy hat, turban, pith helmet, fez?
Materials: Felt, wool, straw, velvet, leather?
Small or wide-brimmed?
Women: Cap, bonnet, veil, hat or hair adornments?

Make-up:
Pale or dark? Ageing? Lines? Youthful?
Men: Beard, moustache, mutton chops?

Accessories:
Men: Ties? Cane? Pocket watch and chain? Spectacles? Gloves? Umbrella? Handkerchief? Bandana?

Footwear:
Men: Leather shoes? Boots? Barefoot?
Women: Slip-on leather shoes? Plain or embellished? Boots? Slippers? Barefoot?

KEY TERMS:

Pith helmet: a round, lightweight helmet worn in hot climates.

Fez: a flat-topped, round, brimless hat, worn in some middle-Eastern countries.

Mutton chops: facial hair style where long thick sideburns cover the cheeks and may connect to a moustache.

Mackintosh: a long waterproof raincoat, sometimes with a short cape over the shoulders.

Download a printable version from Samples & Downloads at www.illuminatepublishing.com.

Set design inspired by context

One of the challenges of designing *Around the World in 80 Days* is capturing the many different settings, from Fogg's home to the Reform Club; from a steamship leaving Japan to a train in the Wild West; from an Indian forest to a Hong Kong opium den. As there are many quick changes of location, you will need to think about how you can suggest these without long, impractical scene changes. Consider how your design will:

- serve the practical needs of the play
- show the period setting and specific location
- contribute to the atmosphere and purpose of the scene.

Some design features typical of late-Victorian wealthy English interiors include:

- dark polished wood
- patterned wallpaper
- fine china
- leather or velvet upholstery
- solid furniture
- fireplaces
- trays for serving food and tea
- gas lamps
- candles
- framed paintings and mirrors.

Some of the settings in foreign countries which cater for British travellers, such as consulate offices and steamships, might also have some of the above features. Locations such as the Indian forest, however, or the American west or the opium den would be distinctly different.

A street in 1890s Enoshima, Japan

TASK 5

The chart below lists some of the main settings of the play. After you have chosen your stage configuration, use it to begin formulating ideas for your set design.

LOCATION: **Phileas Fogg's home**

KEY SCENES: Scenes 1, 4, 30 and 31

DESIGN CHOICES:

1 What colours and materials would capture a 19th-century gentleman's home?
2 What props or set dressings could establish the period setting and Fogg's personality?
3 How could you use the stage space to indicate when Fogg is inside his home and when he leaves it?

LOCATION: **Reform Club**

KEY SCENES: Scenes 1, 3, 8 and 33

DESIGN CHOICES:

1 Will there be particular design features to indicate the wealth and importance of the club?
2 What furnishings will there be? How will fabrics, colours and materials establish the late-19th-century London setting?
3 Where will the whist table and the clock be positioned to give them appropriate importance?

LOCATION: **Trains**

KEY SCENES:

- Scene 10, on the way to Calcutta
- Scenes 24 and 25, across the plains

DESIGN CHOICES:

1 Will you use signage to establish the trains?
2 How would the train seats be constructed and positioned?
3 What colours and textures will you use?
4 Would you try to establish the view outside the train, perhaps with backdrops or projections?

LOCATION: **Boats/ships**

KEY SCENES:

- Scene 7, the *Mongolian*
- Scene 15, the *Rangoon*
- Scene 21, the *Carnatic*
- Scene 23, the *General Grant*
- Scene 28, the *Henrietta*

DESIGN CHOICES:

1 Will you differentiate between the ships?
2 How would you convey that the scenes are at sea?
3 How would you use the setting to enhance musical numbers like 'The Tea Dance' in Scene 15?
4 Portions of the *Henrietta* are burnt. How might your set design show that?

LOCATION: **India**

KEY SCENES:

- Scene 9, Bombay
- Scenes 11 and 12, the forest
- Scene 13, Calcutta
- Scene 14, the trial

DESIGN CHOICES:

1 What materials, colours and shapes would establish the forest?
2 How could you use the stage space, such as levels, ramps, entrances and exits for 'The Elephant Chase'?
3 Would your set help to establish the importance of the judge in the trial?

LOCATION: **Hong Kong**

KEY SCENES:

- Scene 16, arrival
- Scene 17, hotel balcony
- Scene 18, Hong Kong consul's office
- Scene 19, opium den
- Scene 20, docks

DESIGN CHOICES:

1 Would you use any signage, backdrops or projections to suggest this new location?
2 How will you create the hotel balcony and enhance the romantic mood of this scene?
3 How could colours and textures create the atmosphere of the opium den?

LOCATION: **Yokohama**

KEY SCENE: Scene 22

DESIGN CHOICES:

1 How will your set support the presentation of the acrobats?
2 Will you use any shapes or levels?
3 What colours will you choose?

LOCATION: **America**

KEY SCENES:

- Scene 26, on the platform and 'Sledge Ride'
- Scene 27, New York dock

DESIGN CHOICES:

1 What fabrics and colours might suggest the American West?
2 Will you use any backdrops or projections to suggest the wide-open prairie?
3 How will you create the sledge? What materials will you use? How big will it be?

TASK 6

Choose a scene set in London. Describe the set you would create and how it fits the play's context. You could include how your set:

- is appropriate for the chosen scene
- reflects the setting of London in the late 19th century
- functions practically in terms of the action of the scene and other key moments.

▲ A sitar and tabla

Sound and lighting design inspired by context

Sound and lighting can be used to suggest the various locations and the late 19th century in a number of ways, including:

- period music
- musical instruments appropriate for different countries
- sound effects for period trains or ships
- lighting to suggest geographical areas
- lighting effects that look like period lights, such as gas lamps.

Sound

The script has musical numbers specified in it. In addition, a sound designer has many opportunities to enhance the script. Popular late Victorian music includes Gilbert and Sullivan comic operas and music hall songs, as well as lush, romantic classical music. A wide range of instruments were used including piano, violin, brass instruments and drums. Indian instruments include the sitar (a stringed instrument), and tabla drums. In the mid to late 19th century, Western and cowboy songs became popular in the US. These were often accompanied by a guitar or fiddle (violin).

Sound effects which could help to present the time period include:

- steam train whistles and hisses
- street scenes with horses' hooves and crowd noises.

The Indian setting, for example, could be established by:

- sounds of a crowd at the market
- elephant trumpeting
- calls of tropical birds.

CHALLENGE

Research music from three different locations of the play. Find at least one piece of music which would enhance a scene in the play. Consider the mood you want to create and how the music contributes to it.

Lighting

You might wish to use modern technology to create lighting effects which mimic 19th-century lighting. Most of London would have been lit by gas street lamps, and many homes had gas lighting along with candles and oil lamps. Your lighting design could help to establish the time of day and different locations. You might, for example, use different-coloured gels for the scenes set in the American West from those in London or India. Gobos and other equipment can create effects such as leaves and trees, the moon, clouds and architectural features. Also think about how lighting could show the steam and movement of the trains or boats or suggest the weather in certain places.

▲ London's Royal Arcade

TASK 7

a Read Scene 24 in your group. Make notes on possibilities for sound and lighting design.

b Work through the scene, stopping to agree on effects that would be effective for the action and mood of the scene. You should consider:

- music
- sound effects
- lighting effects
- transitions.

Practical explorations of characters, themes and style

When writing about performing, you should demonstrate that you understand the play's characters, themes and style. The practical activities below will help you to explore the play.

Comedy

There are many comic examples in the play, including:

physical comedy

mistaken identity

exaggerated characterisations

Double-act

Fogg and Passepartout form a comic double-act based both on their differences and their dependence on each other.

TASK 8

a Improvise a short silent scene of the pair preparing for their journey. Find ways of exaggerating their differences. Look at posture, pace, facial expressions and gestures. Does one move quickly, for example? Does one appear calm and the other agitated?

b Develop the scene into physical comedy. Could Fogg be unaware that he has knocked something over and Passepartout catches it? Might Fogg carry something very light while Passepartout struggles with something very heavy?

c Share your scene with another group and discuss the relationship and its comedy.

Physical comedy

There are many opportunities for knockabout humour, from the various fights to the tumbling acrobats. Physical comedy might look spontaneous, but it must be carefully worked out. One way of doing this is to divide a sequence into numbered beats which can be performed precisely over and over. For example:

- Beat 1: Step forward
- Beat 2: Look at partner
- Beat 3: Raise fist
- And so on.

TASK 9

a Working in a group, choose a physical sequence, such as the fight with the Guards, the circus performance, or Passepartout and the bandits. Carefully work out the beats for each character. Then, in slow motion, perform each action accurately.

b Gradually speed up until you have found the best rhythm and pace for the scene.

c Discuss what could be improved.

TIP

One comic technique is a **double-take**: when a character sees something, doesn't fully understand what they have seen and quickly looks again. Think about times in the play when humour is increased by the use of a double-take.

TIP

Safety is important with any physical comedy and fights. Everything should be carefully worked out. No blows should actually be landed and there are no uncontrolled falls. Instead, concentrate on the choreography and reactions.

KEY TERM:

Double-take: a reaction when a someone looks at something, looks away, then quickly looks at it again in realisation. In comedy, it is used to show that a character did not at first comprehend something, but suddenly does.

▲ *The acrobats try to maintain their shape (New Vic Theatre, Newcastle-under-Lyme).*

KEY TERMS:

Ensemble: an approach to acting involving everyone working together, rather than singling out 'star' performers. It also refers to a group of actors who play many roles in a play or a chorus.

Stock gestures: stereotypical gestures to signal certain emotions, such as shaking a fist to show anger.

Using multi-role

The play was originally written for a cast of eight. The four **ensemble** actors play many contrasting roles. It is suggested, for example that Ensemble #3's roles include Captain Blossom Von Darius, the Flower-Seller, Miss Singh, the Suez Consul and a Circus Performer, among other roles. This range of characters requires the actors to change physically and vocally.

TASK 10

The hat game

1. Place a wide assortment of hats in a pile.
2. The first two actors randomly take two hats and begin a scene that fits those two hats. For example, an actor wearing a top hat might object to being stopped by an actor in a policeman's helmet.
3. As the scene goes on, two people on the side hand the actors new hats. The actors must suddenly change their characters and scenes to fit their new hat. So, the policeman's hat might be replaced by a flowery bonnet, and the top hat by a cowboy hat. That will inspire two new characters and a fresh interaction.
4. Continue to change hats until a variety of different characters and scenes have been improvised.
5. Two new actors start the game again.

TASK 11

a Look at the 'Suggested Doubling for a Cast of Eight' early in the script and examine the line of parts that one of the ensemble members has. For each character, develop:

- one **stock gesture**
- one vocal quality
- one physical quality.

For example, you might make these choices for a character:

- gesture: hands on hips
- vocal: Cockney accent
- physical: walks with a limp.

b Take a photo or draw a sketch of each character, noting decisions about the character and when this gesture/skill might occur.

Group movement

There are many sequences in the play which could be enhanced by group movement. The script indicates a number of dances and group scenes. There are also opportunities for unison movement during scenes like the Indian market, the tilting boat, the acrobats and the sledge ride.

TASK 12

a In a group, decide on one person to be the leader, with the rest as followers. The leader should 'conduct' the group. When the leader moves their hand to the left, everyone must lean to the left. When they lower their hand, everyone else bends down or kneels. When they wave their hand, everyone shakes in unison with it, and so on.

b When you are working well together, improvise a scene when you are all on a train or boat, with the leader indicating when and how you should move. You might lean back when going fast or bounce up when hitting a rough patch of the journey.

Key characters

Lead characters

Phileas Fogg: a precise, handsome, upper-class Englishman, 'around forty'; the protagonist.

Passepartout: a French former circus performer who becomes Fogg's valet; provides comic relief.

Inspector Fix: a determined Scotland Yard detective who pursues Fogg for a suspected robbery; the antagonist.

Mrs Aouda: a beautiful young widow, saved by Fogg; the love interest.

Selected supporting characters

Mr Naidu: an Indian businessman who travels from Suez to Calcutta with Fogg.

Colonel Stamp Proctor: a prosperous, well-dressed, opinionated American.

Captain Blossom Von Darius: the female captain of the *Tankadere*, heading for Yokohama.

Captain Speedy: captain of the *Henrietta*, heading for Bordeaux.

Flanagan/Stuart/Ralph: upper-class men from the gentlemen's club who play cards with Fogg.

Miss Singh: a local Indian woman who takes the travellers to Allahabad by elephant.

TASK 13

Locate where in the play each character makes their first appearance. Experiment with how they might enter the scene and show their relationship with other characters. Consider what the audience's first impression of the character might be.

TASK 14

a With a partner, choose at least four characters from the list above to study more closely. Discuss your impressions of them.

b Look at the adjectives below and select at least three to describe each character. Explain why you have made those choices.

angry brave sensitive emotional romantic
intelligent calm tempestuous silly old young loyal
secretive deceptive sad protective changeable comic
commanding impetuous unlucky steady sensible
passionate powerful passive cold distant weak
strong plotting peaceful playful moody hopeful
heroic villainous wise greedy rich

Interpretation of character

You will need to show how you can interpret a character. This means that you understand the character's motivations and goals, and the obstacles they face. In your interpretation, you might decide that a character is sympathetic, changeable, villainous, passive, intelligent, funny, emotional, heroic, or a combination. Then you must be able to use your vocal and physical skills to portray the character and create particular effects for the audience, such as tension, romance, surprise, anger, comedy, pity or sorrow.

Use the questions below to begin your interpretation of **Colonel Stamp Proctor**.

TASK 15

a Using the prompt questions below, write two paragraphs of your interpretation of Colonel Stamp Proctor.

b Then create similar questions for a contrasting character, such as Miss Singh or Inspector Fix.

FACTS:

An outspoken American, travelling from San Francisco.

He insults Fogg's card-playing and calls him a 'Limey'. Before he and Fogg can duel, the train is attacked by bandits. He helps Fogg save Passepartout.

As a Colonel, he achieved a high military rank and knows the commander of a local fort in the US.

KEY SCENES:

Act 2, Scene 24: Insults Fogg.

Act 2, Scene 25: Goes with Fogg to help save Passepartout.

Act 2, Scene 26: Says goodbye to Fogg.

POSSIBLE VOCAL CHOICES:

Colonel Proctor is both helpful and troublesome to the travellers.

- What accent/dialect might he use to show his background?
- What changes could he make to volume and tone when he is angry or dominating a situation?
- How might he use diction, pitch, tone or emphasis when saying insulting words?
- How might he use volume, tone or emphasis when he is being kind or helpful?

EFFECT ON AUDIENCE:

- What first impression of Colonel Stamp Proctor should the audience have?
- Do you want the audience to admire him?
- Are there moments when the audience should be amused by him?

POSSIBLE PHYSICAL CHOICES:

He is a confident man of action, quick to enter a conflict.

- How might posture and body language demonstrate his status and confidence?
- What gestures could he use when challenging Fogg?
- When and how does the pace or rhythm of his movements change?
- How could he use body language, posture, eye contact and gestures when he parts from Fogg?

POSSIBLE COSTUME CHOICES:

- How will his costume indicate his nationality and status?
- Will the condition of his costume change after the fight with the bandits?
- Does he adjust aspects of his costumes, such as removing his hat, gloves or jacket?
- Will he have any notable accessories, such a gun holster, a cigar or a flask?

Download a printable version from Samples & Downloads at www.illuminatepublishing.com.

SET PLAY 4:
Around the World in 80 Days
by Jules Verne, adapted by
Laura Eason

4

Performing choices

In Question 2, you will discuss in detail how you would perform a particular line as a given character. For example (in Act 1, Scene 1):

> You are performing the role of **James**.
>
> Describe how you would use your vocal and physical skills to perform the line below and explain the effects that you want to create.
>
> James: Terribly sorry, sir. *(Knowing he's done for.)* I expect that's it for me, then. Shall I place an advertisement for a new man before I go?

In this scene, the audience will see the clock-like precision of Fogg and James's relationship. Throughout, as James, I will have an upright posture and a calm, unemotional manner, deferring to Fogg in every matter. (1) On this line, I know I have let Fogg down. I will drop my gaze, slightly bow and softly say 'Terribly sorry sir.' There will then be a sight pause as the severity of my error sinks in. (2) My voice, which has previously been an imitation of an upper-class one, will slightly slip back to my natural voice when I say, with a hint of a Cockney accent, 'I expect that's it for me, then.' (3) I will turn away to go, then turn back and offer to place an advertisement with a matter-of-fact tone. Throughout my facial expression is blank, matching the lack of emotion of Fogg. (4) The comedy of this exchange is that such a little matter could lead to my being fired and how both of us accept this as natural. The audience will see how comically particular Fogg is and how even someone as precise as James can't always meet his high standards. (5)

1. Understanding of character and context of line; mentions 'posture'
2. Notes use of pause as well as detailed physical skills
3. Highlights vocal skills
4. Describes physical skills (movement, facial expression) and vocal skills (tone), and justifies them
5. Notes effect on audience

TASK 16

a Choose one line from the play spoken by each of these characters:
- Fogg
- Passepartout
- Naidu.
- Aouda
- Fix

Experiment with different ways of performing the chosen lines.

b Answer the following question for each character's line:

Describe how you would use your vocal and physical skills to perform your chosen line and explain the effects that you want to create.

c Check your work by marking or highlighting:

V for each vocal skill you mention

P for each physical skill

E for an effect on the audience.

TIP

It is useful to write in the first person ('I') to help you fully imagine your performance of the role. Do more than describe the vocal and physical skills: also think about how your choices will add to the audience's understanding of the play, characters and relationships.

TIP

You can write about physical and vocal skills in combination rather than physical and then vocal, if that helps you to express your ideas clearly.

Character revision sheet

Below is a partly completed character revision sheet for **Mrs Aouda**.
Copy the grid and complete it.

Character and importance to the play	Mrs Kamana Aouda is the educated daughter of a wealthy merchant. She was married off to an older man she did not love. After his death, she is due to die too at his funeral, but is saved by Fogg. They fall in love. She helps him to connect to his emotions and realise that there is more to life than he had thought.
What do they want?	• To be saved from death • A life companion.
What obstacles do they face?	• Guards are leading her to her husband's funeral pyre. • Fogg finds it difficult to show his emotions to her.
What are their key scenes?	Act 1, Scene 12: She is rescued and accepts Fogg's protection. Act 1, Scene 15: Drinks tea with Fogg. Act 1, Scene 17: Fogg invites her to travel to London with them. Act 2, Scene 23: Discussion about the journey. Act 2, Scene 26: The sledge ride across the plains. Act 2, Scene 31: Asks Fogg if he would like a devoted companion. Act 2, Scene 34: Now married, they look forward to their next voyage.

How might they be costumed?	How might their hair and make-up by done?
Draw a simple sketch or write a description. Consider: • colours • fabrics • shape and fit • personality, background and status.	Draw a simple sketch or write a description. Consider: • length, colour and style of hair • type of make-up (colours; how it is appropriate for character, setting and period).

How might they use body language? • Posture • Gait • Facial expression	
How might they use their voice? • Emotional range (angry, sad, happy, irritated, desperate, dominating) • Pitch and volume (low or high; loud or soft) • Accent or other distinctive features	
Choose one important line and analyse how they might say it.	

TASK 17

Using the grid for guidance, create similar revision sheets for all the major characters, including: Fogg, Passepartout and Fix.

Download a printable version from Samples & Downloads at www.illuminatepublishing.com.

Using the performance space and interaction with others

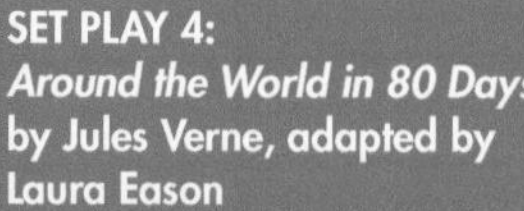

There are many opportunities to explore the stage space and interact with other characters. You might think about, for example, how to:

- establish the developing relationship between Fogg and Mrs Aouda
- portray the conflict with Inspector Fix
- show the effect of different locations on the travellers.

You could reflect on the use of proximity, levels, touch and reactions.

When you are writing about performance space and interaction, make sure that you focus on the effects you wish to achieve for the audience, such as romance, surprise, tension, pity, excitement or comedy.

TASK 18

Look at the photographs on the right and make notes on the use of performance space and interactions. Consider:

- where on the stage actors are positioned
- use of proximity and levels
- gestures
- moments when the characters are touching
- any reactions.

TASK 19

a Look closely at the last two pages of Act 1, Scene 1, from 'Movement sequence continues.' Note suggested or specified actions, such as entrances, reactions or exchanges of items.

b Choose a stage configuration. Sketch this and mark where entrances and any pieces of furniture will be.

c Decide the effects you want to achieve in this scene, for example tension, surprise, comedy.

d How will you use the stage space to help with this? You could try the following interpretations:
- The actors use the whole width and depth of the stage.
- The actors work together in a tight, contained section of the stage.
- Fogg behaves mechanically, ignoring James and not making eye contact.
- Fogg and James act as a team, with James anticipating Fogg's needs and Fogg politely acknowledging him.

e Experiment with different reactions, such as facial expressions, eye contact, gestures and movements:
- What is Fogg's expression when he sighs?
- What gestures or expressions does James make when Fogg enters or says goodnight?
- How is the 'screeching halt' conveyed in terms of movement and facial expressions?
- How does James act when he exits? How does Fogg react to his exit?

f Try different ways of performing the scene, then answer the following question:

> You are performing the role of **James**.
>
> Focus on James's scene with Fogg. Explain how you might use the performance space and interact with the actor playing Fogg to show the audience **the comic relationship between the characters**.

TIP

There are many different ways a scene can be interpreted. These are just a few examples.

Answering a question about character interpretation

If you choose to answer Question 4, you will write about how you would use acting skills to interpret a character both in the extract provided and the play as a whole. An example of this sort of question might be:

> You are performing the role of **Phileas Fogg**.
>
> Describe how you would use your acting skills to **interpret Fogg's character**. Explain why your ideas are appropriate for:
>
> - this extract
> - the performance of your role in the play as a whole.

TASK 20

a Write a response to the question above, based on the extract in Task 19.

b Check that you have discussed:

- vocal skills
- physical skills
- the extract
- the rest of the play
- why your ideas are appropriate.

TIP

Consider if the character you are writing about is consistent throughout the play, or if they change and develop.

TASK 21

Choose a scene in which Passepartout is featured. Use the spider diagrams below to prepare a response about his character in the play.

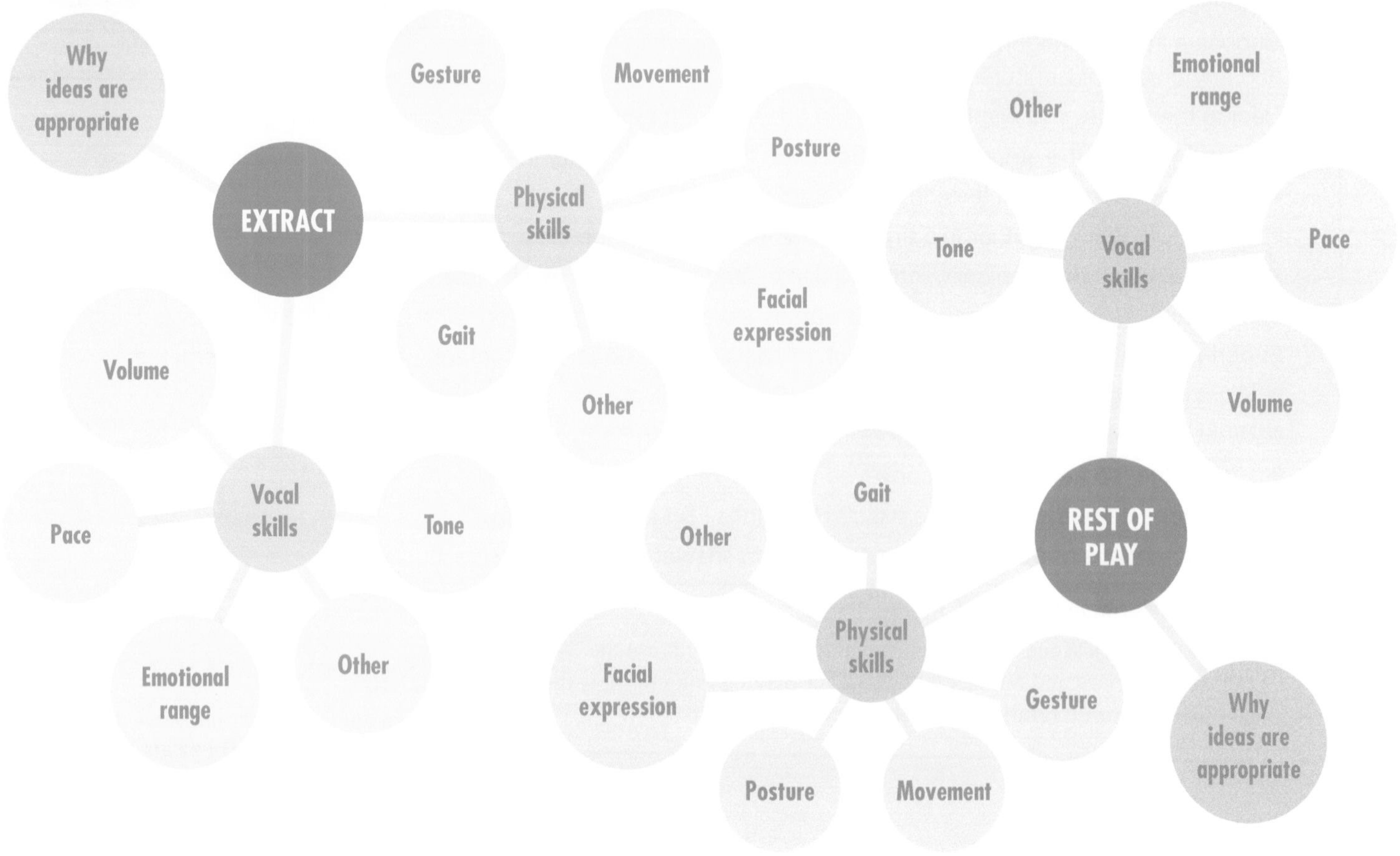

EXTRACT

Why ideas are appropriate

Physical skills: Gesture, Movement, Posture, Facial expression, Other, Gait

Vocal skills: Volume, Pace, Tone, Emotional range, Other

REST OF PLAY

Why ideas are appropriate

Vocal skills: Other, Emotional range, Pace, Volume, Tone

Physical skills: Gait, Other, Facial expression, Posture, Movement, Gesture

Design choices

If you choose to answer Question 5, you will be thinking as a designer and commenting on one aspect of design. For example:

> You are a designer working on **one** aspect of design for this extract.
>
> Describe how you would use your design skills to create effects which **support the action**. Explain why your ideas are appropriate for:
>
> - this extract
> - your chosen design skill in the play as a whole.

You may choose to focus on set, costume, lighting, sound or puppet design. Whichever you choose, you must explain why your ideas are appropriate to the play as a whole. You might refer to the way in which:

- your design contributes to the action of the play and helps to show the nature of the characters
- your design for the extract is consistent with the design requirements for the rest of the play (for example, in style, tone or conventions of the production)
- the technical aspects of your chosen specialism support your design ideas.

Around the World in 80 Days offers many opportunities for imagination, creativity and design flair.

Question 1 of the exam will focus on the late 19th century and a specific location, such as London or India. For Question 5, you may explore this context in naturalistic detail or you may develop a more abstract or symbolic design. Some productions use story theatre conventions, creating the many locations with the inventive use of a few props, chairs and sheets. Whatever choices you make, you need to ensure that you demonstrate an understanding of the play and its particular requirements.

Costume design

For costume design, you might consider:

- style, cut and fit
- colour, fabric, decorative features
- whether realistic or stylised
- condition (worn or new, neat or wrinkled, clean or stained)
- footwear and headwear
- accessories
- the status or social role of character
- make-up and hairstyle.

As costume designer, you will also be responsible for practical choices about the fabrics and fit for the characters. You may want to:

- highlight differences between the English characters and those from other countries
- show the different outfits associated with various jobs or locations
- establish the different ages and personalities of the characters
- help to show if the characters change over the course of the play
- consider how multi-role could be done with efficient costume design.

This traditional Hindu outfit could give you some costume ideas for Mrs Aouda.

If you concentrate on the late-19th-century setting, you could research in detail the types of clothing worn in different countries and how colour, accessories, fabric and fit will convey messages about the characters. On the other hand, you might create a less naturalistic, more fantastical world, and the fabrics and silhouettes you choose will reflect that choice. Make sure, however, that you still consider how the characters and their roles and status in the world of your production are shown by their costumes.

TASK 22

a Sketch costume designs for **three** significant characters in Act 1.

b Choose **one** of those characters and one scene. Write about their costume for that scene and how they might be costumed in the rest of the play.

c Check that you have:

- referred to fabric, colours, shape/silhouette, fit, condition
- included headwear and/or footwear, as appropriate
- considered make-up and hairstyle, if appropriate
- explained how the costume helps the action of the extract
- related your design to the rest of the play.

Set design

For set design, you might consider:

- staging configuration
- the location and atmosphere of the scene
- if there will be any levels, platforms, ramps or stairs
- entrances and exits
- if there will be backdrops, flats or projections
- whether there will be special effects (such as blossoms or confetti dropping from the flies, or a set being suddenly knocked over or pulled apart)
- the colour palette you will use
- how materials, textures and shapes can help to create a suitable setting
- what props or set dressings are needed.

One of the challenges is to decide how realistic or artificial/stylised you want your set to be. Alongside this, you need to know how you will incorporate the different settings into this. You could, for example:

- have a composite set, which represents several settings at once, a minimalistic set or set changes where scenery will be brought onstage
- ask the actors to bring on set items or construct or dismantle parts of the set in front of the audience
- use modern technology, such as projections or a revolve
- suggest themes of the play through **theatrical metaphors**, for example colours, symbols or backdrops associated with travel.

Some designs for the play have used maps on backdrops or projected onto the floor, or have used miniature versions of the ships and trains to represent their journeys.

KEY TERM:

Theatrical metaphor: when comparisons and symbols are used to suggest meaning. For example, a set design which resembles a head might suggest that all the action is a characters' thoughts or dreams.

TASK 23

a Create a set design for a scene in India, Japan or America
b Write a paragraph explaining its effect on the audience. Consider:
- dominant colours and textures
- positioning of important set items or props
- levels
- materials
- the atmosphere you want to create
- how the set supports the action of the play.

TASK 24

Look at the sketch on the right of a theatre in the round. Choose a different scene from that in Task 23 and create a set design for it using this configuration.

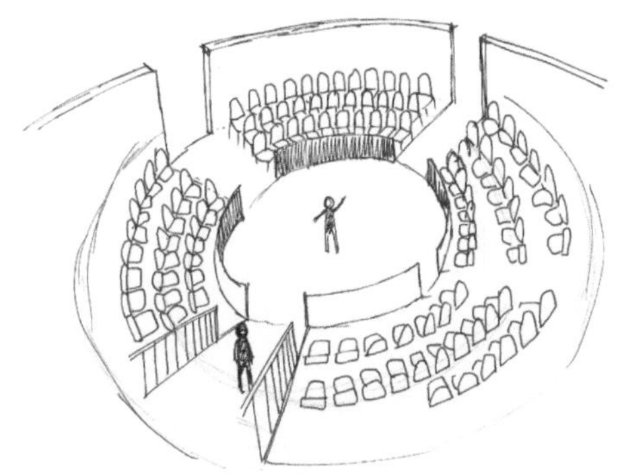

TASK 25

Choose one significant prop or piece of scenery that appears in the play. Sketch several ideas of how it could be designed. Some important items include:
- the whist table
- the hotel balcony
- opium den pillows
- the sledge.

Important props include:
- Inspector Fix's newspaper
- Judge Obadiah's giant law book
- tea cups
- passports.

Lighting design

When designing lighting, you might consider how to create:
- time of day and season
- mood or atmosphere
- the setting, action and characters of a scene (such as a follow spot to focus the audience on a character's journey or backlighting to make them appear mysterious)
- a focus on a particular moment.

Some of your lighting tools are:
- colours
- angles and intensity
- light from onstage sources (candles and lamps)
- use of shadow and silhouette
- special effects
- transitions, blackouts or fades.

The action of the play covers the few days preceding Fogg's departure and the 80 days of his journey. In that time, not only does he travel through a number of different countries, he uses different means of transport, including trains, ships, a sledge and an elephant. Throughout the play, scenes take place at different times, from early morning to late at night, and this, as well as the different locations and moods of scenes, should be supported by the lighting.

TASK 26

Some sample effects a student might want to create are given below. Consider:

- where in the play they might be suitable
- how they could be accomplished technically.

A I want to show that this scene is taking place in a forest. My lighting scheme will make it appear that they are only lit by natural lighting filtered through the trees.

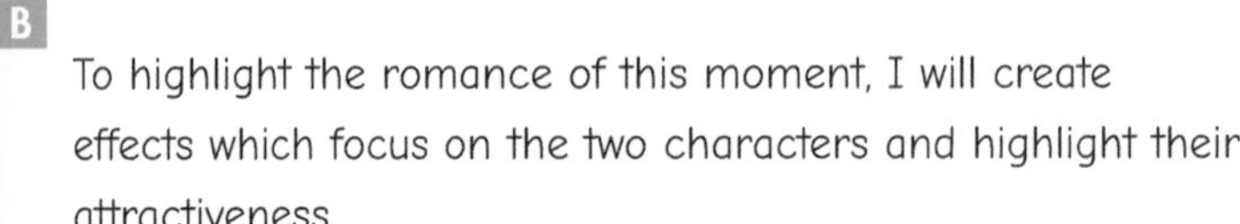

B To highlight the romance of this moment, I will create effects which focus on the two characters and highlight their attractiveness.

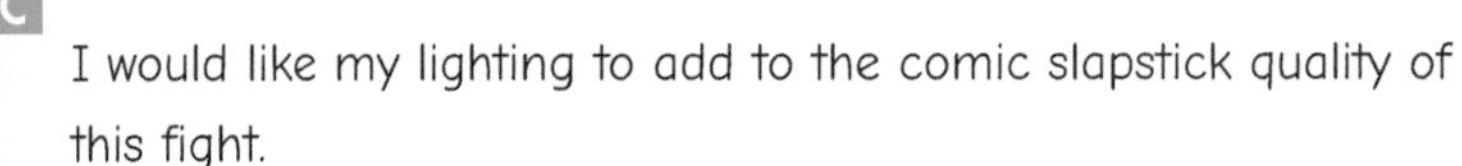

C I would like my lighting to add to the comic slapstick quality of this fight.

D The lighting will give the impression of the train moving quickly.

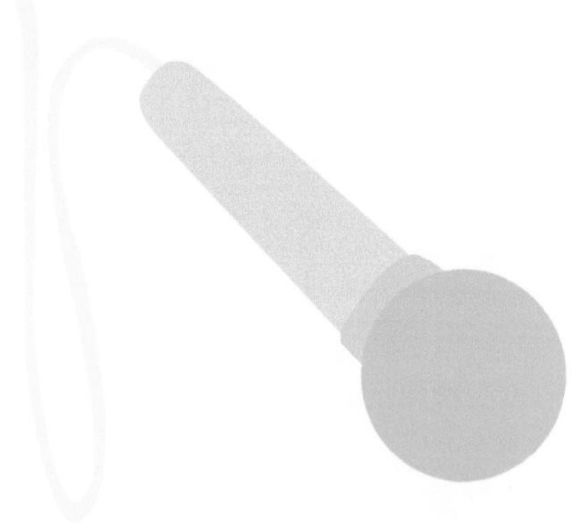

TASK 27

Choose two contrasting scenes from the play. Write down your ideas of how lighting could help to convey the actions of these scenes and the necessary mood.

Sound design

When designing sound for *Around the World in 80 Days*, you should consider how to:

- create atmosphere
- add to the action and emotion of a scene
- contribute to the setting and style of the play
- fulfil the practical needs of the script.

Some choices you can make involve the use of:

- live or recorded sound
- volume/amplification (use of microphones and speakers)
- naturalistic or symbolic sound
- music (recorded, or performed live on- or offstage).

TIP

Remember that only clean (unannotated) copies of the script can be taken into the exam.

TASK 28

Below are some sound effects which could occur in the play. Identify when they might be used and how they could be created:

- music suitable for dancing
- waves
- crowd noises
- sounds to increase tension and suspense
- an elephant trumpeting
- horses' hooves
- romantic instrumental music
- train noises
- whistles.

TASK 29

a Identify two contrasting scenes from the play. Describe what effects you want to create for the audience, such as increasing tension, suggesting romance or adding to the comedy.

b Write a detailed explanation of how your sound design will create these effects. Consider:
- when the sound/music will start and end
- its volume
- how it will be created (live, recorded, onstage or off)
- if it will fade in and out or snap on and off
- what direction the sound will come from (position of speakers, and so on).

Puppet design

Puppetry can be a useful tool to convey the voyage, with opportunities to show the journey and the many people and creatures encountered. If you choose to write about puppet design, you must show how your design ideas will add to the development of the action of the play and be consistent with the style, mood and atmosphere.

Some opportunities for puppet design include:

- trains and ships
- the elephant
- the forest
- the floating gardens
- the American plains.

When designing your puppet, think about the following.

- What type of puppet will it be, for example shadow puppet, marionette, hand-and-rod puppet or a giant backpack puppet that is worn by a puppeteer?
- Materials: wood, cloth, bamboo, willow, papier mâché, string, wire?
- How is the puppet operated onstage? A puppeteer who is 'part' of the character? Held by a performer? Offstage puppeteer?
- How does the puppet tie in with the dramatic intentions for the extract and the play as a whole?

▲ *The elephant puppets in the play* Circus 1903 *are near life-size, realistic and highly believable. They interact very naturally with the human actors, and the audience.*

TASK 30

Choose a scene from the play which you believe would be enhanced by the use of puppetry. Draw a detailed sketch of the puppet and annotate it with explanatory notes about how it would be made and operated. Remember to include: materials, how it would be manipulated, its size and the effect it would create.

▶ For more on puppet design, see pages 269–272.

5 SET PLAY 5: *Noughts & Crosses* by Malorie Blackman and Dominic Cooke

Synopsis

Sephy Hadley, a teenage member of the Crosses, the ruling black class, is on her family's private beach. **Callum McGregor**, a member of the Noughts, the white underclass, joins her and asks if he can kiss her.

Callum has passed the test to join Sephy's school, Heathcroft, and Sephy is tutoring him. After she leaves, Callum speaks to the audience about his family: his older brother, **Jude**, and his troubled sister, **Lynette**, who has been changed by a mysterious incident.

His mother **Meggie** is worried about Callum being educated with the Crosses, but his father, **Ryan**, thinks it is the only way he will succeed.

On the first day of school there is a demonstration against the Nought students being taught at Heathcroft. Sephy tries to intervene to protect Callum and the other Noughts, but ends up offending him, by referring to them as 'Blankers'. Later, he asks her never to use that word again.

At dinner, the Hadleys hear Sephy's father, **Kamal**, who is the Deputy Prime Minister, denounce the Liberation Militia, as an 'illegal terrorist group' run by Noughts. Jude supports the group.

At school, Sephy tries to sit with Callum and the other Noughts at lunch. Callum moves away from her. After school, Callum runs into Sephy on the beach. She accuses him of being a snob and they argue. The next day at school a Cross girl gang bullies Sephy. When Callum hears about the fight he tries to see Sephy, but Sephy's mother, **Jasmine**, denies him entry.

At Callum's house, Lynette and Jude are arguing. Lynette believes that she is black and therefore one of the Crosses. Ryan explains that Lynette and her boyfriend, **Jed**, were attacked by Nought men because Lynette was going out with a Cross. Lynette snaps out of her dream-state and realises that she is two years older than she thought and her boyfriend isn't coming back. Later, she tells Callum that she misses living in a fantasy world.

Lynette then goes missing. Police arrive to say that Lynette has died. At Lynette's wake, Sephy arrives and receives a hostile welcome.

Three months later, Callum tells the audience about the changes in the McGregor household. Jude and his father are going to secret political meetings. Callum is the last of the Noughts to remain at Heathcroft.

Two months after this, Callum calls Sephy and they agree to meet at the shopping centre. However, when Callum gets ready to go out, his father forbids him. Callum realises that something is going to happen at the shopping centre and rushes out. Callum pulls Sephy away from the centre as a bomb explodes.

Back home, Callum and his mother watch a report about the bombing, which was carried out by the Liberation Militia. Meggie confronts Ryan and Jude about their involvement in the bombing. Jude says that everyone was meant to be evacuated but Ryan says he planned that people should die, saying he had no choice as he was protecting his family. Meggie says he has been brainwashed and throws him out of the house. Callum accuses Jude of knowing that their father is covering for him and that Jude was responsible.

Act 2

Sephy is at her house telling the audience about Jasmine's drinking. Her father has a girlfriend and is leaving the family after the next election.

A reporter announces that Ryan has been arrested. Callum and his mother discover that someone is paying Ryan's legal fees. Callum is suspended from school. Callum is a witness at his father's trial. Despite the defence, Ryan is found guilty and sentenced to death. Jasmine insists that they go to watch him being hanged.

At the last minute, he receives a reprieve and instead is sentenced to life imprisonment. Sephy and Jasmine argue about 'duty' and Jasmine's drinking.

That night, Callum's house is burnt to the ground. Kamal announces that he is sending Sephy to boarding school.

Callum sneaks into Sephy's bedroom and tells her how angry he is. She responds that really they love each other. They hug and wonder if they should run away together. They fall asleep. They are awoken by Sarah, the Hadley's secretary, and Jasmine at the door. Sarah helps to hide Callum from the suspicious Jasmine. Callum tells Sephy that she can contact him at his aunt's address. A reporter announces that Ryan was killed trying to escape from prison.

Now September, Callum is sad because he's heard nothing from Sephy. Jude convinces Callum to take part in something that will 'make a difference'. Sarah arrives with a letter for Callum from Sephy, but she misses him. Sephy leaves for boarding school.

Over two years later, Sephy and Callum exchange letters. She then meets him on the beach. They kiss and a group of Noughts, led by Jude, attack and abduct her. The group demand a ransom for Sephy's release. Callum videos Sephy reading a statement addressed to her father.

When they are left alone, Sephy and Callum make love. When Jude and the others come back, they think Callum has raped Sephy and that she will now have to be killed. Jude and Callum fight and Sephy escapes.

Sometime later, Sephy and Callum arrange to meet on the beach. Sephy reveals that she's pregnant. They are surrounded by police and Callum is arrested. Kamal tells Callum he should convince Sephy to terminate her pregnancy and, if he does, he will commute his death sentence to a prison term. Callum refuses. Sephy and Callum declare their love. Callum is hanged.

The play ends with Sephy on the beach holding her baby, Callie Rose.

TASK 1

With your group, create ten still images showing what you think are the most important plot points of the play.

TASK 2

With your group, create a bullet point list of some of the performance and design (costume, lighting, setting, sound) challenges for the play. For example:

- quick changes between the scenes
- establishing different costumes for the Noughts and the Crosses.

Context

The context of ***Noughts & Crosses*** is contemporary **dystopian**. Dystopian theatre presents a world which may have parallels with the contemporary world but highlights the dangers and injustices of it.

Some dystopian stories are clearly set in an imagined future, such as Margaret Atwood's *The Handmaid's Tale and The Testaments* and George Orwell's *1984*.

The play is set at an unspecified time and place. Although the Noughts and Crosses are inventions of the author, much of the play is recognisable to a contemporary audience, such as the technology, the school and the shopping mall. By introducing the powerful Crosses and victimised Noughts, Blackman wants the audience to examine their own expectations and prejudices. She has said she was inspired to write it based on:

> ... a lifetime of experiences. Some of the racist incidents in the book were based on real events from my own childhood. And I also wanted to play with the idea that 'history is luck' to a certain extent. What if Africans had invented trans-oceanic travel and colonised Europe and America?
>
> ('Q&A with Malorie Blackman', www.malorieblackman.co.uk/index.php/qa-with-malorie/)

KEY TERMS:

Dystopian: referring to an imagined world where society is presented in a highly negative light. Writers often create dystopian worlds in order to warn people about present dangers.

Direct address: speaking directly to the audience.

Episodic: a series of loosely connected scenes.

CHALLENGE

Bertolt Brecht famously said that 'Art is not a mirror with which to reflect reality but a hammer with which to shape it.' As a practitioner of 'epic' conventions, he didn't want the audience just to be entertained by the play, but wanted them to be educated and encouraged to take action.

Think about the play *Noughts & Crosses* and write a bullet point list of what you think the author Malorie Blackman and the playwright adaptor Dominic Cooke want the audience to think about after seeing it.

CHALLENGE

Research production photographs of plays with dystopian settings such as *1984* by Headlong or *The Effect* at the National Theatre. Note any design features that you think could be used in *Noughts & Crosses*. Through your design choices, how can you make clear that you are presenting an alternative, negative world, for example by the use of technology or symbols?

The playwright and director, Dominic Cooke, specifies in the script that he wants the 'scenes to flow into one another with no gaps' and that there should be 'a minimum of props and clutter'. There should be 'no blackouts except where stated'. This suggests that the play will have to be staged in a fluent and efficient way that avoids the demands of full detailed sets or lengthy scene changes.

The original production used 'epic' conventions such as **direct address** to the audience and a minimalistic set to accommodate the **episodic** nature of the script.

To reflect the contemporary dystopian context, you could use techniques such as:

- projections or captions
- a clear political or social focus
- minimal or symbolic settings
- emphasis on hardships and injustice
- effects which suggest danger or violence
- clearly defined social groups.

You may choose to create a design that has more detail and props than the original production, but ensure that you explain your reasons for any choices you make.

▶ For more about epic theatre see page 216.

Costume, hair and make-up design inspired by context

SET PLAY 5: *Noughts & Crosses* by Malorie Blackman and Dominic Cooke

5

TASK 3

Using your understanding of the play's context of contemporary dystopian theatre, create a costume for **Jude McGregor** using the prompts below. You might wish to consider if there are any costume details that will indicate Jude's rebellious nature, his identity as a 'Nought' and his family's lack of money. Will you create costumes that reflect fashions today or create altered 'dystopian' fashions? Will you have all the Nought characters dressed similarly or will their costumes reflect their individual personalities?

Headwear: Baseball cap? Beanie? Headphones? Balaclava?

Clothing: Fabrics: Polyester? Wool? Cotton? Lycra? **Colours:** Primary colours? Black? White? Pastels? Khaki? **Prints:** Plain? Stripes? Checks?

Jacket/coat: Long or short? Thick fabric or thin?

Trousers: Sweatpants? Jeans? Combats? Black? White?

Shape and fit: Tight? Baggy? Layers?

Footwear: Boots? Trainers? Loafers? Identifiable brands? **Condition:** Worn or new?

Hair: Short? Long? Neat? Clean? Styled?

Make-up: Colours? Highlight certain features? Scars? 'War paint' in the hide out?

Period: Present day? Futuristic?

Nought identity: Any badges/decals to show they are 'Noughts'?

TIP

When writing about your costume design, remember that you must not only describe it, but you must also justify your choices. How will your choices show that you have understood the character of Jude and the context of contemporary dystopian theatre?

TASK 4

Now consider the character of Jasmine and draw a sketch of a possible costume for her. Remember to consider: headwear, jewellery, hair and make-up, shape and fit, colours, materials, footwear.

Download a printable version from Samples & Downloads at www.illuminatepublishing.com.

Set design inspired by context

Contemporary dystopian theatre offers many opportunities for designers to use their imaginations and current technology. For example, you could use projections to create captions identifying key scenes; video could be utilised to show news reports; a futuristic world could be imagined through choices in colours, materials and architecture. Given the many different locations, you may wish to keep the design simple and flexible. Some scenes occur outside and others inside, so you may consider how your design will reflect this. There may be opportunities for actors to mime objects rather than them being realistically presented. You could think about how the use of levels, steps, ramps or ladders could aid your ability to show the power dynamic in a contemporary dystopian style.

The chart on the following page lists a few of the key locations of the play with some of the requirements suggested by the script (you may discover others) and some of the design questions to answer.

TIP

Your set may suggest objects or locations without fully creating them in a realistic fashion. Recurring colours or materials can make a design consistent. For example, you may associate a certain colour with all the Noughts' locations and a different colour for the Crosses'. You could suggest that everything owned by the Noughts is old and worn, while the Crosses' things are new and clean. You might have an overall concept of a restricted palette of colours or materials giving a futuristic feeling to the play or you could look at a particular time period and base your design on that.

TASK 5

Answer the questions on each setting in the chart on page 123 and add any requirement notes as you discover them.

TASK 6

You are designing props or items of set for Act 2, Scene 21. The props or items of set must reflect the conventions of contemporary dystopian theatre used in *Noughts & Crosses*. Describe your design ideas for the props or items of set.

You should include the ways in which:

- props or items of set contribute to the contemporary dystopian conventions (such as highlighting a political message, use of captions, moving fluently from one scene to the next, highlighting social injustice, emphasising the play's themes, creating an alternative world)
- objects or items of set contribute to the action of this scene.

TIP

Projections are usually considered part of a set rather than lighting design. A gobo projected from a **lantern** of, for example the moon, can be discussed under either lighting or set design.

KEY TERM:

Lanterns: the equipment used to produce light onstage, such as floods, fresnels or profiles.

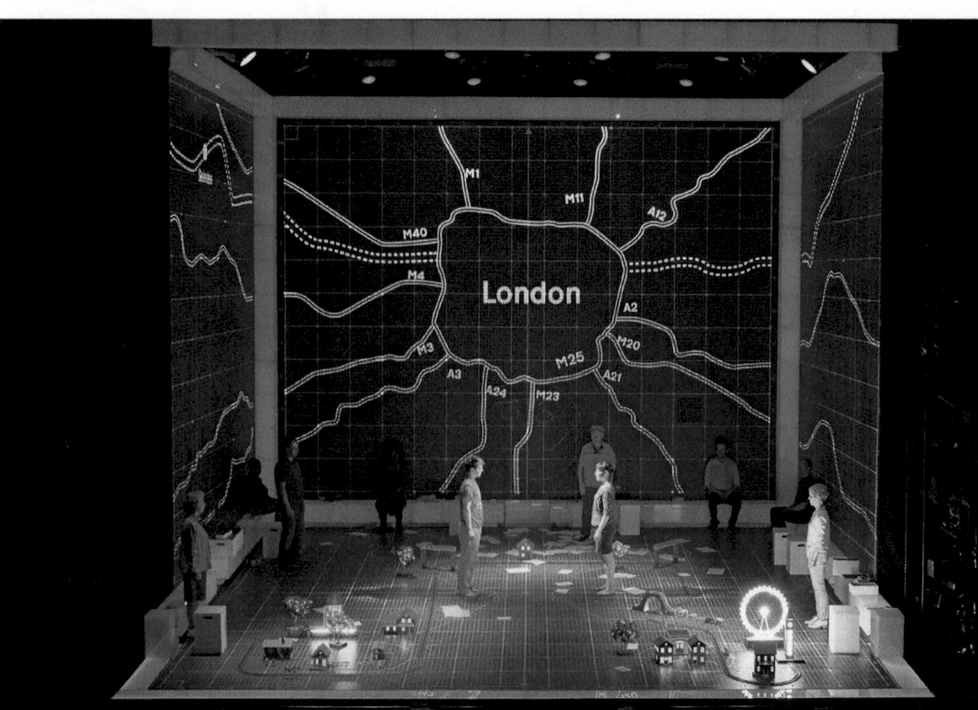

Projections on the walls and floor of the set of The Curious Incident of the Dog in the Night-Time *enhance the minimalistic set.*

LOCATION: Beach

REQUIREMENTS: Give the impression of being outside by the sea. Isolated/private.

DESIGN CHOICES:

1. Where on the stage configuration of your choice would you place this scene?
2. What are the dominant colours and textures that you would use?
3. Are there any practical items of set, such as a sign, fence or blanket, that you would use to identify it as a beach?
4. Is there any technology that you wish to use such as projections or video?

LOCATION: School dining hall

REQUIREMENTS: Area to collect food. Noughts' table. Seats.

DESIGN CHOICES:

1. This is a complex scene – how will you use the stage space to show: the collection of food; sitting at the Noughts' table; '*the dining hall melts away, leaving* CALLUM *alone*'?
2. What colours and materials could you use to convey the atmosphere of the school dining hall?
3. How can you indicate if you are setting this in the present day or a future time period?

LOCATION: Sephy's house

REQUIREMENTS: TV room. Empty chair. Suggestion of wealth and space.

DESIGN CHOICES:

1. How will you handle the reporter's speech? Will you use technology to have either a recorded or live version of the projection? Or will they appear on the stage? Or both?
2. How can you suggest the wealth of Sephy's house? How will it differ from Callum's?

LOCATION: The prison

REQUIREMENTS: Execution chamber. Area for Ryan where he could be hanged. Hood. Noughts on one side of the room, Crosses on the other.

DESIGN CHOICES:

1. Where will you place this on the stage configuration of your choice to give this scene maximum dramatic impact?
2. How will you place the Noughts and Crosses groups to highlight the conflict between them?
3. Where will the entrance for the Prison Governor be to give his announcement dramatic impact?
4. What colours will you use in this scene to highlight its frightening nature?

LOCATION: Callum's house

REQUIREMENTS: Table. Chairs. Family home. Not particularly well-off.

DESIGN CHOICES:

1. Where on the stage configuration of your choice would you place this scene?
2. What are the dominant colours and textures that you would use?
3. What style of tables and chairs would you use in order to indicate if you are setting this in the present day or a future time period?
4. Are there any other objects you would use to identify what the McGregors are like?
5. Would you use any captions or projections in this scene?

LOCATION: Café at Dundale Shopping Centre

REQUIREMENTS: Possibly stool for Sephy in café. Large enough stage area to represent explosion at end of scene.

DESIGN CHOICES:

1. Could signs (neon? wooden? illuminated? logos?) be used in this scene?
2. How can you suggest a busy, public space?
3. How can the space be used to show Callum trying to escape? (Levels? Ramps? Running across a wide stage?)
4. Where on the stage will the explosion take place? Would the set alter to show that an explosion has taken place? (Shattered glass? Broken objects?)

LOCATION: The trial

REQUIREMENTS: Areas for the judge, lawyers, accused witnesses and clerk to sit or stand. TV/VCR.

DESIGN CHOICES:

1. How will you create a courtroom atmosphere?
2. What objects or set pieces are necessary to convey that this is a trial?
3. Will you show the video on the TV screen or have it projected elsewhere?
4. Are there captions that could make this scene clearer or more powerful?

LOCATION: The Hideaway

REQUIREMENTS: A secret place. Isolated. Video camera. Scissors. Hood. TV.

DESIGN CHOICES:

1. How can you create the sense that this is a hidden space?
2. What colours and textures will you use?
3. How can you create the sense that Sephy is trapped here? For example, if there are windows will they be covered or the doors have large locks?
4. How will this location be different from Sephy and Callum's homes?

Writing about your design ideas

Question 1 will ask you to consider an aspect of design for the play in relation to its context. Below is a student's plan for the following question:

You are designing a **costume** for **Kamal Hadley** to wear in a performance of an extract from Act 2, Scene 3. The costume must reflect the conventions of contemporary dystopian theatre used in *Noughts & Crosses*. Describe your design ideas for the costume.

1 Understanding of the character in the play:

Kamal Hadley is the highest-status character in the play and a powerful member of the Cross community. In this scene he has returned home after a break in order to present himself as the perfect father to the press. His costume is a smart suit, crisp white shirt and tie. Polished shoes. A perfect fit, as if it has been personally tailored for him. Gold cufflinks show his wealth.

2 Conventions of contemporary dystopian theatre:

For my design, I have created a slightly futuristic period, so all the characters' clothes will look very streamlined with slim silhouettes and geometric designs on the fabric. Instead of buttoning down the middle, the jackets will button diagonally across the front. The powerful Cross characters will have prominent collars on their shirts giving them a distinguished look. All the Cross characters are associated with the colour blue – so his suit will be navy blue; his tie is blue with a detail of crosses on it. The details of his outfit in contrast to the simpler Noughts, who will be dressed in drab, brown clothing, highlight the political message of inequality, appropriate for the contemporary dystopian context of the play.

3 Relationship to others:

When he first enters the scene, Sephy thinks he's come back to stay, he has his jacket off and looks more fatherly, but once Juno, his PR, approaches, he snaps back into Deputy Prime Minister mode and puts his jacket back on and buttons it. His costume asserts his role as a powerful Cross.

TIP

It is important to know that there are many other interpretations of how Kamal Hadley might be costumed.

TIP

You should aim to justify your ideas. Explain why you are making these specific choices; don't just describe what the character will look like. How do your choices of fabrics, colours, shape and fit, accessories and so on help to convey the character, the play and its conventions?

- Understanding of the character in the play
- Conventions of contemporary dystopian theatre
- Relationship to others.

TASK 7

Using the above plan as a guide, create your own plan for the character of Lola in Act 1, Scene 7:

You are designing a costume for **Lola** to wear in a performance of an extract from Act 1. The costume must reflect the conventions of dystopian theatre used in *Noughts & Crosses*. Describe your own design ideas for the costume.

Practical explorations of characters, themes and style

When writing about performing roles in the play, you must demonstrate that you understand the characters and how they interact. You need to use the performance space to show your understanding of the play. Below are some exercises to help you explore your understanding of the play, its characters and its style.

Non-naturalistic conventions

Throughout the play Sephy and Callum use direct address to express their thoughts and ideas to the audience. Use the Tasks below to experiment with different ways of directly addressing the audience in the play.

TASK 8

Improvise a short scene in which you describe a recent journey you have taken (to school, to the shops, for example). Then experiment with the following different ways of telling your story:

- Stand in one place and tell your story to your group, making eye contact with them as you speak, as if speaking to your best friend.
- Tell your story, but only occasionally look at the audience. The rest of the time you are busy doing another chore (packing a bag or arranging chairs, for example).
- Tell your story, but halfway through stop and begin acting out the ending of your journey, miming the actions and speaking the dialogue.

TASK 9

a Many of the scenes in the play begin with Sephy or Callum speaking to the audience and then stepping into the action of the scene. Experiment with the staging configuration of Act 1, Scene 1, when Sephy moves from her direct address to sitting with Callum on the beach and Act 2, Scene 6, when Callum moves from his direct address to testifying at his father's trial. Experiment with how you will use the performance space, eye contact and interaction with others in the transition from direct address to dialogue.

b Act 2, Scene 23 has a more complicated use of direct address when Sephy and Callum speak directly to the audience mid-scene. Experiment with different ways of performing this scene using stylised movement and never touching each other. For example:

- Both actors kneel two metres apart and say their lines facing the audience.
- Both actors do a series of abstract movements, such as warm-up stretches, while speaking.
- Both actors stand facing each other and alternate between looking at each other and the audience.

c Based on your discoveries, make bullet point notes on how you could answer the following question:

> You are performing the role of **Callum**.
>
> Focus on Act 2, Scene 23 from 'What letter?' to 'Against nature.' Explain how you might use the performance space and interact with the actor playing Sephy to **create a sense of the characters' changing relationship** for your audience.

REFLECTION

Discuss the effects the different ways of using direct address had on those watching. Do you think any of these versions of direct address could be used in a production of *Noughts & Crosses*? For example, do you think Callum and Sephy should stand still and look at the audience throughout the direct address or try one of the other methods of direct address? (There is no right answer, but it is worth exploring different ways of using direct address.)

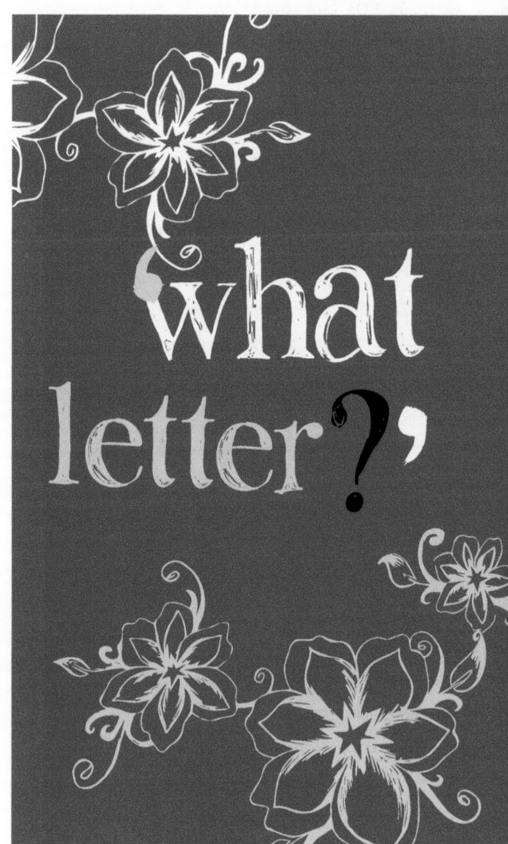

Physical theatre

Physical theatre can help to convey the message of the play in a clear and powerful way. For example, you might want to use a stylised movement sequence to show that a group of people are angry or despairing. You might use slow motion to spotlight a moment or to break it down for the audience. There might be recurring movements in order to create a visual **motif.**

KEY TERMS:

Physical theatre: theatre that emphasises physical movement, such as mime.

Motif: a repeated image or idea.

Soundscape: a collection of sounds that create a setting or suggest a scene, or a drama technique where performers use their voices (and sometimes other items) to create sounds.

TASK 10

a Focusing on Act 1, Scene 20 (the Dundale Shopping Centre), try the following techniques:
   - In a group, create the shopping mall through the use of physical theatre and **soundscapes**. For example, you could physically create a revolving door; create the sounds of the shopping centre such as the espresso machine or centre announcements; create a synchronised movement sequence showing busy shoppers.
   - Use of slow motion: while Callum and Sephy are rushing, everyone else could be moving in slow motion.
   - Choreograph a movement sequence showing the power of the explosion using slow motion and sound effects.

b In your workbook, note any uses of physical skills or the performance space that were particularly effective in showing the tension of this scene.

c Now look at Act 1, Scene 7 and Act 2, Scene 19 and note in your notebooks any opportunities for physical theatre in these scenes.

TIP

Remember that only clean (unannotated) copies of the script can be taken into the exam.

In physical theatre you may use techniques such as slow motion or still images. From On the Waterfront *directed by Steven Berkoff.* ▼

SET PLAY 5: *Noughts & Crosses* by Malorie Blackman and Dominic Cooke **5**

Interpretation of character

You will need to show how you can interpret a character. This means that you understand the character's motivations and goals, and the obstacles they face. Then you must be able to use your vocal and physical skills to portray the character and create particular effects for the audience, such as tension, comedy, romance, surprise, pity or sorrow.

Look at one interpretation of the character of **Lynette** (your own interpretation may differ).

Interpretation:

PHYSICAL APPEARANCE:

Lynette is white, like Callum, but believes she is black. As she mainly stays inside, I imagine her to be very pale. She is forgetful and dreamy, possibly doesn't eat regularly, so may be thin.

VOICE:

Her voice is soft and otherworldly. She uses a high-pitched, 'little girl' voice on lines such as 'Don't you think I'm beautiful, Callum?' (Act 1, Scene 2). In Scene 12, when she says she is no longer 'bonkers', her voice is lower and more direct. Although it may seem she is 'better' than in the earlier scenes she is actually less happy.

BODY LANGUAGE:

She doesn't have much energy and will begin a gesture before it trails off unfinished. In Act 1, Scene 2, she might dance or spin around the room. She frequently looks at her own hands in disbelief. When she sees herself in a mirror she doesn't recognise herself.

PROPS:

Mirror? A colouring book?

EFFECT ON AUDIENCE:

From the first introduction, the audience should see that Lynette is 'away with the fairies'. At first she seems 'peaceful' but changes in Act 1, Scene 10 when she realises the truth. She is a tragic figure whose death triggers the actions of others.

FACTS:

Background: Lynette is Callum's and Jude's 20-year-old sister. Her parents are Meggie and Ryan. She is a Nought. Two years before the beginning of the play, she and her Cross boyfriend were attacked by Noughts. She was in intensive care and has not been the same since.

Job: none.

HAIR:

Blonde, plaited.

COSTUME:

Mismatched, slightly childish outfits. She might wear a child's dressing-up tiara and pyjamas, for example.

TASK 11

Using your own understanding of the characters in the play and how they could be interpreted, create an interpretation of Callum. Use the following headings:

- Age
- Physical appearance
- Voice
- Body language
- Costume
- Hair
- Make-up
- Effect on audience.

Download a printable version from Samples & Downloads at www.illuminatepublishing.com.

Performing choices

In Question 2, you will be asked to discuss in detail how you would perform a particular line as a given character. For example:

TIP

It is a good idea to write in the first person ('I') so you can fully imagine your own performance of the role. Do more than just describe the vocal and physical skills you would use: also think about how your choices will add to the audience's understanding of the play, its characters and their relationships.

You are performing the role of Sephy.

Describe how you would use your vocal and physical skills to perform the lines below and explain the effects you want to create.

> **Sephy:** '*Us* Noughts and *you* Crosses. It makes it sound like ... Like I'm in one world you're in another.'

This is an early sign of the tension between the Noughts and Crosses and the frustration that Sephy feels about these conflicts keeping Callum and her apart. (1) When playing Sephy speaking these lines, I am repeating what Callum has said but with a stronger emphasis. I will say 'Us' and 'You' loudly, with my tone of voice on 'you' making it sound like an accusation. I may mimic his voice in a slightly sarcastic way. My accent is 'posh' or educated upper class, highlighting the difference between Callum and me. (2) I like Callum, so I'm seated close to him. (3) I feel a bit bad for teasing him about what he's said, so my voice is softer on 'It makes it sound like ...' but I don't finish my sentence, possibly because I think what I'm going to say will only make things worse. Instead I touch his arm when I say 'Like I'm in one world and you're in another.' (4) I want to show him how ridiculous it is that two people as close as we are should be considered so totally different. I'll smile at him, hoping he'll be more hopeful about the future. (5) From this, the audience should understand both the problems these two characters face and the attraction they feel for each other. (6)

(1) Understanding of character and motivations
(2) Vocal skills and explanation
(3) Physical skills and effect
(4) Physical skills
(5) Physical skills, facial expression and effect
(6) Understanding of play and characters

TASK 12

Experiment with different ways of using your vocal and physical skills for each of the following lines:

> **Ryan:** We'd appreciate some peace and quiet at the dinner table, please.
> **Meggie:** Well, I'm not as naïve as I used to be. Jasmine Hadley opened my eyes.
> **Sephy:** I'd never fully realised just how powerful words could be.
> **Lola:** I bet it was one of her Blanker friends. Blank by name and blank by nature.
> **Jasmine:** Who d'you think paid for all their legal fees, you stupid girl?
> **Jude:** I didn't think you had it in you, little brother.

TASK 13

a Make notes on the following:
- Vocal skills:
- Physical skills:
- Effects achieved:

b Then, using the example above as a guide, write an answer to the same question, referring to the characters and lines in Task 12.

c Check your work by marking or highlighting:
V for each vocal skill you mention
P for each physical skill
E for an effect on the audience.

Character revision sheet

Below is an example of a character revision sheet based on the character of **Jasmine**, which has been partially completed. Copy the grid and complete it.

Character and importance to the play	Jasmine She is wife of the Deputy Prime Minister, Kamal, and Sephy's and her sister Minerva's mother. She previously employed Callum's mother, Meggie.
What do they want?	To be admired, part of a powerful, high-status family.
What obstacles do they face?	Her husband no longer loves her. Her daughter disobeys her. Her drinking.
What are their key scenes?	Act 2, Scene 1: After arrest of Ryan. Act 2, Scene 3: Kamal returns for public relations interview. Act 2, Scene 7: Tells Sephy to dress up as they are going out. Act 2, Scene 8: Execution chamber when Ryan is reprieved. Act 2, Scene 9: Argument with Sephy. Act 2, Scene 11: Tells Sephy she is being sent to boarding school. Tries to get Kamal to stay. Act 2, Scene 13: Gets Sephy up after she has overslept. Doesn't notice Callum is hiding in Sephy's bedroom.

How might they be costumed?	How might their hair and make-up be done?
Draw a simple sketch or write a description of it. Consider: • colours • fabrics • shape and fit • character's personality and status.	Draw a simple sketch or write a description of it. Consider: • style and colour of hair • type of make-up (realistic or fantasy; colours; how it is appropriate for character, setting and period)

How might they use body language?	
• Posture • Gait (the way they walk) • Facial expression	
How might they use their voice?	
• Emotional range (angry, sad, happy, irritated, desperate, dominating and so on) • Pitch and volume (low or high; loud or soft) • Accent or other distinctive vocal features	
Choose one important line and analyse how they might say it.	Act 2, Scene 11: 'What a lovely family meal! We must do it more often.'

TASK 14

Using the grid for guidance, create similar revision sheets for all major characters including: Callum, Sephy, Kamal, Lynette, Jude, Minerva, Ryan and Meggie.

Download a printable version from Samples & Downloads at www.illuminatepublishing.com.

Using the performance space and interaction with others

There are opportunities to explore the space and interaction with others in many ways in the play. You might think about how you could include the audience in your performance by **breaking the fourth wall** and how you will move from the **direct address** section of the play to the scenes with other characters. You could consider how the conflict between the Noughts and Crosses is shown in their movements.

When you are writing about how you will use the performance space and interaction with others, make sure that you focus on the effects you wish to achieve, such as tension, surprise, humour, suspense, pity or sorrow, and how you will use your skills to achieve them.

TASK 15

Look closely at Act 2, Scene 9 (Jasmine/Sephy).

a Read the scene, taking particular notice of any stage directions.

b Agree what stage configuration you are going to use: end on, theatre in the round, thrust, promenade, proscenium or traverse. Mark where the entrances will be and any pieces of furniture.

c Decide what effects you wish to achieve in this scene. To help you do this, answer the following questions on the following issues:

- What is Sephy's relationship to her mother at this point?
- Why is Jasmine drinking and how much has she drunk before this scene?
- Has Jasmine ever hit Sephy before?
- What are Sephy's motivations in this scene?
- What are Jasmine's motivations in this scene?

d How will you use stage space? Looking at the top of page 79, try the following:

'*Sephy snatches the half-empty bottle from her.*'

- Sephy watches her mother pour another glass. Then, without giving a warning or changing expressions, she suddenly snatches the bottle, hiding it behind her back.
- Sephy explodes in anger when her mother pours another glass and grabs the bottle, holding it up high out of reach from her mother, taunting her.
- Jasmine reaches for the bottle to avoid Sephy's direct eye contact. Sephy moves closer to Jasmine and stares in her eyes as she grabs the bottle. She steps away when her mother moves closer to her.

Jasmine's reaction

- Jasmine tries to maintain her dignity and stands very still when she says with authority, 'Give me that bottle.'
- Jasmine, a bit drunk and woozy, lunges towards Sephy trying to grab the bottle and screams, 'Give me that bottle.'
- Jasmine, humiliated, sags against the table and, without looking at Sephy, says, 'Give me that bottle.'

e Continue working through the scene, experimenting with different staging configuration ideas. When you have finished, answer the following question:

> You are performing the role of **Jasmine**.
>
> Focus on the lines 'You don't know every damn thing, Persephone' to 'And when you realise that, maybe you'll stop judging me.' Explain how you might use the performance space and interact with the actor playing Sephy to **create the tense mother and daughter relationship** for the audience.

Answering a question about character interpretation

If you choose to answer Question 4, you will need to write about how you would use acting skills to interpret a character both in the extract provided and in the play as a whole. For example (in Act 2, Scene 13, from 'Just ... a minute' to 'Just' cause I overslept?'):

> You are performing the role of **Sephy**.
>
> Describe how you would use your acting skills to **interpret Sephy's character** in this extract. Explain why your ideas are appropriate for:
>
> - this extract
> - the performance of your role in the play as a whole.

TIP

It is important to include both vocal and physical skills. Highlight key moments when these skills can be discussed.

Below is a sample student plan for this question.

This extract:

1 Character of Sephy and reasons for acting choices:

Sephy loves Callum and they have spent the night together, but she has fallen asleep before making their plans for the future. At the beginning of the scene, she has overslept and Callum is in danger of being discovered in her room by her disapproving mother.

2 Acting skills: vocal:

I would play the opening still sounding sleepy and uncertain. I would pause between 'Just' and 'a minute' to give myself time to decide what to do. Before I open the door, I would use two different tones and volumes, depending on whether I am whispering to Callum or shouting through the door. My voice when speaking to Sarah and Jasmine will sound calmer and less urgent than when I speak to Callum. I will use a sarcastic teenage inflection on lines like 'Big deal' or 'cause I overslept' which will hide my fear that Callum will be discovered.

3 Acting skills: physical:

While keeping my voice calm I will be frantically active during this scene: waking Callum up, getting dressed, helping to hide Callum. One moment of stillness will occur when I say to Callum that we haven't done 'anything wrong'. We will maintain eye contact. It will be clear from his reaction that I am living in a dream world and I quickly change pace, clumsily throwing on my dress. I will take a split second to make sure I look presentable in the mirror. Although this is largely a serious scene, there is an element of comedy when Callum is nearly discovered and I help to hide him.

Rest of play:

1 Character of Sephy and reasons for acting choices:

Throughout the play, Sephy is bright, passionate and loyal. Caught between her family and her love of Callum. They are like a modern day Romeo and Juliet.

2 Acting skills: vocal:

Anger and sarcasm towards parents, particularly Jasmine. When speaking to audience in direct address I will create an intimacy, explaining my thoughts and feelings. Upper-middle-class accent, confident and articulate at school. Act 2, Scene 21, voice is emotional, frightened. Cries when being filmed for video. Pleading with Callum.

3 Acting skills: physical:

Hunched on the floor in Act 2, Scene 21. In love scene (Act 2, Scene 23) combine direct address to audience (facing them) with stylised miming of undressing and touching, to show love scene with Callum.

TIP

When writing your response as a performer, it is useful to write in the first person. So, 'I would move more quickly here' rather than 'Sephy would move quickly here.' That will help you to fully imagine yourself playing the role. Include the headings below in your plan:

- Character of Callum and reasons for making acting choices
- Acting skills: vocal
- Acting skills: physical.

TASK 16

Using the structure of the plan, on the previous page, for Sephy as a guide, write your own plan for the following question:

> You are performing the role of **Callum**.
> Describe how you would use your acting skills to **interpret Callum's character** in Act 2, Scene 23, from 'Callum: You should eat something' to 'Do you?'
> Explain why your ideas are appropriate for:
> - this extract
> - the performance of your role in the play as a whole.

Design choices

If you choose to answer Question 5, you will be thinking as a designer and commenting on one aspect of design. For example:

> You are a designer working on **one** aspect of design for this extract.
> Describe how you would use your design skills to create effects which **support the action**. Explain why your ideas are appropriate for:
> - this extract
> - your chosen design skill in the play as a whole.

You may choose to focus on set design, costume design, lighting design, sound design or puppet design. Whichever you choose, you must explain why your ideas are appropriate to the play as a whole. You might refer to:

- how your design helps to show the action of the play and the nature of the characters
- how your design for the extract is consistent with the design requirements of the rest of the play
- how you have used design methods that fit in with the mood or atmosphere of the play
- props or anything that the actors may carry onstage.

Noughts & Crosses makes particular demands on the designer because of its short episodic scenes and many different settings. You may choose to have a set upon which specific areas represent certain locations such as a raised area that represents the bedrooms or other intimate scenes and a central area in which all large public scenes, such as the trial or shopping mall, would occur. Another option would be to have a single set upon which simple scene changes could occur by having basic items wheeled onstage or carried on by performers or stage crew. Projections or simple 'flying' of objects such as signs could also aid your design. A revolve could reveal new locations.

The costumes might reflect today's society, with recognisable school uniforms for the students and suits for the politicians or you may make a stylised choice.

Given the many short scenes, music or sound effects could be vital for creating locations, such as crowd noises to establish the busy shopping mall or the sound of waves to create the beach.

Lighting and sound design could be used to emphasise the horror of certain events such as the near hanging of Ryan or the explosion at the shopping mall.

Costume design

For costume design, you might consider:

- style, cut and fit
- colour, fabric, decorative features
- realistic or stylised
- condition (worn or new; neat or wrinkled; clean or stained and so on)
- footwear/headgear
- accessories
- status or social role of character
- make-up and hairstyle.

Below are extracts from sample responses based on Act 1, Scene 7.

A

I want to highlight that this is a non-naturalistic production. All the characters will wear jumpsuits, but Nought characters will wear black jumpsuits with white circles on them while the Cross characters will wear white jumpsuits with black crosses.

B

I am setting my production in the recognisable present day, as if historic events were different, which caused different people to be in power. Each school girl will wear uniform typical of a fee-paying school: bright striped woollen blazer with a distinctive badge, pleated grey skirt, white blouse, knee-length socks, a tie with a cross design. However, Lola is the leader of a gang so will have made adjustments to make her outfit rebellious and different. Her skirt will be shorter than the others and she will wear large non-regulation hoop earrings. Before the fight with Sephy, the girls will take off their blazers, showing that despite their 'posh' uniforms they are willing to get into physical fights.

In my concept, all the characters will wear black trousers and a long-sleeve black T-shirt and simply add one important item of clothing to show the character they are playing. So, in this scene, all the characters will be wearing school blazers with a badge with their character name on it. I feel this fits with the 'epic' nature of the play, as it is non-naturalistic and will help to quickly change from scene to scene.

TASK 17

Read the responses above and write **D** for detailed description of the design and **J** for ideas justified by explanations.

TASK 18

Draw sketches showing three different stages of Sephy's costumes: Act 1, Scene 1; Act 2, Scene 12 and Act 2, Scene 21. Label your sketches showing how her costume reflects the changes in her character throughout the play.

TIP

You might want to consider the following:

- how your costumes will establish the characters of the Nought gang
- how the costumes will reinforce the meaning of this scene and the play
- how the costumes will reinforce the style of the play.

TASK 19

a Write several paragraphs answering the following question as a costume designer:

> Focus on Act 2, Scene 22 from The Hideaway to 'Pete: Good thinking.'
>
> You are a designer working on **one** aspect of design for this extract.
>
> Describe how you would use your design skills to create effects which **support the action**. Explain why your ideas are appropriate for:
>
> - this extract
> - your chosen design skill in the play as a whole.

b Check to make sure you have:

- referred to fabric, colours, shape/silhouette, fit, condition
- included headwear and/or footwear, as appropriate
- considered make-up, hairstyle and/or masks, if appropriate
- explained how the costume helps the action of the extract
- related your design to the rest of the play.

▲ *The choice of fabric, including colour and texture, is important for costume design.*

Set design

For the set design, you might consider:

- stage configuration
- how you suggest the location and atmosphere of the location
- if there will be any levels, ramps or stairs
- the entrances/exits
- if there will be backdrops, flats or projections
- the colour palette you will use
- how the materials, textures and shapes will help to create a suitable setting
- which props are needed.

One of the challenges is to decide how realistic or artificial/stylised you want your set to be and how you will incorporate the many settings of the play.

I was particularly pleased with how the bomb scene [in *Noughts & Crosses*] all came together. At that point we had the first layer of paper ripped off the scaffolding and little bits of paper dropped from the ceiling like debris. It made for a real shock to our audience and then a beautiful moving moment as some music played in the background. Along with the lighting, it made for a really atmospheric end to the first half.

TASK 20

Use the mind maps below to begin working on your ideas for the following two settings: the shopping centre and the Hideaway. Add more legs to the mindmap to incorporate your ideas.

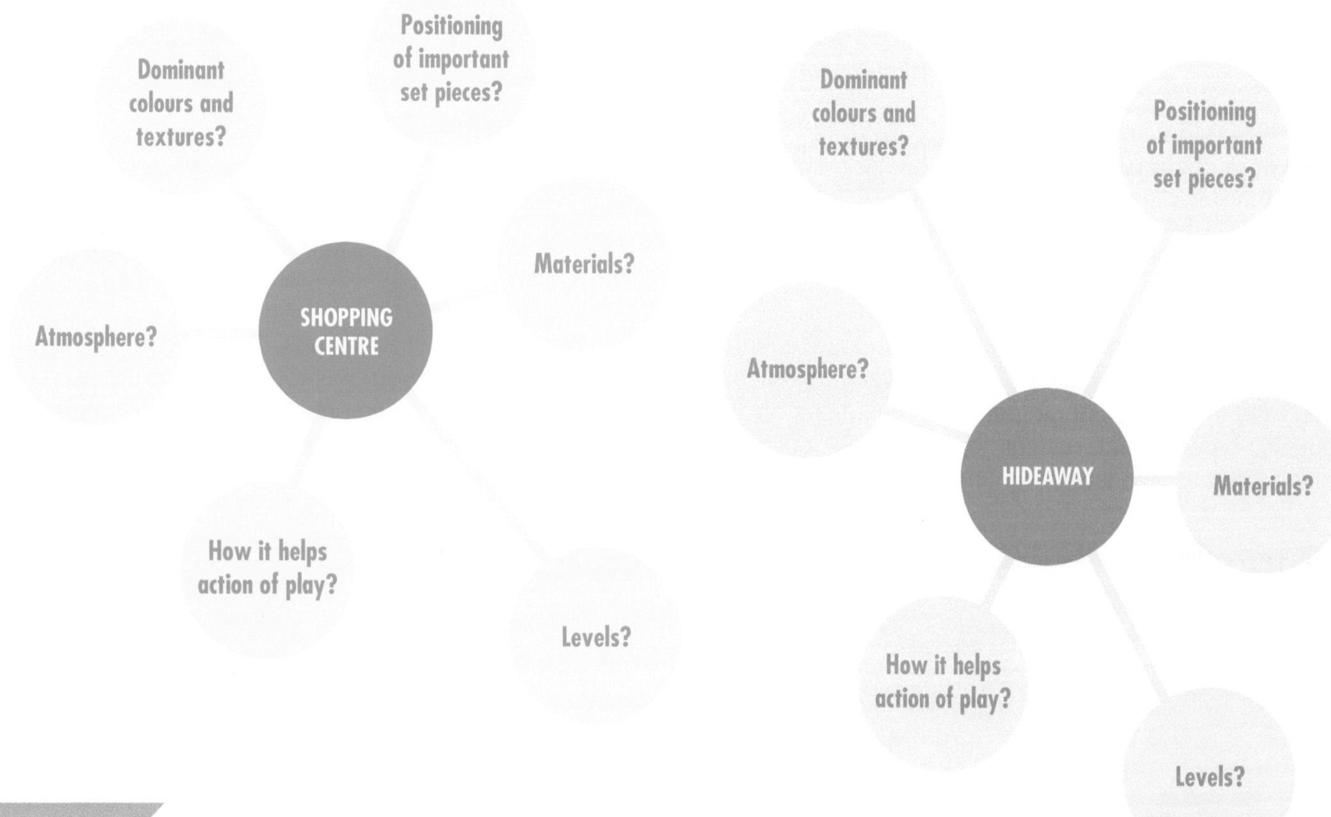

TASK 21

a Choose one significant prop or piece of scenery used in Act 1 and another used in Act 2, and sketch several ideas for how they could be designed. For example, you might choose the school lunch table from Act 1 and Sephy's bed in Act 2. Consider how each item could be used practically and how the design will fit with your other design ideas for the play.

b Create a design for Act 2, Scene 6 from 'The Trial' to 'Callum: She's … friend' for the stage configuration of your choice. Sketch and label your ideas. Remember to consider:

- entrances/exits and areas for key moments
- use of backdrops or projections, if appropriate
- the practical demands of the scene
- the atmosphere and style of your production.

c Then answer this question:

> You are a designer working on **one** aspect of design for this extract.
>
> Describe how you would use your design skills to create effects which **support the action**. Explain why your ideas are appropriate for:
>
> - this extract
> - your chosen design skill in the play as a whole.

Lighting design

When creating your lighting design you might consider how to create:

- time of day and, possibly, season
- mood or atmosphere
- focus to highlight particular moments
- the setting, action and characters of a scene (such as a follow spot to focus the audience on a character's journey or backlighting to make them appear mysterious).

Some of your tools are:

- colours
- angles and intensity
- light from onstage sources (lamps, birdies)
- use of shadow and silhouette
- special effects
- use of blackouts or fades.

TASK 22

Below are some short excerpts from various student responses to the demands of lighting *Noughts & Crosses*. As you read them, highlight in pencil any mentions of: angles, specific types of lanterns/lighting equipment, colours, blackouts/fades, onstage lighting, special effects or shadows.

TASK 23

Read Act 2, Scenes 27 and 28 and note down in your workbook ideas on how lighting could help to convey the actions of these scenes and the necessary tension.

A

In Act 2, Scene 1, I will use a harsh white light, angled sharply diagonally downwards (1) on the Reporter downstage right to replicate filming lights, (2) while the rest of the stage is lit with warmer yellow tinted lights. The harsh lights will flick off at the end of the Reporter's section to show the report is over and the 'TV' has been turned off. (3)

(1) Describes colour and angle of lights

(2) Explains effect

(3) Explains transition and effect

B

The lighting in the Hideaway scenes will be dark. I imagine that the windows would be covered, so I will create the effect that all the lighting is coming from artificial onstage lights such as torches or a small table lamp, which will be used during the videoing section. The torches will cast shadows in the room and, when shone on the characters' faces, make them look frightening.

C

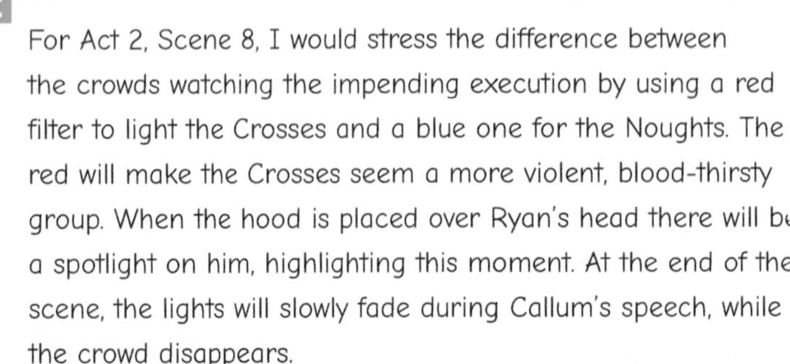

For Act 2, Scene 8, I would stress the difference between the crowds watching the impending execution by using a red filter to light the Crosses and a blue one for the Noughts. The red will make the Crosses seem a more violent, blood-thirsty group. When the hood is placed over Ryan's head there will be a spotlight on him, highlighting this moment. At the end of the scene, the lights will slowly fade during Callum's speech, while the crowd disappears.

Sound design

When designing sound for *Noughts & Crosses*, you will want to consider how to:

- create atmosphere
- add to the action and emotion of a scene
- contribute to the setting and style of the play
- fulfil the practical needs of the script.

Some choices you can make involve:

- live or recorded sound
- volume/amplification (use of microphones)
- naturalistic or symbolic sound
- music.

TASK 24

a With your group, using your voices and any objects you can find, create sound effects for Act 1, Scene 3 (the school gates). Some effects you could make include:
   - the sound of the school bell
   - crowd noises/shouting
   - police car arriving/police siren
   - cheers.

b Perform the scene with one person 'controlling' the volume by indicating when noises should get louder and when softer.

c Then focus on the next scene, Act 1, Scene 4 (the beach), and discuss how the demands of this scene are different. Make notes on the various ways you could use sound to help this scene. Some choices you could make include:
   - adding recorded music in the transition to or under the scene
   - having performers onstage or offstage creating sound effects
   - adding recorded sound effects such as ocean waves or seagulls
   - experimenting with volume (suddenly getting louder or softer)
   - amplifying or distorting voices, by using microphones.

d Experiment with different versions of this scene and then make notes about which choices you thought were most effective.

REFLECTION

Discuss the effect of the sudden silence at the end of the scene in Task 24.

Note any discoveries you have made in your workbook.

6 SET PLAY 6: *Romeo and Juliet* by William Shakespeare

Synopsis

Act 1

After the Chorus introduces the play, servants and family members of the feuding Capulets and Montagues brawl on the streets of Verona. **Prince Escalus** halts the fight and orders, 'on pain of death', that neither family disturbs the peace again. **Romeo**, a Montague, tells his friend **Benvolio** that he is in despair because he is in love with Rosaline who has rejected him.

In the Capulet household, **Paris** asks **Lord Capulet** for permission to marry his daughter, **Juliet**. Lord Capulet invites Paris to that evening's party. The young Montague men learn of the party and decide to attend uninvited. Lady Capulet asks Juliet about her 'disposition to be married', as Paris would be a good match for her.

Mercutio teases Romeo with the tale of 'Queen Mab'. Despite Romeo's misgivings, the young Montagues enter the party. Romeo sees Juliet and is immediately entranced by her beauty. **Tybalt**, Lord Capulet's nephew, suspects Romeo is a Montague, but Lord Capulet tells him not to disrupt the party. Romeo speaks to Juliet and they kiss. Discovering that Juliet is a Capulet, Romeo despairs again, and is hurried out of the party by Benvolio. Juliet asks the **Nurse** to discover who Romeo is and, upon being told he is a Capulet, laments that she loves a 'loathed enemy'.

Act 2

Hiding below Juliet's window, Romeo overhears her expressions of love for him. He emerges and they declare their love for each other. Juliet says that if his love is 'honourable' and his 'purpose marriage', she will send a message to him tomorrow.

Romeo tells **Friar Laurence** that he is in love with Juliet and asks if he will marry them. When Romeo joins his friends, Mercutio teases him for leaving them last night. Juliet's nurse arrives and Romeo instructs her to help Juliet meet him that afternoon at Friar Laurence's cell to be married.

Juliet waits anxiously for her nurse's return. After some comic delays, she delivers Romeo's message. Juliet hurries to the Friar's cell to be married.

Act 3

Tybalt approaches Benvolio and Mercutio, seeking Romeo. When Romeo arrives, he refuses to fight Tybalt. Mercutio finds Romeo's refusal 'dishonourable' and challenges Tybalt. They draw swords as Romeo attempts to stop the fight. Mercutio is stabbed and curses both the Montagues and the Capulets. When Benvolio announces Mercutio is dead, Romeo kills Tybalt and flees. The Prince bans Romeo from Verona.

Juliet is impatiently waiting for her wedding night when the Nurse tells her the news of Romeo's banishment. A distraught Juliet tells the Nurse to ask Romeo for a last farewell.

Friar Laurence tells Romeo of the Prince's ruling of banishment. Romeo despairs at being separated from Juliet. The Nurse arrives with Juliet's message. A desperate Romeo draws a sword to kill himself. Friar Laurence scolds Romeo and tells him to see Juliet.

Lord Capulet tells Paris that Juliet will do as he wishes, so he should prepare to marry Juliet on Thursday.

Juliet and Romeo awake after spending their wedding night together. Romeo reluctantly leaves for Mantua. Lady Capulet informs Juliet that she is to marry Paris on Thursday. Juliet refuses and begs her father not to force her to marry. Furious, he insists she must or he will disown her. When Juliet asks the Nurse what she should do, the Nurse says that, as Romeo is banished, she should marry Paris.

Act 4

Paris speaks to Friar Laurence about his upcoming marriage when Juliet arrives. When Paris leaves, Juliet says that she would rather die than marry Paris. The Friar explains his plan for her to take a potion so that she appears dead. He will write to Romeo so that when she wakes, she can travel to Mantua with him.

Juliet begs her father's forgiveness and agrees to marry Paris. That evening, she nervously drinks the potion. As her parents make preparations for the wedding feast, Juliet is discovered by the Nurse, apparently dead. The Capulet household mourns her death, while Friar Laurence comforts them.

Act 5

In Mantua, Romeo's servant, Balthasar, tells him that Juliet is dead. Romeo determines to go to her tomb and die alongside her. He goes to an apothecary to get poison.

Friar John tells Friar Laurence that he was unable to get the letter to Romeo telling him of the Friar's plan and that Juliet is really alive.

Paris goes to Juliet's tomb. He sees Romeo trying to break into the tomb and suspects him of defiling her resting place. Romeo and Paris fight and Romeo kills Paris.

Romeo enters the tomb, takes the poison and dies. When Friar Laurence arrives, Balthasar tells him that Romeo is in the tomb. When Juliet awakes and discovers Romeo is dead, she takes his dagger and kills herself. The Prince and the two families arrive and Friar Laurence explains the deaths. The Prince tells the Montagues and Capulets that they have been punished for their hate. Lord Capulet and Lord Montague agree to raise statues in remembrance of their dead children.

TASK 1

a After reading the synopsis, work in your group to choose ten important plot points. Create a still image for each. Discuss which moments you think are the most exciting and dramatic.

b Then list some of the performance and design challenges in staging *Romeo and Juliet*. It is important to consider: lighting, sound, costume and set.

You might begin by deciding how to:

- create the period setting
- differentiate between the many characters
- establish the status of different characters
- show the different locations.

▲ *The Piazza dei Signori in Verona*

Context

Romeo and Juliet is set in Verona, a city in Italy. The first performances are thought to have been in 1596–97 at the Curtain Theatre in Shoreditch, just outside London. Shakespeare set many of his plays in Italy, an exotic and romantic location for his audiences. *Romeo and Juliet* has been set in many different times and locations, but for your exam, the context is **late-16th century Verona**. This context will influence your understanding of the play and the possibilities for its design.

Shakespeare's audiences would think of Italians as passionate and hot-blooded, but also ruled by the church, as Italy was staunchly Catholic. This is reflected in the play's plot and the importance of Friar Laurence. After Romeo and Juliet, he has the most lines in the play. Despite their passion, Juliet will not spend the night with Romeo until they are married, and they both turn to the Friar when faced with difficult decisions. Some designers use religious imagery to reinforce the significance of the characters' Catholicism.

▲ *In Baz Luhrmann's 1996 film, religious statues, icons and crosses are depicted. Through the use of modern design, such as neon in the crosses, the period has been updated to the 20th century.*

Italy was also a country with a clear social and political hierarchy, where the Prince was able to make and enforce new laws. Marriage was a way of increasing personal worth and maintaining or improving social status. The role of wife and mother was the goal of most women. As the only daughter of her family, Juliet would be expected to marry someone of at least a similar social standing who was approved of by her parents. Daughters were obliged to obey their fathers. Lord Capulet's outrage when Juliet dares to refuse Paris is so great that he threatens to throw her out of the home. At Romeo's death, the Friar believes the only salvation for Juliet is to live among 'a sisterhood of holy nuns'.

▲ *Medieval architecture and the ruins of the Roman arena in Verona*

Verona is a historic city and has remains from the Roman era, including an arena. 16th-century Italian architecture often displayed classical influences, such as columns and arches. This part of Italy is warm, and many of the scenes in *Romeo and Juliet* take place outdoors. Verona has city squares (piazzas), which would contain fruit and vegetable markets. In Act 3, Scene 1, Benvolio emphasises the heat and its effect on their moods when he says 'these hot days, is like the mad blood stirring'. The public nature of the street brawls is what attracts the stern rebuke from the Prince.

The Renaissance (14th to 17th centuries) was a time of remarkable achievements in art, architecture, music and literature. Famous Italian artists from the 16th century include Veronese, Moroni and Caravaggio. Painters often took their inspiration from classical myths and biblical stories. Art from the period might inspire your design choices, such as the vivid use of colour, draping fabrics and classically influenced architecture. The costumes and sets in Franco Zeffirelli's 1968 film of *Romeo and Juliet* were almost certainly influenced by art from this period.

Status was important in 16th-century Verona. The Capulets and Montagues, described in the first line of the play as 'both alike in dignity', are important and wealthy families. Their status would be reflected in their clothing. Italy had a thriving trade in silks, velvets and other textiles which would be used in clothing for wealthy citizens.

Question 1 in the exam will ask you to describe how a specific design skill could reflect the context of *Romeo and Juliet* in late-16th-century Verona. The following pages explore various design areas and how they could reflect the context of the play.

▲ *Juliet and Paris in Zeffirelli's film version*

TASK 2

The painting below is by Paolo Veronese. Although the subject is the biblical story of the wedding at Cana, Veronese has set it in the context of 16th-century Italy, with influences of Greek and Roman architecture. Work with a partner to note 16th-century details which could be included in a production of *Romeo and Juliet*. Consider:

- costumes
- set dressings
- props
- musical instruments.

▲ *Paolo Veronese,* The Wedding at Cana

TASK 3

Study the images on these pages reflecting Italy in the 16th century. Write a paragraph or draw some sketches explaining how these images could influence a designer's concept for scenes or characters in *Romeo and Juliet*. For example, what colours, shapes and decorative features could inspire the designs?

▲ *A window in the Bartolini Salimbeni Palace in Florence*

▲ *16th-century embroidery depicting the rise of Lazarus, on display in Milan*

▲ *A medieval buckler*

KEY TERMS:

Doublet: a close-fitting padded jacket, which may or may not have sleeves.

Jerkin: a sleeveless jacket, often made of leather.

Breeches: knee-length trousers.

Hose: a garment which tightly covers the legs (similar to thick tights or leggings).

Bodice: the close-fitting upper part of a dress, from neck to waist.

Chemise: a loose-fitting undergarment which resembles a long shirt.

Costume, hair and make-up design inspired by context

In the 16th century, men typically wore a combination of **doublets**, **jerkins** and **breeches**. Women wore gowns comprised of a bodice, sleeves and a long skirt. Outfits would vary depending on social standing, personality and occupation.

A fashionable Italian man at this time might be seen wearing an embroidered cap, a silk **doublet**, a jerkin and silk **hose**. Men, particularly those who wished to emphasise their seriousness and power, often wore dark colours, such as black or dark brown in silk or velvet.

Aristocratic women might wear brighter colours, with red particularly associated with wealth. They might also dress in more elaborately patterned or embellished fabrics. Women's gowns were both decorative and modest, with long sleeves, floor-length skirts and under layers.

Tradesmen and servants might wear a simple tunic over hose, while serving women, for example, would wear a lace-up **bodice** over a **chemise**, possibly adorned with a scarf or shawl and a long, full skirt. Young unmarried women generally wore their hair down, but once married it was put up. Various caps, hats and headdresses were worn, such as small, brimless, velvet caps for men and veils for women.

▲ *Jacopo Bassano,* Portrait of a Franciscan Friar, *c1540–42*

▲ *Giovanni Battista Moroni,* Prospero Alessandri *(1560): a wealthy young man, holding his hat and wearing a doublet, jerkin, breeches and hose, with soft leather gloves to the side.*

▲ *Moroni,* Portrait of a Lady / La Dama in Rosso *(c1556–60): an aristocratic young woman, holding a fan.*

TASK 4

a Choose a main character from the play. Design a costume for them in a key scene. Consider: hair, make-up, fabric, fit, accessories, headwear and shoes.

b Explain how the costume suggests the character's role and the effect their external presentation will have on the audience.

TASK 5

SET PLAY 6: *Romeo and Juliet* by William Shakespeare 6

Use the play's context and the prompts below to design a costume for one male and one female character (different from that in Task 4). Consider the character's status and wealth, as well as suitable colours and fabrics.

Hair:
Men: Long or short? Bald? Colour?
Women: Up or down? Colour? Straight, curled or braided?

Make-up:
Pale or dark? Ageing? Lines? Youthful?
Men: Beards? Moustaches?

Costume:
Men:
Doublet? Jerkin? Tunic? Breeches? Collar or ruff? Robe?
Sleeves: Attached to the doublet or separate?
Colours: Bright or dark?
Fabrics: Velvet, silk, wool, linen?
Women:
High or low neckline?
Sleeves: Full or narrow? Attached to bodice or separate?
Fabrics: Plain or patterned? Velvet, silk, wool, cotton, linen?

Footwear:
Men: Slip-on leather shoes? Boots? Barefoot?
Women: Slip-on leather shoes? Plain or embellished? Barefoot?

Headwear:
Men: Caps, hats: felt, wool, velvet? Small or wide-brimmed?
Women: Caps, veils, adornments

Outerwear:
Men: Mandilion? Cloak? Jacket?
Women: Cloaks? Shawls?

Accessories:
Men: Sword? Gloves? Handkerchiefs? Masks?
Women: Jewellery? Gloves? Lace? Ribbons? Handkerchiefs? Apron? Masks? Fans?

KEY TERM:

Mandilion: a decorative hip-length cloak, usually worn over one shoulder.

TIP

When writing about costume choices, it is important that you show your understanding of the character and the context. For example, you should show that women from this period wore gowns which were floor-length and had long sleeves, or that Friar Laurence would wear an outfit appropriate for a man of the church. You should also demonstrate knowledge of the fabrics available at the time and how choices of colour and material convey messages about the characters.

TIP

Carefully read the stage directions. They might suggest or include costumes or accessories. in Act 1, Scene 1, for example, Sampson and Gregory have 'swords and bucklers' (small round shields). In Act 1, Scene 4, the Montague youths put on masks, and in Act 2, Scene 2, Friar Laurence is carrying a basket.

Download a printable version from Samples & Downloads at www.illuminatepublishing.com.

Set design inspired by context

One of the challenges of designing *Romeo and Juliet* is capturing the many different settings, from street scenes to Juliet's bedroom, a masque ball and a Friar's cell. Consider how your design will:

- serve the practical needs of the play
- show the period setting and specific location
- contribute to the atmosphere and purpose of the scene.

Some design features typical of 16th-century Verona include:

- light-coloured stone and marble
- tapestries
- rich textiles, such as **drapes**
- arches, columns and steps
- religious icons
- dark wooden furniture.

CHALLENGE

Research the architecture and furniture of 16th-century Italy. Based on your research, sketch some items which might be seen in the Capulet household.

TASK 6

The chart below lists some of the main settings of the play. When you have chosen your stage configuration, use it to generate ideas for your set design.

LOCATION: **Verona streets**

REQUIREMENTS: In several scenes, including Act 1, Scene 1 and Act 3, Scene 1. Must be large enough to allow stage-fighting and crowd scenes.

DESIGN CHOICES:

1. What colours and materials would capture the Verona location?
2. What props or set dressings could establish the period Italian setting?
3. Would levels, scale or textures be useful and add impact?

LOCATION: **Juliet's balcony and bedroom**

REQUIREMENTS: The famous balcony scene occurs in Act 2, Scene 1. Juliet's bedroom is the setting in several scenes, including Act 3, Scene 2; Act 3, Scene 5 and Act 4, Scene 3.

DESIGN CHOICES:

1. How far apart are Juliet and Romeo in the balcony scene? What height will the balcony be and where will Romeo hide?
2. Will there be any particular design features to the balcony or the windows, such as patterns on the ledge, curtains or arched frames?
3. What furnishings are in the bedroom? What fabric and colour choices can establish 16th-century Verona?

LOCATION: **Capulets' hall**

REQUIREMENTS: Several scenes might occur in the Hall. The most significant is the Capulet party in Act 1, Scene 4.

DESIGN CHOICES:

1. How can your design show the social status of the Capulets? (You might consider the size of the room, levels, wall decorations and materials.)
2. Where should Romeo and Juliet be positioned on the set when they first meet?
3. How would your design contribute to the mood of the scene?

LOCATION: **Friar Laurence's cell**

REQUIREMENTS: This is a small area where confidential conversations take place, such as in Act 2, Scene 2; or preparations for religious services, as in Act 2, Scene 5, before the wedding.

DESIGN CHOICES:

1. How could you differentiate the purpose and atmosphere of the cell from other locations in the play?
2. What materials and colours would you use?

LOCATION: **Tomb**

REQUIREMENTS: The setting for Act 5. The tomb would be an above-ground structure where members of the Capulet family would be laid to rest after death.

DESIGN CHOICES:

1. What materials, colours and shapes would you use to establish the tomb structure?
2. What set dressings could you use? Might there be plants, flowers, statues, candles, plinths?
3. How would your set add to the atmosphere and action of the play's ending?

TASK 7

Choose a scene from the first two acts of the play. Describe the set you would create and how it fits the context. Explain how your set:

- is appropriate for the chosen scene
- reflects the setting of Verona in the late 16th century
- functions practically in terms of the scene and other key moments.

KEY TERM:

Drapes: curtains or other hanging fabric.

Sound and lighting design inspired by context

Sound and lighting design can suggest the setting of 16th-century Verona in a number of ways, including use of period music, and torches and candles for authentic lighting and creating the appropriate atmosphere for various scenes.

Sound

In the 16th century, musicians and minstrels would be hired to perform for special occasions or would travel around the country. Musical instruments of the time include brass and wind instruments, such as trumpets and **clarions** (which could be used for fanfares), recorders, flutes and pipes; string instruments, such as lutes, harps and **viols**; keyboard instruments like the harpsichord; and percussion, such as tambourines and drums. As sound designer, you might consider how period music, either performed live or recorded, could enhance key scenes.

To reinforce the period setting, you could use sound effects, such as birdsong, wind or horses' hooves, or **soundscapes** of crowds in the market square to create the atmosphere of Verona. You might think about, for example, how bells could ring out, doors clang shut, stones crunch underfoot, or swords clash.

Lighting

There was no electricity or gas in the 16th century, so you might use modern technology to create effects which mimic lighting that would have been available: sunlight, moonlight, lit torches, lanterns and candles.

Your lighting design could establish the time of day of a scene, such as the early morning of Act 3, Scene 5; the hot afternoon of Act 3, Scene 1; or the moonlit garden of Act 2, Scene 1. Using gobos and other specialist lighting equipment, it is also possible to create effects such as leaves, the moon, clouds and architectural features.

KEY TERM:

Clarion: a shrill medieval trumpet.

Viol: a Renaissance stringed instrument, similar to a violin.

Soundscape: a collection of sounds that create a setting or suggest a scene, or a drama technique where performers use their voices (and sometimes other items) to create sounds.

CHALLENGE

Research 16th-century music and find at least one piece of music which would enhance a scene in the play. Consider the mood you wish to create and how the music contributes to it.

Medieval minstrels in their gallery

This design by Matt Kizer (set and projections) and Jaime Mancuso (lighting) uses gobos for leaves and trees and projections for the walls and window. The production combined modern styles and textures with shapes and patterns inspired by the 16th-century Teatrico Olimpico in Vicenza. ▶

TASK 8

a In your group, read Act 1, Scene 4, the Capulet party scene. Make notes on possibilities for sound and lighting design.

b Work through the scene, stopping to agree on effects that would be effective for the action and mood of the scene. You should consider:

- music
- lighting effects
- sound effects
- transitions.

Practical explorations of characters, themes and style

When writing about performing, you should demonstrate that you understand the play's characters, themes and style. The practical activities below will help you to explore the play.

Parents and children

Romeo and Juliet's parents are both shown in the play. Juliet's relationship with her parents develops from obedience to secretiveness to disobedience and deception. Lord Capulet's attitude changes from saying that Juliet is 'the hopeful lady of my earth' (Act 1, Scene 2) to declaring it was 'a curse having her' (Act 3, Scene 5), to mourning her supposed death '…and with my child my joys are buried' (Act 4, Scene 4). Some critics believe that, in the early acts of the play, Juliet's mother is less close to her than her father, due to Lady Capulet's eagerness for Juliet to marry Paris and her reliance on the Nurse to communicate with her.

TASK 9

Working in a group, create three still images which sum up different stages of Juliet's relationship with her parents. Consider how their relationship might be shown through their facial expressions, **proximity**, gestures and body language.

KEY TERM:

Proximity: the distance between people or objects; how near or far.

Feuding families

The feud between the Montagues and the Capulets is at the heart of the play and whenever they meet, there is tension and the potential for violence.

TASK 10

a In a large group, choose a leader to stick a label of either 'Montague' or 'Capulet' on each member's back. The group members will then move around the room to try to discover who is a Capulet or a Montague. When a Capulet finds other Capulets, they may greet them and walk with them, whereas they might sneer at or avoid Montagues.

b After a few minutes, the leader will clap their hands and all Montagues must move to one side of the room and all Capulets to the other. Facing each other, they should create a large tableaux showing how each group feels about the other.

c Afterwards, discuss how you felt being part of a group and how it felt to have 'enemies'.

Status

Verona was a hierarchal society, with Prince Escalus at the top. Noble families, including the Montagues and Capulets, were below him, and various working people below them. When the Prince enters a scene, such as in Act 1, Scene 1, to stop the fight between the Montagues and Capulets, or in Act 3, Scene 1, when he issues the banishment against Romeo, the other characters in the scene recognise his status by the way they behave around him.

TASK 11

a Work in a group to choose one scene in which the Prince appears and decide what other characters are in the scene. In addition to characters who speak lines, these could include members of his 'train' (people who travel with him) and bystanders.

b Assign each character in the scene a number to represent their status. If the Prince is a 10, what would a lord, servant or fruit-seller be?

c Then practise the Prince's entrance into the scene and the reactions of the other characters. Do they bow to him? Try to avoid his glance? Stand protectively close to him? Nod in agreement with what he says? At the same time, try different ways for the Prince to assert his status. Experiment with:

eye contact posture

gesture proximity pace

vocal tone and volume

stage positioning, including entrances and any use of levels.

▲ *Stellan Skarsgard as Prince Escalus in Carlo Carlei's 2013 film version*

Love and hate

Romeo and Juliet must choose between love and hate. In Act 1, Scene 4, Juliet exclaims, 'My only love sprung from my only hate!' The intensity of their love alongside the hatred between their families forces them to make difficult decisions.

KEY TERMS:

Verse: text arranged in lines, often with a regular rhythm.

Iambic pentameter: a line of verse with ten syllables, where the stress falls on the second, fourth, sixth, eighth and tenth beats, forming a 'di-dum' rhythm.

Prose: text without rhythm or rhyme, usually set out in paragraphs.

Sonnet: a 14-line poem with a formal rhyme scheme.

TASK 12

a In a small group, chart a timeline showing the different stages of Romeo and Juliet's love, from their first meeting to their deaths.

b Choose five of these key moments and create a still image for each.

c Then, use thought-tracking. A group member should point at Romeo or Juliet for them to say what they are thinking and feeling at that moment.

d Consider how their emotions change during the play and how that might be shown in their body language and voices.

TASK 13

Two instances when the young lovers must make difficult choices are when Juliet makes the decision to take the potion and when Romeo, believing that Juliet is dead, decides to kill himself.

a Create a conscience alley, with group members on either side of 'Juliet'. As she walks down the 'alley', pondering her decision, group members should call out reasons why she should or should not take the potion.

b At the end, 'Juliet' should discuss why this is a difficult decision for her and why she makes the choice she does.

c Repeat the exercise with an actor playing Romeo.

Speaking verse

Most of the play is written in a type of verse called **iambic pentameter**, though a few characters, such as the Nurse, speak mostly in **prose**. Some speeches have formal rhyme schemes, such as the Chorus's opening speech, which is written as a **sonnet**, with lines of alternating rhymes and ending with a rhyming couplet.

An actor must be aware of the way the text is written and the different ways it can be spoken. The language's beauty, meaning and believability are all important. One way of exploring the verse is to choose one word in each line, ideally one of the stressed beats, to emphasise.

"Two households, both alike in dignity"

TASK 14

a Choose a speech from the play and select one word from each line that you believe is the most important. Experiment with how you can interpret each of the selected words in order to convey meaning and emotion. You might consider:

- volume, such as whispering a word or shouting it
- pace – saying the word more slowly or quickly
- tone/emotional range – colouring the word with a certain emotion, such as love, anger or fear
- pitch – using a higher or lower pitch.

b Perform the speech using your choices.

c Make notes on what was particularly effective.

SET PLAY 6:
Romeo and Juliet by
William Shakespeare

6

Key characters

Lord Capulet
A nobleman and father to Juliet.

Lady Capulet
A noblewoman and mother to Juliet.

Juliet
The 13-year-old only daughter of the Capulets who falls in love with Romeo.

Tybalt
Juliet's 'fiery' cousin, kills Mercutio and is killed by Romeo.

Nurse
Juliet's long-time nurse/nanny and confidante, who often provides **comic relief**.

Prince Escalus
The most powerful authority figure in Verona.

Mercutio
Romeo's restless, mocking noble friend, who is killed by Tybalt.

Paris
A nobleman who wishes to marry Juliet.

Friar Laurence
A Catholic friar who is a confidante to Romeo and Juliet.

Lord Montague
A nobleman and Romeo's father.

Lady Montague
A noblewoman and Romeo's mother.

Romeo
A young nobleman who falls in love with Juliet.

Benvolio
Romeo's cousin and friend, who often acts as peace-maker.

TASK 15

Locate where in the play each character makes their first entrance. Experiment with how they might enter the scene and show their relationship with other characters. Consider what the audience's first impression of the character might be.

KEY TERM:

Comic relief: characters or interludes which provide light moments in contrast to more serious events.

TASK 16

a With a partner, choose at least four characters from the list above to study more closely. Discuss your impressions of them.

b Look at the adjectives below and select at least three to describe each character. Explain why you have made those choices.

angry brave sensitive emotional romantic intelligent calm tempestuous
silly naïve old young loyal secretive deceptive sad protective
changeable comic commanding impetuous unlucky steady sensible
passionate powerful passive cold distant weak strong plotting peaceful
playful moody hopeful heroic villainous religious wise strong independent

TASK 17

a Using the prompt questions below, write two paragraphs of your interpretation of Lord Capulet.

b Then write similar questions for a contrasting character, such as the Nurse, and answer them.

Interpretation of character

You will need to show how you can interpret a character. This means that you understand the character's motivations and goals, and the obstacles they face. In your interpretation, you might decide that a character is sympathetic, changeable, villainous, passive, intelligent, funny, emotional, heroic, or a combination. Then you must be able to use your vocal and physical skills to portray the character and create particular effects for the audience, such as tension, romance, surprise, anger, comedy, pity or sorrow.

Answer the questions below to begin your interpretation of **Lord Capulet**.

FACTS:

- A married, wealthy, middle-aged nobleman of Verona.
- Married to Lady Capulet, with one daughter, Juliet.
- The head of the Capulet family, who have a long-time feud with another noble family, the Montagues.

KEY SCENES:

Act 1, Scene 2: With Paris: expresses his protective love for his daughter.

Act 3, Scene 4: After Tybalt's death, agrees that Paris should be speedily married to Juliet.

Act 3, Scene 5: Is furious with Juliet for refusing to marry Paris.

Act 4, Scene 2: Makes excited arrangements for the wedding and is pleased by Juliet's obedience.

Act 4, Scene 4: Despairs at Juliet's apparent death.

Act 5, Scene 3: Mourns Juliet's actual death and is reconciled with the Montagues.

POSSIBLE VOCAL CHOICES:

Capulet experiences a wide range of emotions. What vocal skills could help to portray his character?

- What accent/dialect might show his status?
- How would volume and tone change when he is angry or dominating a situation?
- How would diction, pitch, tone or emphasis add impact to insulting words?
- What volume, tone or emphasis would suit his expressions of love for his daughter?

EFFECT ON AUDIENCE:

- What first impression of Lord Capulet should the audience have?
- Are there moments when you want the audience to:
  - be sympathetic to Capulet
  - pity him
  - judge him harshly
  - be angry with him?

POSSIBLE PHYSICAL CHOICES:

Lord Capulet is referred to as 'Old Capulet', which separates him from the young noblemen Romeo and Tybalt, yet he is still a powerful presence, who does not shy away from physical encounters.

- How might Capulet's age affect his movements?
- How could his posture and body language demonstrate his status?
- What gestures might encourage people to obey him?
- When and how does the pace or rhythm of his movements change?
- How could he use body language, posture, eye contact and gesture to show his reconciliation with Montague?

POSSIBLE COSTUME CHOICES:

- How will his costumes show his age, wealth and status?
- Will he be costumed differently for the party scene? If he wears a mask here, what might it be like?
- Does he dress differently when outside?

Download a printable version from Samples & Downloads at www.illuminatepublishing.com.

SET PLAY 6:
Romeo and Juliet by William Shakespeare

6

Performing choices

In Question 2, you will discuss in detail how you would perform a particular line as a given character. For example (in Act 1, Scene 1):

> You are performing the role of **Sampson**.
>
> Describe how you would use your vocal and physical skills to perform the line below and explain the effects you want to create.
>
> Sampson: Is the law of our side, if I say ay?

In this scene, Sampson and Gregory are Capulet servants eager to show the Montagues how much they despise them. Throughout the scene, as Sampson, I will employ a swaggering gait, and a working-class accent appropriate to my role as a servant of this feuding household. (1) However, to show my concern at staying on the right side of the law, before I speak this line, there will be a slight pause and my body language and stage position will change. I will turn away from the Montague servants, hunch my shoulders and step closer to Gregory so that my enemies cannot see my doubt. (2) I will speak the line softly and urgently to Gregory, which will be a comic change from my previous bravado. (3) I will emphasise the word 'law' because I want to go as far as I can but don't want to be punished. I will raise the pitch of my voice at the end of the line to stress the importance of the question. (4) This is a moment of comedy for the audience as they will understand how my anger can be turned off and on. (5)

(1) Understanding of character and context of line, mentions gait and accent

(2) Use of pause as well as detailed description of physical skills

(3) Vocal skills and their effect (comic)

(4) Vocal skills

(5) Effect on audience

KEY TERM:

Bravado: the appearance of boldness or extreme confidence.

TASK 18

a Choose one line from the play spoken by each of the following characters:

- Juliet
- Friar Laurence
- Nurse.
- Romeo
- Mercutio

Experiment with different ways of using vocal and physical skills for the chosen lines.

b Answer the following question for each character's line:

Describe how you would use your vocal and physical skills to perform your chosen line and explain the effects you want to create.

c Check your work by marking or highlighting:

V for each vocal skill you mention

P for each physical skill

E for an effect on the audience.

TIP

It is a good idea to write in the first person ('I') to help you fully imagine your own performance of the role. Do more than just describe the vocal and physical skills you will use: also think about how your choices will add to the audience's understanding of the play, its characters and their relationships.

Character revision sheet

Below is a partly completed character revision sheet for **Romeo**. Copy the grid and complete it.

Character and importance to the play	Romeo. Romeo and Juliet are the co-protagonists. The audience follows Romeo's journey from mourning an unrequited love, to his falling in love with and marrying Juliet, to killing Tybalt and finally himself.
What do they want?	To be in love and loved in return.
What obstacles do they face?	• He falls in love with someone unacceptable because of the feud between their families. • His impetuous nature means he takes action before thinking.
What are their key scenes?	Act 1, Scene 1: Tells Benvolio he is sad because Rosaline doesn't love him. Act 1, Scene 4: Attends Capulet party and falls in love with Juliet. Act 2, Scene 1: Balcony scene. Act 2, Scene 2: Asks Friar Laurence to marry him to Juliet. Act 2, Scene 3: Mercutio teases him and Nurse delivers the message. Act 3, Scene 1: Mercutio is slain by Tybalt and Romeo kills him. Act 3, Scene 3: Romeo despairs because he has been banished. Act 3, Scene 5: He departs after spending his wedding night with Juliet. Act 5, Scene 1: He is told of Juliet's 'death' and visits the apothecary. Act 5, Scene 3: At Juliet's tomb, Romeo kills Paris and commits suicide.

How might they be costumed?	How might their hair and make-up by done?
Draw a simple sketch or write a description. Consider: • colours • fabrics • shape and fit • personality, background and status.	Draw a simple sketch or write a description. Consider: • length, colour and style of hair • type of make-up (colours; how it is appropriate for character, setting and period).

How might they use body language?	
• Posture • Gait • Facial expression	
How might they use their voice?	
• Emotional range (angry, sad, happy, excited, desperate, despairing) • Pitch and volume (low or high; loud or soft) • Accent or other distinctive features.	
Choose one important line and analyse how they might say it.	

TASK 19

Using the grid for guidance, create similar revision sheets for all the major characters.

Download a printable version from Samples & Downloads at www.illuminatepublishing.com.

SET PLAY 6:
Romeo and Juliet by
William Shakespeare

Using the performance space and interaction with others

There are many opportunities to explore the stage space and interact with other characters. You might think about, for example, how to establish:

- the 'love at first sight' between Romeo and Juliet
- their developing relationship
- the pain of their parting.

You could consider how scenes involving a lot of characters or movement could be staged, such as the street fights and the Capulet's party. You could reflect on how to use proximity, levels, touch and reactions.

When you are writing about performance space and interaction, make sure that you focus on the effects you wish to achieve for the audience, such as romance, surprise, tension, sorrow, pity or comedy.

TASK 20

Look at the photographs below and make notes on the use of performance space and interactions. Consider:

- where on the stage actors are positioned
- use of proximity and levels
- gestures
- moments when the characters are touching
- any reactions.

▲ *Close-quarter fighting with rondel daggers from Hans Talhoffer's* Fechtbuch*, a combat manual from 1467*

CHALLENGE

Research some images of medieval sword fighting or fencing. Using them as inspiration, either sketch or explain how you could stage some of the fight scenes in the play.

▲ *Bette Bourne, Tim Carroll and John McEnery in a 2004 production at the Globe Theatre*

▲ *Ellie Kendrick and Adetomiwa Edun at the Globe in 2009*

▲ *An engraving from* The Illustrated Library Shakespeare *(1890), showing Romeo with the Apothecary*

TIP

There are many different ways a scene can be interpreted. These are just a few examples.

TASK 21

a Look closely at the scene between Romeo and the Apothecary in Act 5, Scene 1. Note any suggested or specified actions, such as entrances, reactions or exchanges of items.

b Choose a stage configuration. Sketch this and mark entrances and any pieces of furniture.

c Decide the effects you want to achieve in this scene, for example tension, surprise, comedy.

d How will you use the stage space to help with this? You could try the following interpretations:

- Romeo quickly circles the Apothecary as he speaks, while the Apothecary stands still or moves very slowly.
- The Apothecary tempts and teases Romeo by holding the poison just out of his reach.
- Romeo falls to his knees to beg for the poison.
- Romeo throws money at the Apothecary as he exits.

e Experiment with different reactions, such as facial expressions, eye contact, gestures and movements:

- What is Romeo's reaction when he first sees the poison?
- How does the Apothecary respond to Romeo's speeches?
- How does Romeo behave when he gets the poison?
- What does the Apothecary do on receiving the money?

f Try different ways of performing the scene then answer the following question:

> You are performing the role of the **Apothecary**.
>
> Focus on Romeo's scene with the Apothecary. Explain how you might use the performance space and interact with the actor playing Romeo **to create suspense** for the audience.

Answering a question about character interpretation

If you choose to answer Question 4, you will write about how you would use acting skills to interpret a character both in the extract provided and the play as a whole. An example of this sort of question might be:

> You are performing the role of **Romeo**.
>
> Describe how you would use your acting skills to **interpret Romeo's character**. Explain why your ideas are appropriate for:
>
> - this extract
> - the performance of your role in the play as a whole.

TASK 22

a Write a response to the question above, based on the scene specified in Task 21.

b Check that you have discussed:

- vocal skills
- physical skills
- the extract
- the rest of the play
- why your ideas are appropriate.

TASK 23

Choose a scene in which Juliet is featured. Use the spider diagrams below to prepare a response about her character in the play.

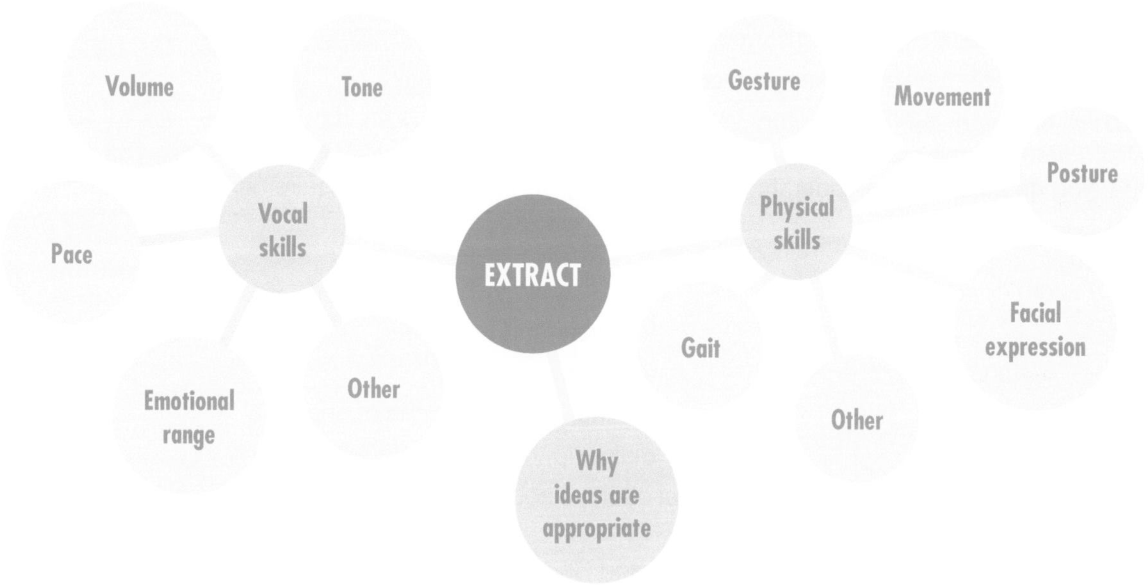

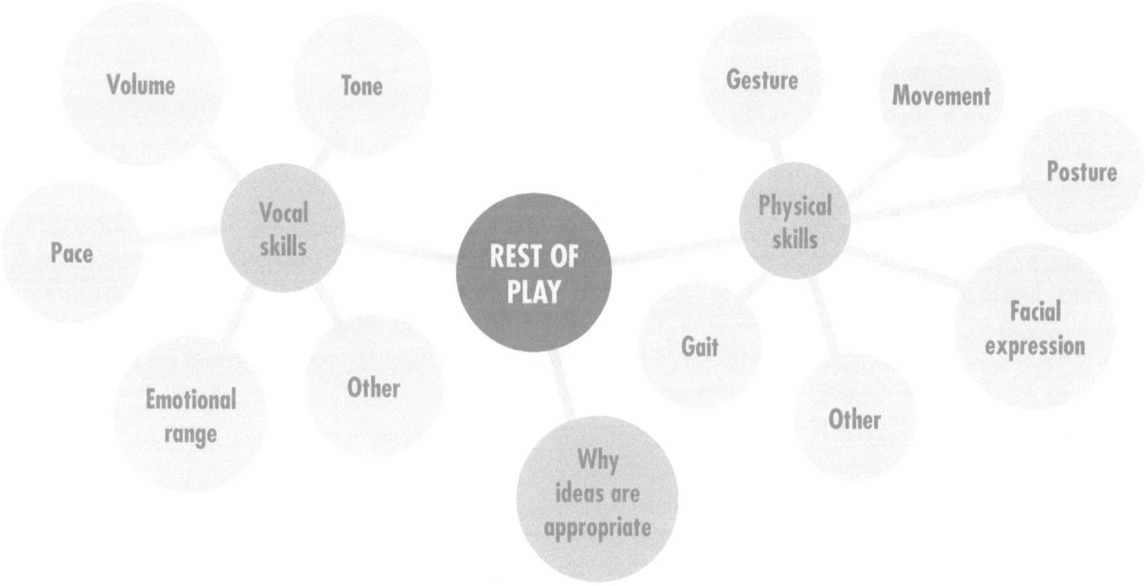

EXTRACT

- Vocal skills: Volume, Tone, Pace, Emotional range, Other
- Physical skills: Gesture, Movement, Posture, Facial expression, Gait, Other
- Why ideas are appropriate

REST OF PLAY

- Vocal skills: Volume, Tone, Pace, Emotional range, Other
- Physical skills: Gesture, Movement, Posture, Facial expression, Gait, Other
- Why ideas are appropriate

Design choices

If you choose to answer Question 5, you will be thinking as a designer and commenting on one aspect of design. For example:

> You are a designer working on **one** aspect of design for this extract.
>
> Describe how you would use your design skills to create effects which **support the action**. Explain why your ideas are appropriate for:
>
> - this extract
> - your chosen design skill in the play as a whole.

TIP

Consider if the character you are writing about is consistent throughout the play, or if they change and develop.

You may choose to focus on set, costume, lighting or sound design. Whichever you choose, you must explain why your ideas are appropriate to the play as a whole. You might refer to the way in which:

- your design helps to show the action of the play and the nature of the characters
- your design for the extract is consistent with the design requirements for the rest of the play (for example, in style, tone or conventions of the production)
- the technical aspects of your chosen specialism support your design ideas.

Romeo and Juliet offers many opportunities for imagination, creativity and design flair.

Question 1 of the exam will focus on late-16th-century Verona as the setting. For Question 5, you may wish to explore this context in naturalistic detail or you may develop a more abstract or stylised design. Whatever choices you make, you need to ensure that you demonstrate an understanding of the play and its particular requirements.

Costume design

For costume design, you might consider:

- style, cut and fit
- colour, fabric, decorative features
- whether realistic or stylised
- condition (worn or new, for example)
- footwear and headwear
- accessories
- the status or social role of character
- make-up, hairstyles and masks.

As costume designer, you will also be responsible for practical choices about the fabrics and fit for the characters. You may want to:

- highlight differences and similarities between the Montagues and Capulets
- demonstrate the hierarchy of society portrayed in the play
- establish the different ages of the characters
- help to show any changes the characters undergo during the play
- disguise a character's appearance, such as with a mask.

If you decide to retain the original setting, you could research in more detail the types of clothing worn in the period and how colour, accessories, fabric and fit convey messages about the characters.

On the other hand, you may choose to update the setting, and the fabrics and silhouettes you choose will reflect that. There are challenges to this approach, however, and you must still make sure that your costumes show the characters, their roles and status in the world created. In an updated production, would the Montagues wear different colours or types of clothing from the Capulets, for example? How would you establish the Prince's importance and power? Remember, that if you choose to change the time or location of the play, your choice must be appropriate for the whole play and you must be able to convey your ideas succinctly.

TIP

Some productions use masks to impressive effect. You could consider masks the characters might wear to the ball, such as decorative masquerade half-masks, or ones suggesting animals or mythological beings.

TASK 24

a Sketch costume designs for **three** characters who appear in Act 1, Scene 4 (the party scene).

b Now choose **one** of the characters. Write about their costume for that scene and how they might be costumed in the rest of the play.

c Check that you have:

- referred to fabric, colours, shape/silhouette, fit, condition
- included headwear and/or footwear, as appropriate
- considered make-up, hairstyle and masks, as appropriate
- explained how the costume helps the action of the extract
- related your design to the rest of the play.

SET PLAY 6:
Romeo and Juliet by
William Shakespeare

Set design

For set design, you might consider:

- staging configuration
- the location and atmosphere of the scene
- if there will be any levels, platforms, ramps or stairs
- entrances and exits
- if there will be backdrops, flats or projections
- the colour palette you will use
- how materials, textures and shapes can help to create a suitable setting
- what props or set dressings are needed.

One of the challenges is to decide how realistic or artificial/stylised you want your set to be. Alongside this, you need to know how you will incorporate the different settings of the play. You could, for example:

- have a composite set, which represents several settings at once,
- a minimalistic set
- set changes where scenery will be brought onstage
- use modern technology, such as projections or a revolve
- suggest themes of the play through **theatrical metaphors**, for example by using colours and symbols associated with love or violence.

'Juliet's tomb'

KEY TERM:

Theatrical metaphor: when comparisons and symbols are used to suggest meaning. For example, a set design which resembles a head might suggest that all the action is a characters' thoughts or dreams.

TASK 25

a Design a set for the ending of play.

b Write a paragraph explaining its effect on the audience. Consider:

- dominant colours and textures
- positioning of important set items or props
- levels
- materials
- the atmosphere you want to create
- how the set supports the action of the play.

TASK 26

Look at the sketch on the right of a theatre in the round. Choose an earlier scene from the play and create a set design for it using this configuration.

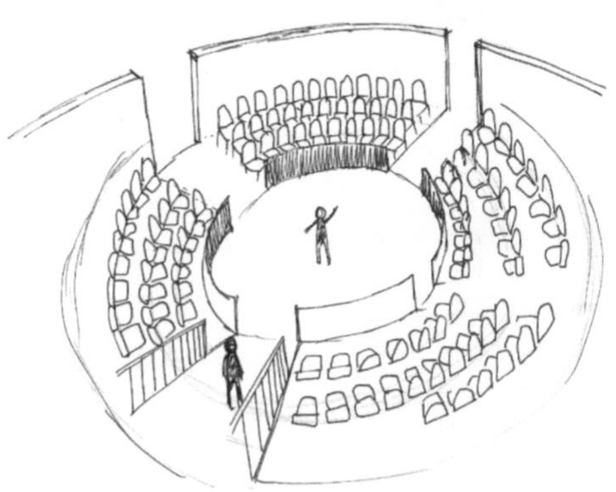

TASK 27

Choose one significant prop or piece of scenery that appears in the play. Sketch several ideas of how it could be designed. Some important items include:

- potion or poison bottles
- swords
- a dagger
- a lantern
- Juliet's bed
- a banquet table
- the balcony.

▲ *Bright torches in John Gielgud's 1935 production at the New Theatre, with Laurence Olivier as Romeo*

Lighting design

When designing lighting, you might consider how to create:

- time of day and season
- mood or atmosphere
- the setting, action and characters of a scene (such as a follow spot to focus the audience on a character's journey or backlighting to enhance a romantic silhouette)
- a focus on a particular moment.

Some of your lighting tools are:

- colours
- angles and intensity
- light from onstage sources (candles and lit torches)
- use of shadow and silhouette
- special effects
- transitions, blackouts or fades.

The action of the play covers only four days. In that time, the protagonists meet, fall in love, marry, part and die. Throughout the play, Shakespeare references particular times of day, from early morning to late at night, as well as the different locations and moods of scenes.

TASK 28

Some sample effects a student might want to create are given below. Consider:

- where in the play they might be suitable
- how they could be accomplished technically.

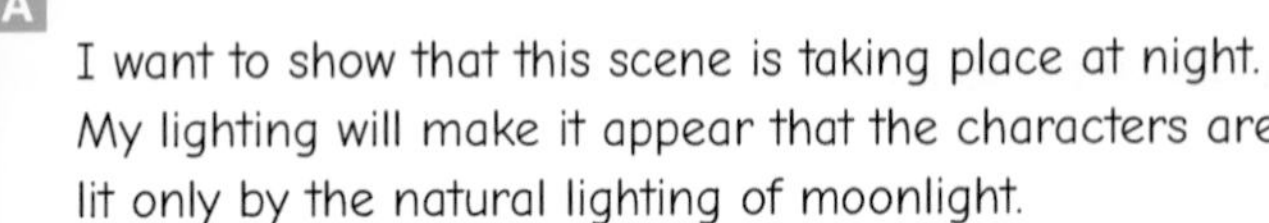

A I want to show that this scene is taking place at night. My lighting will make it appear that the characters are lit only by the natural lighting of moonlight.

B At this stage, this character seems dangerous, so I will backlight him to appear as a dark silhouette against a red background.

C To highlight the romance of this moment, I will create effects which focus on the two characters and highlight their youth and beauty.

D My aim is to show the violence of this scene, so I want the lighting to be exciting.

E My lighting reflects the grandeur of the period setting and wealth of the characters in several ways.

TASK 29

Choose two contrasting scenes from the play. Write down your ideas of how lighting could help to convey the actions of these scenes and the necessary mood.

Sound design

When designing sound design for *Romeo and Juliet*, you should consider how to:

- create atmosphere
- add to the action and emotion of a scene
- contribute to the setting and style of the play
- fulfil the practical needs of the script.

Some choices you can make involve the use of:

- live or recorded sound
- volume/amplification (use of microphones and speakers)
- naturalistic or symbolic sound
- music.

TASK 30

Below are some sound effects which could occur in the play. Identify when they might be used and how they could be created:

- music suitable for dancing
- birdsong
- clashing swords
- crowd noises
- religious music
- an echo effect
- sounds to increase tension and suspense.

TASK 31

a Decide if you are retaining the late-16th-century setting or choosing another time. Research music from your choice of period.

b Consider the different moods in the play, including romantic, violent, comic and tragic, and choose pieces of music to underscore at least **four** different moments.

TASK 32

a Identify two contrasting scenes from the play. Describe what effects you want to create for the audience, such as increasing tension, suggesting romance or provoking sorrow.

b Write a detailed explanation of how your sound design will create these effects. Consider:
   - when the sound/music will start and end
   - its volume
   - how it will be created (live, recorded, onstage or off)
   - if it will fade in and out or snap on and off
   - what direction the sound will come from (position of speakers, and so on).

TIP

Remember that only clean (unannotated) copies of the script can be taken into the exam.

SET PLAY 7: *A Taste of Honey* by Shelagh Delaney

Synopsis

Act 1, Scene 1

In Salford in the late 1950s, **Helen** and her teenage daughter, **Jo**, move into a shabby flat. Helen has a drink and complains about her cold. They bicker about Jo's future plans. Helen discovers some of Jo's drawings and praises them, saying she should go to art school. Jo asks why they are always moving and accuses Helen of running away from someone. **Peter**, a car salesman arrives and asks Helen to marry him. Jo tells Peter not to marry Helen as she is 'a devil with the men'. Peter tells Jo to look after her mother while she's ailing and leaves. Helen asks Jo what she would do if she got married again. Jo replies she'd have her locked up.

Act 1, Scene 2

On the street outside, Jo and her boyfriend, **Jimmie**, a black sailor, have a playful conversation. He asks if she will marry him and, when she agrees, he gives her a ring. Jimmie laments that Jo's mother will be prejudiced against him and that they won't have much time together as he is in the Navy. Agreeing to meet the next day, they kiss goodnight. In the flat, Helen quizzes Jo about her boyfriend. Jo asks Helen about her ex-husband. Helen says, 'He was a rat!' Jo says she would throw out a wife if she had a baby by another man. Helen announces that she is going to marry Peter. Peter arrives and Jo attacks him. Helen intervenes and asks Peter to leave a pound for Jo as they might go to Blackpool for the weekend. When they leave, Jo cries. Jimmie enters and makes Jo a milk drink as a cold cure. Jo asks him if he thinks Helen is beautiful and if they are alike. Jo invites him to stay.

To the sound of wedding bells, Helen enters with boxes containing her wedding clothes. Helen chides Jo for having a cold on her wedding day. Helen sees the ring Jo is wearing on a cord around her neck. Helen tells Jo she is 'only a kid' and should learn from her mother's mistakes. Jo asks about her father and Helen says he was 'a bit stupid'. Helen explains that her husband was a 'Puritan' and that it was the 'first time' with Jo's father. Helen goes off to find Peter.

Act 2, Scene 1

A pregnant Jo and her friend **Geof** enter the flat. Geof says he has been thrown out by his landlady for being behind with the rent. Jo teases Geof, but says he can sleep on her couch. Jo admits that she is pregnant. Geof wonders how she will manage. He asks about her boyfriend and says he will stay the next day to look after her.

A 'month or two later', Geof is making a baby's gown, while an unhappy Jo complains about the heat and her worries about motherhood. Playfully, Jo asks Geof if he would like to be the father of her baby and he says he would. He says he has never kissed a girl and despite Jo's struggles, kisses her. He asks her to marry him and she refuses. Jo wonders if Geof should leave.

Helen returns. Jo is angry when she realises Geof has involved Helen. Helen declares that she wants nothing to do with the grandchild. Helen and Jo argue and Helen begins chasing her around the room. Helen threatens to kill Jo, and Jo threatens to jump out of the window. Geof tries to stop the fight, and the women turn on him, telling him to go, which he does. A drunken Peter enters. Helen invites Jo to come and live with her and Peter, but Peter says she and Geof would not be welcome. Peter leaves and, after a momentary hesitation, Helen follows, saying she will send Jo money.

SET PLAY 7:
A Taste of Honey by Shelagh Delaney
7

Act 2, Scene 2
In her ninth month of pregnancy, Jo is reading a book while Geof bakes a cake and cleans the flat. Jo tells Geof that Helen said her father was 'the village idiot', which Geof doesn't believe. Geof gives Jo a baby doll to practise with and she throws it to the ground because it is the wrong colour. She says she doesn't want to be a mother. Helen enters with her luggage. She announces she is moving back and asks to speak to Jo alone. Jo guesses correctly that Peter has thrown Helen out. When Geof returns with groceries, Helen criticises him. Geof says he will go, but asks Helen not to frighten Jo. Helen throws the groceries back at him and he exits. When Jo wakes up, she wonders where Geof is. Helen says he hasn't come back yet. Jo tells Helen that her baby will be black. Alarmed, Helen says she needs to go out for a drink. Alone, Jo remembers a nursery rhyme she heard from Geof.

TASK 1

a After reading the synopsis, work in your group to choose ten important plot points. Create a still image for each. Discuss which moments you think are the most exciting and dramatic.

b List some of the performance and design challenges of staging *A Taste of Honey*. It is important to consider: lighting, sound, costume and setting. You might begin by deciding how to:
- create the period setting
- establish the characters through costume, hairstyles and make-up
- contribute to the changing mood and atmosphere of the scenes
- handle transitions and passages of time.

Context

The context of ***A Taste of Honey*** is **working-class Salford in the late 1950s**. This context will influence your understanding of the play and its possibilities for design.

The playwright, Shelagh Delaney (1938–2011), was from Salford. Despite a noted flair for writing, she left school at 17 and tried a number of jobs, including as an usherette and in a photography research department. After seeing a play by Terrence Rattigan, she was inspired to write a play herself, believing she could do better. She wrote the first draft of *A Taste of Honey* in a fortnight and sent it to the influential and experimental director, Joan Littlewood. The play underwent a development period before being produced in 1958 at the Theatre Royal Stratford in London and eventually transferring to London's West End.

The playwright and the protagonist were both young working-class women, but *A Taste of Honey* is not autobiographical. Delaney said it was '25 per cent observation and 75 per cent imagination' (Selina Todd, *Tastes of Honey*).

During the 1950s, there was a theatrical movement focused on 'Angry Young Men' plays, such as *Look Back in Anger* by John Osborne. These explored the plight of working-class characters and the injustices of British society. They were performed with gritty realism, which was also associated with 'kitchen sink' drama because of its depiction of the characters' living conditions. This was in opposition to the glamorous, escapist drawing-room dramas that were popular West End fare. Like many of the Angry Young Men plays, *A Taste of Honey* focuses on working-class characters in difficult circumstances and with limited opportunities. Delaney's voice was unique, however, in being from a young woman's perspective.

Salford is an area of Greater Manchester. At one time, it was a thriving industrial town, supported by a number of factories and the busy docks. Lowry's *Coming Home from the Mill*, which hung in one of Delaney's classrooms, gives an impression of the busy Salford landscape. Salford's fortunes began to decline in the 1920s, and a 1931 survey found that it had many of the worst slums in England. Salford was also bombed during the Second World War, leaving some areas as bomb sites for many years.

▲ *LS Lowry,* Coming Home from the Mill, *1928*

The flat Helen has found is described as 'comfortless'. It has a view of the gasworks, a looming, unattractive metal construction. The flat is cold and has a gas heater which they operate by inserting shillings. There is only one bedroom and a communal bathroom. They can also see the city's slaughterhouse and Jo thinks she can smell the river. Jo describes the flat as an 'old ruin', suggesting that it is in a Victorian terrace, rather than one of the new estates.

Helen recalls a happier time of 'bonfires in the street' and 'gingerbread', which seems far removed from Jo's insecure, lonely childhood. The soap opera *Coronation Street* is set in what is believed to be a fictionalised version of Salford, on a street of terraced houses built in 1902. Much of the *Coronation Street* social life takes place in the Rovers Return Inn, just as Helen goes to the pub for a drink to escape the flat.

A Taste of Honey was considered ground-breaking in several ways: it portrayed women living outside society's norms; it featured an inter-racial relationship and it sympathetically portrayed a gay character. In the 1950s, women generally chose between being a wife or work. However, at the play's opening, Helen is neither. She has experienced the social and financial embarrassment of being divorced by her 'Puritan' husband and is now a careless single mother. She says to Jo, 'There's two w's in your future. Work or want, and no Arabian Knight can tell you different.' She, however, avoids work and appears to go off with Peter for his money. Jo decides to leave school, despite a talent for art, feeling that 'it's too late'. She follows Helen in having an illegitimate child, attracting more attention because of the baby's mixed race. She is worried about people 'staring' when she is pregnant, and Helen is shocked at the idea of a black baby, suggesting it should be drowned or adopted.

With the busy docks and the artery of roads, many different nationalities were present in Salford, with one local referring it to it as 'the Barbary Coast' because of its diversity (Selina Todd, *Tastes of Honey*). Jimmie, however, is not 'from Africa', as Jo asks, but Cardiff. He is doing his **national service** in the Navy. Though they speak of marriage, his temporary role in Jo's life is likely to be understood, to some extent, by both of them. Although depictions of interracial relations are common now, it would have been unusual and most likely shocking to audiences of the 1950s.

SET PLAY 7:
A Taste of Honey by Shelagh Delaney
7

In 1957, the Wolfenden Report recommended that 'homosexual behaviour between consenting adults in private should no longer be a criminal offence', but before this, there were many convictions, with over 1000 gay men imprisoned in 1954. It was extremely unusual for an openly gay person to play an important role in public life – or on the stage. Geof, who is arguably the most empathetic character in the play, has experienced prejudice. Jo guesses he is homeless because his landlady found him with a man. Helen refers to him as a 'pansified little freak'. Geof receives a grant to study at art school, where he would have been likely to find more open-minded and unconventional fellow students. Meanwhile, the head of the Arts Council, John Maynard Keynes, declared that culture was not a 'luxury', but 'essential to the creation of a fair and civilised society' (Selina Todd, *Tastes of Honey*).

Question 1 in the exam will ask you to describe how a specific design skill could reflect the context of *A Taste of Honey* set in working-class Salford in the late 1950s. The following pages explore various design areas and how they could reflect the context of the play.

▲ *Terraced houses with the 'gasometer' in the background*

TASK 2

Study the images on these pages related to mid-20th-century Salford. Work with a partner to list contextual details which could be included in a production of *A Taste of Honey*:

- costumes, hairstyle, make-up
- props
- set and set dressings.

KEY TERM:

National service: Compulsory military training and duties. From 1947 to 1963, healthy men aged 18 or over were required to serve 18 months in the armed services.

Costume, hair and make-up design inspired by context

In 1950s Britain, women's fashions were often highly 'feminine', possibly reflecting the end of austerity after the Second World War and a return to previous social roles. Shoulders were softer and more rounded. Necklines varied, sometimes with decorative details such as bows. Skirts were either very full, with **petticoats** underneath, or slim, pencil skirts. Both had defined waists and ended just below the knee. To emphasise a more 'traditional' hourglass-shaped silhouette, corsetry was used, including **girdles** and **waspies**. Waist-length cardigans or jackets were popular as were three-quarter coats or full-length **swing coats**. Bright colours, pastels and small prints were frequently seen. Hair was usually curled and hats were often worn when going out.

State-school students wore uniforms, with girls typically wearing a dark wool **gymslip** over a white shirt, or a skirt and shirt, with a cardigan or blazer and a tie. When not at school, teenagers were often influenced by American culture, such as the '**beatnik**' style of turtlenecks and slim trousers. Girls would sometimes assume a '**gamine**' look with short hair, cropped trousers and flat shoes.

Jo complains that she needs 'new clothes' and only has one coat which she must use for school and dates. Women would often make their own clothes using inexpensive patterns and fabrics. Helen suggests that Jo invest in 'a needle and some cotton' and notes that all of Jo's clothes are 'held together by a safety pin or a knot'.

A coat pattern from the 1950s

Men in non-manual jobs would usually wear two or three-piece suits to work, while, for more casual occasions, they would wear separate jacket/trouser combinations, with flannel trousers. Students might wear more informal clothes, such as knit waistcoats, corduroy trousers, turtlenecks and zip-up jackets, and their hair might be slightly longer or less styled than more conservative men, who would generally have a 'short back and sides'. Brylcreem or other hair **pomades** were often used to keep hair neat or styled. Sailors would wear a navy-blue uniform of wool trousers, a long-sleeved, V-neck tunic and a cap, though they might wear more casual clothes when off duty.

KEY TERMS:

Petticoats: underskirts used to give fullness to a dress or skirt.

Girdle: stretchy undergarment which holds in and shapes the waist, stomach and hips.

Waspies: corsets, shaped like a wide belt, worn from hip to under the bust, which cinch in the waist.

Swing coat: A coat which is fitted at the shoulders but wide and flowing at the bottom.

Gymslip: A sleeveless knee length dress (pinafore dress), worn over a shirt.

Beatnik: an anti-establishment youth sub-culture from the 1950s to early 1960s associated with poetry and jazz. Typical clothing included black turtlenecks, striped tops, berets and sunglasses.

Gamine: derived from the French word for 'waif' or 'urchin', the gamine look was popularised by Audrey Hepburn in the 1950s. It is associated with short hair, a slim figure and youthfulness.

Pomade: a waxy, greasy or creamy substance used to style hair. It holds hair in place and adds shine.

Jo (Rebekah Brockman) and Jimmie (Ade Otukoya) play with the toy car in the Pearl Theatre production.

TASK 3

Use the play's context and the prompts below to design a costume for one male character from the play and one female character. Consider the character's role and personality when making your choices.

SET PLAY 7: *A Taste of Honey* by Shelagh Delaney 7

Hair:
Men: Long or short? Colour? Styled?
Women: Up or down? Colour? Straight or curled? Long or short?

Make-up:
Pale or dark? Ageing? Lines? Youthful?
Women: Lipstick? Eye make-up? Rouge? Powder?
Men: Shaved or unshaven? Moustache?

Main costume:
Men:
Jacket? Trousers and shirt? Turtleneck? Uniform?
Fabrics: Wool, flannel, corduroy, cotton?
Colours: Black, navy, brown, white, other?
Women:
High or low neckline?
Long or short sleeves?
Fit: Tight or loose? Fitted at waist?
Fabrics: Plain or patterned? Wool, cotton, linen, polyester?
Formal or informal: Pyjamas? Robe? Wedding dress? School uniform?

Footwear:
Men: Slip-on shoes? Brogues? Boots?
Women: Heels or flats? Slippers? Colour? Condition? Stockings? Ankle socks? Knee socks?

Headwear:
Men: Caps or hats? Colour? Wide or narrow brim?
Women: Hats: wide-brimmed or small? Berets? Headbands? Hair ribbon?

Outerwear:
Men: Overcoat? Pea coat? Jacket?
Women: Swing coat? Three-quarter jacket? Waist-length jacket or cardigan?

Accessories:
Men: Spectacles? Eye patch? Watch? Gloves? Cigars? Cigarettes? Belts?
Women: Jewellery? Gloves? Cigarettes? Scarf? Handbag? Belts?

KEY TERM:

Pea coat: A heavy woollen coat, usually navy blue and mid-thigh length, often worn by sailors.

TIP

When writing about costume choices, you need to show understanding of character and context. For example, you should demonstrate awareness of the typical silhouette and dress-length for women's fashions at this time or how fabrics, colours and styles reflect the character's income and priorities. It is important to Helen that she is attractive to men, so, how might her outfits show that? In later scenes, Jo is pregnant: how might her costumes reflect her attitude towards her pregnancy?

TIP

Carefully read the stage directions and dialogue. They might suggest or require certain costumes or accessories. In Act 1, Scene 2, for example, Jimmie presents Jo with a ring which she hangs around her neck. The dialogue refers to Helen having a fur and Peter wearing an eye patch. As a designer, it is up to you to decide how these items look.

Download a printable version from Samples & Downloads at www.illuminatepublishing.com.

TASK 4

a Choose a different character from those you used in Task 3. Design a costume for them in a key scene. Consider: hair, make-up, fabric, fit, accessories, headwear and shoes.

b Write a paragraph explaining how the costume suggests the character's role in the play and the effect their external presentation will have on the audience.

Set design inspired by context

One of the challenges of *A Taste of Honey* is designing a set which believably creates the play's world while also accommodating the moments when the action breaks out of the four walls of their flat. For example, how will the setting of the first scene between Jimmie and Jo, which occurs outside, be staged? Where will the musical interludes take place? Will the musicians appear onstage? As a designer, you will need to consider how your design will:

- serve the practical needs of the play
- show the period setting
- suggest the atmosphere and purpose of the setting.

KEY TERM:

Formica: a hard, durable plastic laminate used for worktops and cupboard doors.

Linoleum: an inexpensive, durable and easy-to-clean floor covering.

Antimacassar: A cloth, often decorative, placed over the headrest or arms of a chair or sofa to protect the fabric underneath from staining or wear.

Although there is a single set for *A Taste of Honey*, it does change. At the beginning, it is an uninhabited, barely furnished flat. As the play goes on, it changes, as Jo and Helen, and eventually Geof, occupy it.

In terms of domestic interiors, in the era after the Second World War, there continued a 'make do and mend' attitude, and this would be especially true in the case of this flat where none of the furniture would be new or particularly fashionable. Geof describes the flat as 'enormous', and it might have curtains or screens rather than doors separating its different areas. Furnishings might be patched, mended or mismatched. Some 1950s British design features include:

- print fabrics, including geometric or nature-inspired designs
- **Formica** for surfaces like tables or counters which need to be hard-wearing and can be wiped clean
- patterned area rugs and wallpapers
- **Linoleum** flooring
- net curtains
- small decorative objects, such as ash trays or vases
- large upholstered armchairs and sofas, sometimes protected with **antimacassars**
- electrical or battery-powered objects like radios or clocks.

TASK 5

With a partner, study the image on the left. Note any features which you feel particularly make this room appear to be a 1950s design.

TASK 6

When listing the benefits of the flat, Helen says that the wallpaper is 'contemporary'. Look at the samples below and discuss which would be most appropriate for the flat and why. What condition do you think the wallpaper might be in?

TASK 7

Choose a staging configuration, then use the prompts below to consider how your design could support the action of specific scenes in the play.

Act 1, Scene 1	• Would you have windows in your set? If so, what would be the view Helen refers to? Will the set have any features like backdrops or projections to suggest the Salford neighbourhood? • Peter sums up the district as 'tenements, cemetery, slaughterhouse'. How might your design reflect this? • Where would the different areas of the flat be? The door, bedroom and kitchen? • What are the dominant colours and textures in the room? • What key pieces of furniture are there?
Act 1, Scene 2	• This scene begins 'on the street'. Where will that be located on your set? • How will your set aid the transition to inside the flat? Where will Helen dance? • How is the flat different now that Helen and Jo have unpacked and settled in? • Where does Jimmie enter? • Jimmie describes the flat as 'the dirtiest place I've ever seen'. How could your set design reinforce that impression?
Act 2, Scene 1	• What style and size would the balloons be? Where would they be put? • Geof remarks on the 'state' of the flat. How messy is it? • Where are the sheets and blankets kept? • How does Geof's presence change the flat?
Act 2, Scene 2	• Where will Geof's dance with the mop and bucket occur? • How has the flat changed in the months since the previous scene? How much has Geof cleaned it? What items has he added? • What does the doll that Geof gives to Jo look like?

TASK 8

Choose several pages from the first act to explore. Describe the set and how it suits the play's context. You could consider how your set:

- is appropriate for the chosen scene
- reflects 1950s Salford setting
- functions practically in terms of the action of the scene and other key moments.

CHALLENGE

Research the architecture and furniture of 1950s Britain. Based on your research, sketch some items which you believe could be seen in Jo and Helen's flat.

Sound and lighting design inspired by context

Sound

Sound can be used to suggest 1950s Salford setting in a number of ways, including:

- period music
- urban sound effects
- using sound to create the appropriate atmosphere for various scenes.

As a sound designer, you might consider how period music, either performed live or recorded, could enhance key scenes. In *A Taste of Honey*, jazz music is mentioned in the stage directions. Music is used in the transitions, and the stage directions indicate that the actors dance on and off to it. In the original production, each character had a piece of music associated with them. Many productions make a feature of the music, including having a jazz trio onstage, performing well-known or specially composed songs. Other productions use recorded music or a more understated soundtrack.

To reinforce the Salford setting, you could consider sound effects to reinforce the location of the flat, including the neighbours and nearby factories. You could also use more abstract sounds to suggest characters' moods or a change in the atmosphere.

CHALLENGE

Research 1950s jazz music and choose at least one piece which would enhance a scene in the play. Consider the mood you want to create and how the music contributes to it.

Lighting

Lighting can help to create the period and setting. Lighting could, for example:

- suggest the light from the urban location and how it enters the flat
- show different times of day or seasons
- differentiate when the characters are inside or outside.

Through your choice of colour gels, you might suggest the coldness of the flat, the weather outside or a change of mood.

You may wish to use some practical period lights, such as table or standard lamps or the 'unshaded electric light bulb dangling from the ceiling' to illuminate some scenes.

TASK 9

a In a group, carefully read your choice of approximately ten pages of Act 2. Make notes on any possibilities for sound and lighting design, especially those which reflect the context of working-class Salford in the 1950s.

b Work through the section, stopping to agree any effects that would support the action and mood of the scene. You should consider:

- music
- sound effects
- lighting effects
- transitions.

Practical explorations of characters, themes and style

When writing about performing, you should demonstrate that you understand the play's characters, themes and style. The practical activities below will help you to explore the play.

Mother and daughter

The relationship between Helen and Jo is at the heart of the play. When Delaney began writing the play she had 'only two people in it – the mother and daughter' ('Commentary' *A Taste of Honey*). They are the most developed characters in the play. Helen has generated many different responses, from those who see her as a restless, rebellious woman seeking happiness, to those who consider her a negligent and cruel mother. Whatever interpretation you arrive at, it is important to understand that the play begins and ends with the mother and daughter and that their relationship is complex and variable.

Some critics have judged Helen very harshly. Delaney, despite her own description of her as a 'semi-whore', had to defend Helen from accusations of sex work. Instead, she saw her as someone seeking fun and happiness, that 'taste of honey' which Jo also desires.

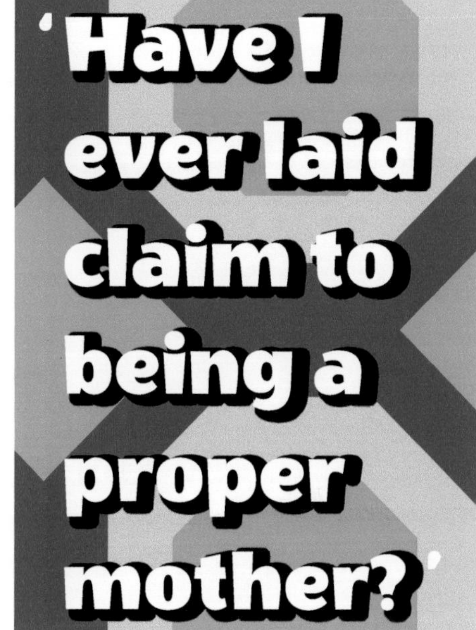

TASK 10

Working in a small group, create five still images which you believe sum up different stages of Jo and Helen's relationship. Consider how the relationship might be shown through their facial expressions, **proximity**, gestures, body language and use of levels.

KEY TERM:

Proximity: the distance between people or objects; how near or far.

TASK 11

In your group, use hot-seating to discover more about Helen and Jo.

a Let one person play Helen and the others ask her questions about her past, including her childhood, her own mother and her marriage. 'Helen' should give full, believable answers based on their understanding of the play and including relevant details.

b Then put 'Jo' in the hot-seat and ask about her feelings towards her mother, her boyfriend and her future.

c Afterwards, read the end of Act 1, Scene 2. Discuss how your understanding of the characters could influence how this scene is interpreted.

Love

Different types of love are explored in the play, from the young love between Jo and Jimmie, the friendship between Geof and Jo, the lustful relationship between Peter and Helen and the complex mother-daughter love of Helen and Jo. There are also moments in these relationships which tip over into anger and animosity.

TASK 12

Choose one line for each of these pairs to express how they feel about each other. With a partner, explore how you could use your vocal skills to show what your character is feeling at that moment.

TASK 13

a Working in a pair, choose part of a scene in which there is a range of emotions between two of the characters. For example, pages 48–49 for Jo and Geof; pages 24–25 for Jimmie and Jo; and pages 18–19 for Helen and Peter.

b Face each other, about three metres apart, and begin reading the scene.

c Take a step closer on each line when you think your character is feeling emotionally closer to the person they are speaking to. Take a step back if they are feeling hostile or angry. Take a step to the side if they are feeling neutral.

d Afterwards, discuss when the characters' emotions changed and how they could use physical skills to show this.

Acting styles

Naturalism

A groundbreaking aspect of *A Taste of Honey* was its blending of naturalism and more stylised techniques, such as music hall turns and 'breaking the fourth wall'. Joan Littlewood, the play's original director, used a variety of techniques in rehearsal.

One technique Littlewood used was a naturalistic pre-scene, where the actors playing Helen and Jo carried heavy bags and suitcases around the theatre so that they would enter the scene appropriately exhausted for the play's beginning.

▲ *Rita Tushingham as Jo holds a sparkler at the fairground.*

TASK 14

a Choose one scene and improvise a pre-scene to it of what the characters are doing before the dialogue begins. For example, what did Geof and Jo do at the fairground, or what has Peter been doing before he enters in Act 2, Scene 1?

b Repeat your improvisation, and lead it into the play's dialogue.

c Discuss how the pre-scene affects the character's actions and emotions.

To explore a character's objectives, you need to decide what they want in the scene, what obstacles there are to their achieving it and how they attempt to overcome the obstacles. There are many instances of conflicting objectives in scenes, for example when Helen is caught between what Peter and Jo want. Objectives can be stated as verbs, so a character's objectives might be 'to force X stay', 'to comfort X', 'to demonstrate my love' or 'to clean the room'. Objectives may change throughout a scene and a character may try many ways of achieving their objectives.

TASK 15

Choose a small section from the script and decide what each character wants at that point and what is keeping them from getting it.

Physical skills

Littlewood used **Laban** techniques to encourage highly physical work from her actors. One of these techniques is 'The Eight Basic Efforts', where actors explore actions using different types of 'effort' The efforts are:

- flicking
- wringing
- dabbing
- punching
- floating
- slashing
- gliding
- pressing.

TASK 16

a Improvise a scene in which Jo and Geof are tidying the flat. What efforts would each character make? Would one punch a cushion, while the other flicks away some dust? Experiment with the different efforts and decide which suit the characters best.

b Then experiment with using different efforts when each character makes their entrance.

Comedy

Littlewood used music-hall features, such as songs, dances and comedy. Helen and Jo's double-act banter; Geof's dance with a mop and bucket and Peter's drunken offstage falls all contribute to the play's comedy. There are also moments when a character will break from a scene to speak to the audience, thus breaking the fourth wall, such as at the play's end, when Helen says to the audience, 'I ask you, what would you do?'

TASK 17

Focus on the beginning of Act 2, Scene 2 and improvise a music-hall-style physical comedy scene between Geof and Jo. How can you use props along with exaggerated movement, near misses and falls to create an entertaining scene?

Symbols

Delaney uses several symbols to explore Jo's hopes and fears for the future, such as the flower bulbs she hides in a dark place, hoping to plant them later. Having something which might bloom in six months' time could represent her hope for the future. When the bulbs die, it might indicate the loss of her dreams. Other symbols could include their suitcases, which show how they are always on the move, the references to coffins and cemeteries and the children seen and heard outside the flat.

TASK 18

Focus on the flower bulbs, or another symbol for the play, and draw some sketches of how these could be used in the design of the play and what themes they might reinforce.

KEY TERM:

Laban: a type of movement analysis created by Rudolf Laban (1879–1958) which influenced modern dance and actors' training.

Key characters

Peter: Helen's younger boyfriend. He is a 'brash car salesman' who lost his eye when he was a private in the army. He pursues Helen and asks her to marry him.

Helen: the divorced, working-class, hard-drinking mother of Jo.

Jo (Josephine): a 17-year-old working-class girl with a talent for art, who becomes pregnant and leaves school.

Geof (Geoffrey): a gay art student who moves into the flat and looks after Jo.

Jimmie: a 22-year-old black sailor from Cardiff who has a brief relationship with Jo. He 'proposes to her', but leaves her.

TASK 19

Locate where in the play each character makes their first entrance. Experiment with how they might enter the scene and show their relationship with other characters. Consider what the audience's first impression of the character might be.

TASK 20

a Working with a partner, choose three characters to study more closely. Discuss your impressions of them.

b Look at the adjectives below and select at least three to describe each character. Explain why you have made those choices.

angry brave sensitive emotional romantic
intelligent calm silly careless young loyal
secretive drunk rude changeable comic thoughtless
loving unlucky sensible passionate weak strong
playful moody hopeful lecherous talented cruel
neglected lost greedy vulnerable helpful
sensual unpredictable reliable fickle

Interpretation of character

You will need to show how you can interpret a character. This means that you understand the character's motivations and goals, and the obstacles they face. In your interpretation, you might decide that a character is sympathetic, changeable, villainous, passive, intelligent, funny, emotional, heroic, or a combination. Then you must be able to use your vocal and physical skills to portray the character and create particular effects for the audience, such as tension, romance, surprise, anger, comedy, pity, tenderness or sorrow.

Answer the questions below to begin your interpretation of **Jimmie**.

FACTS:

A 22-year-old 'naval rating', from Cardiff, completing his national service as a 'male nurse in the Navy'. He was a nurse in a hospital and can 'sing and dance'. He is going away and won't return for at least six months when he next has leave. He carries a toy car and has brought a ring for Jo.

KEY SCENES IN THE PLAY:

Act 1, Scene 2

POSSIBLE VOCAL CHOICES:

- Would he speak with a dialect or accent?
- Are there times when he would speak softly and other times more loudly?
- When he is joking, will his tone or pitch change?
- What is the pace of his dialogue when he discusses marriage?
- How might he change his voice when he quotes Shakespeare?

EFFECT ON AUDIENCE:

- What first impression of Jimmie do you want the audience to have?
- Are there moments when you want the audience to be:
  - charmed by him
  - amused by him
  - critical of him?

POSSIBLE PHYSICAL CHOICES:

- How athletic and confident are his movements? How easy is it for him to swing Jo 'through the air'?
- How does he use the space when he proposes to Jo and gives her the ring?
- How might he react physically to how dirty Jo's flat is?
- How could he use eye contact and facial expressions to show Jo how attracted he is to her?

POSSIBLE COSTUME CHOICES:

- Will his costume indicate his job?
- Will he wear the same outfit for both scenes?
- Does he dress differently outside?

TASK 21

a Using these prompt questions, write two paragraphs of your interpretation of Jimmie.

b Then write similar questions for a contrasting character, such as Helen and answer them.

Download a printable version from Samples & Downloads at www.illuminatepublishing.com.

Performing choices

In Question 2, you will discuss in detail how you would perform a particular line as a given character. For example (in Act 1, Scene 1):

> You are performing the role of **Helen**.
>
> Describe how you would use your vocal and physical skills to perform the line below and explain the effects that you want to create.
>
> Helen: Everything is seen at its best in the dark – including me. I love it. Can't understand why you're so scared of it.

In my interpretation of Helen in this scene, she tries to make the best of her ill-judged and hasty decision to move into this flat. Although Helen is often seen as heartless, here she is trying to cheer up Jo. (1) As Helen, I will speak with a working-class Manchester dialect and have a low-pitched, slightly hoarse voice, as I have a cold. (2) I would stand casually, with my hand on my hip, and smile at Jo. (3) There would be a slight pause before I say 'even me' because I'm making a joke at my own expense about my age. (4) When Jo doesn't laugh, I would double-down on my enthusiasm, by opening my arms and declaring loudly, 'I love it!' (5) When that doesn't work, I will momentarily furrow my brow, wondering why Jo is so fearful. I will take Jo by the shoulders, make eye contact and say softly, 'Can't understand...' (6) This is a brief interlude where Helen shows her concern for Jo and the audience see a warmer and softer side of her character. (7)

1. Understanding of character and context of line
2. Chooses vocal skills appropriate for context
3. Describes physical skills of posture and facial expression (smile)
4. Use of pause and justification for it
5. Gesture and volume
6. Facial expression, gesture, eye contact and volume
7. Notes effect on audience

TIP

It is a good idea to write in the first person ('I') so you can fully imagine your own performance of the role. Do more than describe the vocal and physical skills you will use: also think about how your choices will add to the audience's understanding of the play, its characters and their relationships.

TASK 22

a Choose one line from the play spoken by each of the following characters:

- Jo
- Helen
- Geof
- Jimmie
- Peter.

Experiment with different ways of using vocal and physical skills for these lines.

b Answer the following question for each character's line:

> Describe how you would use your vocal and physical skills to perform your chosen line and explain the effects that you want to create.

c Check your work by marking or highlighting:

V for each vocal skill you mention

P for each physical skill

E for an effect on the audience.

Character revision sheet

SET PLAY 7:
A Taste of Honey by Shelagh Delaney
7

Below is a partly completed character revision sheet for **Geof**. Copy the grid and complete it.

Character and importance to the play	Geoffrey Ingram. Although not introduced to the audience until the second act, Geof is an important ally to Jo, who supports her while temporarily finding a home for himself. He is an art student and takes on domestic tasks like cleaning, shopping and sewing.
What do they want?	Geof wants to create a home for Jo, her baby and himself.
What obstacles do they face?	• Geof's sexuality means that they cannot be a conventional romantic couple. • He experiences prejudice. • Jo's unpredictable moods affect him. • Helen objects to him being in the flat.
What are their key scenes?	Act 2, Scene 1: Returning from the fairground and agreeing to stay with Jo. Act 2, Scene 1: They discuss Jo's pregnancy and feelings for her boyfriend. Act 2, Scene 1: Geof is looking after Jo and planning for the baby. Act 2, Scene 2: Geof reassures Jo about her father and they discuss love. Act 2, Scene 2: Helen puts pressure on Geof to leave.

How might they be costumed?	How might their hair and make-up by done?
Draw a simple sketch or write a description of costume. Consider: • colours • fabrics • shape and fit • personality, background and status.	Draw a simple sketch or write a description of it. Consider: • length, colour and style of hair • type of make-up, if any (colours; how it is appropriate for character, setting and period).

How might they use body language?	
• Posture • Gait • Facial expression	
How might they use their voice?	
• Emotional range (angry, sad, happy, irritated, desperate) • Pitch and volume (low or high; loud or soft) • Accent or other distinctive features	
Choose one important line and analyse how they might say it.	

TASK 23

Using the grid for guidance, create similar revision sheets for all the major characters: Jo, Helen, Peter and Jimmie.

Download a printable version from Samples & Downloads at www.illuminatepublishing.com.

Using the performance space and interaction with others

There are many opportunities to explore the space and to interact with other characters. You might think about, for example, the quiet, intimate scenes between Jo and Jimmie or Jo and Geof and how these contrast with scenes of Helen and Jo or Peter and Jo arguing.

When you are writing about performance space and interaction, make sure that you focus on the effects you wish to achieve for the audience.

▲ *Gemma Dobson and Stuart Thompson, National Theatre*

▲ *Rachel Botcha and Rebekah Brockman, Pearl Theatre Company*

TASK 24

Look at the photographs on the left and make notes on the use of performance space and interactions. Consider, for example:

- where on the stage actors are positioned
- use of proximity and levels
- gestures or moments when characters touch
- any reactions.

TASK 25

a Look closely at the short scene between Peter and Jo in Act 1, Scene 2. Note any actions required, such as movements, use of props, reactions or physical contact.

b Choose a stage configuration. Sketch this and mark where entrances and pieces of furniture will be.

c Decide the effects you want to achieve here, for example tension, comedy, conflict, insight into characters.

d How will you use the stage space to help with this? You could try the following interpretations:
- Jo flirts with Peter and playfully tries to provoke him
- Jo is furious with Peter and wants to drive him away
- Peter is trying to get close to Jo and win her over
- Peter tries to ignore Jo and treats her like a young child.

e Experiment with different reactions, such as facial expressions, eye contact, gestures and movements:
- How does Jo react to the chocolates? Will she eat them secretly or boldly?
- How will Peter react to Jo throwing the lid at him? Does he go to strike her? Does he rub where it hit him?
- How close are Peter and Jo when she attacks him? Does she use her fists or slap him? Where does she make contact?
- Where is Jo when she says 'You leave me alone'? What is her expression? Does she make eye contact?

f Try different ways of performing the scene then answer this question:

> You are performing the role of the **Peter**.
>
> Explain how you might use the performance space and interact with the actor playing Jo to show the audience **Peter's attitude towards Jo**.

TIP

There are many different ways of interpreting a scene. These are just a few ideas.

Answering a question about character interpretation

If you choose to answer Question 4, you will write about how you would use acting skills to interpret a character both in the extract provided and the play as a whole. An example of this sort of question might be:

> You are performing the role of **Jo**.
>
> Describe how you would use your acting skills to **interpret Jo's character**. Explain why your ideas are appropriate for:
>
> - this extract
> - the performance of your role in the play as a whole.

TASK 26

a Write a response to the question above, based on the scene between Jo and Peter in Task 25.

b Check that you have discussed:

- vocal skills
- physical skills
- the extract
- the rest of the play
- why your ideas are appropriate.

TASK 27

a Choose another scene in which Jo is featured. Use the spider diagrams below to prepare a response about her character.

b Repeat the exercise for the other characters in the play.

TIP

Consider if the character you are writing about is consistent throughout the play, or if they change and develop.

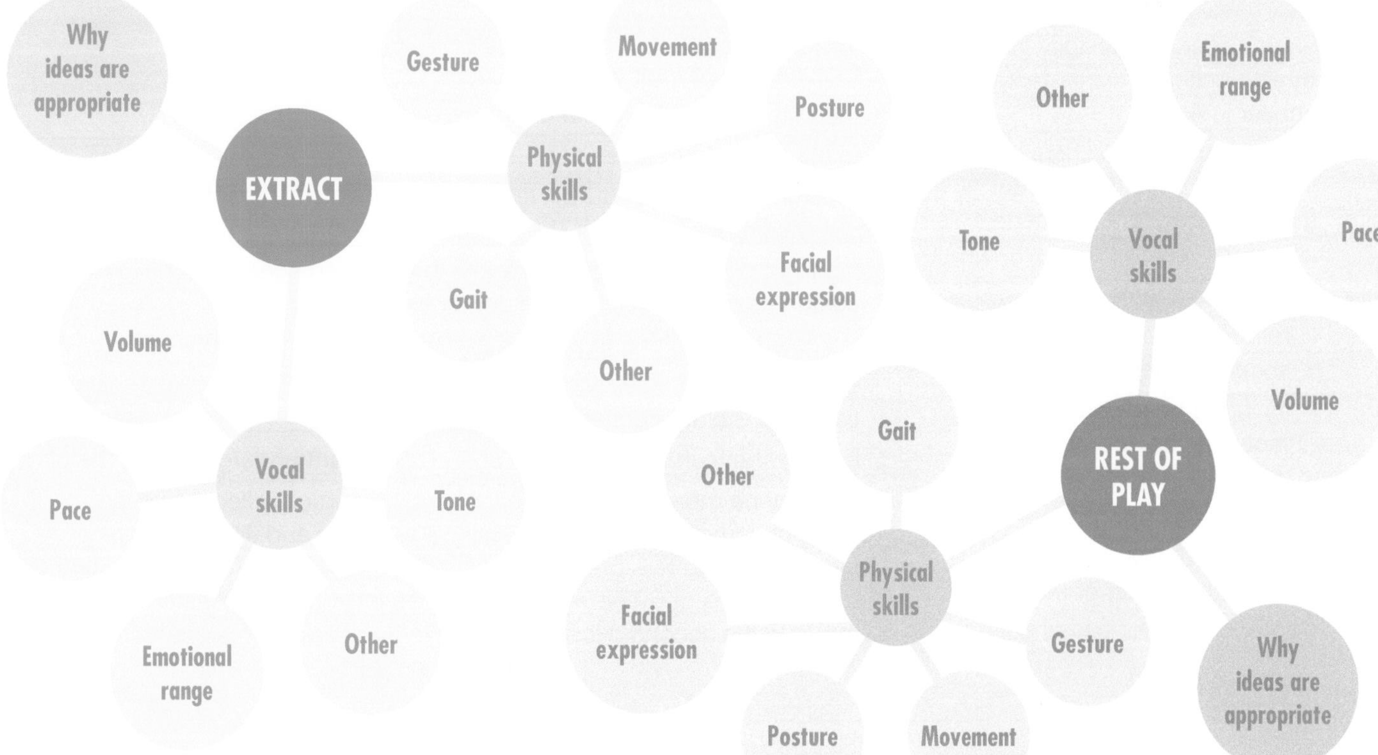

▲ *Jodie Prenger as Helen in the National Theatre production. Compared with Jo, she is glamorous, with false eyelashes, curled hair, and bright lips and nails. Do such costume and make-up choices suggest she is self-absorbed and vain, or lonely and in need of fun and distraction...? Think about design choices alongside the performer's expressions, gestures, attitude and use of props.*

Design choices

If you choose to answer Question 5, you will be thinking as a designer and commenting on one aspect of design. For example:

> You are a designer working on **one** aspect of design for this extract.
>
> Describe how you would use your design skills to create effects which **support the action**. Explain why your ideas are appropriate for:
>
> - this extract
> - your chosen design skill in the play as a whole.

You may choose to focus on set, costume, lighting or sound design. Whichever you choose, you must explain why your ideas are appropriate to the play as a whole. You might refer to the way in which:

- your design helps to show the action of the play and the nature of the characters
- your design for the extract is consistent with the requirements for the rest of the play (for example, in style, tone or conventions of the production)
- the technical aspects of your chosen specialism support your design ideas.

A Taste of Honey offers many opportunities for imagination, creativity and design flair.

Question 1 of the exam will focus on working-class Salford in the 1950s as the setting of the play. For Question 5, you may explore this context in a naturalistic way or use it in a more abstract or symbolic design. Whatever choices you make, they must be appropriate for the play and its themes.

Costume design

For costume design, you might consider:

- style, cut and fit
- colour, fabric, decorative features
- whether realistic or stylised
- condition (worn or new, neat or wrinkled, clean or stained)
- footwear, headwear and accessories
- the status or social role of character
- make-up and hairstyle.

As costume designer, you will also be responsible for practical choices about the fabrics and fit for the characters. You may want to:

- highlight differences and similarities between the characters (How could costumes contrast Helen and Jo, for example?)
- indicate the wealth and social class of the characters (How could costumes show who does and does not have money?)
- establish the different ages of the characters
- help to show changes that the characters might undergo during the play.

There may be moments when characters' costumes reflect their very specific circumstances, such as Helen's wedding and Jo's pregnancy. Consider if characters dress one way when they are in the flat and another if they are going out. The weather changes from winter in the first act to summer in the second. How might that influence what the characters wear?

TASK 28

a Sketch costume designs for **three** significant characters who appear in Act 1.

b Choose **one** of the characters from one scene. Write about their costume for that scene and in the rest of the play.

c Check that you have:
- referred to fabric, colours, shape, fit, condition
- included headwear and/or footwear, as appropriate
- considered make-up and hairstyle as appropriate
- explained how the costume helps the action of the extract
- considered the whole play.

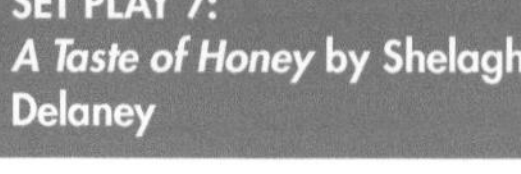

Set design

For set design, you might consider:

- staging configuration
- the location and atmosphere of the scene
- if there will be any levels, ramps or stairs
- entrances and exits
- any backdrops, flats or projections
- the colour palette you will use
- how materials, textures and shapes can help to create a suitable setting
- what props or set dressings are needed.

One of the challenges is to decide how realistic or artificial/stylised you want your set to be and how it will be used to best effect in the various scenes. You could use, for example:

- a naturalistic box set
- an abstract set which suggests the world outside the flat or themes you wish to emphasise
- technology, such as projections or a revolve.

You might also want to consider how your set could enhance the music sequences or audience interaction. One production replaced the first row of seats in the auditorium with broken sofas to bring the audience more fully into the world of the play.

TASK 29

a Create a design for a key scene of the play.

b Write a paragraph explaining its effect on the audience. Consider:
- dominant colours and textures
- positioning of important set items or props
- levels
- materials
- the atmosphere you want to create
- how the set supports the action of the play.

TASK 30

Look at the sketch of a theatre in the round. Choose another scene from the play and design a set for it in this configuration.

TASK 31

Choose a significant prop or piece of scenery from the play. Sketch several ideas of how it could be designed. Some notable props are:

- tea-making equipment
- suitcases
- balloons
- flowers
- groceries
- the baby's gown
- the mop.

Lighting design

When designing lighting, you might consider how to create:

- time of day and season
- atmosphere
- the setting, action and characters of a scene (such as a follow spot to show a character's isolation or backlighting to emphasise silhouettes)
- a focus on a particular moment.

Some of your lighting tools are:

- colours
- angles and intensity
- light from onstage sources (table lamps, for example)
- use of shadow and silhouette
- special effects
- transitions, blackouts or fades.

The action of the play covers more than nine months, from the rainy day when Helen and Jo move into the flat, followed by the Christmas when Jo becomes pregnant, then up to very near her delivery date. There are scenes which take place in light and others in near darkness; some in winter and others summer; many inside and at least one outside.

TASK 32

Below are some lighting effects a student might wish to create. Identify where in the play they might be used and how they could be created.

TASK 33

Choose two contrasting scenes from the play and make notes on how lighting could help to convey the action of the scenes and the necessary atmospheres.

A I want to show that this scene is taking place at night in a dark flat.

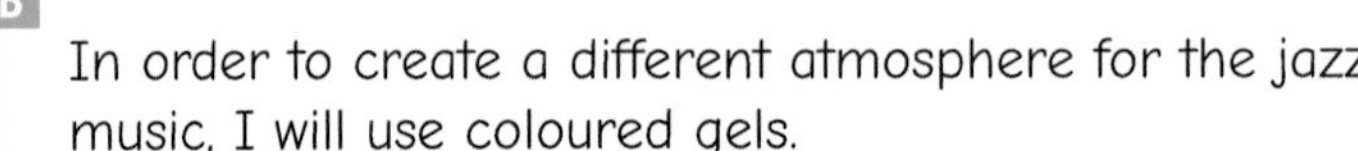

B In order to create a different atmosphere for the jazz music, I will use coloured gels.

C To emphasise Jo's isolation, I will use a slow fade.

D To capture the period, I will use practical lamps and lighting fixtures that would be seen in the 1950s.

E Shadows will suggest how cold and empty the flat is.

F Lighting design is very important to show the passage of time.

G I want to highlight the urban location and the grubbiness of the flat.

Sound design

When designing sound for *A Taste of Honey*, you should consider how to:

- create atmosphere
- add to the action and emotion of a scene
- contribute to the setting and style of the play
- fulfil the practical needs of the script.

Some choices you can make involve the use of:

- live or recorded sound
- volume/amplification (use of microphones and speakers)
- naturalistic or symbolic sound
- music.

Some productions of *A Taste of Honey* use sound in adventurous ways, such as having an onstage DJ playing music or commissioning specially composed songs. A production might create a nightclub atmosphere for the show and have the actors singing into microphones. Sound can also be used in an abstract way to show the tension between the characters or their emotional states.

TASK 34

Below are some sound effects which could occur in the play. Identify when they might be used and how they could be created:

- jazz music
- rain
- a kettle whistling
- a door slamming
- transition music
- wedding bells
- 'here comes the bride' fanfare
- fairground music
- tugboat hoots
- children playing and singing
- an offstage crash
- a siren.

TASK 35

Decide if you are retaining the 1950s jazz music suggested in the play or choosing other appropriate music. Consider the different moods in the play, including romantic, violent, comic and dramatic, and research pieces of music to underscore at least **four** different moments.

TASK 36

a Choose two contrasting scenes from the play and describe what effects you wish to create for the audience, such as increasing tension, suggesting romance or provoking sorrow.

b Write a detailed explanation of how your sound design will create these effects. Consider:

- when the sound/music will start and end
- its volume
- how it will be created (live, recorded, onstage or off)
- if it will fade in and out or snap on and off
- what direction the sound will come from (position of speakers, and so on).

TIP

Remember that you can only take clean (unannotated) copies of the script into the exam.

WHAT HAVE I LEARNED?

CHOICE OF SEVEN PLAYS

VOCAL SKILLS
- Accent
- Pace
- Pause
- Emotional range
- Pitch
- Intonation
- Inflection

DESIGN
- Costume
- Lighting
- Sound
- Set

PHYSICAL SKILLS
- Body language
- Posture
- Gesture
- Facial expression
- Eye contact
- Movement

CONTEXT
- Location
- Mood
- Atmosphere
- Time
- Period

USE OF PERFORMANCE SPACE
- Interaction with others
- Interpreting character
- Creating effects for audience

EXAM
- Everyone answers Questions 1, 2 and 3
- THEN Choose Question 4 (Performance) OR Question 5 (Design)

CHECK YOUR LEARNING

If you are uncertain of the meaning of any of the terms above, go back and revise.

Use this summary as a basis for your own checklist of what you have learned: Samples & Downloads at www.illuminatepublishing.com.

SECTION C

LIVE THEATRE PRODUCTION

THE SPECIFICATION SAYS...

- Students must learn how to analyse and evaluate the work of live theatre makers (performers and/or designers).
  - How the play has been interpreted in the production seen and what messages the company might be trying to communicate.
  - The skills demonstrated by the performers and how successfully meaning was communicated to the audience by the performer.
  - The design skills demonstrated in the production and how successfully meaning was communicated to the audience through design.

ASSESSMENT FOCUS

AO3: Demonstrate knowledge and understanding of how drama and theatre is developed and performed.

AO4: Analyse and evaluate the work of others.

TIP

The play for Section C **must not** be the same play as the one you studied for Section B.

TIP

You will never be asked to retell the plot of the play you see. You will need to analyse the production, **not** the story.

KEY TERM:

Evaluate: to judge or form an opinion of something, such as explaining what effect was created and how successful it was.

For Section C of the exam, you will be asked to answer one of three questions based on a live or digital theatre production you have seen.

To prepare for this question you will:

- view a production of live or digital theatre
- make notes on different performance and design elements
- analyse how the performers' acting skills or designer's choices helped to communicate the characters, action and style of the play to the audience.

What to look for in a live theatre production

Usually, when people go to the theatre they go for one reason: to be entertained. They may not break down the different elements of the play that made them laugh, cry or gasp in surprise. They simply know if they were interested in what they saw and if, in their opinion, it 'worked'. As a student of drama, you must learn to separate the different elements of the production and then **evaluate** to what extent they contributed to the success of the performance.

One of the exciting aspects of going to the theatre is that, although the audience is experiencing the event together, everyone's reaction to it will be slightly different. You only need to read theatre reviews to realise that even professional theatre-goers disagree on the quality of what they saw. Many things can influence your perception of a play, including:

- how familiar you are with the play
- if the content of the play is relevant or of interest to you
- if you know about the actors in the play
- how much people around you are enjoying the play.

For Section C, regardless of how much you enjoyed the play, you must be able to show that you have understood the contribution of the actors or designers, and that you can analyse and evaluate their work.

Audiences are influenced by a variety of production elements, including the actors and design.

Production elements

This mind map gives you an idea of the different elements you should be analysing. You can use it for the basis of your notes for any show you see. Add more legs to the mindmap to incorporate your ideas.

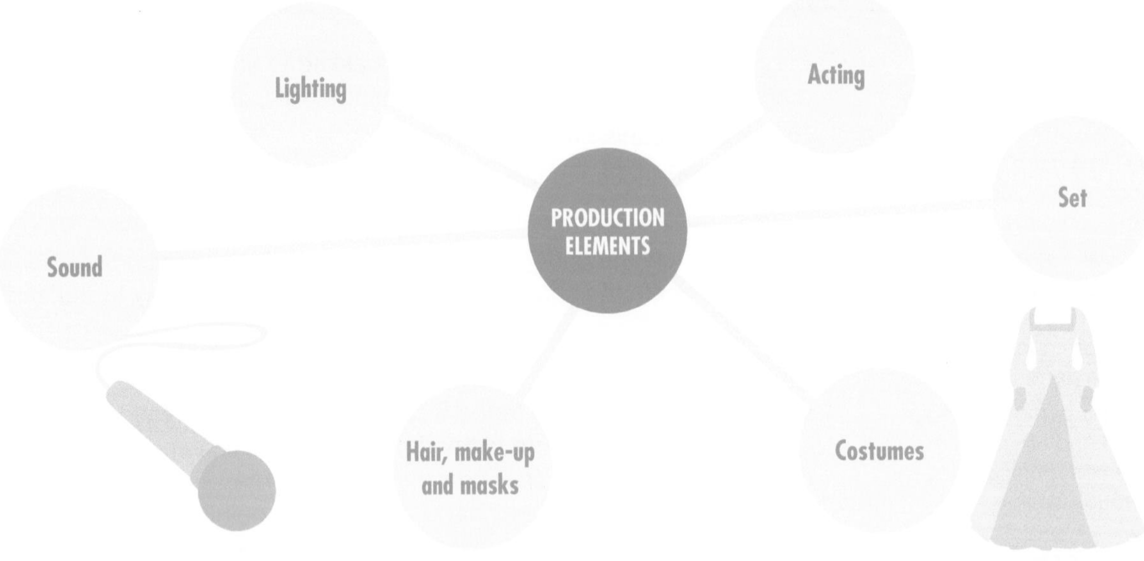

TIP

Your area of focus may either be on performance or design.

In order to write with insight about the production, it will help if you are familiar with:

- the plot and characters
- the features of the style/genre of the production
- the context of the play/production.

The best responses will come from students who have developed an understanding of the play and production. Some ways of doing this include:

- reading reviews (some people prefer to read these after seeing the play, so that their own opinions are not influenced in advance, while others prefer to read them beforehand so that they can look out for particular moments when watching the performance)
- reading interviews with the performers or creative team, such as the director or designers
- finding and studying production photographs.

All of these activities will help you to be a more critically aware audience member.

KEY TERMS:

Performance conventions: techniques used in a particular type of performance, such as soliloquies in Shakespeare or direct address in an epic play.

Soliloquy: a speech when a character is alone onstage.

Aside: when a character breaks out of a scene to speak briefly to the audience.

Writing about performers

Typically, you will be asked to evaluate one or more actors' use of voice and physical skills**,** use of space and if they created convincing characters. Depending on the style of the play, you may observe different **performance conventions**, such as: direct address, when they speak directly to the audience; audience interaction, when they involve the audience in the production; or choral speech, when the performers speak together as a group. Different periods and types of plays use different conventions. For example, in Shakespearean plays, you may notice conventions such as **soliloquies**, when a character speaks alone onstage, or **asides**, when they address a remark to the audience before returning to the scene.

Performers' vocal interpretations

Performers' vocal interpretation of character, such as:

- accent
- intonation
- pitch
- volume
- timing
- pace
- delivery of lines
- phrasing
- emotional range.

Actors are trained to use their voices. On a very basic level, an actor must have the skill to project their voice at an appropriate volume and to **enunciate** clearly enough so that they can be heard and understood by all the audience, no matter how large the theatre is. But, beyond that, their voices are essential for expressing the play's characters and actions.

KEY TERM:

Enunciate: to pronounce or articulate words.

Accents

The use of accents conveys many aspects of their character's background, such as:

- education
- where they were brought up
- social class
- occupation.

When an actor is using an accent, consider why this choice was made:

- Does the accent say something about where the character is from?
- Does it suggest something about the period or setting of the play?
- Does it give an indication of the character's education or attitudes?

But accents are only one small part of an actor's job. They must also use their voice to show feelings and to create effects such as tension or comedy. Actors achieve effects through many different uses of their voices and there is no easy formula where you can simply say, 'He spoke loudly, so he was powerful' or 'She spoke quickly so she was funny.' However, it is worth beginning to break down the ways the actors you hear use their voices.

THEATRE MAKER ADVICE

Alex Harland, performer

I recently saw Glenda Jackson playing King Lear at the Old Vic. It's a tricky part for any actor to play, and I have often seen actors resort to shouting a lot as they attempt to portray Lear's frustration and descent into madness. In Glenda Jackson's performance, she managed to avoid this whilst encapsulating Lear's growing impotence. So good was her performance that the fact she was playing what is traditionally a male role ceased to be relevant.

Examples and effects of vocal skills

TASK 1

Use the chart on the following page to identify and analyse the vocal skills you observe, although there are, of course, many possible variations. You will not hear all of these examples, but the prompts should help you consider vocal skills in detail. After noting your observations, think about the effects achieved. If someone shouts, for example, the effect might be to convey authority or anger. If someone speaks with a high-pitched voice, they could be showing youthfulness or fear. If someone speaks slowly, they might be uncertain or creating tension.

VOCAL SKILLS	EXAMPLES	POSSIBLE EFFECTS
Volume	**1** Speaks loudly/shouts	
	2 Speaks softly/whispers	
	3 Voice suddenly gets louder or softer	
Pitch	**1** Uses higher vocal **register**	
	2 Uses lower vocal register	
	3 Changes pitch – such as suddenly going up or down at the end of a line	
	4 Changes pitch to imitate another character	
Timing/pace	**1** Speaks slowly	
	2 Speaks quickly	
	3 Pauses at a particular moment	
	4 Speaks at a different or the same tempo as another character	
Intonation	**1** Speaks warmly or tenderly	
	2 Speaks sharply or aggressively	
	3 Emphasises certain words	
Phrasing	**1** Hesitates at the beginning of a line or mid-line	
	2 Emphasises the verse of a line	
	3 Makes the poetry of a line clear and attractive	
	4 Speaks informally/casually 'throwing lines away'	
Emotional range	**1** Voice breaks/sobs	
	2 Giggles or laughs while speaking	
	3 Speaks with control (such as attempting to control anger or sorrow)	
	4 Speaks romantically	
	5 Screams	

Download a printable version from Samples & Downloads at www.illuminatepublishing.com.

TASK 2

Read the following responses to performances and decide if the actors, through their use of vocal skills, have created a serious or a comic effect.

KEY TERM:

Register: the vocal range of the voice (upper, middle or lower registers); the variety of tones of voice.

The actor's voice suddenly broke and there was a long pause as if he was unable to continue. After a second, he softly said, 'She was my daughter.' He emphasised the words 'was' showing that was in the past and said 'daughter' tenderly making it clear that his daughter was no longer alive. Behind him, the chorus of women began a gentle wailing sound that gradually increased in volume until it was over-powering.

The two actors worked in a tight partnership. Their dialogue consisted of a series of rapid-fire exchanges. The actor playing Rob used his lower register and had a booming voice, while Jenny's voice was higher pitched and more cutting. Their use of their voices in the trial scene was very confident and the characters acted as if they were experienced court officials, but when they suddenly paused and looked blankly at each other and then at the audience, it was clear that they were talking nonsense. Together they asked persistent, forceful questions of the defendant, but their mispronunciation of longer words showed how silly they were. Their pompous attitude was punctured by the witness's simple answer, 'I don't know.'

TASK 3

Re-read the responses on the previous page. Note examples of actors using pitch, volume, timing, pace, pause and emotional phrasing to achieve either a comic effect or a dramatic effect.

Delivery of lines

Delivery of lines simply means how an actor says their lines and conveys their meaning. One way of writing about vocal skills is to discuss how certain lines were said (or delivered) by the actors and the effect on the audience. If you have the opportunity to read the play beforehand, you may want to note a few lines that you want to listen out for in particular, in order to note how they are delivered. On the other hand, while you are watching the play certain lines may stand out. Try to note your impressions of these as soon as you can as it is easy to forget after even a very short passage of time.

TIP

When writing about physical actions, don't just note what the actions are, but consider how they help to tell the story. For example, instead of just writing 'He has his arm around her waist' you could write, 'He tries to restrain her by protectively putting his arm around her waist.'

KEY TERM:

Describe: to write what you saw, heard or experienced.

Performers' physical interpretation

Performers' physical interpretation of character, such as:

build age height facial features movement postures facial expression gesture

The type of physical skills you see will depend in part on the style of play you are viewing. You may be seeing a stylised piece that makes demands on the actor's physical skills. They may be required to mime, create physical theatre or differentiate between a range of characters when using multi-role. On the other hand, a more naturalistic production may offer more subtle physical opportunities, where actors can express emotions by something as small as a shrug, a change in posture or a raised eyebrow.

Many directors feel that, before an actor speaks, a large part of their job is done simply by how they look and their stage presence.

▲ People, Places, Things, *National Theatre, 2016*

TASK 4

Think of a line you have seen delivered memorably from a play or film and write in as much detail as you can about how it was delivered and what the effect was.

TASK 5

Look at the photographs on the right and on the following page and try to **describe** the characters' physical stage presence and the physical interaction between them. Think of as many descriptive words as you can for each example.

▲ The Curious Incident of the Dog in the Night-Time, *2016*

The Chronicles of Kalki, *Company One, 2015*

Zastrozzi, *Williamstown Theatre Festival*

Song for a Future Generation, *Williamstown Theatre Festival*

TASK 6

Copy and complete the chart below to suggest some possible effects of performers' physical interpretation of characters in the performance you see (there are, of course, many others you might see, so this list can be extended and altered to suit the production you view).

PHYSICAL INTERPRETATION: Movement

POSSIBLE EXAMPLES:	EFFECTS:
Gait/way of walking: 1 Graceful 2 Limp/stagger 3 Awkward 4 Hurried 5 Slow/shuffling	

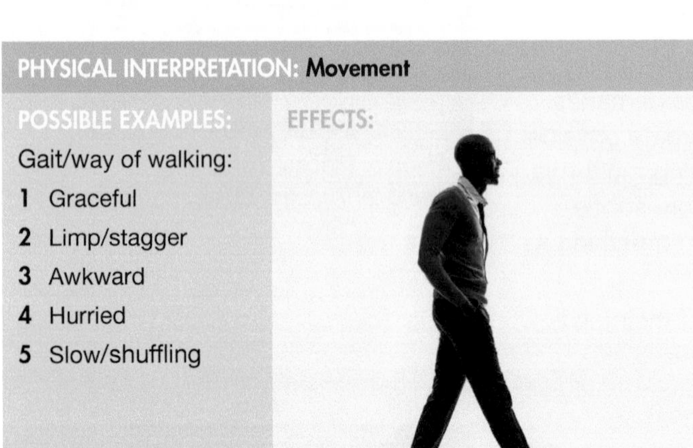

PHYSICAL INTERPRETATION: Posture

POSSIBLE EXAMPLES:	EFFECTS:
1 Upright 2 Hunched 3 Stiff 4 Off-centre/crooked	

PHYSICAL INTERPRETATION: Gestures

POSSIBLE EXAMPLES:	EFFECTS:
1 Pointing 2 Outstretched arms 3 Wringing hands 4 Fist	

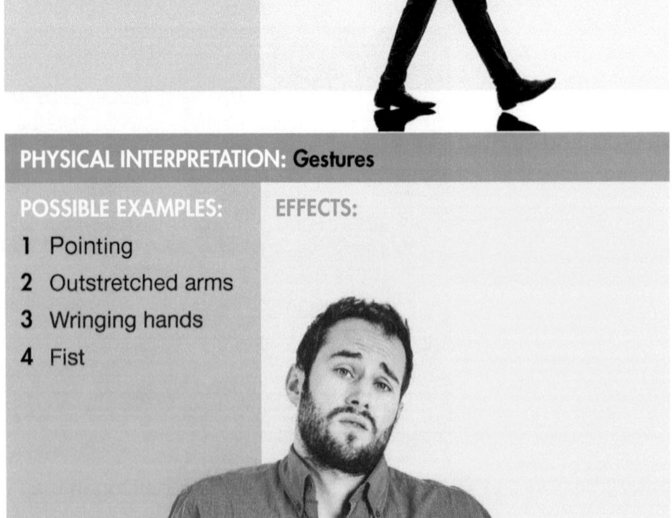

PHYSICAL INTERPRETATION: Facial expression

POSSIBLE EXAMPLES:	EFFECTS:
1 Smiling 2 Pleading 3 Sad 4 Tense 5 Shocked	

Download a printable version from Samples & Downloads at www.illuminatepublishing.com.

Evaluating an actor's performance

Use the figure and questions below to note details of an actor's performance you are evaluating.

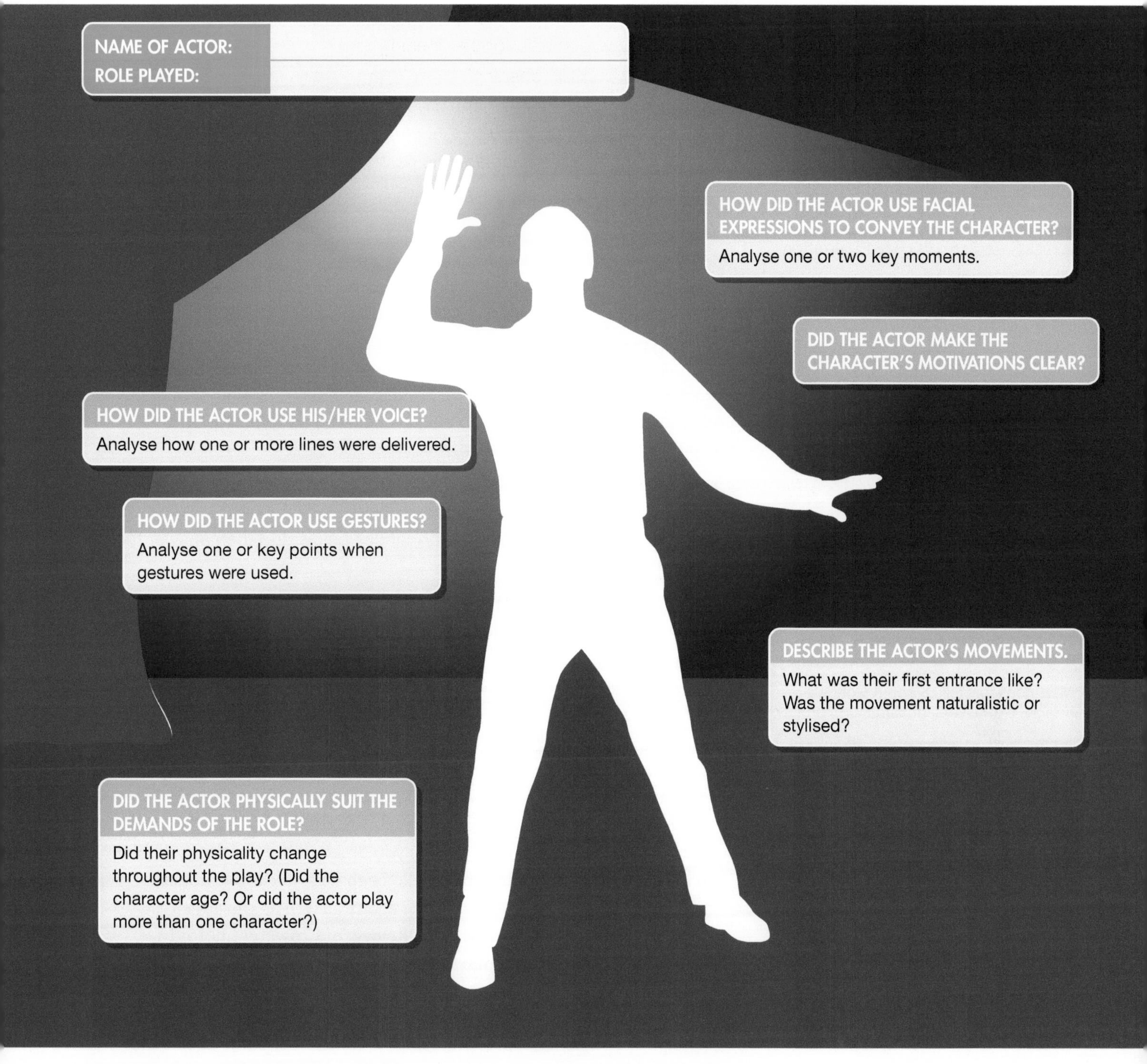

NAME OF ACTOR:

ROLE PLAYED:

HOW DID THE ACTOR USE FACIAL EXPRESSIONS TO CONVEY THE CHARACTER?

Analyse one or two key moments.

DID THE ACTOR MAKE THE CHARACTER'S MOTIVATIONS CLEAR?

HOW DID THE ACTOR USE HIS/HER VOICE?

Analyse how one or more lines were delivered.

HOW DID THE ACTOR USE GESTURES?

Analyse one or key points when gestures were used.

DESCRIBE THE ACTOR'S MOVEMENTS.

What was their first entrance like? Was the movement naturalistic or stylised?

DID THE ACTOR PHYSICALLY SUIT THE DEMANDS OF THE ROLE?

Did their physicality change throughout the play? (Did the character age? Or did the actor play more than one character?)

Write at least three sentences summing up your impression of how effective this actor was in meeting the demands of portraying a character in this production.

TIP

Write about the acting as someone who is knowledgeable about theatre and not as a fan. You need to weigh up how successful specific elements of the performance were, using the correct terminology.

Download a printable version from Samples & Downloads at www.illuminatepublishing.com.

Analysis and evaluation of a performance

In the exam, you won't be asked to simply **describe** what you saw, you must also **analyse** and **evaluate** it. Many students find it difficult to tell the difference between these three skills.

1 Description
2 Analysis
3 Evaluation

Example:

In Act 1, the actor playing Chris was **tall and thin**, and walked in a **hesitant, stooping** way. 1 **Whenever a new character appeared onstage**, his **gestures** would become more jagged and **vocally** he showed his uncertainty by **stuttering, particularly when Sally appeared**, which **emphasised** how tongue-tied he was in her presence. 2 This **worked well** as it showed his transformation in Act 2, when he threw off his previous shyness and **convincingly** became the dashing hero of Sally's fantasies. 3

Evaluating theatre is something that professional theatre critics do every day. Their responses are not exactly like those you will be writing for your examination, as they will be writing about many different elements of a production and they often aim to entertain as well as to evaluate, but reading their work can provide an inspiration for your own writing.

TASK 7

Choose an actor whose work you have enjoyed and write a paragraph evaluating how they used their acting skills to convincingly create a character.

TASK 8

Read the excerpts of actors' performances below and then answer the questions in the margin.

Still, it is Gough who is the major pull. She comes on – snorting, smoking, eyes so screwed up they barely function – 1 looking as if she has been badly assembled from an Ikea kit. Caught between wrath and terror, she seems to rear away even as she stoops forward. 2 ('Review of Denise Gough in People, Places & Things' by Susannah Clapp, 6 September 2015, *The Observer*)

1 What does this tell us about Gough's use of facial expression, gestures and props?

2 What does this tell us about her use of physical actions and performance space?

Delivering the verse with a warm expressiveness, Ejiofor's magnificent, exotic-accented Othello 3 exudes a calm charisma and has the kind of spiritual presence that would make you dread doing anything shabby in his presence. Never has an Othello been less quick to jealousy, nor has more movingly revealed the agony as well as the anger in his mistaken sense of betrayal. 4 ('Review of Chiwetel Ejiofor in First Night: Othello, Donmar Warehouse, London' by Paul Taylor, 4 December 2007, *The Independent*)

3 What does this tell us about Ejiofor's speaking voice and use of accent?

4 What do you learn about Ejiofor's characterisation and portrayal of emotions from this?

It helps of course that at 17, Radcliffe is exactly the same age as the character he is playing, and he superbly lays bare the sheer rawness of youth, the sudden mood swings of adolescence, and that intense unforgettable feeling that you are in a hostile world all on your own 5 ... The actor keeps turning the emotion on a sixpence, switching from sullen anger to raw vulnerability, or from terrible pain to a sudden childlike innocence and charm. 6 ('Review of Daniel Radcliffe in Equus' by Charles Spencer, 28 February 2007, *The Telegraph*)

5 What does this tell us about Radcliffe's believability in playing this role in terms of conveying the character's youth?

6 From this description how effective do you think Radcliffe's performance was? Pick out key words and explain whether this gives you a positive or negative impression of the performance.

A critical evaluation of an actor's performance

The examples on the previous page were all of reviewers giving a positive evaluation of a performance they have seen. However, you may see a performance in which an actor gives, in your opinion, a disappointing performance. You may wish to write about this, but make sure that you support your opinion with evidence from the performance you saw. Here are two critical evaluations of actors' performances.

From the moment the actor playing Hamlet walked onstage I suspected he wouldn't be up to the job. (1) He didn't look like a Hamlet to me – he was far too old. (2) The costumes were very old-fashioned and middle-aged. (3) He looked the same as his father's ghost! Also he was really boring in all of his long speeches. (4) I don't think I was the only one in the audience who was happy rather than sad when he died at the end. (5)

1. Very informal
2. Could make a more informed statement by explaining how old Hamlet should appear to be
3. Moves away from acting and instead criticises costumes
4. Beware of saying something is 'boring' – this may suggest more a lack of effort from you in trying to engage with and understand the play. If it is boring, explain why. His voice? Actions?
5. Makes a general point without any supporting evidence

Unlike Ophelia, the actor playing Hamlet was less successful in convincing the audience that he was a young person in mental torment. (1) Although there were some believable interactions between him and other characters, particularly in the play scene, when he would alternate between playful comments and deeply distressing ones, (2) elsewhere he struggled with the verse-speaking. (3) He took the 'O, what a rogue and peasant slave am I' soliloquy at such a fast pace and had such poor diction, he was difficult to understand, making it impossible to sympathise with him. (4) In scenes with Polonius, his attempts at humour seemed forced, with exaggerated use of gestures and facial expressions. (5) However, in the closet scene with Gertrude, and particularly, the final fight, he seemed to find a depth of emotion that had previously evaded him and the entire audience froze when they saw in his tormented expressions and rigid body the dreadful effects of the poisoned sword. (6)

1. Compares his performance to another actor's in the play, which suggests evaluation and questions the believability of an aspect of the performance
2. Mentions interaction and gives an example, although this could be more detailed
3. Evaluates a vocal skill (speaking verse)
4. Chooses a particular scene and gives detailed comments on vocal skills and effect
5. Provides examples, locating a particular scene and notes gestures and facial expressions, although these could be more detailed
6. Chooses a clear example and explains effect achieved

TASK 9

Write a short paragraph evaluating a performance that you thought could have been improved and remember to give clear examples from the performance and focus on the acting skills.

TIP

It is important to focus your evaluation on the actors' performance skills. In most cases, they are not responsible for the costume they are wearing or the script they are speaking.

KEY TERM:

Diction: how clearly and precisely words are spoken.

Evaluating design

Analysing the performance space

As soon as you take your seat in the auditorium, you will begin forming impressions of the play you are about to see. For example, you might note the following:

- What the relationship is between the audience and the stage. Is the audience close to the stage or far away?
- Is it an end on or proscenium stage where everyone looks at the stage from the same direction, or is it a traverse, thrust or in the round stage where views may differ, or is it a promenade production where the audience may stand and follow the performers?
- What is the shape and size of the stage and how might that influence the type of performance you are going to see?
- Is there a stage curtain hiding the set or is the set on view before the play begins?
- If you can see the set, where are the entrances and exits? What else do you notice about it?
- Can you tell if the actors enter from a backstage doorway or will they enter through the audience?

From the opening moments of the production you will be influenced by elements of the design. From the design you may learn the:

- period (present-day? a period from the past? the future?)
- style (naturalistic? stylised? abstract? comic? epic? storytelling?)
- mood/atmosphere (mysterious? humorous? tense? playful?)
- staging possibilities (levels? entrances? large acting space?)
- background or occupations of the characters (a working-class household? a city office? a police station?).

TIP

Try to find production photographs from the show you have seen to help you analyse design features. These are often available online, in programmes or in reviews.

▲ Dracula

▲ What It's Like When Two Geeks Love Each Other

TASK 10

Look at the production photographs above and then write a few sentences explaining what you learn about the play and its design. You might begin:

From the first image, I can tell that this play is ...

Remember to include what you notice about the:

- possible period of the play
- type of costumes
- set
- lighting
- possible style of performance.

TIP

Notice the different stage configurations used in these two designs. One is an end on stage in an outdoor space; the other is a traverse stage in a small indoor space. How might the type of theatre affect the design?

Use the Live theatre evaluation sheet to make notes on the design of the production you see: Samples & Downloads at www.illuminatepublishing.com.

Analysing and evaluating costumes, hair and make-up

The use of costumes, hair and make-up can transform an actor. When analysing and evaluating these elements of a production, consider:

- if the use of costume is to establish period or setting
- whether there are costume changes, especially if this suggests a transformation of a character, for example from poor to rich or young to old
- if the choices are naturalistic or stylised
- how the choice of colours, fabrics and textures create effects
- if hairstyles suggest a period, style or character
- if make-up is naturalistic or stylised
- if the make-up is subtle or has special effects, such as the use of **prosthetics**
- if a mask contributes to characterisation or mood.

Use the figure on this page to note the costume, hair and make-up of the characters in the play you see.

Is hair worn up or down? Is it long or short? Does it change at any point? What does it suggest about the character?

Is the make-up distinctive in any way? Is it used to show age? To show character or style? Is it natural or exaggerated/fantastical?

What is the silhouette of the costume? Is anything distinctive about the length or fit of the costume? What colours and fabrics are used?

Are there any notable accessories such as hats, shawls, ties or handbags?

What footwear is worn? Does this suggest an occupation, period or character trait?

KEY TERMS:

Prosthetics: make-up that uses moulds and sculptural techniques to create special effects, such as scars or a false nose.

Silhouette: the outline or shape created by a costume on a figure.

Download a printable version from Samples & Downloads at www.illuminatepublishing.com.

▶ See pages 267–268 for more information.

Sample student responses writing about costumes

TASK 11

Read the student responses to the following question about the costumes in the production they saw. Rate them 1 to 3 (1 being the best) and then explain why.

> Describe how costumes were used to help create the style of the production. Analyse and evaluate how successful the costumes were in helping to communicate the style of the production to the audience.

Which response was the best at:

- describing details of the costumes
- analysing how the costumes helped to establish the style and period of the play
- evaluating how effective they were?

TIP

If the production takes place in a certain period, you might research that period to make sure you get the terminology correct, such as 'singlets' or 'drop-waist' in the examples on this page.

CHALLENGE

Research the costume and set designers of the production you saw (some designers do both, while others specialise in one or the other). Often designers have websites or other online sources you can access, which will have examples of their work. Some contemporary theatre designers to explore include Tim Shortall (whose advice is found in this book), Alison Chitty, Nick Omerod, Miriam Buether, Tom Scutt, Rob Howell and Es Devlin.

A

The designer of the costumes for Chariots of Fire at the Hampstead Theatre, Michael Howells, created the 1920s period in a naturalistic style through his clever use of fabric and colours. The runners wore outfits very different from contemporary exercise gear. Instead of lycra, they wore simple cotton off-white shorts and singlets. I felt this made them look very vulnerable, almost as if their differences were stripped away when they ran, while also establishing the period setting. When they weren't running, the differences between the characters were highlighted: the formal black dinner jacket that Harold Abrahams wore in the dining scenes contrasted with the rough woven brown country jacket and trousers of Eric Liddell. The fit and styling of Abraham's dinner jacket, in particular, gave him a long silhouette and emphasised his status.

B

One of the themes of the play is social class and the contrasting personalities of the two main runners. One, Harold Abrahams, came from a wealthy, ambitious background and was often shown wearing dinner jackets, a white silk scarf casually hanging around the neck. The other, Eric Liddell, was the very religious son of a Scottish missionary. He was shown in rougher brown clothes. However, both men were dressed similarly when they ran. Liddell's sister wore a simple drop-waist dress.

C

The runners' clothes looked almost comic to me. There was one scene where Abrahams was stripped down to just a pair of shorts and a sleeveless T-shirt while his trainer and a man who seemed to be a butler in a waistcoat looked on. There was also his girlfriend who wore a 1920s style hat and a long dress. Her prettiest dress was the one she wore in the dining scene.

Analysing and evaluating sets

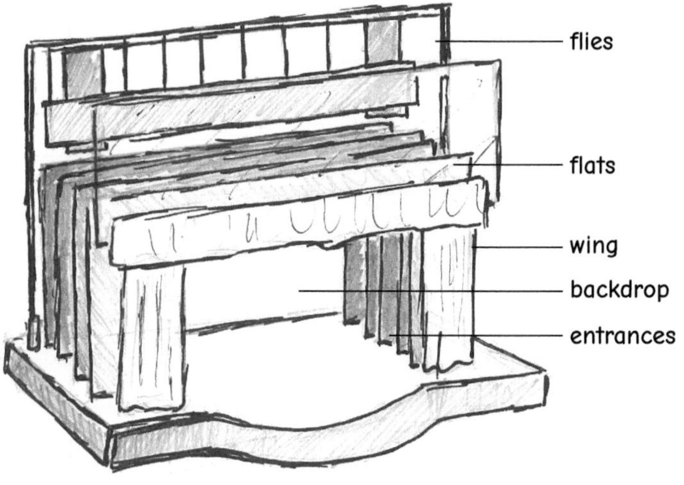

There are many different sorts of sets that designers might be hired to design. The production might be a small, touring production of a naturalistic play or a large West End musical with many special effects. Whatever the production, there are some very basic common elements, such as:

- entrances/exits
- acting areas
- colours/textures to suggest a mood/location.

Writing about sets

Naturalistic

You watch a performance that is highly naturalistic. Some sets have so much believable detail that it is as if you have walked into someone's front room. These sets are sometimes in the style of box sets where you have three walls with doors and windows realistically presented.

Stylised

Stylised sets may have as much detail as a naturalistic set, but their goal is not to replicate a believable place, but to suggest a setting without representing it exactly. For example, the set may not have walls or may be angled or proportioned in an unusual way. It may have symbolic features, where the set represents an idea from the play.

Minimalistic

Minimalistic sets are simple, basic sets with little stage furniture and only basic backgrounds. They may be as simple as a black stage with a single light overhead.

Sets may also combine naturalistic, stylised and minimalistic elements.

A naturalistic box set with period furniture in June Moon

A stylised set with exaggerated use of colour in Shockheaded Peter

A minimalistic set with a black background and simple painted stage in Take the Car

Set design terminology

Some of the technical elements you may look for in a set design include:

Cyclorama: a large piece of stretched fabric upon which lights or images can be projected.

Scrim: a piece of gauze that is used as a screen. Depending on how it is lit, it can either be transparent or opaque.

Floor covering: what is placed on the floor of the stage. This could range from linoleum to sand; carpet to wood chips. There may be a design painted on the floor or images projected onto it.

In addition to the set itself, consider how it is used. For example:

- Are there set changes? If so, how are they handled? Do trucks bring on new scenery? Is there a **revolve**? Or does one set represent many things?
- Are there different levels to the set?
- How do the actors enter and exit the stage?

KEY TERM:

Revolve: a large turntable device that can be turned to reveal a different setting.

For more information about sets go to pages 260–264.

Useful terms

Following are some useful terms to use when analysing sets:

Backdrop: a large painted cloth hung as part of the scenery.

Drapes: curtains or other hanging fabric.

Flat: a piece of scenery mounted on a frame.

Furnishings: furniture on the set, such as chairs, cushions, tables.

Multimedia: film or other media technology used in a live theatre production.

Projection: a film or still image used to form a theatrical backdrop.

Set dressings: items on the set not actually used as props, but that create detail and interest in it, such as vases or framed paintings on a wall.

Truck: a platform on wheels upon which scenery can be mounted and moved.

Analysing sets checklist

Ask yourself the following questions when analysing sets:

- ✓ Is there one set that incorporates all the action or several?
- ✓ Are there a few complete set changes, many minimal set changes or no set changes at all? Do the actors complete the set changes or backstage crew?
- ✓ Does the action take place on one level or several levels?
- ✓ What are the main colours used in the set? Do they suggest a certain mood or theme (for example, red for danger or passion; white for purity or innocence)?
- ✓ Does the set help to establish the location and period?
- ✓ Does the set tell the audience something about the theme of the play or the lives of the characters?

Evaluating sets checklist

Ask yourself the following questions when evaluating sets:

- ✓ If the set was naturalistic, how believable did you find it? Were there any details that were particularly effective?
- ✓ If the set was stylised, how positively did it show the style and action of the play?
- ✓ If the play was minimalistic, did it help to focus the audience on the characters and plot of the play?
- ✓ Can you pick out any moments when the set was used effectively?
- ✓ How well did the set contribute to the mood/atmosphere of the production?

Sample student response writing about a set

Describe how the set was used to support the action in the production. **Analyse** and **evaluate** how successful the set was in helping to communicate the action of the production to the audience.

It was a bold, large-scale set on two levels. (1) Most of the acting took place on the lower level, which served as the living room for the main characters. However, with a few additions of furnishings, such as a bed in the second act, brought on by trucks, that level also served as a park, a phone box and a living room. The set was only minimally dressed, with two modern, low-slung, brown leather chairs and a round, white fur rug. The upstage platform was accessed by two curving ramps and was used for the monologues addressed to the audience. (2) Above it, a large abstract painting slowly turned, symbolically emphasising the wealth of the two main characters and their preoccupation with art. (3) The modern architecture, furniture and art used in the set added powerfully to the production, helping to locate it in the rich Manhattan neighbourhood of the play and reinforcing the theme of art. (4)

(1) Description

(2) Description

(3) Analysis

(4) Evaluation

Analysing and evaluating sound

Sound design is an important aspect of theatre. From the moment you walk into the auditorium there may be music playing. Throughout the play there are likely to be sound cues. These may be practical, realistic sounds, such as doorbells, ringing phones or gunshots. They may be more suggestive, such as the **amplified** sound of water dripping or a ticking clock to show the passing of time. Microphones in musicals are common, but increasingly they are being used in non-musicals as well, sometimes simply to amplify voices, but at other times to create special effects such as capturing the actors' breathing or to heighten the importance of between-scene **narrations**.

Look at the mind map below to note the types of sound you might notice in a production. Add more legs to the mind map to incorporate your ideas.

KEY TERMS:

Amplification: how sound is made louder.

Narration: providing the audience with background information or commentary on the action of the play.

Reverb: an echoing effect.

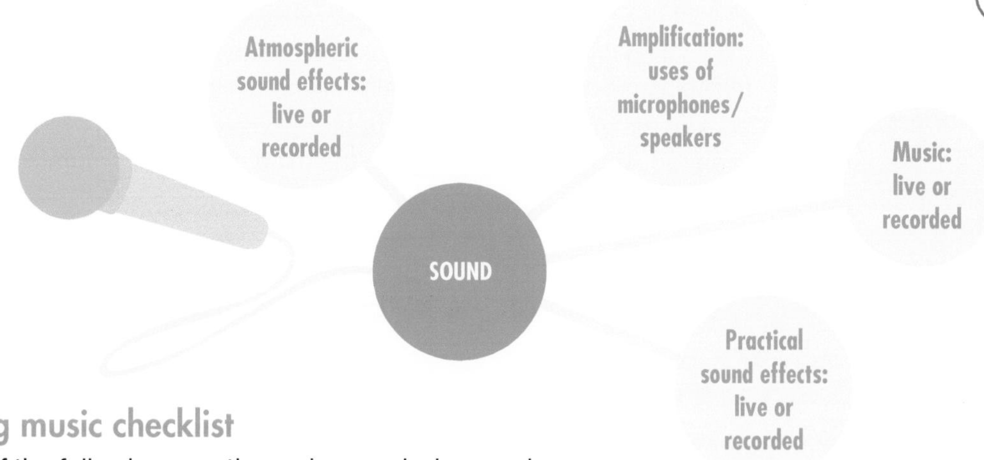

Analysing music checklist

Ask yourself the following questions when analysing music:

- ✓ Does it help to establish the period or setting of the play?
- ✓ Does it help to establish the mood of the play?
- ✓ Is it recorded or performed live?
- ✓ Does the sound of the music surround the audience or come from a single or several sources?
- ✓ Does it affect the action onstage (for example, do the characters move in time with it or refer to it in any way)?
- ✓ Does the volume increase or decrease at certain points?

Analysing sound effects checklist

Ask yourself the following questions when analysing sound effects:

- ✓ Do they help to establish the time of day, period or location of the play?
- ✓ Are they important to the plot (such as gunshots or phone calls)?
- ✓ Are they natural sounding or have they been distorted (such as use of **reverb** or other special effects)?
- ✓ Do they come from one direction or many directions?
- ✓ Does the volume of the sound affect the audience's experience of it?

Evaluating music and sound effects checklist

Ask yourself the following questions when evaluating music and sound effects:

- ✓ In a naturalistic production, did the music seem appropriate for the time and location or how believable were the sounds?
- ✓ In a stylised production, did they add to the style of the production? Did they make it more comic? Frightening? Tense?
- ✓ Were there choices made by the sound designer that actively enhanced the audience's experience of the play?
- ✓ How well were the sound effects achieved – were the timing, volume and quality correct for the play?

▸ For more information about sound go to pages 256–259.

Analysing and evaluating lighting

The type of lighting you see in your live production may depend on the equipment available at the theatre and the requirements of the play. In most indoor theatres, the audience enters with the **house lights** on. When the play begins, these are turned off, so that the audience is in the dark and the stage is lit. Some theatres have advanced state-of-the-art equipment with computerised systems using **LED lights**. Smaller, more basic theatres will operate a basic **lighting rig** in which a limited number of lights are used. In advanced systems, each light can produce many different colours or effects; whereas, in a basic rig, lanterns have coloured **gels** placed in front of them and can only be used for that colour. Some theatres, such as the Sam Wanamaker Theatre at the Globe in London, which is a re-creation of an early 17th-century theatre, are experimenting with productions that are lit solely by candles. Some productions have a combination of lights from the lighting rig and onstage lamps and candles. Outdoor productions, which take place in daylight, traditionally use no or limited lighting effects.

Look at the mind map below to note the types of lighting you might notice in a production. Add more legs to the mind map to incorporate your ideas.

KEY TERMS:

House lights: lighting that makes the audience visible.

LED lights: light-emitting diodes (LEDs) are light sources that have a high light output but use relatively little power.

Lighting rig: the structure that holds the lighting equipment in the theatre.

Gels: coloured transparencies used to create different-coloured lighting.

Transitions: moving from one lighting state to another, such as a fade to darkness or a sudden blackout.

Blackout: in lighting, suddenly switching all the lights off.

Strobe: a lamp that produces rapid flashes of bright light.

Fade: in lighting, gradually getting lighter or darker.

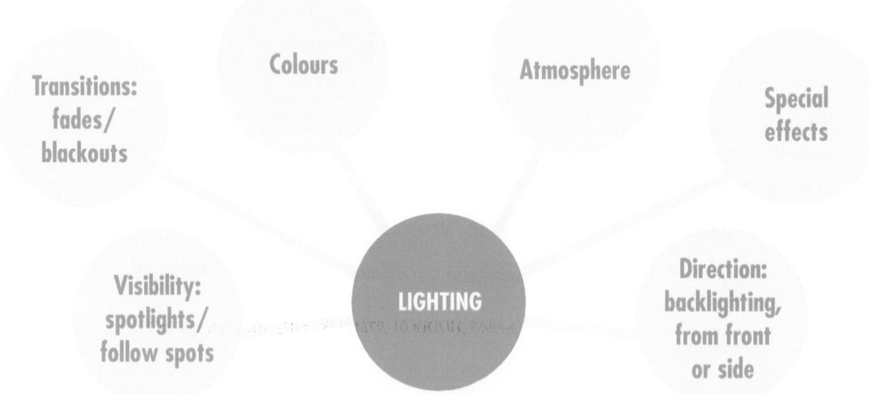

TASK 12

Look at the short excerpts from the sample responses below and decide if the student is commenting on: direction, **transitions**, visibility, special effects, atmosphere or colours (it may be more than one of these).

A In this scene, the actor playing the leading role was backlit, (1) making his silhouette clear, (2) as water poured down on him.

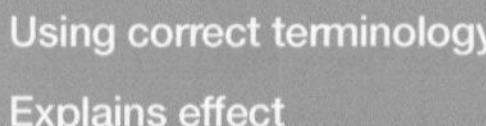

B On the darkened stage, only Ariel was lit by a follow spot. As he spoke his last lines, the spot got smaller, so, in the end, only his face was visible.

C The last image of the play was the actors facing the audience, looking shocked, and then a sudden **blackout**.

D

After the previous harshly lit scenes, the rosy gentle sidelighting of the breakfast scene, produced by a lighting rig in the wings, established the calm family life in this country kitchen.

E

During the fight scene, strobe lighting was used, which made the violence look particularly shocking.

Analysing lighting checklist

Ask yourself the following questions when analysing lighting design:

- ✓ How did the lighting designer create certain effects (types of equipment, transitions and so on)?
- ✓ How did the lighting designer use colour?
- ✓ What directions/angles were used in the lighting?
- ✓ Were any special effects created?
- ✓ Was lighting used to suggest time of day, location. character, period?

Evaluating lighting checklist

Ask yourself the following questions when evaluating lighting design:

- ✓ Did any choices made by the lighting design enhance the audience's experience of the performance?
- ✓ Did the lighting help to focus the audience on certain elements of the performance?
- ✓ Did the lighting enhance the mood or atmosphere of the performance?
- ✓ Did the lighting help to convey the action of the performance?

TIP

Using the correct terminology, such as the key terms shown on the facing page, will help to demonstrate your ability to analyse lighting with insight.

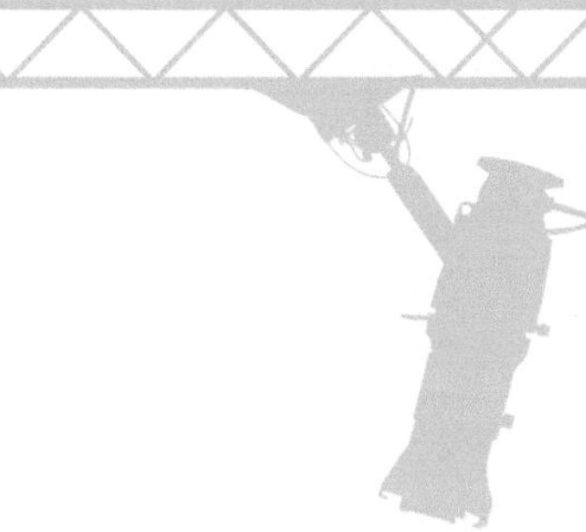

Applying your learning

You will need to be able to use correct terminology in your response. The examiner wants to see if you can describe, analyse and evaluate what you have seen.

TASK 13

Read the following excerpt for this student's response and write:

- **D** next to any description
- **E** next to any evaluation.
- **A** next to any analysis

The lighting designer created an image of a phone box simply by having a sharp-edged box of light. This was created by a profile spot, which made the light harsh and clearly focused. It was a simple but powerful effect, as the actors could step into the square of light and the audience immediately believed that they were in a separate contained space. The scene ended with a sudden blackout. This made the last image the audience saw the actor's happy expression, which I think was more surprising and appropriate than a slow fade.

▸ For more information about lighting look at pages 252–255.

PRACTICE QUESTIONS FOR SECTION C: LIVE THEATRE PRODUCTION

Answer one question from this section.

State the title of the live/digital theatre production you saw.

You must answer on a different play from that in Section B.

1 Describe how one or more actors used their vocal and physical acting skills to create effective characters. Analyse and evaluate how successful they were in communicating their character to the audience.
You should make reference to:

- the use of voice
- physical skills
- the actors' use of space. [32 marks]

OR

2 Describe how lighting was used to support the action in the production. Analyse and evaluate how successful the lighting was in helping to communicate the action of the production to the audience.
You should make reference to:

- the types of lighting
- the colour and intensity of the lighting
- any special effects. [32 marks]

OR

3 Describe how the set was used to help create the style of the production. Analyse and evaluate how successful the set was in helping to communicate the style of the production to the audience.
You should make reference to:

- the appearance of the set
- any changes in the set
- how it was used by the actors. [32 marks]

TASK 14

Write an answer to one of the questions above. Then either mark your own work or swap papers with someone else and mark their work. Read through it and write:

- **D** next to any description
- **A** next to any analysis
- **E** next to any evaluation.

At the end, write at least one thing that you or they did well and one thing that could be improved.

TIP

It is easy just to describe what you have seen. Remember to analyse and evaluate it. Some words to use when evaluating might include:

believable, powerful, disappointing, convincing, portrays well, conveys, surprises, moving, atmospheric, appropriate, adequate, impressive.

Improving your written work

Whatever aspect of the production you are writing about make sure that you:

- Give **specific examples and details** from the production.
- Use relevant **technical terminology**.
- Explain how the performance or design choices helped to **communicate meaning** to the audience.
- Explain whether or not the choices were **successful and why**.

ASSESSMENT FOCUS

In your response you must demonstrate that you:

- understand how theatre is developed and performed **(AO3)**
- can analyse and evaluate the work of others **(AO4)**.

When there are bullet points in the question, you must respond to each of them.

Planning your response

A common feature of successful responses is that there is evidence of at least some planning in order to organise ideas and make sure the question is fully answered. There is no one set way of planning your answer, but below are some approaches that work for other students.

Annotate the question

Use the question and make notes around it.

For example:

Describe how the set was used to help create the <u>style of the production</u>. (1) Analyse and evaluate how successful the set was in helping to <u>communicate</u> (2) the style of the production to the audience.

You should make reference to:

- the <u>appearance</u> of the set (3)
- any <u>changes</u> in the set (4)
- how it was used by the <u>actors</u>. (5)

(1) Twelfth Night, Shakespearean production, 17th-century costumes, stylised.

(2) Romantic and comic. Created a beautiful setting, emphasis on nature. Comic potential in Malvolio/Olivia scenes.

(3) Large scale; use of blue; sheets create waves; projections for storm.

(4) Revolve used for change to second setting. After the excitement of the opening, scene is calmer.

(5) Comedy created in overhearing scene. Use of sundial. Hedges where actors could suddenly appear.

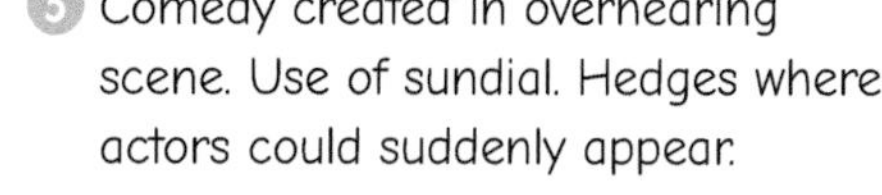

An updated production by Emma Rice of Twelfth Night, Globe Theatre, 2017

TIP

To **analyse** something you are breaking it down and looking at it closely. To **evaluate** something is to write about the effects that were achieved and if they were successful. You must do both of these.

Making a mind map

Another way of planning your response is to create a mind map.

Planning paragraphs

You could write a quick paragraph plan (below is just one example, the requirements of the question you have or the production you saw may vary):

Introduction: Style of production

Paragraph 1: Appearance

Paragraph 2: Changes

Paragraph 3: Use by actors

Paragraph 4: Analyse what was communicated and evaluate how successful.

Avoiding common errors

Check the list below to see if you have made one or more the following common errors:

- ✓ No (or incorrect) technical language (for example, referring generally to lighting without anything more specific).
- ✓ General comments without giving examples from the production.
- ✓ Saying something is good without explaining why.
- ✓ Only writing about one or two moments from the play.
- ✓ Only descriptive with no analysis or evaluation.
- ✓ No discussion of effect on audience.
- ✓ Little understanding of the requirements of the play.
- ✓ One or two points repeated with no development of ideas.

WHAT HAVE I LEARNED?

LIVE THEATRE PRODUCTION

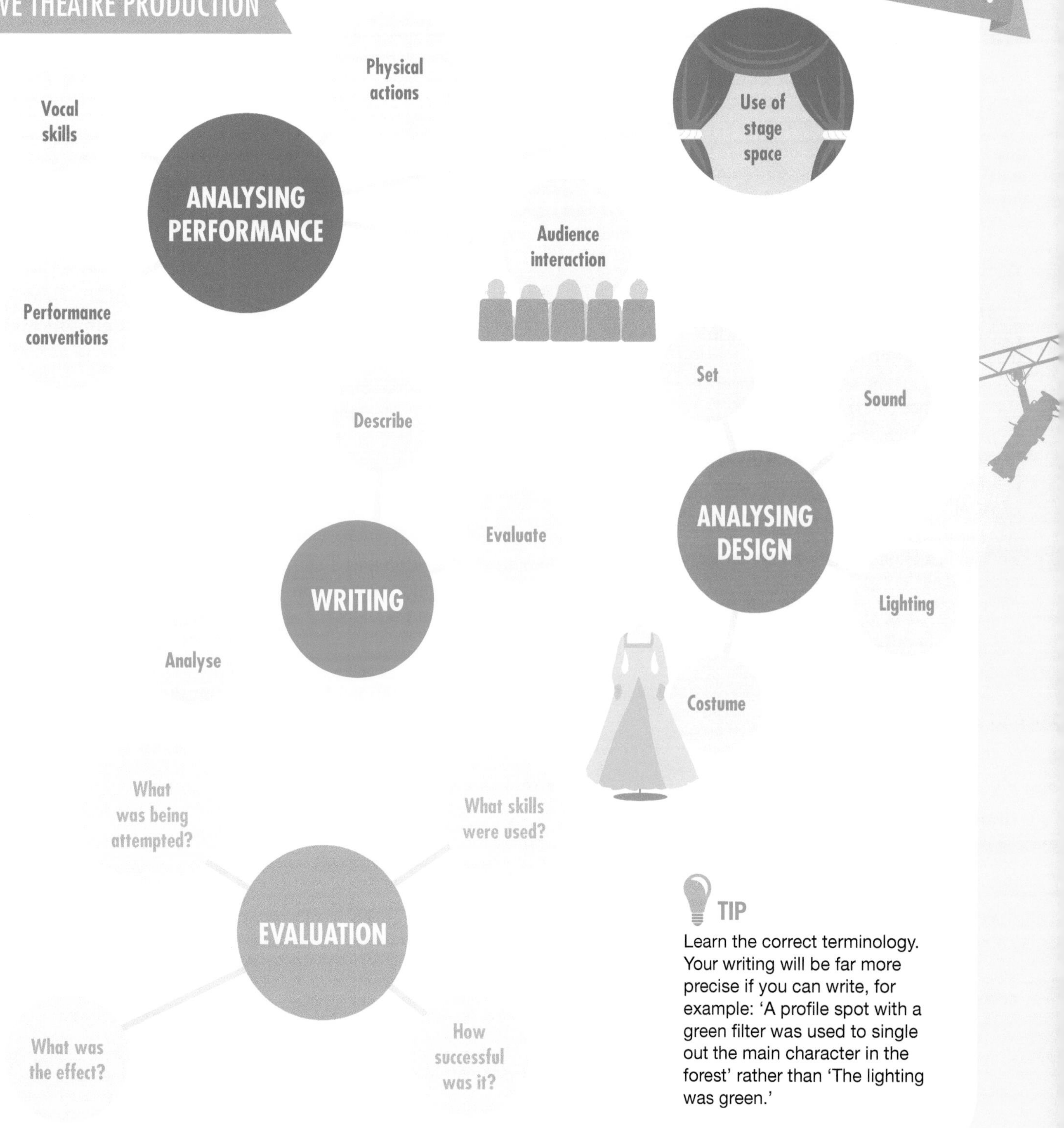

ANALYSING PERFORMANCE
- Vocal skills
- Physical actions
- Performance conventions
- Audience interaction
- Use of stage space

ANALYSING DESIGN
- Set
- Sound
- Lighting
- Costume

WRITING
- Describe
- Evaluate
- Analyse

EVALUATION
- What was being attempted?
- What skills were used?
- What was the effect?
- How successful was it?

TIP

Learn the correct terminology. Your writing will be far more precise if you can write, for example: 'A profile spot with a green filter was used to single out the main character in the forest' rather than 'The lighting was green.'

CHECK YOUR LEARNING

If you are uncertain of the meaning of any of the terms above, go back and revise.

Use the downloadable version of this summary as a checklist of what you have learned: Samples & Downloads at www.illuminatepublishing.com.

COMPONENT 2

DEVISING DRAMA

THE SPECIFICATION SAYS...

Students must learn how to create and develop ideas to communicate meaning in a devised theatrical performance.

Students must learn how to contribute to a devised drama in a live theatre context for an audience. They must contribute as either a performer or designer.

ASSESSMENT FOCUS

This is a practical component in which students are assessed on their ability to create and develop ideas to:

- communicate meaning for theatrical performance **(AO1)**
- apply theatrical skills to realise artistic intentions in live performance **(AO2)**
- analyse and evaluate their own work **(AO4)**.

What this means is that you will be working in a group, either as a performer or a designer, to create an original devised piece that will then be performed and evaluated. You will perform your piece in front of an audience and write a production log.

KEY TERMS:

Devising: a way of creating drama that begins not with writers or a script but is based on the collaborative efforts of a group of people.

Improvise: to act without a script.

Stimulus: a resource in drama used to start a creative process by providing context, inspiration or focus.

What is devising?

THEATRE MAKER ADVICE

Kerry Frampton, director/performer/designer, Splendid Productions

Devising is problem solving in the most beautiful and practical way – the pursuit of the clearest way to communicate an idea.

Devising is a way of creating drama without starting with a script. Instead, usually beginning with an idea and a stimulus, actors and designers research, **improvise**, develop and shape scenes until they have a complete piece of drama ready for an audience.

How do we begin?

You will be presented with a range of stimuli. A **stimulus** is something that will spark ideas, discussion and creativity. For example, it could be a:

- photograph, painting or sculpture
- poem, news article or short story
- song or piece of instrumental music
- recent or current event
- theme, such as 'Time' or 'War'
- myth or fairy tale
- cultural event such as a festival, carnival or ceremony.

How will we be assessed?

You will be marked on your Devising log, which is divided into three sections:

- Section 1: Response to stimulus: (20 marks) (AO1)
- Section 2: Development and collaboration (20 marks) (AO1)
- Section 3: Analysis and evaluation (20 marks) (AO4)

You are also marked on your contribution to the Devised performance, as a performer or designer (20 marks for AO2), giving a total of 80 marks.

Collaboration and group work

What type of group member are you?

Group work is an essential element in devising (as well as other aspects of drama). Use the exercise below to consider what type of group member you are and how you can improve.

TASK 1

In a small group, choose a topic for a short scene to be performed at an event, such as an assembly. You have five minutes to agree on the topic of the scene, assign parts and write the first few lines.

REFLECTION

How easy did you find that task? Did your group manage to meet the deadline? What helped or hindered you?

When identifying your strengths and weaknesses in group work, it is good to reflect on your natural attitudes towards group work. Below are descriptions of typical group members:

LEADER: You have ideas and are happy to express them. You enjoy being in charge. You may sometimes be frustrated if others aren't following you or disagree with you.

HELPER: You don't usually lead a group, but you are happy to put forward ideas and work with others. You may assist Leaders to see their ideas through or you may encourage others to take part.

PASSENGER: You don't want to lead and you aren't confident about putting your ideas forward. However, you will go along with what the group wants to do.

BLOCKER: You find group work frustrating and you don't positively help the group. You might tend to argue with others, refuse to cooperate or become distracted.

REFLECTION

Thinking back to your actions in Task 1, which description best fits you?

Moving forwards

If you are a Leader, make sure you:

- listen to others
- check that everyone feels included
- are flexible about adjusting your ideas or compromising.

If you are a Helper, make sure you:

- have your ideas heard
- think about leading part of a task
- are challenged by the work.

If you are a Passenger, make sure you:

- contribute ideas
- are active and not passive
- complete work that is challenging for you.

If you are a Blocker:

- 

Blockers frustrate others because they keep them from fulfilling their potential, but most of all they hurt themselves. Some people are Blockers because it is the only way they feel they can get attention or perhaps they lack confidence in their own work. However, you will receive much more positive attention and learn so much more if you can work productively with others.

TIP

Keep reflecting on how you work in groups. Groups need Leaders but they should aim to ensure that everyone is included in the process. Passengers can't just coast – drama is active!

Staying positive

'Yes, and ...'

Being positive is a vital part of successful group work. No one wants to work with someone who is blocking their ideas or making them feel foolish. The game below, 'Yes, and ...' is great for encouraging creativity and cooperation. Remember you can't say 'no'!

Working with a partner, start with one of the following scenarios (there are many others you can use):

1 You are in a car that has broken down in the middle of nowhere.
2 You have locked yourself out of your house.

Whatever is said, the other person must say, 'Yes, and ...' and add a point. For example:

The car has broken down.

Yes, and I think I know how to fix cars.

Yes, and I have a car manual somewhere.

Yes, and it says we need a spanner.

And so on ...

REFLECTION

Were you positive and did you keep the ideas flowing?

At any point did you block your partner?

What would you improve for the future?

Deciding if you wish to perform or design

If there are only two students in a group, then both must be performers, as the minimum performance size for a group is two. In any larger group, you have a choice to be a designer instead of performer.

Potential designers should consider:

- Will you have access to the equipment you need to create a lighting design, assemble a costume or construct a puppet, for example?
- Do you have an idea for a design that will have a positive impact on a performance?
- Are you willing to develop your practical skills in order to realise a completed design?
- Will you contribute fully to the devising of the piece?

Potential performers should consider:

- Are you happy to develop your theatrical skills in order to perform in front of an audience?
- Are you able to learn lines and do you have a positive attitude about rehearsals?
- Will you try to provide a performance that will have a positive impact on the live performance?
- Will you contribute fully to the devising of the piece?

TIP

If you are unsure about whether to choose a performance or design specialism for this component, your teacher can help you choose what will potentially be most successful for you.

Typical plan for devising

There is no one way to organise a devised piece. Below is just one way that you may approach developing your piece. You might find once you are working that you would like to go back to an earlier stage, such as research or devising, in order to improve a section of your work.

INTRODUCTION TO STIMULI
You will become familiar and work with a range of stimuli such as photographs, articles or music.

CHOOSE STIMULUS
You will decide which stimulus will be the basis of your piece. You will write about this in your Devising log.

RESEARCH STIMULUS
You will work in your group to research different aspects of your stimulus, such as its context, theme, visual images. You will note your research in your Devising log.

DEVISING
Your group will begin devising scenes for your piece. Designers will begin researching and developing their designs. You will improve the structure of the piece. You will agree how your stage will be configured. You will chronicle your discoveries in your Devising log.

REHEARSAL
Your group will agree and set the stage movement and learn lines. Designers will contribute their ideas and skills. You will receive and respond to feedback. You will continue making improvements in the piece. You will note your changes and developments in your Devising log.

TECHNICAL REHEARSAL
You will have a rehearsal to test and adjust any technical elements such as lighting and sound. Design candidates will take a lead role to ensure that all technical/design elements work correctly.

DRESS REHEARSAL
You will have a full rehearsal in costume and with all technical elements in place. Some groups choose to have a small invited audience for this in order to receive last-minute feedback and make final adjustments.

PERFORMANCE
You will perform the piece in front of an audience and the assessor.

REFLECTING/EVALUATING
Review and evaluate your work.

TIP

Throughout the process you will be making notes, diagrams or recording comments for your Devising log. The final section of your Devising log is an analysis and evaluation of your work.

Getting started with devising

THEATRE MAKER ADVICE

Kerry Frampton, director/performer/ designer, Splendid Productions

We specialise in creative adaptations of existing plays or novels, they must have a strong spine of politics or a question about society that we want to explore. Our current production is centred around Leadership, which is pertinent to our current political situation. Normally, we read lots of options and then one will stand out above the others.

Our structure is quite tight, so there are some logistical elements to consider in our choice of material:

- Could this be done with a cast of three?
- What would we like an audience to consider/ponder/ question and feel like?
- What is the problem we are trying to solve?

KEY TERM:

Hot seat: one performer sits in a chair and, in character, answers questions.

▲ *The blinded cyclops in Splendid Productions'* The Odyssey

When beginning your devised work, you will be exposed to a range of stimuli. You should select one or more of these for your devised piece. Your exploration of the stimulus should be active and creative. There is no one best way of devising but here are some examples to get you started:

- Create a series of still images based on the stimulus and discuss any storylines that may result from those images.
- Choose one character inspired by the stimulus and **hot-seat** that character to establish a back story.
- Create a location inspired by the stimulus, exploring the sounds and sights in the space.
- Research the context of the stimulus (when it occurred, why it was important) and create a scene based on that context.
- Create a series of quick-fire scenes based on the theme or title of your stimulus.
- Choose several characters from the stimulus and write a monologue for each.
- Introduce a prop or piece of costume to an improvised scene based on the stimulus.

Response to a stimulus

THEATRE MAKER ADVICE

Kerry Frampton, director/performer/ designer, Splendid Productions

Normally I'm drawn to something that I can see. As a visual learner, if I can see it I can make it, so there has to be a strong image in there somewhere.

For *The Odyssey* [an ancient Greek tale] I had an idea about how we might blind a Cyclops – which ended up not being in the final piece – I also wondered if we could tell this HUGE fable without the central figure being present. *Odyssey*, with no Odysseus. How do we tell that story? Whose stories are ignored in the original? Where are the women? What about the villains? It then becomes a vehicle of telling everyone else's version of events.

In your Devising log you will be asked to write about the different stimuli that your teacher presented and the stimulus you chose. You will need to then explain:

- Your first response to the stimuli.
- The different ideas, themes and setting you considered and how and why you reached your final decision.
- What you discovered from your research.
- What your own dramatic aims and intentions are (for example, if you are a performer, what you want to achieve in your portrayal of a character).
- What the dramatic aims and intentions of the piece were (for example, what theme your piece might explore or what message it would deliver).

Stimulus example

Read the following poem by acclaimed poet Lemn Sissay twice. The first time, read it aloud so you experience the sound and rhythm of the words and any ideas that stand out. The second time, try to locate the poet's message to the listener.

What if? by Lemn Sissay

A lost number in the equation
A simple, understandable miscalculation
And what if on the basis of that
The world as we know it changed its matter of fact
Let me get it right. What if we got it wrong?

What if we weakened ourselves getting strong?
What if we found in the ground a file of proof?
What if the foundations missed a vital truth?
What if the industrial dream sold us out from within?
What if our unpunishable defense sealed us in?
What if our wanted more was making less?
And what if all of this wasn't progress?

Let me get it right. What if we got it wrong?
What if we weakened ourselves getting strong?
What if our wanting more was making less?
And what if all of this wasn't progress?
What if the disappearing rivers of Eritrea,
the rising tides and encroaching fear
What if the tear inside the protective skin
of Earth was trying to tell us something?
Let me get it right. What if we got it wrong?
What if we weakened ourselves getting strong?
What if the message carried in the wind was saying something?

From butterfly wings to the hurricane
It's the small things that make great change
In the question towards the end of the leases
no longer the origin but the end of species

Let me get it right. What if we got it wrong?
What if the message carried in the wind was saying something?

CHALLENGE

The poet Lemn Sissay (pictured above) has spoken extensively about his interesting life and appeared on the radio show *Desert Island Discs*. Research his life to see if that could enrich your devised piece.

TASK 2

a In your group discuss what you think the poet is saying about the world and the dangers that we face.

b Read through the poem again and underline in pencil any words or phrases that seem important to you.

c Choose five phrases from the poem and, as a group, create still images for them (such as 'message carried in the wind' or 'industrial dream'). Discuss the images and if any of them suggest a way you could use this stimulus in a dramatic way.

d Write a list of questions you have for the speaker, such as: Who are you speaking to? What made you so worried about the world? What do you think we can do?

e As a group, hot-seat one member who will imagine they are the speaker. That person will think about the speaker's background and experiences. The rest of the group will ask questions. What can you discover about the speaker? Why are they choosing to speak out?

f The poet seems concerned about changes in the environment. Go online and try to discover what he means by 'disappearing rivers of Eritrea', 'rising tides' and 'end of species'. Research climate change and note any ideas that you think might inspire or contribute to a devised piece.

g Discuss where you could set a piece based on this poem. Would it be in the present day, the past or the future? Would it be in an existing country or an imagined one?

h What would you like to achieve in a piece based on this poem? For example, would you like to design a set that would show how the world's environment is changing or would you like to play one of several characters in conflict about climate change?

i What would you like a devised piece based on this poem to achieve? Would it have a political message about the environment or leaders? Or would it be a personal piece about a character making a discovery or finding a reason to be hopeful? Do you want the audience to have a greater understanding of the issues suggested by the poem or do you want them to be more interested in the emotional journey of the characters?

j If there are designers in your group, do they have ideas about how design could contribute to an exploration of this stimulus, such as a sound design or type of costume that they would like to explore or are there effects they could create with lighting or puppetry?

k Make notes for your Devising log explaining your ideas from your initial response to the stimulus.

TIP

Make notes about your work from the beginning. It will make it much easier to explain the process if you have detailed notes that you can shape into your Devising log responses.

CHALLENGE

Try to extend your research beyond the most obvious internet pages. Visit a library, interview people, listen to music and discover images.

THEATRE MAKER ADVICE

Kerry Frampton, director/performer/designer, Splendid Productions

Sometimes I have a niggle of a thought, an idea that to me is exciting and it'll just be sat in my brain and as I'm going about my daily business I'll have other ideas, or something I'm doing will feed into that. The idea grows and changes and expands. The seeds of each piece are planted and I see what grows and what doesn't.

Examples of stimuli and themes

Below are examples of stimuli and related themes that you could use for a devised piece.

Photography

The photo on the right shows British athlete Dame Kelly Holmes winning Olympic Gold. Use that as a starting point for your devising.

POSSIBLE THEMES: **competition, women in sport, strength, overcoming hardship, images of women, triumph and defeat.**

Dame Kelly Holmes winning gold in the 2004 Olympics

Poetry

A Poison Tree by William Blake

I was angry with my friend;
I told my wrath, my wrath did end.
I was angry with my foe:
I told it not, my wrath did grow.

And I waterd it in fears,
Night & morning with my tears:
And I sunned it with smiles,
And with soft deceitful wiles.

And it grew both day and night.
Till it bore an apple bright.
And my foe beheld it shine,
And he knew that it was mine.

And into my garden stole,
When the night had veild the pole;
In the morning glad I see;
My foe outstretched beneath the tree.

POSSIBLE THEMES: **friendship, conflict, anger, hypocrisy, consequences.**

Music

'The March of the Knights' from the ballet *Romeo and Juliet* by the Russian composer Sergei Prokofiev.

POSSIBLE THEMES: power, conflict, tribes, families.

Myths

The Greek myth of Eurydice and Orpheus. Orpheus was the son of the god Apollo and a highly gifted musician. He loved Eurydice. One day, Eurydice was bitten by a serpent and died. She descended to Hades in the Underworld. Orpheus was so sad that he begged Hades to let him have his loved one back. He played such sweet music that Hades gave permission to Orpheus to bring Eurydice back to Earth. But there was one condition: he was not allowed to look back at her as they rose from Hades. When they were almost back on Earth, Orpheus looked back to see if Eurydice was still there. Hades snatched her back to the Underworld. Orpheus spent the rest of his days playing sad music and was said to be the inspiration guiding those who wrote mournful tunes.

POSSIBLE THEMES: love, death, trust, journeys, danger.

Art

Yinka Shonibare is a Nigerian-British artist who lives in London. His work explores ideas about cultural identity, often by reimagining situations in a surprising way.

POSSIBLE THEMES: Victorian age, society, fashion, culture, contrasts.

▲ Diary of a Victorian Dandy *by Yinka Shonibare*

Image courtesy Stephen Friedman Gallery, London.

Film

Slumdog Millionaire is a 2008 British film directed by Danny Boyle and starring Dev Patel as Jamal Malik, a young man who grew up in an Indian slum who appears on the gameshow *Who Wants to be a Millionaire?* Despite his humble beginnings, Jamal has an amazing ability to answer the difficult quiz questions. He is accused of cheating, but through a series of flashbacks the reason for his knowledge is revealed.

POSSIBLE THEMES: luck, prejudice, intelligence, gameshows, overcoming obstacles.

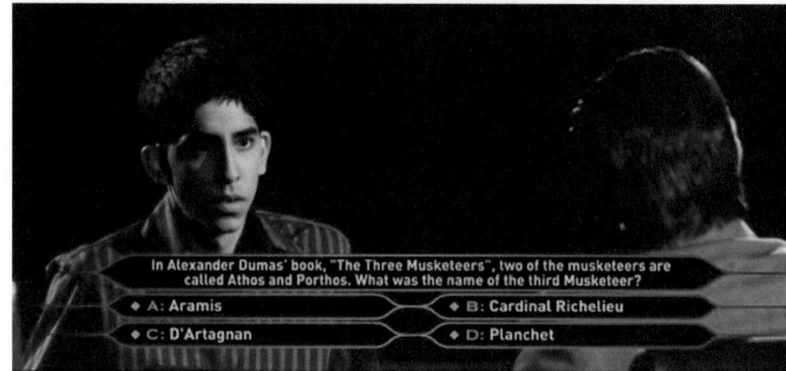

▲ *Slumdog Millionaire*

Novels

Face by Benjamin Zephaniah explores the life of Martin Turner, a popular teenager whose life is transformed after a car accident leaves his face disfigured. He discovers that the change in his appearance affects how even his closest friends treat him. The novel traces the obstacles Martin faces in hospital and when he returns to school.

POSSIBLE THEMES: physical appearance, friendship, overcoming obstacles.

News

Stephen Sutton was diagnosed with terminal cancer at the age of 15. In response, he decided to do two things: compile a 'bucket list' – all the things he wanted to do before he died – and to raise money for charity. In the last years of his life, supported by his family, he: skydived, got a tattoo, became a Guinness World Records holder, hugged an elephant, and played the drums in front of a huge crowd at Wembley. As his popularity grew through social media and celebrity attention, the donations flooded in. By the time he died in 2014, at the age of 19, he had raised more than £3.2 million for charity.

POSSIBLE THEMES: overcoming obstacles, goals, health, social media, families.

History

Suffragettes

In the late 19th century and early 20th century, suffragettes fought for the right for women to vote in elections. Two famous British suffragettes were the sisters Emmeline and Christabel Pankhurst. They believed in 'deeds, not words', and held rallies and protests. In 1909, their group used tactics such as hunger strikes, and some had to endure force-feeding. In 1918, women in Britain over the age of 30, with a few restrictions, were given the right to vote. In 1928 this was extended to women over the age of 21.

POSSIBLE THEMES: women's rights, protests, politics.

Musical

The musical *Hamilton* takes a modern approach to the life of one of America's founding fathers, Alexander Hamilton. It traces his life from his humble origins as an orphan in the Caribbean to his death in a duel. You could research different figures from history and create a short musical based on their lives. But remember, it took Lin-Manuel Miranda, the creator of *Hamilton*, seven years to write the musical, so be realistic about what you can accomplish in the time available.

POSSIBLE THEMES: ambition, politics, overcoming obstacles.

Cultural

Weddings

Different cultures celebrate weddings with different wedding customs, superstitions and rules. For example, a Pakistani wedding typically takes several days, as there are four different ceremonies. A traditional Chinese wedding is arranged between families and may include a 'bride price' – money or gifts given to the family of the bride. In some regions of Sweden, the bridesmaids carry bouquets of weeds to ward off trolls. There are many television programmes devoted to the experiences of those hoping to find love, preparing for marriage or competing for a prize of a wedding or honeymoon. You could use the backdrop of a wedding or series of weddings to shape your piece.

POSSIBLE THEMES: love, money, tradition, family.

REFLECTION

What makes a stimulus interesting to explore? How can you ensure that an idea has enough substance to serve as the basis for your piece?

CHALLENGE

There are some excellent resources available to stretch your ability to devise. One helpful book is *Drama Games for Devising* by Jessica Swale, which provides lots of interesting exercises and games for the various stages of devising. Alternatively, visit the websites of companies that specialise in devising, such as Complicite and Splendid Productions (whose artistic director offers advice in this chapter), that provide useful online resources and DVDs.

TASK 3

a Read the above possible stimuli and in your group discuss which ones appeal to you most and why.

b Choose one of the stimuli and create a mindmap diagram of ideas based on it. At this stage be very free with ideas, but think about characters, locations, themes and plots that appeal to you.

Research

Once you have decided on your stimulus and topic you will want to research it in order to develop your ideas. There are many ways of researching a topic. These include:

books videos

newspaper articles documentaries music

online articles museums

interviews photographs

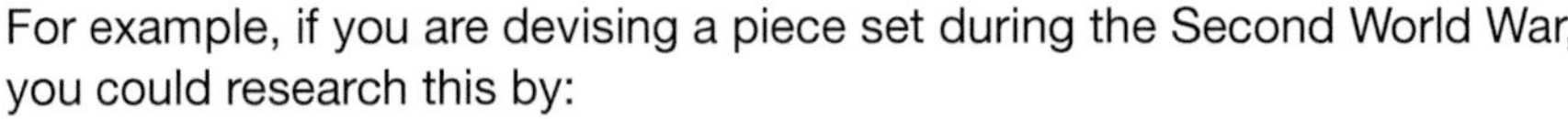

For example, if you are devising a piece set during the Second World War, you could research this by:

- visiting or looking at the online resources of a museum, such as the Imperial War Museum
- watching a documentary about the war
- reading history books or magazines about the period
- finding images of wartime fashions
- listening to popular songs from the period
- watching a film either set in the period or made during that time
- locating images of advertising from the period
- interviewing relatives or someone in your community who remembers it.

How to use your research

Some groups find it best to assign different research responsibilities: one person may be researching music, while another could be reading articles or finding visual images. If you are a designer you should take an active role in helping research areas that will influence the design of the piece. Everyone should contribute to the research process, as you need to show how you have assisted the development of the piece in your Devising log.

Once you have gathered some research, you should share it with the group. then choose the aspects that you think are most useful.

For example, in order to improvise a scene in which a mother worries about whether or not to evacuate her children to a safer location you might use wartime posters such as the two on the left for inspiration.

After finding a piece of music from the Second World War, use it to create a scene in which the mother says goodbye to her children.

Genre/style

Many groups find that their work is more interesting and focused if they choose a genre or performance style for their piece. This will help you to create a piece with a more consistent tone and should aid the audience in understanding the type of theatre they are seeing. Some groups combine two genres or styles in order to create variety. Below are some genres you might consider.

Comedy

Theatre that makes the audience laugh is one way of keeping an audience interested and involved. Some common features of comedy include:

misunderstandings

physical humour (such as disguises that go wrong or accidents that cause embarrassment)

comic timing (the use of pace and pause to make the audience laugh)

exaggeration

However, do not be misled into thinking that comedy is easy. It is common to mistake something that is a bit silly or a private joke as being something that will have a wide appeal to an audience. Comedy can be used to explore serious issues and many successful devised pieces combine humour with a serious message. For example, you might make a serious political point by comically exaggerating the arguments on both sides or by creating larger-than-life characters.

Tragedy

Tragic pieces deal with large issues that have a sad outcome.
Some common features of tragedy include:

a sympathetic or worthy protagonist who experiences a downfall

warnings that things may go wrong

conflict

serious tone

A tragic subject has to be important – it would be difficult to create a tragic piece based on something trivial such as losing a shoe. You need to make sure you can sustain the tone so that it leads to a moving conclusion.

Melodrama

Melodrama is a type of theatre with exciting situations and exaggerated characters. Features of melodrama include:

characters whose role and personality are clear from their first entrance

an exaggerated acting style

a hero and a villain

dangerous situations

good usually triumphs over evil

Victorian melodramas featured 'stock' or stereotypical characters and often involved the hero saving the heroine from the villain. Modern melodramas can be altered to fit the story you wish to tell and may have a more comic tone.

Commedia dell'arte

Commedia dell'arte is a type of theatre that was particularly popular in the 16th–18th centuries, but has influenced many other types of drama. It was performed by a travelling group of actors in distinctive costumes. Features of commedia dell'arte include:

- **stock characters**, such as comic servants, old men, young lovers and boasting soldiers
- use of physical gestures and physical comedy
- tragedy
- tasks
- improvisation.

Once the style and rules of commedia dell'arte are learned, they can be applied to a number of situations. Often, much comedy can result from the master/servant relationship or the misunderstandings of the 'old men' characters.

KEY TERM:

Stock characters: easily recognised, stereotypical characters.

Breaking the fourth wall: breaking the imaginary wall between the actors and performers by speaking directly to the audience.

▲ *A commedia-influenced production of* Once Five Years Pass

Naturalism

Naturalism is a type of theatre that creates the illusion of reality, so the audience fully believes the characters and the situations in which they find themselves. Features of naturalism include:

- believable characters
- gestures and vocal patterns that imitate those experienced in real life
- situations that are recognisable to the audience
- realistic props and settings
- situations that may involve ordinary people who unexpectedly experience a crisis.

Naturalism can be an appealing choice, as much acting that we know from films and television is highly naturalistic. However, onstage you must make sure that this choice will give you the opportunity to demonstrate your physical and vocal skills. Remember that naturalism does not mean simply repeating real life; it is just as crafted, edited and shaped as any other dramatic form.

Epic theatre

Epic theatre is a type of theatre associated with the German writer and director, Bertolt Brecht. He rejected naturalism and instead used techniques to draw the audience's attention to the fact that they are watching a play. Features of epic theatre include:

- captions or projections with slogans or scene headings
- political goals
- comedy, sometimes even when dealing with apparently serious matters
- exaggerated characters
- **breaking the fourth wall** by speaking directly to the audience
- use of song and music.

Brecht believed that theatre should inspire the audience to action, so he created techniques to keep them alert and interested. He wrote about political or social injustice using narration, songs and physical comedy.

Documentary theatre

Documentary theatre is drama that consists entirely or in part of factual materials, such as the words of interviews, newspaper articles or government reports. As much as possible the material is not altered but is presented **verbatim** – that is, the actual words are used. Some documentary theatre uses 'verbatim' sections contrasting with fictional situations. Features of documentary theatre include:

- careful and accurate research
- social or political themes
- recreation of an actual time or event
- naturalistic acting.

Some documentary theatre makers interview people after an important event and then carefully edit the material into a piece of drama. For example, Gillian Slovo interviewed protesters, community members and police after the 2011 riots in London. Other documentary theatre makers have edited trial transcripts to create a piece of theatre.

KEY TERM:

Verbatim: using exactly the same words as were used originally.

Physical theatre

Physical theatre is a type of non-naturalistic drama that emphasises movement such as mime, dance, clowning and mask-work in order to tell its story. Features include:

- stylised movement
- use of music and dance
- strong use of stage pictures and images
- less emphasis on dialogue.

▲ *Physical theatre and clever use of props can create impressive effects, as in this production of* Jonah, a Musical Detour

Physical theatre can be used on its own or it may be joined with another genre of theatre. For example, you may wish to have a stylised slow motion movement section to show a difficult journey or a rapid, chaotic movement scene in order to show a character's mental state. A piece could combine a verbatim report being spoken while others mime what is in the report.

▲ *Splendid Productions' performance of* Antigone

Theatre-in-Education

Theatre-in-Education (also called TIE) is a show with an education focus designed for school audiences or other groups to teach them about a certain issue. TIE productions usually have the following elements:

- a small-cast
- low-budget
- inventiveness, such as using multi-role or creative use of props
- audience interaction
- issue explored from many viewpoints
- factual information
- a strong, clear message
- simple set and props that can easily be moved to different venues.

The audience of a TIE piece needs to be one of your key starting points. Are you aiming to educate a young audience about the dangers of social media or the importance of healthy eating? A play aimed at seven-year-olds would need to be very different from one aimed at 16-year-olds. You should have a learning objective, such as, at the end of this show, the audience will now understand what the dangers of unhealthy eating are; or how to recognise healthy eating habits; or easy ways to prepare a well-balanced meal and so on.

TIP

Working in a particular style can help the audience and those assessing your work to understand your intentions.

TIP

You could devise a piece influenced by theatre makers such as Brecht or Kneehigh.

TASK 4

Create a simple scene, such as your journey to school, and then perform it in different styles. For example:

- Documentary theatre: recreate the exact words that were spoken to you.
- Physical theatre: create a bus and mime the actions of the passengers and driver.
- Epic theatre: write captions for each stage of your journey and speak directly to the audience.
- Naturalism: recreate the gestures and words spoken when people are waiting for the bus.
- Melodrama: create an exaggerated hero and villain for your journey and exaggerate the extreme danger you were in.

REFLECTION

Which performance styles did you think added the most to the piece? Which do you think will fit in best with your devised piece?

Development and collaboration

Working with others and developing ideas are part of the pleasure of drama, but these can also be difficult. Make sure that, throughout the process, you are all contributing and meeting your responsibilities. For your Devising log you need to explain:

- How you developed and refined your ideas and those of the others with whom you worked.
- How you developed the piece in rehearsals.
- How you developed and refined your own theatrical skills (performance or design) during the devising process.
- How you responded to feedback.
- How you used your refined theatrical skills in the final piece.

TIP

The word 'refined' means that the Devising log should note the progress and changes you have made during the devising and rehearsal process. Think about how you respond to setbacks and overcome obstacles. Did you make any changes after receiving feedback?

Rehearsal techniques

Devising is an active process and involves a great deal of 'trial and error' while you test ideas and see what works for you. Below are some rehearsal techniques to help you to develop your ideas.

Objectives

Create a short scene in which two characters have different **objectives.** Before the scene begins, clearly state what your objectives are, for example:

KEY TERM:
Objective: what the character wants.

CHARACTER 1 (Employee): I want a pay rise.

CHARACTER 2 (Boss): I want to leave work early to go to a football game.

REFLECTION

Discuss if the objectives and conflict are clear in the example on the right. What could be improved?

As you improvise the scene, think about how many different actions (the things you actually do) you can make to achieve your goal. For example, the employee might block the boss from leaving the room or show him a folder of all the work he has done. The boss might pretend to agree so he can leave or rush by the employee trying to ignore him.

First line/last line

As a group, agree the first line last line of a scene. Improvise a scene in which the characters take actions to get logically from the first line to the last. For example, the first line could be:

I'm fine, really, don't worry about me.

The last line could be:

I don't think you are ready to go back to school.

Between these you could devise a scene in which someone who is upset pretends they are fine, but then breaks down and can't carry through with their plan.

Another variation on this technique is to agree opening and closing positions for a scene. This might be two still images, such as a first image of one character on the floor, arms outraised to the other character whose back is turned. The second image might be the first character walking towards the door while the second character sits huddled in a chair. The challenge is to discover how the characters journeyed from the first image to the second.

Using performance conventions

Depending on the style of your piece, you may want to introduce various conventions. As you develop your piece you wish to try the following:

- Still images: these might be based on images you have researched or ones that you develop, which will help you to tell your story. You might use still images to start or end a scene or to emphasise a particular moment.
- Movement sequences: you could use synchronised movement, slow motion, mime, dance or other physical theatre. For example, you could recreate a protest using a silent slow motion sequence showing different people in a crowd or you could show how the internet works by having actors represent the journey a message makes through virtual space.
- **Choral speaking**: you could have a group of actors commenting together on a scene or you could share out lines in a speech among a number of people. You could highlight one word by having everyone saying that single word together.
- Breaking the fourth wall: you could use narration or opportunities to speak directly to the audience by introducing or interrupting the scene to comment on it.
- Split screen or **cross-cutting**: this is when you either have two scenes happening at the same time or you cut between the two scenes.

As you develop your piece, keep thinking about the meaning of it and what effect you want to have on the audience. You might think about using one of these conventions to help you get your meaning across. For example, you might want to highlight the turning point in a character's life, so you could use narration, slow motion or a still image to pinpoint that moment.

KEY TERMS:

Choral speaking: a group of people speaking together or sharing a speech.

Cross-cutting: alternating between two different scenes.

TIP

Avoid putting conventions in that do not help to advance your piece. Sometimes students will put in long dance or song sequences that do not help to tell their story. Part of the process is editing out anything that is irrelevant to your piece.

TASK 5

Choose a moment from your piece and rehearse it using at least two of the conventions above. Discuss which conventions work and if you could use them at other parts in your piece.

Contributing to development and collaboration as a designer

In most conventional theatre productions (and in Component 3), designers take their initial design inspiration from an existing text. However, designing for devised pieces has special challenges, especially in your ability to demonstrate your contributions to the development of the piece and to meet the practical demands of completing your work in time for the first performance. In script-based productions, if you read a script and see that you need to create a life-like, baby puppet or a sound design to depict a storm, you can plan in advance how much time and what materials you will need to complete the design.

However, with a devised piece, there will most likely be a longer period before you know what will be required. One way of avoiding a last-minute panic is to take an active role in the development of the piece. Here are some suggestions:

- Use design as part of the devising experience. For example, bring in music or sound effects to inspire rehearsals or aid movement sequences. Offer photos/artworks to prompt devising.
- Be an active participant in rehearsals and suggest how your design ideas could help the storytelling. For example, if there is a lengthy exposition section, which is slowing down the piece, could you offer to replace it with a shadow puppet show to convey the back story? Could you, as a sound designer, suggest using amplification or a distorting effect to make a moment more climactic or frightening?
- Take an active interest in the genre/performance style of the piece as this will affect your design choices.
- Establish any major design needs as early as possible. Even if the piece has not been fully devised, the group can decide on central concepts early on that you can begin developing while the script is being finalised. For example, a recent devised play had a major set change at the end, which had been agreed early in the devising process, so that everyone knew that was what the piece was leading to and the designer could begin the construction.
- Offer to lead rehearsals to develop a specific element of the production such as set changes, positioning onstage, use of props or puppetry.
- Provide rehearsal props/costumes/puppets/music, so that the actors are able to rehearse effectively.
- Involve the rest of the group in aspects of your design. For example, you could arrange a session with the whole group to record sound effects or a group trip to a charity shop to source costumes or props.
- Be flexible. Remember that ideas can change completely, especially in the early stages of devising.

TIP

Take an active interest in the whole piece. Don't think of yourself as less important than the performers. Your point of view about how the piece can be developed and shaped is as important as anyone else's.

TIP

Refer to Component 3 for more ideas on the types of design choices you can make, the materials you will need and the health and safety requirements.

Collaboration

Kerry Frampton, director/performer/designer, Splendid Productions

I'm a collaborator and not precious, there are normally as many people outside watching with opinions as there are onstage. It is a collaborative process in Splendid. There are techniques that I know will just work beautifully, particularly if they're centred around what we would like an audience to do. There are some things that just don't quite work for that specific piece, so I'll hold onto them for another performance.

Creative people often have strong opinions and this can lead to conflict. However, in drama it is important to find a way of resolving these potential conflicts. In the professional theatre, it is usually the director who settles these issues, but in group work, where everyone has an equal stake in the outcome, it can be a bit more difficult.

As a designer, you must work with the performers to ensure that your design is supporting the entire piece and the performers have an obligation to ensure that your creativity and input are seen and effective. It is no good designing a beautiful hat, if the actor refuses to wear it because they feel it hides their face or might fall off.

The designer and performer need to work together and arrive at a solution. Could the hat be refitted or altered so it fits more securely or is tilted off the face? Could the hat be worn for part of the scene and then taken off?

TASK 6

Look at the following design/performer collaboration problems and suggest how they could be resolved:

- You are the costume designer. You know the piece is set in the 1960s, but otherwise haven't learned enough about the characters to begin working on a costume design or sourcing items. You are worried that you won't have time to arrange the costumes if you don't get some guidance soon.
- You are a puppet designer. You are confident about making a puppet but aren't comfortable being onstage operating it. No one else in the group has volunteered to operate it.
- You are a set designer. You are excited about doing a set design, but the group has said they want a complicated and expensive set that you don't feel you could do.
- You are a lighting designer. Your idea is for the whole piece to be very dimly lit, but the costume designer says that means their costume/make-up design cannot be properly seen.
- You are a sound designer. You want music playing underneath several scenes, but the actors say they fear their dialogue won't be heard.

TIP

The best pieces are when all the elements work together. Don't think of yourself as in competition with the rest of the group. The goal is for everyone to succeed!

How to rehearse

THEATRE MAKER ADVICE

Kerry Fampton, performer/designer/ director, Splendid Productions

This one is one of my favourite Splendid moments in a rehearsal room, it was the *Seven Stages of Man*. There were three of us and a sheet. We wanted the Everyman character (played by me) to be manipulated and dressed using this sheet to represent each stage:

Birth – through a slit in the sheet a BIG baby is born.

1. **Infancy – sheet becomes nappy.**
2. **Child –becomes a cape.**
3. **Lover – sheet becomes a bed cover.**
4. **Worker – the sheet becomes a counter, or production line.**
5. **Wisdom – the sheet becomes a robe like a Greek scholar.**
6. **Old Age – the sheet is now a gigantic beard.**
7. **Dependency – it becomes a nappy again and we start at the beginning.**

There is no set way to rehearse, and professional theatre companies vary in how they approach rehearsals. Below are some approaches that you might find helpful:

- Start with a short warm-up such as a quick game or physical exercise to get focused.
- Agree an aim for a rehearsal such as:
  - 'creating the beginning'
  - 'staging the journey scene'
  - 'trying out the props'
  - 'working with music in the protest scene'.
- If possible, take it in turns to stand outside the scene and make constructive comments. Students acting as designers can helpfully comment on the work of the performers and vice versa.
- Spend a few minutes at the end of the rehearsal discussing how the rehearsal went.
- Assign tasks for people to do as homework such as:
  - 'research fashion for this period'
  - 'find a piece of music for the opening'
  - 'learn lines for the opening'.
- Have one or more people in the group act as a **scribe** to write down or pull together any bits of script that emerge from the work.
- Agree what you will rehearse in the next session.

KEY TERM:

Scribe: someone who writes documents.

Avoiding common rehearsal problems

Common rehearsal **errors**:

- Rehearsing one section of the piece at the expense of the other scenes. Some groups end up with a perfect opening scene – and nothing else.
- Spreading the work unevenly – make sure that everyone is important to the success of the piece.
- Spending too long talking rather than getting up and doing. Often you can only tell if an idea will work by trying it.
- Having too many scenes with characters sitting down talking. Some groups avoid this by restricting the number of chairs in their piece and choosing active scenes where the characters have to be doing something.
- Having pieces that are under-researched. If you have set something in the 1920s it will be very confusing if you have people using mobile phones or talking about television.
- Getting discouraged and constantly changing ideas. It is normal to have some rehearsals that are less successful than others. However, if you were enthusiastic about an idea, don't give up the first time you hit an obstacle.

If you get stuck, try one of the following **solutions**:

- Check to see if there is clear conflict in the scene. Apply the 'objective' rehearsal technique discussed earlier.
- See if there is a convention, such as using mime or music, that will make the scene more exciting.
- Write a bit of dialogue or a monologue that could kick-start the scene.
- Make sure you have agreed what the message and purpose of your piece is.

The Wonderful World of Dissocia *by Anthony Neilson, costumes designed by Alice Smith in collaboration with Jasmine Swan*

TIP

Make notes in your notebook as you go through the process of rehearsals to help you in completing your Devising log.

THEATRE MAKER ADVICE

1 When preparing to play a character, my advice would be: Keep your eyes open! A lot of inspiration can be drawn from observing other people, for example in the supermarket, in cafes or on public transport. I was once playing a character who was never seen without a cigar. On the way to rehearsal one day I was sitting behind an old man who was wearing a cloth cap pushed right back on his head with a cigarette stuffed behind his ear. It occurred to me that I could use the same combination for my character, and from that time onwards in rehearsal I was never without a cap and a cigar jammed behind my ear. It helped me a lot.

2 The more ways you can rehearse a scene the better. it's easy to go stale when you rehearse the scene with the lines as written. One technique I have found useful is to replace the actual words with gibberish. For example the line How are you? could become Bee da su? This helps with uncovering the underlying rhythms of the text, which is often as important as to what is actually being said.

3 In rehearsal, there is no such thing as wrong. If you persevere when things aren't going well, often interesting developments can arise, which allow you to take the scene in a different direction.

Alex Harland, performer

The 'objective' rehearsal technique can be found on page 218.

TIP

You can use a sheet like this to make notes that will help you write your Devising log. Look at what needs to be shown in your Devising log and then note on your sheet when you have done this. For example: initial response, research, aims and intentions, responding to feedback, developing and refining ideas.

Designers' and performers' rehearsal note-taking sheet

Some designers and performers find it helpful to use a grid like the one below to keep track of their progress (it is understood that elements of this will change and develop as rehearsals progress; also, the time you have to rehearse will vary from centre to centre). This will help you to complete your Devising log.

Title of piece: *2008*

Style of piece: epic/physical theatre

Date of first performance: 1 November

Role: set designer

KEY TERM:

Chairography: choreographed movements involving chairs.

WEEK OF REHEARSALS	WHAT HAVE I LEARNED?	WHAT DO I NEED TO DO?	WHEN DOES IT NEED TO BE COMPLETED?
WEEK 1	▶ STIMULUS: news report about the financial crash of 2008. INITIAL RESPONSE: People carrying boxes, lives changed, office environment. ▶ OUR IDEAS: the piece is going to be set in an office building in 2008. Showing the effect of the economic crash.	▶ RESEARCH: design for 2008, offices/office furniture. Research other plays with office sets (online). ▶ CONTRIBUTION: Bring in photos of office as stimulus for a rehearsal. ▶ Source some rehearsal furniture.	Week 2
WEEK 2	▶ AIMS AND INTENTIONS: The style of the piece is going to be epic. (COMMUNICATE MEANING) ▶ Create sympathy for those who cannot cope with the change. Are we too focused on money/material things? ▶ Direct address. Use captions/projections? ▶ Boxes used as a recurring motif?	▶ Make notes of scenes so far and discuss with performers possible captions. (COLLABORATION) ▶ Research what economic graphs look like for possible design idea. Sketch possible design for wall (keep copy for Devising log) (DESIGN SKILLS, CREATING AND DEVELOPING IDEAS)	Week 3
WEEK 3	▶ Make prop lists (doughnuts, telephones, pens, paper). (PRECISE DETAILS) ▶ Feedback on design for back wall. Discuss how it could be used by performers. (COLLABORATION)	▶ Arrange materials (flat/paint) for back wall. Schedule time in art room for painting. Arrange volunteers to help. (DESIGN SKIILLS)	Painting to be completed by Week 5, other tasks by Week 4
WEEK 4	▶ Discuss set changes with group. How can these be accomplished? Can sound designer provide music to accompany these? (COLLABORATION) ▶ Source chairs on casters. (PRECISE DETAIL)	▶ Make a plan for set changes. ▶ Arrange for one rehearsal with group to organise these. ▶ Bring in remaining props. ▶ Prepare for feedback session.	Next rehearsal or next week (coordinate with sound designer)
WEEK 5	▶ Change the lettering and size of captions – currently they can't be read easily. (RESPONDING TO FEEDBACK/PRECISE DETAIL) ▶ Set changes too slow!	▶ Finish back wall set (take photos for Devising log). ▶ Rehearse set changes again (simplify!). ▶ Re-do caption slides. (RESPONDING TO FEEDBACK) ▶ Create prop list.	Next rehearsal or next week
WEEK 6	▶ Set is fully painted – but needs to dry. ▶ Located chairs that can be rolled on – and go up and down (possibly incorporate in movement/**chairography**?).	▶ Get set up. ▶ Locate new tray and set of mugs. ▶ Rehearse actors for tearing down graph scene. ▶ Ask for volunteers to help with technical rehearsal.	Set and props: tomorrow Actors: next rehearsal Volunteers: technical rehearsal

Download a printable version from Samples & Downloads at www.illuminatepublishing.com.

Giving and responding to feedback

As you rehearse you will need to help each other to improve your performance or design. Giving and receiving feedback is an art, as you have to be constructive and helpful, while also being truthful. You also have to be open to hearing comments that may disappoint you. A good technique is to give feedback with the following structure:

One thing you liked

One thing you didn't understand

One thing that could be further developed/you'd like to see more.

So, for example, your feedback might be:

- I liked the tension in the opening scene because it made me wonder what was going to happen next.
- I didn't understand why the parents were fighting.
- I would like to see the characters when they are out of the home setting.

Or your comments might be more technical:

- I liked your use of an accent in the first scene.
- From the way you positioned yourself onstage, I couldn't tell how you felt about the other character.
- I would like to see you use your excellent comedy skills more, for example in the restaurant scene.

Or the feedback on a design might be:

- I liked the period music used at the beginning of the show, which helped me to picture when it was happening.
- I didn't know if there was meant to be sound effect in the second scene or if that was a mistake.
- I would like to have heard more effects that established the location – something that made clear what a busy, hectic place it was.

Once you receive feedback, you need to consider how to address any issues that arise. Of course, the person giving feedback could be wrong, but be open to the possibility that they are trying to help you. You might schedule extra rehearsals to address any problems or discuss with the rest of your group any common areas of concern.

Another way to give feedback is to use Buddy Assessor forms.

What this means is that groups get together and each person gets a Buddy Assessor from another group. At certain stages during the rehearsal process, the Buddy Assessors will watch and comment on each other's work. After receiving your Buddy Assessor's comments, you can target how you will develop and improve your work. Evidence of this process can then be recorded in Section 2 of your Devising log to show how you developed and refined your piece and theatrical skills during the rehearsals.

Buddy Assessor form – devised piece

Name of performer/designer:

Name of assessor:

What did the performer/designer do well? Please give clear examples.	
What would you like to see developed more? Explain in as much detail as possible.	
Performers: what vocal skills did the performer demonstrate? What physical skills did the performer demonstrate? Designers: did the designer demonstrate a range of skills (think about design ideas; use of technical equipment; creativity)? Provide examples.	
Performers: did the performer create one (or more) roles convincingly? Designer: did the designer add to key moments of the piece? Provide examples.	
Did the performer/designer contribute to the piece as a whole (for example, by clearly knowing cues/lines; working positively with others)? Provide examples.	
What did you think was the message or theme of the piece? Explain.	
Any comments on the piece as a whole?	

TIP

Once you have been assessed, write up your notes for your Devising log and set targets for areas needing development and improvement.

Download a printable version from Samples & Downloads at www.illuminatepublishing.com.

Structuring your piece

Kerry Fampton, performer/designer/ director, Splendid Productions

Peter Brook [a respected director] has a lovely phrase 'Hold on tightly, let go lightly.' If it doesn't serve the piece, if it doesn't do what we need it to do for an audience, then it can't stay in. Our work is lean, the aim is always clarity and truth.

In Splendid we always know **what** we are showing/telling an audience, **why** they need to be shown or told that and finally **how**. The **how** is what theatrical technique will tell that section in the clearest way: song, naturalism, direct address, chorus, narration. The **how** is normally what we work through in the rehearsal room.

THEATRE MAKER ADVICE

Once you have arrived at the basis of your piece, you will want to consider its structure. Some basic structures are:

- **Linear**: this is when a piece goes in chronological order. For example, it might show, in order, the events of one day or one week or one year.
- **Non-linear**: this is when events are not in chronological order but may jump around in time. For example, there could be a scene set in the present day, then one set a century ago and then another in the future.

Other structural devices you might consider:

- **Narration:** having one or more characters speaking to the audience.
- **Bookending:** having the first and last scenes connected in some way.
- **Flashbacks:** providing scenes from the past that give extra meaning to the main story.
- **Sub-plot**: a secondary story that runs alongside the main story, so, for example, the main story may be political, but there is a romantic sub-plot.

A typical structure of a play is:

- **Exposition**: when you introduce the setting and main characters and what they want.
- **Complication**: where the obstacles to the characters' objectives are developed.
- **Climax**: the point of greatest tension and conflict.
- **Resolution**: when the plot comes to its conclusion.

An example of students using this structure would be:

- **Exposition**: Four different characters are shown on a summer day rushing for a bus. Each has an important appointment that day.
- **Complication**: Each character has obstacles that make them anxious and fearful they will have problems on that day. There is a flashback for each character showing why today is so important to them.
- **Climax**: There is a dramatic accident on the bus. A slow-motion sequence shows the accident.
- **Resolution**: Some survive and some do not. The survivors reflect on their feelings.

▲ *Spendid Productions' production of* The Trial, *telling the audience what to do.*

KEY TERMS:

Chronological: Showing events in the order in which they occurred.

Sub-plot: a secondary or less important plot in a story.

Charting the structure of your piece

It is likely that you will find you want to alter the structure of your piece. One way of refining the structure is to get a large sheet of paper and chart a graph like this:

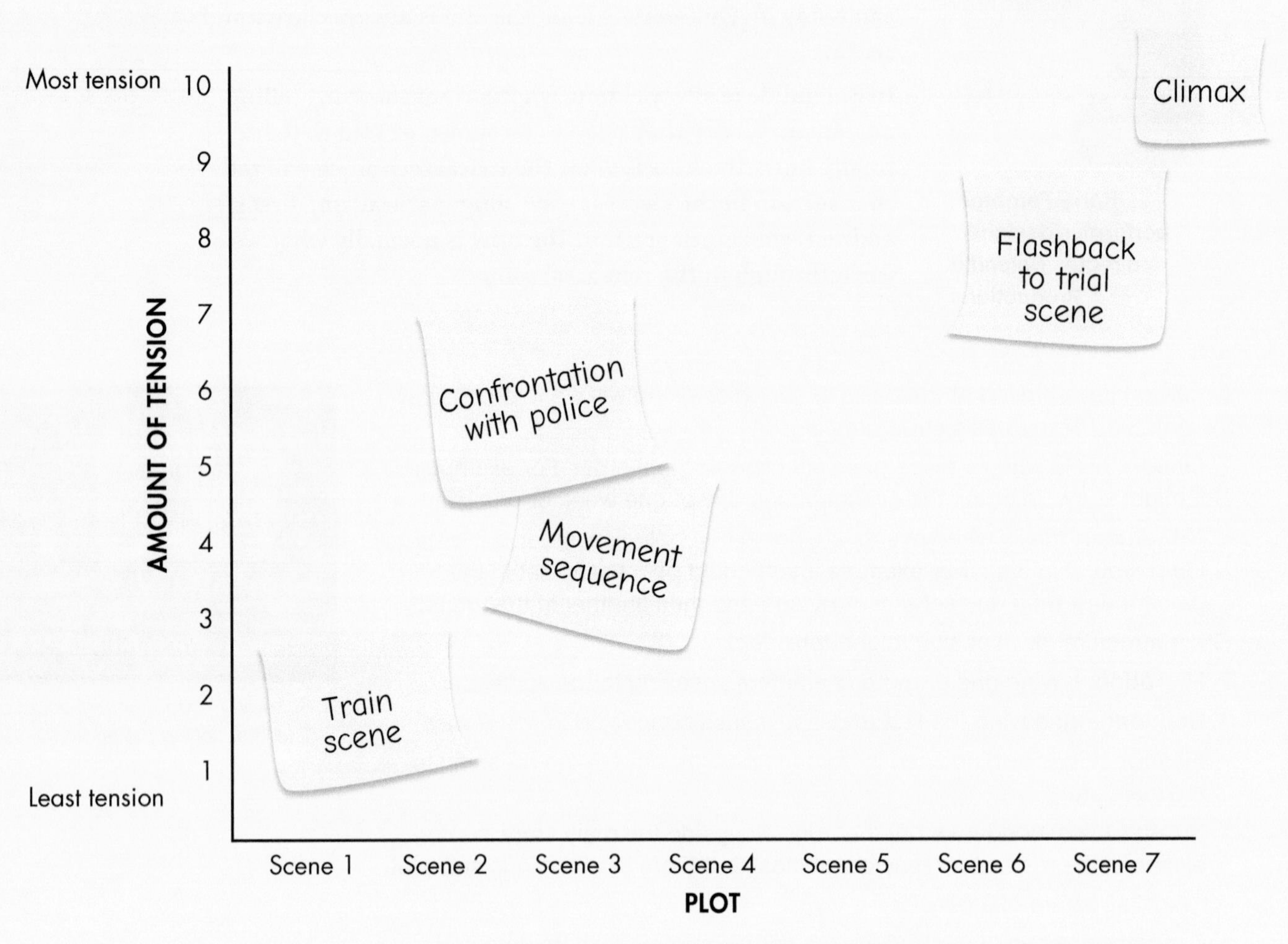

Write down each of your scenes on sticky notes and place them on the graph. As you work, you may discover that the scene you thought would be your climax doesn't work or that you want to introduce a different opening or ending scene. Keep adjusting the structure until you feel it works and there are no unnecessary scenes.

Download a printable version from Samples & Downloads at www.illuminatepublishing.com.

The devised performance

For the devised performance, you will be contributing either as a performer or a designer. The assessed performance may be a duologue – a performance by just two people – or a group performance of three to six performers. If there are designers in the group they can choose between the following options:

- lighting
- sound
- set
- costume
- puppets.

There can only be one designer for each specialist area. So you may have a lighting and set designer in the group, but you cannot have two set designers, for example.

The length of the devised piece depends on the number of performers in the piece.

The designers' work must be seen in the live performance. This means, for example, that if you are a lighting design student then your lighting must be seen as part of the devised piece. Design students are assessed on their design, not on their practical ability to operate the equipment associated with the design. However, design students are encouraged to improve and develop their theatrical skills as much as possible and to realise their designs in a practical way as much as they are able to within any limitations they may discover.

TIP

You will complete a Statement of Dramatic Intentions, where you specify what you, as a designer or performer, want to show and what you want the audience to understand from the performance.

TIP

Keep checking the timing of your piece. In the final weeks you should keep a close eye on its length in order to decide if you need to edit or add material.

Theatrical skills – performance

Performers must develop and perform one character or, if it suits the style of the play, more than one role.

You will be marked on the following:

- level of use of theatrical skill
- range of theatrical skills demonstrated
- contribution to the effectiveness of the piece
- inventiveness of your work
- success in realising individual artistic intention.

For a performer, theatrical skills you will aim to show should include:

- vocal skills
- physical skills
- characterisation
- interaction and communication with audience and other performers.

Your 'artistic intention' will be judged against your Statement of Dramatic Intentions, which you will provide before your performance. Be as accurate here as you can.

TIP

It is important that your Statement of Dramatic Intentions is accurate.

How to demonstrate vocal skills

At the very least, you must ensure that your speech is clear and easily heard by the audience. But other aspects of vocal ability you might experiment with are:

- **Tone:**
  - Are you able to adjust the tone of your voice to express the situations your character is in?
- **Pace and pause:**
  - Can you vary the pace of your speech as appropriate for the situation?
  - Can you use techniques such as pausing to heighten tension, suggest hesitation or create comic timing?
- **Variation in voice:**
  - If you are playing more than one role, can you differentiate between characters by using vocal skills, such as accent, pitch or volume?
  - If you have a character who behaves differently in certain situations can you show that by a change in voice?

TIP

Before rehearsals and performances do a short vocal warm-up, including exercises to free your vocalisation and tongue twisters to improve diction (see page 246).

Common vocal problems

It is no accident that drama schools spend years working on improving their students' vocal skills, such as breath control, diction and pitch, as these are so important for a performance. Here are some common problems for young actors:

Monotone:

- Speaking everything on the same note.
- **Effect:** dull.

Volume:

- Speaking too softly to be heard.
- **Effect:** confusing and frustrating.

Diction:

- Speaking indistinctly and running words together.
- **Effect:** confusing and irritating.

Pitch:

- Speaking either on too high or too low notes to be fully expressive.
- **Effect:** unpleasant, irritating or dull sound.

Lack of emotion:

- The tone of voice not matching the excitement of the dramatic situation.
- **Effect:** doesn't convey character or situation

TASK 7

Choose a section of the devised piece and experiment with different ways of delivering the lines. Check the list of common errors and make sure you are avoiding those.

▸ Go to pages 246–247 for more advice about vocal work.

How to demonstrate physical skills

You may devise a piece that demands advanced physical skills such as mime or synchronised movement. However, even a naturalistic piece offers you the ability to show physical skills. You will be assessed on how well your physical skills add to your characterisation and the piece as a whole. Some ways in which you can show physical skills include:

use of gesture

use of stage space

body language and stance

variation in movement

Common physical skills difficulties for student actors:

- tight, self-conscious movement
- areas of tension inappropriate for the character or situation, such as raised shoulders or clenched hands
- repetitive movements
- wandering onstage or other movement without purpose
- inappropriate movement for character, such as too young for an older character or too hesitant or informal for a powerful, high-status character.

TASK 8

Choose a scene from your piece and take out all the dialogue. See if you can convey the meaning and emotions of the scene with no words at all.

REFLECTION

What movements help you to establish your character and what they want? Can you vary your physical choices to give the scene more impact?

▲ Dental Society Midwinter Meeting, *feeling the cold*

Theatrical skills: design

THEATRE MAKER ADVICE

Kerry Frampton, director/performer/ designer, Splendid Productions

I normally design our work – again because my strongest ideas about character and story and atmosphere come from images or colours – every choice we make for the production then feeds into the design.

Fifty-five percent of communication is visual, the Greek root of the word theatre is 'to see', so we must think carefully about the information we are placing before the eyes of the spectator.

In a practical way there is no room for surplus set, as we are taking down and putting up our set twice a day in a selection of spaces. It must also be able to fit into the boot of a car.

With *The Odyssey* – we needed a clear, linear, visual way to plot the 20-year journey from War to Home for Odysseus. So a blue washing line (the colour of the sea) was rigged across the back and each stop was a way of exploring another **archetypal** quality demonstrated by the hero, each archetype had an emoji-like picture at the top [see photo below] so that you could clearly understand which stop had happened.

Again, because the story was so complicated and moved around, we needed something simple that would allow an audience to feel safe. To see the progression of the piece as well as Odysseus. He was going home, we were too.

KEY TERM:

Archetypal: a typical example of someone or something; associated with an original or mythic quality of someone or something, eg, 'he was the archetypal businessman' or 'it was the archetypal battle between good and evil'.

Splendid Productions' The Odyssey ▶

TIP

Your 'artistic intention' will be judged based on your Statement of Dramatic Intentions, which you will provide before your performance. You will be asked to write briefly what you aim to show in the performance and what you want the audience to take away from the performance. Be as accurate as you can.

You will be marked on the following:

- Level of theatrical skill.
- Range of theatrical skills demonstrated.
- Contribution to the effectiveness of the piece.
- Inventiveness of your work.
- Success in realising individual artistic intention.

Design specialism and requirements

Specialism chosen:
Lighting designer

Requirement: Must create **one** lighting design. The design must show a range of lighting effects/states and cues/transitions designed to meet the demands of the devised piece being performed.

Specialism chosen:
Sound designer

Requirement: Must create **one** sound design. The design must show a range of sound effects and cues/transitions designed to meet the demands of the devised piece being performed.

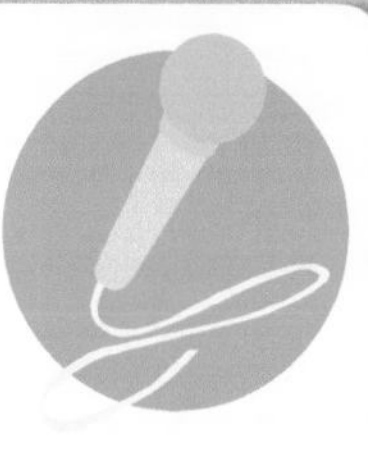

Specialism chosen:
Set designer

Requirement: Must create **one** set design. The design must be for one setting, showing dressings and props designed to meet the demands of the devised piece being performed.

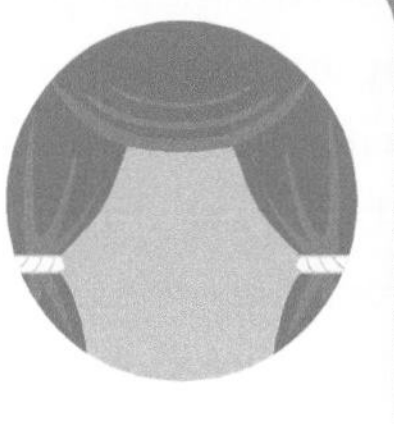

Specialism chosen:
Costume designer

Requirement: Must create **one** costume design for one performer. The design must show clothing and accessories (and hair, make-up and masks if applicable) designed to meet the demands of the devised piece being performed.

Specialism chosen:
Puppet designer

Requirement: Must create **one** puppet design. The design must show a complete puppet designed to meet the demands of the devised piece being performed.

Your designs will be assessed in the live performance so must be visible in it.

How to show a range of theatrical skills

You may wonder how, if you are creating a single design, you can show a range of skills. Here are some suggestions:

- **Costume design:** you might think about using different fabrics or stitches to show a range of skills. You could choose accessories or create a make-up design to show more skills. You may choose a design that shows that you have thought about fit/shape. You might create a costume that is suitable for a quick change or can be modified for different scenes.
- **Lighting design:** you might demonstrate that you know how to use colours, different lanterns or special effects. Your cue sheet should be detailed and accurate. The timings should be clear, for example indicating if it is a sudden blackout or a slow fade.
- **Puppet design:** you could create a puppet that shows advanced skills in its design and how it is manipulated by the puppeteer. It might have a range of movements or show a well-chosen, imaginative use of materials.
- **Set design:** in addition to the main set design, you could provide stage furniture or other set 'dressing' to show more theatrical skills. For example, if the piece is set in a particular period, you might source or create items, such as a particular prop for the set to reinforce that.
- **Sound design:** you should create a detailed cue sheet showing your understanding of the needs of the devised piece. You might create original sound effects or research a variety of music to create your sound design.

Analysis and evaluation

THEATRE MAKER ADVICE

Kerry Frampton, director/performer/designer, Splendid Productions

Often we find that the simpler the idea, the better it is. Our simplest ideas are the ones that our audiences think are the most clever.
Simple and obvious are my two tips for devising. In fact here is my main preach for young devisers:

1. If your topic/stimulus/starting point is **complex** your way of telling the story must be **simple**.
2. If your topic/stimulus/starting point is **simple** the way of communicating your piece can be **complex**.

Taking something complex and then communicating it in a complex way just makes the audience hate you. Communicating an idea clearly is important. If you don't know what you are doing and why then an audience won't either. It just becomes an annoying mystery that makes the spectator feel like they don't 'get it'.

TIP

When writing your Devising log, don't be afraid to use the word 'I'. However, don't take credit for work you didn't do or work that didn't occur.

In the context of this section:

- To 'analyse' is to identify and investigate.
- To 'evaluate' is to assess the merit of the different approaches used and formulate judgements.

Section 3 of your Devising log gives you the opportunity to show your skills at analysing and evaluating your devised work. You need to include:

- how far you developed your theatrical skills
- the benefits you brought to the pair/group and the way in which you helped to shape the final piece
- the overall impact you personally had on the devising, rehearsals and performance.

You should also consider the areas of the devising that didn't go as well as you had hoped or could have been further developed.

In order to write concisely about how well you succeeded, you need to be very clear about what you hoped to achieve.

Here is an example of a performer analysing and evaluating their work:

KEY TERM:

Stage business: the small movements an actor might do onstage, such as opening a book, brushing hair or straightening cushions. These may add to the naturalism of a scene or provide insight into the characters.

> I knew that my role was a comic one, so I worked hard with Sam to get the timing of the office scene correct. (1) There was a tricky piece of physical comedy where I spilled a drink on him, which didn't work at first. It seemed unbelievable and sloppy. (2) However, I suggested that Sam should do some stage business with the folders so he seemed to be caught more by surprise and the spilt drink caused more damage. (3) I was pleased with that scene in the final performance. Judging by the audience's laughter, it worked very well. (4)

(1) Analysis
(2) Evaluation
(3) Analysis
(4) Evaluation

Here is an example of a costume designer analysing and evaluating their work:

As our piece was set in the 1950s, I spent a long time making sure that I got every period detail as correct as possible. I found a vintage clothing shop and purchased a small handbag for Ruth that was perfect for the period (1) and looked great with her dress. (2) However, I was frustrated that despite studying magazines for the period, I never got her hairstyle exactly right. (3) With a larger budget, we might have thought about using a wig or perhaps I needed more training in how to get a beehive look. (4) However, the overall look was clearly of the period, and there were excellent details like the colour of her nail polish. (5)

Analysis (1)
Evaluation (2)
Evaluation (3)
Analysis (4)
Evaluation (5)

TASK 9

Choose an aspect of your contribution to the final piece and write a paragraph explaining:

- what you did
- what was successful about it
- what could have been improved.

KEY TERM:

Beehive: a hairstyle popular in the 1950s and 1960s for which hair was back-combed into a high cone shape.

Audience questionnaire

Name of piece:

1. When and where did you think this play was set?
2. What moments did you particularly like and why?
3. What did you think could have been improved and why?
4. Please provide some comments on the performances.
5. Please provide some comments on the design (set, costume, lighting, sound and puppet, as appropriate).
6. What do you think the message of the piece was?
7. On a scale of 1 to 10 with 1 being the worst and 10 the best, what score would you give this piece?

TIP

To improve their analysis and evaluation section, some groups find it helpful to have the audience complete a questionnaire. You should write the questionnaire specifically to suit your devised piece. For example:

- If you set the piece in a particular time period, did the audience understand that?
- If your piece had a message, did they know what it was?
- If you created a comedy, did they think it was funny?
- If you had audience interaction, did they engage with that?

Checking your Devising log

Your Devising log must be your own work. Even though you have devised as part of a group, you must put together your Devising log on your own. Your work may be presented in written form or a combination of recorded evidence and written, or entirely recorded.

As you are preparing your Devising log, frequently look over the following checklist:

- [ ] Have I written or recorded three sections with the appropriate headings?
- [ ] Are the sections roughly the same length?
- [ ] Have I stayed within the final word count/length?
- [ ] Have I provided evidence of research?
- [ ] Have I stated my dramatic aims and intentions?
- [ ] Have I shown how I developed and refined ideas?
- [ ] Have I explained how I helped the group?
- [ ] Have I shown how I responded to feedback?
- [ ] Have I demonstrated that I have developed my theatrical skills?
- [ ] Have I explained how I positively shaped the final piece?
- [ ] Have I used correct theatrical terminology to explain my thoughts?
- [ ] Have I given specific examples to back-up my points?
- [ ] Have I analysed and evaluated my work?

TIP

Often students discover that one section of their log is weaker than others. Go back to that section and look at it critically. Seek out anything important that you might have missed. Some students make basic errors such as forgetting to discuss the stimulus or what they hoped to achieve with the piece.

CHALLENGE

In order to succeed at a high level, you need to provide precise details and an impressive amount of creativity. Check your work to make sure your creative journey is clear and that you have backed it up with specific details.

TIP

The Devising log may be written, an audio/visual or audio-visual recording or a combination of the two. If you are unsure which method of creating your Devising log would be best for you, discuss this with your teacher. Don't assume that speaking in a recording is necessarily easier than writing, as it will require the same preparation and organisation. No matter which method you choose, you should make sure that your work does not exceed the maximum length or timing. Your work may be accompanied by:

- photographs and/or
- sketches/drawings and/or
- cue sheets.

WHAT HAVE I LEARNED?

DEVISING DRAMA

CHOICE OF STIMULI
- A poem, news article or short story
- A song or piece of instrumental music
- A recent or current event
- A photograph, painting or sculpture
- A theme, such as 'Time' or 'War'
- A myth or fairy tale
- A cultural event, e.g. festival or ceremony

CHOICE OF GENRE
- Comedy
- Tragedy
- Physical theatre
- Melodrama
- Documentary theatre
- Commedia dell'arte
- Epic theatre
- TIE
- Naturalism

CHOICE OF SPECIALISM
- Performer
- Designer
  - Set
  - Lighting
  - Sound
  - Costume
  - Puppet

HOW TO DEVISE
- Generate ideas
- Respond to feedback
- Research
- Rehearse
- Polish and refine
- Design

DEVISING LOG
- Section 1: Response to stimulus
- Section 2: Development and collaboration
- Section 3: Analysis and evaluation
- The devised performance

CHECK YOUR LEARNING

If you are uncertain of the meaning of any of the terms above, go back and revise.

Why not use the downloadable version of this summary as a basis for your own checklist of what you have learned from Samples & Downloads at www.illuminatepublishing.com.

COMPONENT 3

TEXTS IN PRACTICE

THE SPECIFICATION SAYS...

This component is a practical component in which students are assessed on their ability to apply theatrical skills to realise artistic intentions in live performance.

For this component students must complete two assessment tasks:

- Study and present a key extract (monologue, duologue or group performance).
- Study and present a second key extract (monologue, duologue or group performance) from the same play.

Each student must choose to be assessed as a:

- performer or
- lighting designer or
- sound designer or
- set designer or
- costume designer or
- puppet designer.

You must choose the same specialism for both extracts.

ASSESSMENT FOCUS

AO2: Apply theatrical skills to realise artistic intentions in live performance.

CHALLENGE

If performing, choose a role that will give you sufficient opportunities. There are many ways in which you could show an excellent range of skills by attempting roles with at least some of these qualities: emotional depth; physical precision; an interesting context; vocal variation. If you are playing two different characters in the extracts, make sure you have differentiated between them. If you are playing the same character, there may be the opportunity to show how that character has grown or changed from the earlier extract.

TIP

Keep track of the length of your piece.

Getting started

You must decide on your specialism and the play text you will be studying and presenting. **The play you choose cannot be one you studied for Component 1 and cannot have the same playwright, genre description, performance style or time period as your Component 1 play.** This is in order to give you a varied experience of drama. It will allow you to learn about different plays and styles.

You may prepare monologues, work with one other performer on a duologue or you may perform in group pieces with up to five other students. If you choose to design, you will be designing for the extracts being performed by others.

How you will be assessed

Whether you are a designer or a performer, you will be assessed on the following contribution to the performance in both extracts:

- Range of skills demonstrated.
- Skills deployed precisely and in an effective way.
- Personal interpretation that is appropriate to the play as a whole.
- Personal interpretation that is sensitive to context.
- Artistic intentions are achieved.
- The length of your piece is dictated by the number in your group.
- If you are performing a monologue, your performance of each monologue should be between 2 and 5 minutes.
- If you are producing a duologue, the extracts should be between 3 and 10 minutes.
- If it is a group performance, each extract should be between 4 and 20 minutes.

Simple costumes and a clever set in a school play

Performers

If you choose to be a performer, you must perform and interpret one role or character per extract – or more than one role if, for example, it is a multi-role. You may perform the same character in both extracts or perform different characters in each extract. For example, a performer in two extracts from *A Midsummer Night's Dream* could play Bottom in both extracts or Bottom in the first extract and another character such as Puck or even Helena in the second extract. You may play a character of any age, gender or background.

How to approach a script

Whatever script you perform, you will need to study it carefully in order to decide how the characters can be interpreted. Below are examples from three different genres of playscript with initial questions that an actor might ask and suggestions of rehearsal techniques to explore the scenes further. These could be used with a wide variety of scripts.

A naturalistic script

The scene on the following page is the opening of *Citizenship* by Mark Ravenhill (2006), a play about teenagers and their fumbling journey towards adulthood. In it, Amy is getting ready to pierce the ear of her friend, Tom.

Try the following rehearsal exercises using the extract on the following page.

Sense memory

One common rehearsal technique is to recall physical conditions and relive them. In this scene, Tom swallows Nurofen, takes a swig of vodka and puts an ice cube on his ear. All of these need to be realistically recreated by the actor. Focusing on those three actions, recall times when you:

- found it hard to swallow a pill – how did it taste and feel?
- tasted something that was surprisingly strong, sour or unpleasant – how did you feel?
- were suddenly very cold – how did that feel?

Working individually, go through the motions of swallowing a pill, taking a gulp of an unpleasant or surprising drink and putting something very cold on your ear (some people find it helpful to do this with their eyes closed). What sensations could you remember? What physical reactions did you have? Apply those sensations to the relevant parts of the scene.

TIP

There is no one right answer to these questions, but how you personally decide to answer them is the basis for your interpretation of the characters.

Actions

From this scene there are hints about Tom and Amy's relationship. One way to explore this is by playing different actions. That means to agree what the character wants to achieve in the scene. For example, Amy's action for the scene might be 'to get close to Tom' or 'to help Tom' or 'to show Tom how much I like him'. With your partner:

- Decide if your character wants the same thing throughout the scene or if it changes at some point.
- Choose a verb to describe what your character wants, such as 'to reassure', 'to command', 'to console' or 'to approach', for each section of the scene.
- Play the scene and explore how your choice of action words might affect your performance. If you chose 'to get close to', does your character find excuses to be near or touch the other character? If you chose 'to help', does your character speak in a calm and reassuring way to the other?

TIP

In naturalistic acting, the audience will want to see how believable you can make the characters and their reactions to situations.

Citizenship

One

Amy, Tom

Amy: You got the Nurofen? (1)

Tom: Yeah.

Amy: Take four.

Tom: It says two.

Amy: Yeah, but if you're gonna really numb yourself you gotta do four.

Tom: I dunno. (2)

Amy: Do you want it to hurt?

Tom: No.

Amy: Then take four. Here. (3)

[Amy *passes* Tom *vodka. He uses it to wash down four Nurofen.*] (4)

Amy: Now put the ice cube on your ear.

[Tom *does this.*] (5)

Amy: Now you gotta hold it there till you can't feel nothing.

Tom: Thanks for helping. (6)

Amy: It's gonna look good.

Tom: Yeah?

Amy: Yeah, really suit you.

Tom: Thass good.

Amy: You got a nice face. (7)

Tom: I don't like my face.

Amy: I think it's nice.

Tom: Sometimes I look in the mirror and I wish I was dead. (8)

Amy: I got rid of mirrors.

Tom: Yeah.

Amy: Mum read this feng shui thing and it said I wasn't supposed to have them. (9) You numb now?

Tom: Almost. You got a nice face.

Amy: You don't have to lie. (10)

Tom: I'm not. You're fit.

Amy: I know I'm plain. But that's okay. I talk to my therapist. (11)

(1) Where is this scene happening?

(2) From this opening, what do you think the relationship is between Tom and Amy?

(3) These lines are very short. What might that suggest about Amy at this point?

(4) What might Tom's facial expression be when he drinks vodka?

(5) How can the actor portray what it feels like to have a cold ice cube on his ear?

(6) Why do you think Tom says this line?

(7) How easy is it for Amy to say this? How might Tom react?

(8) What effect could be created on this line? What will the effect on the audience be?

(9) What does this line tell us about Amy's home life?

(10) How does Amy react to being told she has a nice face?

(11) How does Amy feel about herself?

A stylised script

A stylised script can make different demands on the actor, as you may be creating exaggerated characters or use techniques such as physical theatre or choral speaking.

The play *The Trial* (1970) by Steven Berkoff, adapted from a novel by Franz Kafka (published in 1925), is about a bank clerk, Josef K, who is arrested without knowing of what crime he has been accused. Berkoff uses many stylised conventions, such as a narrator, chorus, soundscapes and physical theatre.

TIP

There is no one way to play these roles. There are many aspects of personal interpretation for you to consider. For example, you may choose to use a particular accent or a certain gesture that you believe is appropriate.

TIP

As you can have no more than six performers in your group, you will need to use multi-role if you choose this script as there are many characters.

The City [Act One, Scene Two]

Sound of ticking clocks made by the Chorus. *'Josef K' sung.* (1)

Narrator: It was eight o'clock. The city came to life. (2)

[*Cacophony of city life.*] (3)

Chorus 1: Someone must have been lying about Josef K.

Chorus 2: For without having done anything wrong ...

Chorus 3: He was arrested one fine morning.

Chorus 4: His landlady who always brought the breakfast at eight o'clock ...

Chorus 5: Failed to appear. (4)

K: That had never happened before. (5)

Chorus 1: K waiting a little longer.

Chorus 2: People opposite seemed to be staring at him with distinct curiosity.

Chorus 3: Then feeling put out and hungry, he rang the bell.

[Chorus *as bell reaches threatening crescendo.* (6) Two Guards *enter in bowler hats.*] (7)

Guard 1: You rang?

K: I rang for the maid.

Guard 1: What's your name?

K: Josef K.

Guard 2: He's the one.

Guard 1: Wouldn't you know anyway.

Guard 2: Pale as fear.

Guard 1: Are you frightened, K?

K: What have I done ... Why! (8)

1. How can the Chorus create the sound of the ticking clocks? Should they perform a movement sequence for this section?
2. Is the Narrator one of the Chorus or a separate figure? Should he step out of the group and address the audience directly?
3. How can the Chorus use vocal and physical skills to create city life?
4. How will the Chorus move during this sequence? Will they stand in one place or move around the stage? Will they move as individuals or as a group?
5. How will Josef K stand out from the other characters? Is he less exaggerated and more realistic? Does he have particular mannerisms to make him seem unassuming and 'ordinary'?
6. How can the Chorus use their vocal skills to create the sound of the bell ringing?
7. How can two members of the Chorus transform into the two Guards? Will they change their body language and way of walking?
8. How can the performer playing Josef K make his fear and confusion clear by using vocal and physical skills?

Splendid Productions' Josef K ▼

Rehearsal techniques

Choral movement

Follow the hand: have one person in your group be the leader. The rest of the group faces the leader. The leader raises their hand, palm towards the group, and the group must follow it, while staying in the same position in the group. So, if the leader's hand moves to the right, the group leans to the right. If the hand goes low the group squats down. If the hand trembles, then the whole group quivers in time with it.

Apply this technique to the clock sequence. The leader should conduct the group to move in time with the 'tick tock' sounds. They can experiment with changing levels or tempo.

REFLECTION

Discuss points in the script where it would be effective to have the Chorus working in unison.

A double act

Have the performers playing two guards experiment with pair work by trying the following:

- Create movements in the scene where you mirror each other.
- Create movements where you seem to be opposites. For example, one of you takes little steps and the other very large ones; one of you moves very quickly and the other very slowly.
- Create movements that show you are such a team that you are always in contact with each other. No matter how much you move some part of you is in contact with the other: a foot, an elbow, a hand, a knee, a forehead and so on.

REFLECTION

The Guards are both comic and frightening. Consider how you can best use your vocal and physical skills to create these effects.

A period script

Using scripts from different periods, such as ancient Greek, Elizabethan or Victorian, offers you the opportunity to demonstrate particular acting skills. Your interpretation of the character and scene must be appropriate for the play's context.

In the Victorian comedy, *The Importance of Being Earnest* (1895) by Oscar Wilde, two men, Jack and Algernon, pretend to be named Earnest in order to win the affections of Gwendolen and Cecily respectively. In this scene, Gwendolen, who lives in London, has travelled to the country house of Jack. She has met his **ward**, Cecily. At first the two women seem to like each other, but upon discovering that they are both engaged to Earnest (although in reality two different men pretending to be named Earnest) they now loathe each other. However, due to the manner in which they have been brought up, they believe they must maintain the pretence of being polite. Cecily's servant, Merriman, has just served them both tea in the garden.

TIP

When working on a stylised script with choral movement, make sure that your work is well-rehearsed, so that in sections where movement is meant to be in unison no one is out of time. This will help you to show that your skills are used in a precise and effective way.

KEY TERM:

Ward: someone, usually a young person, who has a guardian or other legal authority responsible for them.

The Importance of Being Earnest

1 **Gwendolen:** Personally I cannot understand how anybody manages to exist in the country, if anybody who is anybody does. The country always bores me to death.

Cecily: Ah! This is what the newspapers call agricultural depression, is it not? I believe the aristocracy are suffering very much from it just at present. It is almost an epidemic amongst them, I have just been told. 2 May I offer you some tea, Miss Fairfax?

Gwendolen [*with elaborate politeness*]: Thank you [*Aside.*] 3 Detestable girl! But I require tea!

Cecily [*sweetly*]: Sugar?

Gwendolen [*superciliously*]: No, thank you. Sugar is not fashionable any more. [CECILY *looks angrily at her, takes up the tongs and puts four lumps of sugar into the cup.*] 4

Cecily [*severely*]: Cake or bread and butter?

Gwendolen [*in a bored manner*]: Bread and butter, please. Cake is rarely seen at the best houses nowadays. 5

Cecily [*cuts a very large slice of cake and puts it on the tray*]: Hand that to Miss Fairfax. 6

[MERRIMAN *does so,* 7 *and goes out with footman.* Gwendolen *drinks the tea and makes a grimace. Puts down cup at once, reaches out her hand to the bread and butter, looks at it, and finds it is cake. Rises in indignation.*] 8

Gwendolen: You have filled my tea with lumps of sugar, and though I asked most distinctly for bread and butter, you have given me cake. I am known for the gentleness of my disposition, and the extraordinary sweetness of my nature, but I warn you, Miss Cardew, you may go too far.

Cecily [*rising*]: 9 To save my poor, innocent, trusting boy from the **machinations** of any other girl there are no lengths to which I would not go.

Gwendolen: From the moment I saw you I distrusted you. I felt that you were false and deceitful. I am never deceived in such matters. My first impressions of people are invariably right. 10

Cecily: It seems to me, Miss Fairfax, that I am trespassing on your valuable time. No doubt you have many other calls of a similar character to make in the neighbourhood. 11

1 Gwendolen is insulting Cecily who lives in the country. How could this line be delivered without making the insult too obvious, yet ensuring it has the required effect on Cecily? How could Cecily react?

2 Cecily is very young and has apparently misunderstood what agricultural depression is (when farmers are suffering economically) and instead suggests that Gwendolen is depressed because she is in the country. How would Gwendolen react to this?

3 An 'aside' is when an actor speaks directly to the audience. How should the actor make clear that they are speaking the character's thoughts? How might her tone of voice be different in the aside than it is when she speaks to Cecily?

4 How will the actor playing Cecily handle the props to make clear they are intentionally giving Gwendolen too much sugar?

5 What are Gwendolen's motivations for saying this line?

6 How can this moment be made comic?

7 How will Merriman behave at this point? Will he keep a straight face or react to what Cecily has done? Will he pause or pretend nothing has happened?

8 How can Gwendolen show her mounting anger?

9 Does Cecily 'rise' in the same way as Gwendolen? Should Gwendolen and Cecily's movements ever mirror each other?

10 Although both Cecily and Gwendolen are in conflict and angry with each other, this is also a source of comedy as they have gone so quickly from an apparently polite conversation to anger. How could this be played to show how completely their opinions of each other have changed?

11 Cecily is dismissing Gwendolen, in effect, telling her to 'go away'. How could this line be delivered while still maintaining the conventions of Victorian good manners?

KEY TERM:

Machinations: plots, conspiracies or schemes.

Rehearsal exercises

Rehearsal costumes and props: to help recreate the movement appropriate for a piece set in Victorian England, use ankle-length rehearsal skirts so that you can experience how that will alter your movement. For example, Victorian women such as Gwendolen and Cecily would be unlikely to cross their legs or slouch in their chairs.

Also use prop cups, saucers and cutlery so that you can practise handling them with ease. Consider what other props might be used such as Cecily's books or Gwendolen's parasol.

The Importance of Being Earnest

Comedy of manners

One of the sources of humour in the scene is that while outwardly the two women are being very polite to each other, inwardly they are both furious. As a rehearsal technique improvise a scene in which two characters are being incredibly polite to each other. From all external signs, anyone watching them would think that they liked each other. However, despite their smiles, they are saying horrible things to each other.

Now apply any discoveries you have made about how manners can cover real feelings and play the scene as politely as possible.

How can the comedy of the scene be emphasised through the characters' elaborate use of good manners?

Approaching monologues

If you choose to perform a monologue, you will be assessed on the same basis as you would performing a duologue or a group piece, including showing a range of skills and an understanding of the context. In addition, you will have some specific choices to make. Decide the following:

- Is your monologue being addressed to the audience or to one or more characters?
- If your monologue is addressed to one other character, where should you 'place' that character (where you imagine they are sitting or standing) so when you are speaking to them your eye line is consistent and your facial expressions clearly seen. If addressed to several characters, how will you make that clear?
- Where is your monologue located? How will your character use the performance space?
- If your monologue is directed to the audience, what is your attitude to the audience? Are you explaining things to them? Confiding in them? Entertaining them?
- How does your monologue fit into the play as a whole?

TIP

Avoid spending much of your performance with your back to your audience or in profile. In order to demonstrate a range of skills, seek out opportunities to use appropriate facial expressions, gestures and movement.

A naturalistic monologue

Set in Chicago, *A Raisin in the Sun* (1959) by Lorraine Hansberry deals with an African-American family's financial struggles during a time of emerging awareness of civil rights and the fight against segregation. In this naturalistic monologue from Act 3, Joseph Asagai, a bright, personable, ambitious Nigerian student, is challenging the attitudes of Beneatha (who he calls Alaiyo), including what he considers her very American attitude towards money and her African heritage. He begins by questioning her family's expectation to receive insurance money when her father died. Before this speech, Beneatha despairs because her brother, Walter, has squandered the money that would have gone towards her education.

A Raisin in the Sun

Asagai: (1) Then isn't there something wrong in a house – in a world – where all dreams, good or bad, must depend on the death of a man? I never thought to see you like this, Alaiyo. You! (2) Your brother made a mistake and you are grateful to him so that now you can give up the ailing human race on account it! You talk about what good is struggle, what good is anything! Where are we all going and why are we bothering!

Beneatha: AND YOU CANNOT ANSWER IT! (3)

Asagai [*shouting over her*]: I LIVE THE ANSWER! [*Pause.*] (4) In my village at home it is the exceptional man who can even read a newspaper ... or who ever sees a book at all. I will go home and much of what I will have to say will seem strange to the people of my village. But I will teach and work and things will happen, slowly and swiftly. At times it will seem that nothing changes at all ... and then again the sudden dramatic events which make history leap into the future. And then quiet again. (5) **Retrogression** even. Guns, murder, revolution. And I even will have moments when I wonder if the quiet was not better than all that death and hatred. But I will look about my village at the illiteracy and disease and ignorance and I will not wonder long. And perhaps ... perhaps I will be a great man (6) ... I mean perhaps I will hold on to the substance of truth and find my way always with the right course ... and perhaps for it I will be butchered in my bed some night by the servants of empire ... (7)

Beneatha: *The martyr*! (8)

Asagai [*He smiles*]: ... or perhaps I shall live to be a very old man, respected and esteemed in my new nation ... (9) And perhaps I shall hold office and this is what I'm trying to tell you, Alaiyo: Perhaps the things I believe now for my country will be wrong and outmoded, and I will not understand and do terrible things to have things my way or merely to keep my power. Don't you see that there will be young men and women – not British soldiers then, but my own black countrymen – to step out of the shadows some evening and slit my then useless throat? (10) Don't you see that they have always been there ... that they always will be. And that such a thing as my own death will be an advance? They who might kill me even ... actually replenish all that I was. (11)

1. Asagai is speaking to Beneatha in her living room. At the start of the scene where should he be positioned? Where will he look when referring to Beneatha? What furniture or props might he use?
2. What are Asagai's motivations for speaking to Beneatha like this?
3. For a monologue, this line would be cut.
4. His tone changes after this pause. Why?
5. Throughout the speech talks of contrasts, such as 'swiftly and slowly' or 'dramatic' and then 'quiet'. How could vocal skills emphasise these contrasts?
6. What might his facial expression be like when he dreams about being a great man?
7. This is a shocking idea. Would he say this in a casual, matter-of-fact voice or play it for dramatic effect?
8. For a monologue this line would be cut.
9. How does he change the mood on this line?
10. How could tension be built up through this section?
11. What might his final physical position be at the end of this speech?

KEY TERM:

Retrogression: going backwards, to an earlier time or state.

Rehearsal techniques

Subtext:

A. There are a number of mood shifts in Asagai's speech. Go through it and break it into smaller bits each time you think his motivations change. For example, for the first few lines his motivations might be 'to shame Beneatha' or 'to scold Beneatha'. Later sections might be 'to impress her', 'to shock her', 'to show her a different way of life' and so forth. Then experiment with playing the scene with those intentions.

B. After this speech, Asagai asks Beneatha to go to Nigeria with him. Experiment with ways of performing this scene with the subtext of making Beneatha love him and want to be with him.

Characterisation:

Asagai comes from a different background from the other characters in the play. This influences his accent, manners and attitudes. Experiment with specific choices, such as a Nigerian accent (accents can be researched online), a very strong, upright posture and powerful gestures.

TIP

It is your responsibility to time your monologue/duologue/group piece and make sure that each is the correct length. Depending on how quickly you speak or how much movement you put in the performance, performers doing exactly the same material may find that the performance length can differ widely. If a piece is too long then you must make some edits and if it is too short, you should either include a wider selection from the script or make sure that you aren't rushing your performance.

Vocal warm-ups

Whatever piece you choose you will be expected to display your vocal skills. One way to improve your vocal ability is to undertake vocal warm-ups. These help to free up your voice, increase your vocal range and **resonance**, and improve your diction.

1. **Breathing:** making sure that your neck and shoulders are relaxed, place your hands on your **diaphragm**. Breathe in slowly for ten counts and then out for ten counts. Make sure that your shoulders and chest are not rising up and down when you breathe. The action should come from your diaphragm.
2. **Vowels:** slowly breathe in and then breathe out making the vowel sounds (A, E, I, O, U), with an 'm' sound in front: Mah, Mee, Mie, Moh, Moo. The 'M' sound should help you to bring your voice forwards and the vowels should sound open and free.
3. **Diction:** over-enunciate tongue-twisters such as:

KEY TERMS:

Resonance: the quality, strength and depth of sound.

Diaphragm: the large muscle that stretches across the bottom of the rib-cage.

THE LIPS, THE TEETH,
THE TIP OF THE TONGUE

NEW YORK UNIQUE,
UNIQUE NEW YORK

ROUND THE RAGGED ROCKS
THE RAGGED RASCALS RAN

Baker Mukasa, actor

I find sighing for a minute or two at the beginning of the warm-up very useful as it's a gentle way to ease into a vocal warm-up. As well as this, making a noise like a siren on an 'ng' is very good to warm up the range of the voice. Finally, making an 'ooo' sound on a really low note whilst in a squatted position is good for focusing the sound lower in the body so I am grounded and more resonant.

Physical warm-ups

Physical warm-ups are useful to relax areas of tension and increase flexibility and energy. Try the following:

1. **Gentle head rolls:** standing, drop your head to your chest and then gently roll it up to one side and then back to the other so that you are making half-circles from side-to-side.
2. **Shoulder rolls:** gently roll both shoulders backwards several times and then forwards several times. Then straighten one arm and swing that in wide circles, checking that your shoulder is relaxed while you are rotating your arm. Then repeat on the other side.
3. **Loosen up:** lay on the floor and, starting with your feet and working upwards, tense and then relax each part of your body. End with scrunching up your face and then relaxing it.
4. **Shake out:** standing up, shake out each arm and leg eight times, counting aloud as you go. Then repeat for a count of four. Then for a count of two. Lastly, a count of one. Then shake your whole body out.
5. **Mirror:** facing your partner, take it in turns to mirror each other's actions and then switch leaders. See if you can become so in tune with each other that eventually you can continue without knowing who is the leader. This exercise is good for focus and teamwork.

TIP

As with any physical exercise, know your limits and be particularly careful with any work involving your neck and spine. When rising from the ground, don't spring up, but roll to one side, bend your knees and stand up one foot at a time.

Actors perform a range of physical and vocal warm-ups before rehearsals and performances, like this cast.

THEATRE MAKER ADVICE

Baker Mukasa, actor

Rolling down the spine is a great way to begin a physical warm-up, as it increases the mobility of the spine and makes you feel more connected to your body. The more mobile and connected you are to your spine the more you will be able to not only physicalise other characters convincingly but also avoid injuries that may occur due to the physical demands of a play.

Swings are great full body warm-ups. Raise arms above head and then drop upper body towards the floor letting legs bend and arms brush the floor as they swing back and then up again bring you back to standing. It warms up and releases tension in your shoulders, warms up your legs and gets you heart rate up.

Doing high knees is a great warm-up to get the heart rate up and give you the energy you need in order to go onstage.

Characterisation

Your performance must show your understanding of the characters, the play and its context. In order to show this understanding, make sure you understand what has happened before your excerpt begins and what will follow it. What is the world of the play (date, location and so on) and how does your character fit into this world?

THEATRE MAKER ADVICE

Baker Mukasa, actor

I look at first understanding the basic story, what are the key themes and ideas expressed and where does the action of the play take place. From there, I then focus specifically on my character by listing what my character says about others, what my character says about himself, what other characters say about my character and what does my character do in every scene. This will act as the foundation of ongoing character work and help me understand how he is perceived and his relationships with everyone around him.

In *A Raisin in the Sun*, the fact that Asagai comes from a different society and disapproves of the values of the American characters is important to the play. Performers can show this through their use of accent, tone, body language and gestures.

The very different rules of Victorian society influence the vocal and movement choices of the performers in *The Importance of Being Earnest*.

Although *Citizenship* is a more modern English text, character choices, such as a choice of accent and use of teenage body language, will allow you to show characterisation.

The Trial is set in a nightmarish world in which your character might be a victim or a tormentor, which will guide your choices, for example if you are a tormentor you might be obviously dominant in your movements or you might hide your intentions.

Baker Mukasa, actor

When I was playing Harry Dalton, a stable owner in *Equus*, I was struggling to find the weight he would have commanded. As he was a stable owner, used to commanding and taking care of horses, he needed to be grounded. To try and lock into this I did an animal study of a horse to inform how I characterised him, as they are very heavy and have a commanding presence. I used how heavily they breathed and their stance to inform how I played Dalton. Using the horse as a reference really helped me to key into Dalton's character and play him truthfully.

TASK 1

Think of an animal that might share some of the characteristics of your character. Are they proud as a peacock or as timid as a mouse? Can you find ways of adding these characteristics to your character?

Rehearsal techniques for developing and polishing your performance

Below are common performance problems and suggested rehearsal techniques to help.

PROBLEM	POSSIBLE REHEARSAL TECHNIQUE
Lack of tension	Focus on reactions. Use numbered cards to increase the reactions, with the higher the number the more intense/extreme the reaction. How is a '5' reaction different from a '10'? Which is appropriate for this play?
Rushed	Focus on pause and pace: try using pauses to increase tension or allow for reactions. Try a subtext exercise, such as **thought-tracking**, making sure you know what the character is thinking on every line.
Slow/dull	Run through in double-time: perform all the lines and actions but in double-time. Did this help you to discover any wasted moments/slow transitions? Increase the stakes: give the characters a deadline/time limit. If they don't convince the other character of X by Y amount of time it will be the end of the world, for example.
Lack of commitment/ not believable	Create the world of the character: use props or costumes that will help you to put yourself fully into the character's shoes.

Dealing with performance stress

Nerves and stage fright are common for even the most experienced of actors. It would be a very unusual actor who hasn't felt that tightening of muscles, the dry mouth and shaking hands that go with the stress of performing. Learning to manage nerves is part of an actor's job. Below are some techniques to help you:

- Know your role inside out so that you could do it in your sleep or standing on your head if you had to.
- If you are still struggling with lines shortly before the performance even the slightest distraction can throw you off.

KEY TERM:

Thought-tracking: speaking aloud the thoughts of the character.

- Imagine what your character is doing right before they enter. Have they run in from the rain or argued with a parent? Whatever they have done, bring a bit of that world onstage with you. For example, if appropriate for your character and their situation, you might enter shaking out your umbrella or jog on out of breath. Focusing on actions will help prevent self-consciousness.
- If you are performing with others, really listen and react to them onstage. Create a bubble of concentration that excludes distractions.
- When performing, imagine that someone supportive is in the audience and keep that image in your mind.

THEATRE MAKER ADVICE

Baker Mukasa, actor

I deal with the stress by doing things which immerse me in the story of the play I am in and the character's journey. If I am focusing on that then I won't focus on the things that tend to stress me out, for example what will people think, will I remember everything? One thing that helps me do this is I find music that echoes the atmosphere of my first scene, so if it's a confrontational scene I will listen to something aggressive and energetic. By shifting the focus away from the anxiety I am feeling and just focusing on the story it helps me to feel less stressed.

What if something goes wrong?

In theatre, sometimes things go wrong. A prop might be dropped, a line forgotten, a door won't open or a costume rips. These accidents do not have to be a disaster if dealt with well.

The best course of action is prevention. Make sure that you have tried out all your props and costumes before your first performance. Double-check that costumes fit and are not pulling at the seams or causing you to trip. Some props, which are not handled by the actors, may be secured to the set so that they don't accidentally fall over. None of the technical elements of the production should come as a surprise during the performance and any glitches should be ironed out beforehand.

If something still goes wrong, if possible, stay in character. For example, if someone in your group forgets a line, it is far better to stay in character and help them to find their place by either **ad-libbing** a line that will help them to remember where they are or to carry on to your next line rather than dropping out of character and telling them what their line is.

KEY TERM:
Ad-libbing: saying lines that aren't in the script.

If a prop is dropped, you will need to make a quick calculation whether to pick it up or leave it. If you do pick it up, do so in character.

Whatever happens, don't judge or give up on your performance if there are mistakes. Recovering from a mistake and carrying on with confidence is always the best course of action.

Health and safety

As you plan your performance, make sure you consider any possible health and safety considerations. Some common risks and actions are listed below (but you may discover many others).

RISK	ACTIONS
Slipping onstage	Make sure the stage is dry. If, in the course of a scene, liquid is spilt, avoid that area of the stage and then ensure the floor is dried before the next scene. If the stage itself is slippery, consider if the surface needs to be altered. If using a rug as part of the set, ensure it is stuck down and won't cause actors to trip. Ensure that chairs and other set furniture are not set too close to the edge of the stage, where they might tip off.
Injuries during stage fights/physical actions	Any stage fights need to be carefully choreographed. Using techniques such as slow motion can create a more effective and safer fight. **Never** use actual weapons or sharp objects onstage. There should be no actual contact on slaps or punches. Focus instead on acting the reactions.

TASK 2

Go over the demands of your script and list any possible health and safety issues and decide what the solutions should be.

Avoiding errors checklist

Checking your work and avoiding common errors:

- ✓ Do you know all your lines?
- ✓ Do you know all your movements?
- ✓ Do you understand the play from which your excerpts come?
- ✓ Do you project and vary your voice?
- ✓ Do you stay in character even when you are not speaking?
- ✓ Do you listen and react to others?
- ✓ Are you confident about what comes next (rather than looking to others for direction)?
- ✓ Do you maintain your focus and energy throughout your performance?
- ✓ Do you establish your character by the way you speak and move?
- ✓ Do you help to create the world of the play (its location, period, style and themes) through your use of the performance space?
- ✓ Do you achieve your artistic intentions for the role (for example, if you have stated it is a comic role, have you refined the comedy to amuse the audience or if your character is heroic, have you managed to create a character with whom the audience has a sympathetic response)?

Design

As a designer you will be working collaboratively with performers to help convey the meaning of the extracts that are being performed. Throughout the process, you must work together making sure that the end product allows everyone to show their theatrical skills and demonstrate a sensitive insight into the extracts.

Lighting designer

If you choose lighting design for your specialism, you must create one lighting design per extract. Your designs should show a range of effects and **lighting states** and **cues/transitions** designed to meet the demands of the extracts being performed. Your design must be appropriate to the play as a whole and its context.

KEY TERMS:

Lighting states: the settings and positioning of lighting to create certain lighting conditions, such as a bright afternoon or a moonlit scene.

Cues: instructions indicating when a change in lighting should occur.

Transitions: moving from one lighting state to another, such as a fade to darkness or a sudden blackout.

Sample stages of work

Below is a sample of the order in which you might approach the various demands of lighting design.

1. Read the play and make notes on the excerpts of various opportunities for lighting.
2. Explore the lighting capabilities of the performance space, such as available lights/lanterns, size of space and location of audience.
3. Draw a plan of the stage configuration and make notes on what areas need to be lit (angles, direction and so on).
4. Experiment with various colour and intensity options.
5. Consider any special effects you may wish to create.
6. Hang, set and focus any lights as appropriate.
7. Create an initial lighting cue sheet.
8. Work with performers and, if appropriate, other designers to ensure that lighting is effective. For example, can the actors be seen, is the correct mood created, is the set appropriately lit?
9. Run a technical rehearsal to ensure that all lighting timings are correct.
10. Finalise lighting cue sheet.

TIP

Be sure that your lighting is appropriate for the chosen stage configuration. For example, for an in the round configuration, make sure you avoid lights shining into the eyes of the audience.

Approaching a script

THEATRE MAKER ADVICE

Gavin Maze, lighting designer and technician

When I've designed shows, my first step is to read through the script and highlight any mention of location, weather, atmosphere and so on. Some play texts/authors are very specific and will give direct instructions about sunlight, for example coming through windows. I actually prefer the more vague instructions as it lets me put my own stamp on it.

▸ There is additional guidance on working collaboratively through the rehearsal process on page 221.

The play *Macbeth* by William Shakespeare begins in a battlefield where three witches discuss Macbeth, who has successfully defeated the enemy.

Below are sample lighting designer annotations on one version of the play, which begins with the following stage direction:

1 Dark, grey lights, soft (fresnel), not sharp lines, to create grim battlefield. Possible use of gobos to create eerie patterns.

> 1 *The battlefield: thunder and lightning.* 2
> *Enter three witches.* 3

2 Use of strobe or other flashing lights to create lightning effects.

3 Three distinct pools of light (downlighting, profile spots) one for each witch, green filter to make them look otherworldly or else possibly have each witch enter with a handheld light?

Later in the script the witches describe the weather:

> **ALL:** Fair is foul and foul is fair
> Hover through the fog and filthy air. 4
> **Exeunt.** 5

4 Should this be from the beginning of the scene? Green side lighting to highlight effect of fog (can we use dry ice or other smoke machine effect)?

5 Blackout or fade for their exit? Possible cross-fade?

TASK 3

Go through the excerpts you are working on and make notes for any possible lighting effects. You might consider how you create the time of day, location and season. You might want to use lights to pick out particular characters or to add to the atmosphere of a scene.

Lighting equipment

Depending on where your performance will be held, you may have a fully operational professional lighting set-up with computerised controls or you may be working with a basic lighting rig with a manually controlled dimmer board. The lighting equipment that you may have access to could include:

- **Floodlight**: typically a light without a lens so it cannot be focused, but it throws out a large amount of light. They can be used to light a backscreen or to provide a 'wash' (an undefined light) over a large area.
- **Profile spots**: provides more sharp-edged spots of light. They have a lens and are easy to focus. They usually come with a 'gate' which can hold gobos to create special effects.
- **Strobe light**: a device which produces flashes of lights. The number and timing of the flashes can be controlled. These are often used to create effects such as lightning or reporters' flash bulbs or to break up movement so that the audience only sees it in flashes. Health and safety warnings must be issued when these are used as some people have negative reactions to flashing lights.
- **Follow spots**: these are usually manually operated lights which are used to highlight performers and follow their movements onstage. Most have changeable colour filters which can tint the light.

KEY TERM:

Fresnel: a common stage lantern which provides a soft-edged beam of light. It can be used to cover a large area of the stage creating a 'wash' of light'. They often have 'barn doors', which are metal flaps at the side to provide some control of the spillage of light. They are usually fitted with a colour slot in which colour filters can be inserted.

Gobos: metal cut-outs that are used on lanterns to project patterns, such as leaves, stars, swirls or waves.

Filters: also sometimes called 'gels', sheets of plastic used to alter the colour of stage lighting.

Cross-fade: fading lights out on one area of the stage while simultaneously bringing them up on another area.

- **Colour filters**: also sometimes called 'gels', are sheets of plastic used to alter the colour of stage lighting. These are made in hundreds of different colours and can be combined to achieve just the right colour.
- **Gobos**: metal, plastic or glass cut-outs which are used to project patterns, such as leaves, stars, swirls or waves.

THEATRE MAKER ADVICE

Gavin Maze, lighting designer and technician

Whilst at university one of the spaces we used had a massive pillar in the middle of the performing space. On a production of 'Into the Woods' we did in that space, we turned it into a tree and used a few different gobos to create some cool shadows and the illusion of leaves and branches. Don't let a building quirk get in your way – think of a way you can bring it in, the director will probably thank you!

TIP

Early in your design you may begin thinking about the colours and brightness you will use.

Specific effects can be achieved with handheld lights, as used in The Old Man and the Old Moon.

Making choices as a lighting designer

Even for the simplest lighting there are a number of choices you will make including:

- Where will the lights be positioned?
- What colours will be used?
- What will be the direction or angle of the light?
- What will be the intensity of the light?

An instruction of 'light comes in from the window' can be interpreted in many different ways:

TIP

In addition to standard stage lighting, you may use other sources of light such as torches, fairy lights or a 'disco ball' if these will create the effects you desire.

Gavin Maze, lighting designer and technician

For light through a window, generally a fresnel would be good, but this can be achieved with a profile too. You'd need to think about time and location. If the play was set abroad somewhere traditionally hot, the sun might be a bit brighter and 'whiter', whereas say it was an autumnal sunset you'd try and pick a lovely orangey/amber. Generally, the light would be rigged in a way behind the window but it all depends on angles and accessibility. Barn doors would be used here to direct the light in the way you'd want it if you had a fresnel, if you were using a profile lantern you'd use the shutters.

THEATRE MAKER ADVICE

Extract from a sample lighting cue sheet

CUE NUMBER	PAGE NUMBER	CUE	NOTES
1	2	**Preset**	FOH lights up. Single **spotlight** onstage
2	2	**Opening Act 1 Afternoon**	Room brightly lit
3	4	**Darkens to dusk**	Over the scene the room darkens to dusk
4	5	**Gunshot**	Sound cue: blackout
5	5	**Sally stands centre stage**	Visual: actor arrives centre stage. Spotlight up
6	7	**Car approaching**	Sound cue (car): headlights flash through windows of room

Note: FOH = Front of House

Gavin Maze, lighting designer and technician

Look for any ideas that could enhance a scene; for example, is someone entering a room and turning on various light switches, what type of cue will that be (a visual cue or a called cue depending on if you've got someone [like a stage manager] **calling the cues** to you). Try and attend as many rehearsals of the show as you can as you'll pick up on something new each time.

THEATRE MAKER ADVICE

KEY TERM:

Spotlight: a lamp projecting a narrow intense beam of light directly onto a performer or area of the stage.

Call the cues: announce instructions, for example telling technicians when lighting or sound changes should occur.

Health and safety

There are many aspects of health and safety which you should consider. Below are just a few:

RISK	SOLUTION
Burns	Wait a few minutes after switching off before removing colour filters and gobos or touching a lamp. The lamps get extremely hot and can cause injury.
Electric shock	Any work involving electricity should be done with approved equipment known to be safe. Make sure that power is off when hanging or adjusting lights.
Falls	If working on a ladder to place or adjust a lantern, make sure that someone is with you, ensuring that you are safe. Do not put lighting in any location where it could easily fall. All brackets and so forth must be checked by a professional.
Tripping over wiring or cables	Ensure that all wiring, which could cause performers or audience members to trip, has been taped down. None should be placed in locations, such as entrances, where tripping would be most likely.

KEY TERM:

Sound plot: a list of the sound effects or music needed and sound equipment that will be used. This is usually organised scene-by-scene and contains information such as cues and volume.

Sound designer

If you choose sound design for your specialism, you must create one sound design per extract. This means that you will create two different **sound plots**, demonstrating a range of skills, one for each extract. Your design must show a range of sound effects and cues/transitions designed to meet the demands of the extract being performed.

Your sound design may be recorded or performed live and may include sound effects and music. Your design must be appropriate to the play as a whole and its context.

How to approach a script

THEATRE MAKER ADVICE

Max Perryment, sound designer

After reading the script, I'll talk to the director about specific themes and characters of the play, the overall directorial vision and what are the important things that an audience will need to understand. I'll then go through the script and mark every moment, however vague, where sound could be used. I'll usually mark moments that will create a sense of time and place and also opportunities where sound can be used to create certain mood or atmosphere.

Naturalistic or abstract sound design

The play *Kindertransport* (1993), by Diane Samuels, offers opportunities for both naturalistic and abstract sound design choices. In the play, Eva, a young German girl, travels to England by train. Throughout the play a frightening character from a storybook, *The Ratcatcher*, appears, symbolising her fears. There are sounds necessary to establish location or events and others that show how the characters are feeling or to establish an atmosphere.

Here is an excerpt with example designer notes:

1 Abstract: ominous theme to accompany every appearance of Ratcatcher.

4 Naturalistic: train whistle – probably recorded but could it be live?

1 **Ratcatcher:** I will take the heart of your happiness away.

[*The* Ratcatcher *plays his music.* 2

The sounds of the railway station become louder and louder. 3

Another train whistle.] 4

Eva: Mutti! Vati! Hello! Hello! See. I did get into the carriage. I said I would. See. I'm not crying ... 5

2 Abstract: a haunting tune. Perhaps played live on a recorder or flute?

3 Naturalistic: recorded sounds to establish train station: crowd noises, bustling.

5 Abstract: under this speech soft orchestral theme, increases in volume as speech continues.

Sound equipment

The sound equipment you will need depends on your design for the excerpts. Some typical equipment might include:

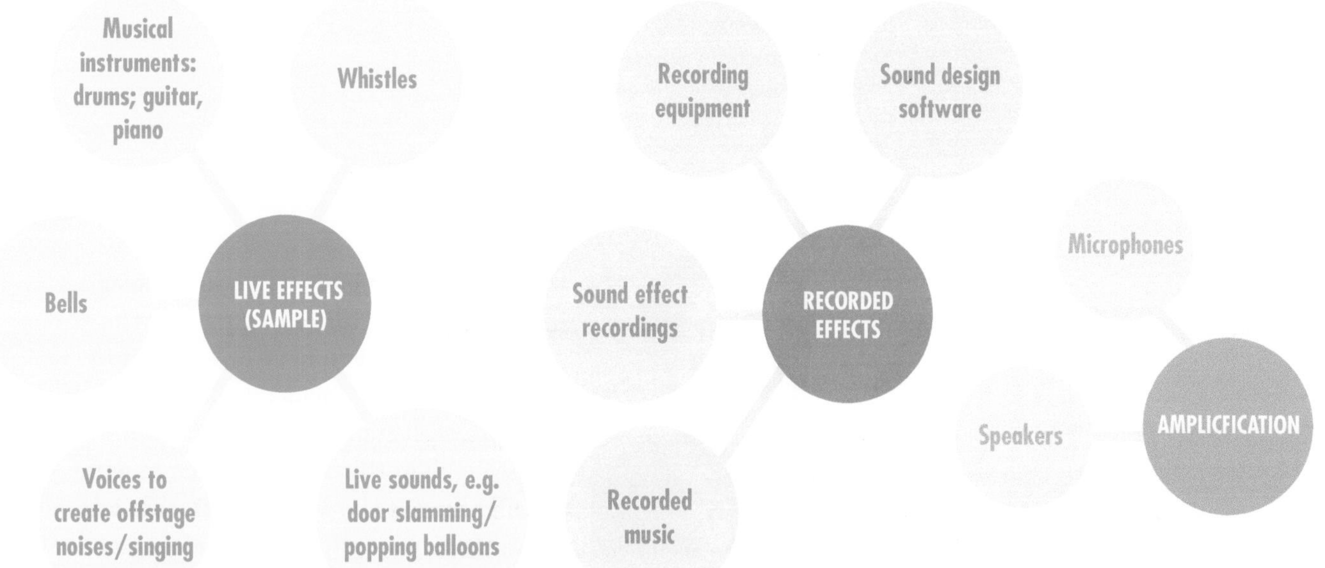

Use of microphones and musical instruments may form part of your sound design, as in The Old Man and the Old Moon. ▼

Possible opportunities to use music or sound

SOUND OPPORTUNITIES

- Beginning of or during scenes (establish locations)
- Create atmosphere during scenes (shrill noises, ominous thuds)
- Note key plot events (gunshots, doorbell, phone ringing)

MUSIC OPPORTUNITIES

- Before play begins
- During scene changes/ transitions
- The curtain call
- A theme when certain characters appear
- Underneath dialogue/action to underscore mood or create an effect (tension, comedy)
- Part of the performance (e.g. in a musical)

THEATRE MAKER ADVICE

Max Perryment, sound designer

Whatever the budget, a sound designer is responsible for telling part of the story. Even if you have one speaker and an iPhone, focus on the story and the overall concept of your design, rather than thinking in terms of what will impress the audience. Decide very carefully where it may be better to have no sound at all or perhaps where sound could be used subliminally underneath scenes. Think about where you want to be naturalistic or abstract in the sound world you create. Whatever your approach your decisions will change the way the audience experiences the play.

A vital piece of software to get to know is QLab, which you can download for free. It is an industry-standard and it enables you to be very creative with sound very easily.

TIP

There are a number of sound effects and sound mixing products available online. Technology is advancing all the time and many of the resources are free or inexpensive.

KEY TERM:

Subliminally: so that it barely registers; the audience is affected without consciously being aware of what is affecting them.

TIP

You may use sound equipment to create special effects such as a 'reverb', which is an echoing effect. This can create an ominous mood or could suggest a location, such as a large empty building.

Creating original sound effects

You may choose to use pre-recorded sound effects or you may record your own. Using easy to find materials you can create the sound of rain, wind or a noisy crowd.

Max Perryment, sound designer

On using sound design to create atmosphere, location and character:

I think a sound designer aims to do exactly these things throughout the entire duration of the play. As an example, I recorded several solo French horn drone-like noises for the play *Creditors*. The French horn at its quietest was reminiscent of a boat foghorn, and since the play was set near a harbour it worked as a little reminder, although quite abstractly, of the location. Additionally, there's a character called Gustav, who slowly and cruelly manipulates the other two characters. The sound that began as a distant horn became more dissonant and menacing, conveying his growing power and control over the other characters.

Sample working order

1. Read script and note sound/music ideas.
2. Discuss ideas with performers and, if appropriate, other designers.
3. Decide which sounds, if any, will be recorded and which live.
4. Record or source recorded sound effects/music or locate materials for live sound effects/music.
5. Create cue sheets noting volume and duration of sound.
6. Arrange any technical requirements such as microphones, speakers or amps.
7. Decide if there are any live cues and rehearse them.
8. Rehearse cues making any necessary adjustments.
9. Have a technical rehearsal making sure all cues are accurate and all health and safety considerations have been followed (such as taped-down wires).

TIP

In addition to the volume you might consider the direction of the sound. By placing your speakers in certain positions, you may create the effect that the audience is surrounded by sound or that a sound is coming from a certain place.

KEY TERMS:

Visual: a cue that the technician must judge by watching the action onstage.

Snap: quickly on or off.

Sample sound cue sheet

CUE NUMBER	PAGE NUMBER	CUE	NOTES	DURATION
0.5	11	**Preshow music**	Preshow music. Quiet	20 mins
1	11	**Preshow music stops**	Loud ringing	Slow fade
2	21	**Alarm clock**	Visual cue when Sally switches on tablet	**Visual**. Until Sally hits alarm clock
3	24	**'You don't know love'**	Visual cue. Headlights through window	Throughout scene
4	51	**Car approaching**	Reverb increases throughout	10 secs
5	58	**Dripping water**	Crunching gravel	End cue: SALLY: No, it wasn't like that
6	76	**People approaching**	Line cue: SALLY: Stand back everyone	10 secs
7	87	**Firework bang**		**Snap**
8	87	**Firework bang x3**		Snap

Health and safety

There are many aspects of health and safety that you should consider:

RISK	SOLUTION
Tripping over wires	Ensure that any sound equipment wires are carefully taped down. Notify all performers and backstage staff of their location.
Electric shock	Any work involving electricity should be done with approved, safe equipment. Before adjusting speakers, amps and other equipment make sure that they are turned off.

Set designer

If you choose set design for your specialism, you must create one set design per extract. This means that you will either create two different sets to suit the two extracts or you will adapt a single set to suit each extract. The design must show dressing and props designed to meet the demands of the extract being performed.

Below are suggestions on how to approach the process of set design.

THEATRE MAKER ADVICE

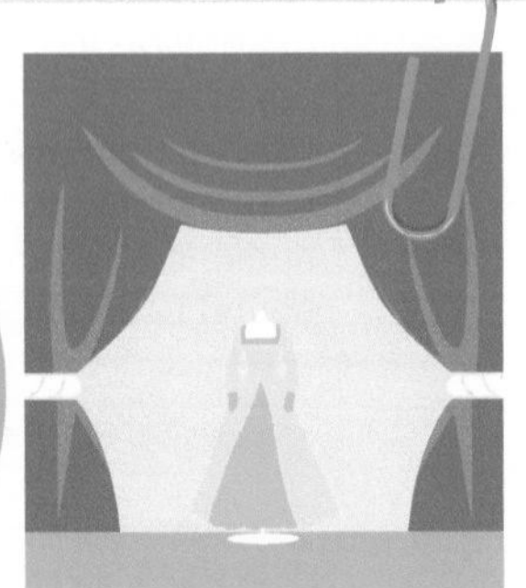

Tim Shortall, set and costume designer

Q. How do you research your ideas?

A. It would depend entirely what is required.
A contemporary UK setting, for example, may be something I am already familiar with, or, if not, may be set somewhere I can visit, for first-hand experience – beats any amount of online and other research, as you get an immediate personal response to that environment, involving touch, smell and so on, as well as merely the visual.

If it's a 'period piece' I will mostly do research online, and through museums, books, documentary film.

Below are typical stages for a set design:

1 Carefully read the script. Note the practical requirements of it and first impressions of possible settings and style.
2 Discuss with the rest of the group the possible setting requirements and the atmosphere and style of the piece.
3 Research, which could include: art books, the internet, visits to museums, trips to locations, taking photographs and so on.
4 Put together initial 'mood boards' – collections of inspirations and ideas, usually mounted on a large board. They might include: sample colours; architectural details; samples of furniture, textures and patterns; inspiration from other theatre designs.
5 Make first sketches and discuss with rest of the group.
6 Measure the stage area and make a **ground plan.**
7 Optional: create a card model (**model box**) of the set. Use this to experiment with colours, textures and placement of set furniture.
8 Make a ground plan and then work with the performance group to make sure the set will work with their requirements. For example, are the entrances and exits in the right place? Is there enough room for any physical actions?

KEY TERMS:

Ground plan: a bird's-eye view of the set showing the scale of the stage and set and where key elements of the design will be located, as shown in the illustration opposite.

Model box: a three-dimensional scale-model of the set that shows how the real set will look and work.

9 Begin creation and assembling of actual set. This may involve a number of tasks from locating pieces of furniture, painting scenery, making drapery or a backdrop, adapting existing pieces of set and so forth.

10 Check your work for health and safety issues.

11 Have a technical rehearsal to make sure that the set operates correctly and that any scene changes can be done safely and efficiently. Make any necessary adjustments.

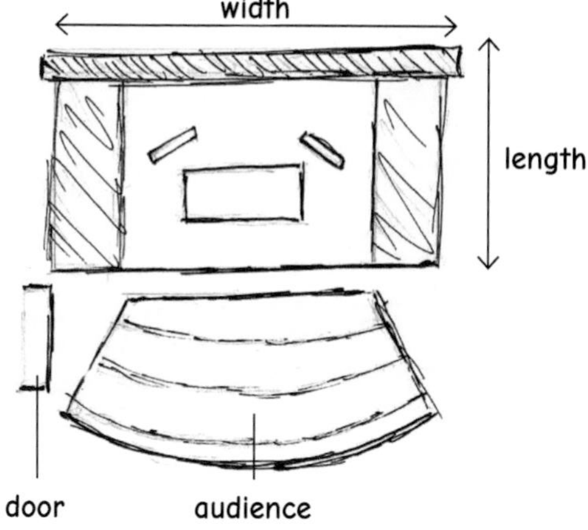

An example of a ground plan

TASK 4

Create your own ground plan for the text you are creating a set design for.

Mark the following on it:

- Where the audience will be.
- Where the entrances/exits will be.
- Where any large pieces of scenery will be (flats/backdrops/ large high-backed pieces of furniture).

Then check your work:

- Do any pieces of scenery block entrances/exits?
- Will the scenery fit on the stage and leave enough room for acting?
- Will the audience have clear sightlines of the action?
- Can any technology you may wish to use, such as projections, work successfully?

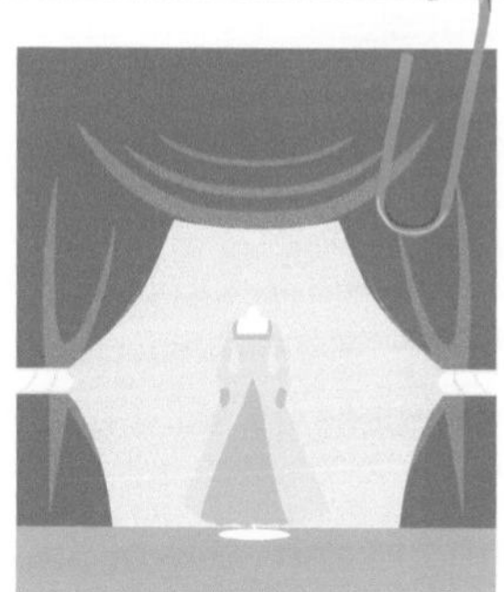
Tim Shortall, set and costume designer

Q. Can you explain how important colour and texture are in a design?

A. The power of colour to affect mood is very well known, of course. And texture can transform and give life to an otherwise dull surface, and, by providing contrast, it will give layers of interest, To give an extreme example: say I'm designing a play set in a grand Victorian house. I've researched the period, and I've tried to recreate every little detail to give as accurate a portrait as I can of the lives these people would have led at the time. There are heavily patterned wallpapers, lots of detailed mouldings, thick drapes at the tall windows, dark colours, brown woodwork and paneling. But when it's finished, I think it lacks 'life' – it doesn't get to the 'heart' of the play, for me. It's too naturalistic. Without changing the structure in any way, I decide to paint the entire thing blood-red. Walls, cornicing, floor, ceiling. All in layered shades of deep, dark reds. I make the paint look as though it's peeling off the surfaces. The floor I paint in a high-gloss red, but cracked all over like a shattered mirror, reflecting the decaying surfaces in kaleidoscopic detail ... The dramatic alteration in colour and texture has changed the visual impact of the entire play. So colour and texture are both powerful tools.

▲ *Sample set designs by Tim Shortall, for* Sweet Charity, *under the Manhattan Bridge (left) and* Pitcairn *(right)*

▲ *Drop-down windows for an end on staging configuration*

▲ *Painted mountain backdrop for thrust staging*

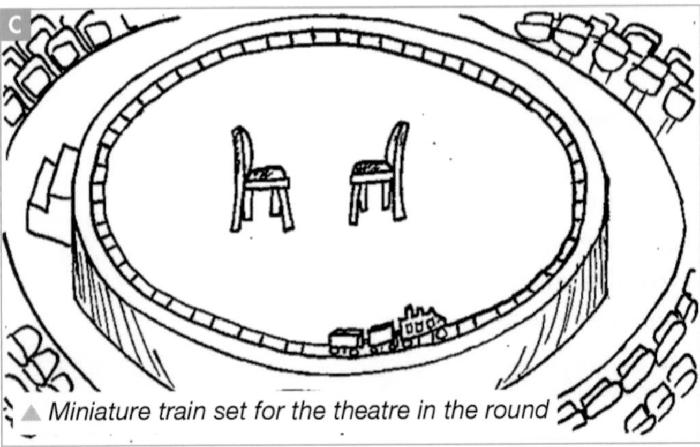

▲ *Miniature train set for the theatre in the round*

Sample work

On the left are the first sketches of a student who is designing the set for a performance where scenes take place on a train. At this point, the group has not decided what theatre configuration or style of performance it will have so the designer is just experimenting with ideas.

All of these ideas would probably have practical challenges in a school setting, but sketches like these are a good way of beginning to develop your ideas. Some questions you might ask yourself about your initial designs include:

- Is this a set that could be created within the time and budget available?
- Do I have (or can I obtain) the necessary skills and equipment to create this set?
- Is this set appropriate to the mood and style of the performance piece?
- Will the sightlines be good for the audience?
- Will the set be safe for the performers and audience?

TASK 5

a Based on the extracts with which you are working, quickly draw several sketches showing different ways you could approach the set design. At this stage, don't worry about how practical the designs are, just use this as a way of getting ideas down on paper.

b Note any ideas that you particularly like.

c Discuss with your group the practicalities of the space in which you are working, your budget, your skills and amount of time you have. Based on these discussions, note any ideas that you think could be further developed.

TIP

Many designers consider the descriptions of a set in a play as suggestions rather than requirements that cannot be altered. Often designers read the description for clues and hints as to what the playwright believes the atmosphere or the set should be and it is up to the designer to interpret these hints.

Working with a script

It is the role of the designer to interpret the requirements of the play. Some playwrights offer no description of what the set should be like, while others will give detailed descriptions. However, no matter how detailed the description is, the designer interprets this in order to create the desired effects.

Minimalistic or abstract sets

In *The Trial*, the playwright Steven Berkoff describes the set requirements as follows, with sample designer notes provided in the margin:

The stage is bare. Ten screens and ten chairs and a rope are the set. (1) The screens are the structure of the city – lawcourts, houses and endless corridors. (2) They are a maze and a trap – they are mirrors and paintings (3) – they are external and internal worlds. (4) The cast are the environment of K. The rope is his route as well as his death. (5)

(1) We have a cast of five, so will only use five chairs and five screens. What style of chair? All the same colour or different?

(2) How big should the screens be? Should they all be the same size? Is it easier to create the impression of a city, with different or the same heights?

(3) Screens need to move, so lightweight or possibly on wheels for quick changes

(4) Screens can be painted differently – one side black, the other representing different images

(5) Where should rope be onstage? Should it be used in different scenes and then hung as a noose later? Check health and safety considerations

▲ *Use of projections in the set of* Once Five Years Pass

TIP

While this designer plans to use the idea of chairs, screen and rope in Berkoff's suggestions, another designer might ignore this advice. For example, if the staging configuration is in the round or traverse, the designer might think that the screens would block too much of the set. Another designer might want to incorporate technology such as projections or videos.

Period settings

The example below describes a Victorian set for Oscar Wilde's *The Importance of Being Earnest* (the beginning of Act 2) with sample designer notes.

Garden at the Manor House. 1 A flight of grey stone steps leads up to the house. 2 The garden, an old-fashioned one, full of roses. 3 Time of year, July. 4 Basket chairs, and a table covered with books, are set under a large yew-tree. 5

Miss Prism discovered seated at the table. 6 Cecily is at the back, watering flowers. 7

1 Flats used upstage to show back of house or doorway into house?

2 Cut steps, not needed

3 Use pots with artificial rose trees?

4 Use pastels, yellows and pinks, to highlight season

5 Need at least two matching chairs. Wicker table and chairs or wrought iron? Do we need tree? Possibly make a wooden two-dimensional cut-out one?

6 Position table downstage, slightly stage right

7 Watering can needed. Where best to position roses? Stage left?

THEATRE MAKER ADVICE

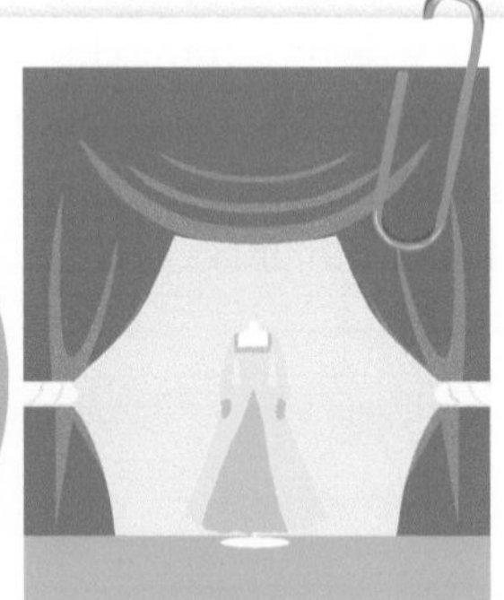

Tim Shortall, set and costume designer

For designers working on very small budgets, the fact that you have almost no money to play with means you are forced to think differently, and to spend very selectively and wisely – what is most important, what can you simply not do without.

TIP

You need to show your interpretation of the play and your artistic intentions. Your set needs to be more than purely functional. Even if you are doing a minimalistic set, you need to demonstrate your skills through the choice of materials and style of design.

TASK 6

a Using the excerpts you are working on, make a list of the minimum requirements of the script. Be precise. If it requires chairs, how many? If it says 'a table' is the table used or is it just for decoration or scene setting – in which case do you need it?

b What dressings (additions to the set) and props (things that are handled by the actors) are required by the script?

c Can you think of one additional item of dressings or props that would add meaning or impact to the script? For example, the set of *The Trial* might have a large clock hanging above it to show how time is running out for Josef K. Or *The Importance of Being Earnest* might have a tea trolley that could be wheeled on (which could be used for comic business for Merriman) or a curved arbor covered in vines and flowers (to highlight the beauty of the garden and provide an entrance and exit point).

Health and safety

There are many aspects of health and safety that you should consider. These are just a few:

RISK	SOLUTION
Injuries when moving the set	Avoid making set pieces that are too heavy. Ensure that you have a sufficient number of people for any set changes and rehearse these so that they go smoothly for the performance. When possible, use 'hand trucks' or other wheeled devices.
Broken glass	Avoid, when possible, using glass in your designs. If necessary (for example, a wine glass), ensure that it is handled and stored carefully. If any glass breaks onstage, it must be carefully swept up to avoid injuries. If it is a requirement of a script that a glass or bottle is broken, then specially purchased 'breakaway' glass made from a plastic resin or 'sugar glass' should be used.
Injuries due to falls	If any parts of the set involve constructing steps, platforms, ladders and so forth, ensure that they are reinforced and suitable for weight-bearing. The stage floor should not be slippery.
Set falling down	Any flats that are used in the set need to be properly bracketed and weighed down to ensure that they don't fall over.
Sharp edges	Avoid having any sharp edges on the set, as these could be dangerous if actors (or set-movers) fall or bump into them.

Costume design

If you choose costume design as your specialism you must create one costume for one performer per extract. This means that you will either design two different costumes, one for each extract, or adapt a single costume for each extract. The design must show clothing and accessories, and hair, make-up and masks, if appropriate, which meets the demands of the extract being performed.

TIP

It is important to know that collaboration with the actors is vital. There is no point in designing a costume that contradicts the performer's ideas about the character, restricts their ability to move or does not fit appropriately.

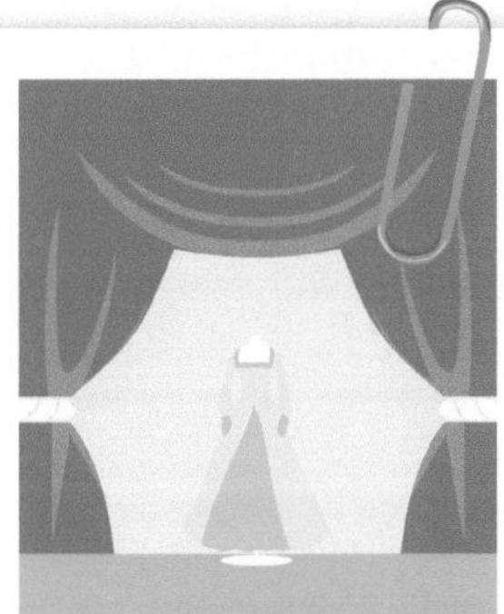

Tim Shortall, set and costume designer

Costume designs will be ongoing during this lead-up to the start of rehearsals. If it is a 'period' piece, it is likely I will have done a considerable amount of work prior to this, especially if the costumes are to be made, as this will involve a great deal of design, fabric and trim sourcing, and the timescale to start the makers will be very tight.

On a modern show, I much prefer to wait to do the costumes until I can talk in detail with each actor, to see what their view of their character is, and what they think they should wear. There is no point trying to give an actor a modern-day outfit without at least knowing in what direction they are heading with their characterisation! They need to feel absolutely comfortable and 'right' with the choice of clothes I have given them.

KEY TERM:

Trim: in sewing, this refers to any extra decoration such as ribbons, thread, lace, tassels, braid and cord.

Possible stages for your costume design:

1. Carefully read the script. Note its practical requirements and your first ideas of possible costumes.
2. Discuss with the performers the possible costumes and choose which costumes you will design.
3. Research, which could include: art books, the internet, visits to museums, magazines, taking photographs and so on.
4. Put together initial mood boards. These might include: sample colours, swatches of fabric, photographs from books or magazines, examples of textures and patterns, inspiration from other costume designs, sample silhouettes, make-up and hairstyle examples.
5. Take measurements of performer(s).
6. Create initial sketches.
7. If appropriate, make pattern for costume.
8. Source and obtain necessary materials such as fabrics and trim.
9. Begin making actual costume.
10. Arrange costume fittings and make any necessary adjustments.
11. Source any necessary accessories.
12. If appropriate, experiment with hair, make-up and mask design.
13. At dress rehearsal make sure that the costume fits correctly and creates necessary effect. Make any necessary adjustments.
14. Check all details of costume, accessories, hair and make-up before first performance.

TIP

At any rehearsals or performances when the costume is being used, have a small sewing kit to hand, including thread, needle, safety pins, scissors and so on, in order to make last-minute repairs.

TASK 7

Using the extracts you are working on, draw a few quick initial sketches of possible costumes. Once you have completed them, check your ideas against the following checklist:

- ✓ Are these costumes that could be created within the time and budget available?
- ✓ Do I have (or can I obtain) the necessary skills and equipment to create these costumes?
- ✓ Are these costumes appropriate for the character and style of the performance piece?
- ✓ Will the costume work practically onstage in terms of movement and comfort of performer?

Working with a script

It is the role of the designer to interpret the requirements of the play. Some playwrights offer no description of what the costumes should be like, while others will give detailed descriptions. Sometimes requirements of the costume are mentioned in the dialogue. For example, Eddie Carbone in *A View from the Bridge* complains about his niece, Catherine, wearing high heels, so for that moment to make sense, she must wear high heels. However, no matter how detailed the descriptions and dialogue are, the designer interprets these in order to create the desired effects.

The best costumes will reveal aspects of the character, and the style and meaning of the play.

Naturalistic period costumes

Kindertransport has scenes set both in the 1930s and in recent times.

The play begins with Eva, a nine-year-old German girl, and her German-Jewish mother, Helga, as they prepare for Eva to travel to England. Below are sample designer notes on the descriptions of the characters in the script:

> Eva, dressed in clothes of the late thirties, (1) is sitting on the floor, reading. The book is a large, hard-backed children's story book entitled *Der Rattenfanger*.
>
> Helga, holding a coat, (2) button, needle and thread, is nearby. She is well turned-out in clothes of the late thirties. (3)

1. What sort of dress would a nine-year-old girl wear in the 1930s? Fabric? Length? Colours?
2. Eva's coat; she will put this on later
3. What does 'well-turned out' mean for the 1930s? Fur? Jewellery? Skirt suit? Make-up?

Later in the script, Eva is further described:

> Eva *puts on her coat and hat* (4) *and label with her number on it – 3362.* (5)

4. What type of hat? Hairstyle? Plaits? Loose?
5. What should the label be made from? Cardboard? String or chain or pin to attach? Handwritten number or printed?

TASK 8

From the script extracts that you are working on, choose either a description of a character or any information you can gather about a character such as occupation, age, location and time period. Then, basing your ideas on the types of questions listed above, write any questions or observations you have about possible costumes for the character.

▲ Animal Farm

Fantasy or stylised costumes

The 1985 adaptation of George Orwell's novel *Animal Farm* presented many challenges for the costume designer, as it depicts animals who speak and, in many ways, behave like humans. In his adaptor's note about the original production, director Peter Hall writes:

> The actors wore black, except for brightly coloured elements – their animal masks, tails and feet. Until the end of the play, they went on all fours, using crutches of varying heights on their hands. The 'human' characters also wore masks. This was one solution to the production of the play. There are many others.

TASK 9

You have been asked to design a costume for one of the following animals in *Animal Farm*:

- Old Major, a large old pig
- Boxer, a huge cart horse
- Moses, a tame raven.

However, in your design you choose not to use masks or crutches as you fear these will impede the actors' ability to speak or move freely. Sketch at least two other solutions to creating an animal costume.

Hair and make-up

In addition to costumes, styling of hair and make-up can greatly increase the visual impact a character makes. It's difficult to imagine a 1950s costume looking truly effective if it is not accompanied by an appropriate period hairstyle.

Some considerations:

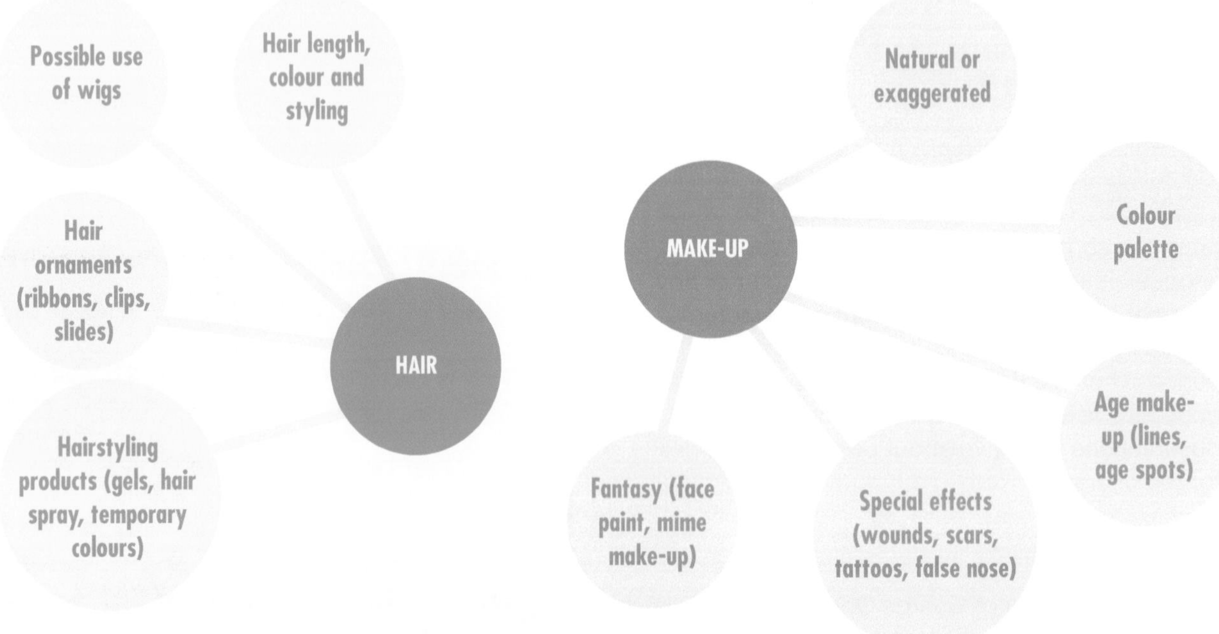

TIP

In order to demonstrate a range of skills you may wish to design hair and make-up as well as costumes.

Health and safety

There are many aspects of health and safety that you should consider. Below are just a few:

RISK	SOLUTION
Tripping	Check that length of costume does not pose a trip hazard. Ensure that actor has enough time working in costume to be comfortable moving in it.
Impeded vision	Ensure that any masks or head coverings have eye holes large enough for unimpeded vision. Check that the fastenings (elastic and so on) are secure so that they do not slip.
Sharp objects	Scissors should be used with care and put securely away when not being used. No loose pins should remain in costumes (safety pins can be used, if securely closed).

Puppet designer

If you choose puppet design as your specialism you must create one puppet per extract. This means that you will either design two different puppets, one for each extract, or adapt a single puppet for each extract. The design must show a complete puppet, designed to meet the demands of the extract being performed.

Types of puppets

One of your first choices will be what type of puppet you wish to make. Below are just some examples:

Shadow puppets

Shadow puppets are two-dimensional puppets that are operated between a light and screen. They can be jointed to create movement.

The photo on the right shows the use of shadow puppets in Pigpen Theatre Company's storytelling theatre production of *The Old Man and the Old Moon*.

A hand puppet

A cloth puppet worn over a hand, traditionally the puppeteer's thumb serves as the jaw of the puppet's face.

Marionette

A puppet, usually made from wood controlled by wires or strings.

Hand and rod puppets

Where the puppeteer uses one hand to control the mouth and rods to control the arms of the puppet.

Backpack puppets

Large puppets attached to the puppeteer by a backpack-like device.

Below is an example of Nikki Gunson's puppet designs for *Sinbad the Sailor* at Stratford East Theatre, including a hand and rod monkey puppet and two large backpack puppets.

▲ *Shadow puppets in PigPen Theatre Company's production of* The Old Man and the Old Moon

◀ *Nikki Gunson's puppet designs for* Sinbad the Sailor *at the Stratford East Theatre. Director Kerry Michael; Designer Hattie Barsby; Photographer Sharron Wallace; Puppet Designer Nikki Gunson; Lighting Designer David Plater*

THEATRE MAKER ADVICE

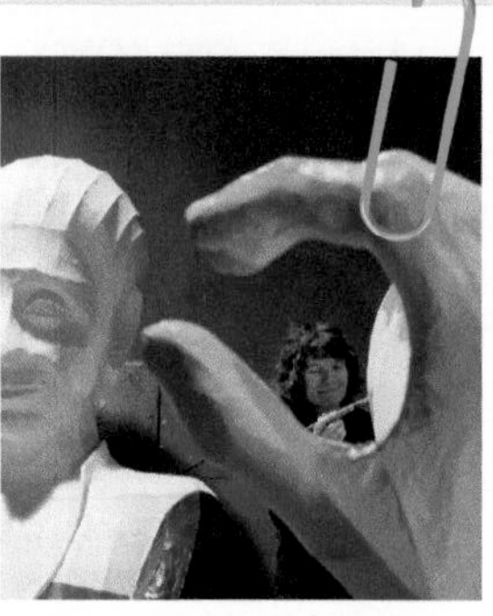
Nikki Gunson, puppet designer

There are few things I look at when deciding what sort of puppet to make:

- Where is the puppet to be performed? – Theatre, street or bus?
- What is the puppet? – Human, animal, mythical or talking chair?
- Size? 8 or 8000 cm?
- The part they play?
- Their character, what they need to be able to do, animation required? – Simple flapping Snow Geese or all-singing and dancing parrot?
- How it needs to be operated and by how many people? – A giant octopus operated by nine people or one person? Three blind mice operated by one person or three people?

Q. What are the basic stages of the design process for you?

A 1 Receive brief/script for – or on the odd occasion decide what – character is to be created.
2 Collect images and ideas, from all sorts of places: brainstorming, books, internet, photos, sketched thoughts and ideas.
3 Working drawings – when I start my working drawings, I work on squared paper and sketch to scale.
4 First draft – starts as a rough sketch, using brief and research images to get an idea of look/style, possible materials, where to put joints, estimate cost of and time taken to build.
5 Rub out and work on until sketch is readable enough to have puppet design approved.
6 Second draft – Drawing is larger, and while sketching I am working out, how and where to animate and what materials could be used, drawing certain things like joints and how they work to the side or on a separate piece of paper.
7 I build up my drawing in the same way I build puppets, constructing it in my mind – Skelly [Skeleton]/joints, Muscles Skin: materials, techniques and style used, varies depending on the needs of each puppet.

Materials

Puppets may be created with a wide variety of materials. For example, if creating a puppet with a three-dimensional head, materials you could consider using include:

foam rubber **polystyrene** wood

papier mâché (paste and paper)

plaster filler and muslin (a type of thin cotton fabric)

Additionally, you will want to think about whether or not your puppet is costumed, which will lead you to thinking about different fabrics. You may want to give it its own costume, and limbs that either hang limply or can be operated separately with a rod.

Working with a script

In Tim Supple's adaptation of Carol Ann Duffy's *Grimm Tales* (1994), one of the tales is 'The Golden Goose'. In the original production, a puppet was used to create the goose.

The goose is described in the script as follows:

> Dummling went straight over to the tree and cut it down, and when it fell there was a goose sitting in the roots with feathers of pure gold. He lifted her out, tucked her firmly under this arm, and set off for an inn where he intended to stay the night.
>
> Later in the play the landlord's daughters become fascinated with the goose and want to steal its feathers. Each of the three daughters becomes stuck to the goose and, as the story progresses more and more people become stuck to the goose as Dummling carries it to show the king.

TASK 10

From this description, copy and complete the following mind map by adding more branches to it to incorporate your ideas:

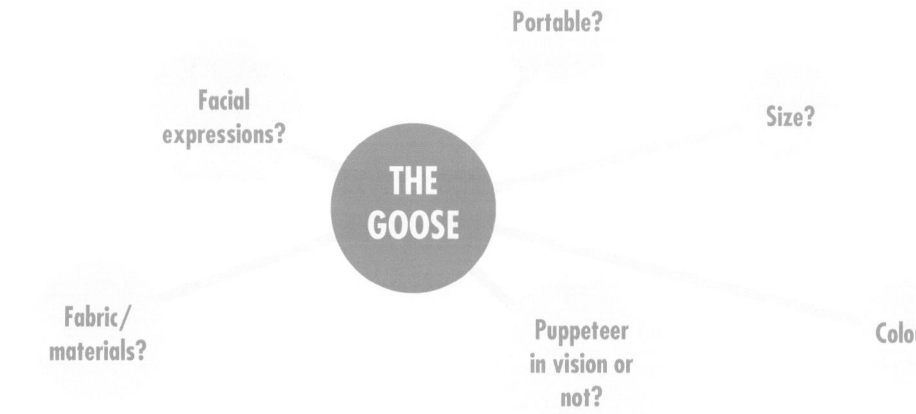

THEATRE MAKER ADVICE

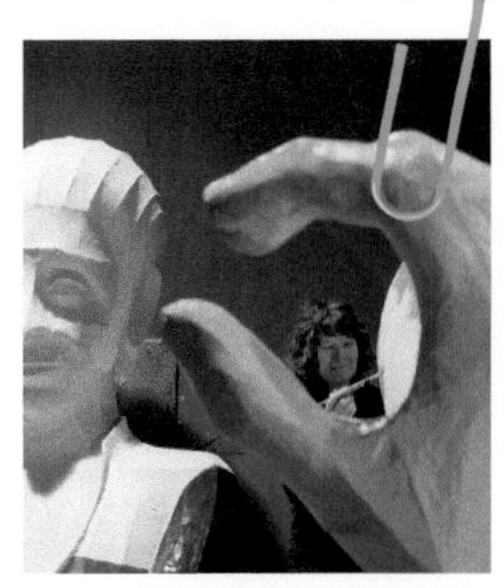

Nikki Gunson, puppet designer

Q. Any advice for making effective puppets?

A. Depends on venue and puppet: for large spaces – go larger than life; striking, bold and simple; don't get bogged down with too much detail that won't be noticed: Bright is always good, you can't beat a bit of glitter.

Exaggerate – head, face, eyes and hands, bring attention to the parts of the puppet you use interact/communicate with.

Finish – paints; satin is my finish of choice, matt tends to flatten and dull, gloss is good for the wet look, gloss varnish on eyes, reflects light, makes them look moist and brings them to life.

Puppeteers

If you or someone else is operating the puppet you must decide if the puppeteer will be in vision or not. It may be that the script will dictate this. For example, in the extract on the previous page, the actor playing Dummling would usually operate the goose puppet, as the script requires him to carry it from place to place. You may choose to have an onstage character working the puppet; an onstage puppeteer who isn't a character in the piece operate the puppet; or the puppet may be operated offstage by an unseen puppeteer, for example by wires or strings.

THEATRE MAKER ADVICE

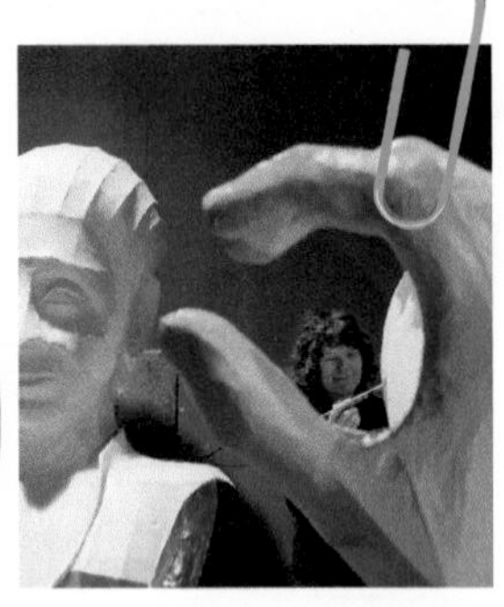

Nikki Gunson, puppet designer

With the puppets I make and operate, the puppeteer is usually in sight, I tend to wear black, shadow-like clothes, not wanting to distract from the puppet (unless a costume is part of the puppet) – sometimes I wear a veiled hat.

To me the magic of being a puppeteer is, even if you are in plain sight, you become invisible. It happens whether operating a large backpack puppet or a small rod puppet – I have a photo of me clearly visible operating a 10ft backpack and people ask 'Where are you?'

Health and safety

There are many aspects of health and safety that you should consider. Below are just a couple:

RISK	SOLUTION
Danger to audience	If there is any audience interaction (particularly with young or vulnerable people) make sure that you use soft, non-toxic materials.
Danger to puppeteer	With backpack puppets, use light materials, such as willow, rather than metal rods to build the frame, so there is not too much weight on the puppeteer's back. Use secure padded straps to attach the puppet. Ensure puppet doesn't obscure view of puppeteer and that they can clearly see any hazards.

TIP

Write your Statement of Dramatic Intentions with care. You will need to express what you, as a performer or designer, want to show and what you want the audience to understand in terms of characterisation, context, atmosphere and meaning.

Texts in practice: checking your work and avoiding common errors

- [ ] Have you allowed enough time for your work to be completed?
- [ ] Have you taken into account the equipment and skills available to you to complete your design/performance?
- [ ] Have you considered any health and safety implications?
- [ ] Have you displayed a range of skills? (For example, if you have only created a single costume of a black leotard or a set that consists of one chair, it will be difficult to demonstrate a range of skills.)
- [ ] Have you used your skills precisely and in a highly effective way? (For example, are the sound cues accurate and at the appropriate volume? Does the costume fit? If there is group movement are you on time and precise?)
- [ ] Is your interpretation appropriate for the play as a whole? (For example, if the play is a non-naturalistic play in which frightening things happen, does your music help show that or have you just inserted popular songs you like?)
- [ ] Is your interpretation sensitive to the context of the piece? (For example, if it is set in a certain period do your costumes and music reflect that? If the scene takes place on a moonlit field, does your lighting help to convey that?)
- [ ] Are your artistic intentions entirely achieved? (Have you completed what you said you would or is the work incomplete or entirely different? For example, if you said you would create a beautiful backpack dragon puppet, have you instead made a glove puppet?)

WHAT HAVE I LEARNED?

TWO EXTRACTS
- Each can be
  - Monologue
  - Duologue
  - Group (up to six performers)

CHOICE OF SPECIALISMS
- Performer
- Lighting
- Designer
- Sound designer
- Set designer
- Puppet designer
- Costume designer

ASSESSED ON
- Personal interpretation appropriate to play as a whole
- Range of skills
- Skills used precisely and effectively
- Artistic intentions achieved
- Personal interpretation sensitive to context

WORKING WITH A SCRIPT
- Naturalistic?
- Minimalistic?
- Fantasy
- Abstract?
- Stylised?
- Period?

TIP

Check that you understand the demands of the script and that your artistic intentions are clear.

CHECK YOUR LEARNING

If you are uncertain of the meaning of any of the terms above, go back and revise.

Why not use the downloadable version of this summary as a basis for your own checklist of what you have learned from Samples & Downloads at www.illuminatepublishing.com.

GLOSSARY OF KEY TERMS

Abstract: not realistic or life-like, but instead using colours, shapes, textures, sounds and other means to achieve an effect.

Accent: a way of pronouncing words that is associated with a particular country, region or social class. This includes foreign accents, such as American or German.

Ad-libbing: saying lines that aren't in the script.

Amplification: how sound is made louder.

Analyse: to examine something, perhaps by looking at the different elements of it, and to explain it.

Antimacassar: a cloth, often decorative, placed over the headrest or arms of a chair or sofa to protect the fabric underneath from staining or wear.

Apron: the area of the stage nearest the audience, which projects in front of the curtain.

Archetypal: a typical example of someone or something; associated with an original or mythic quality of someone or something, i.e. 'he was the archetypal businessman' or 'it was the archetypal battle between of good and evil'.

Aside: when a character breaks out of a scene to speak briefly to the audience.

Audience interaction: involving the audience in the play, for example, by bringing them onstage, going into the audience to speak with them or passing them props to hold.

Backdrop: a large painted cloth that serves as scenery, often at the back of the stage.

Beatnik: an anti-establishment youth sub-culture from the 1950s to early 1960s associated with poetry and jazz. Typical clothing included black turtlenecks, striped tops, berets and sunglasses.

Beehive: a hairstyle popular in the 1950s and 1960s for which hair was back-combed into a high cone shape.

Blackout: in lighting, suddenly switching all the lights off.

Blocking: the movements of the actor. These are often written down by the stage manager to ensure that they can be repeated. For example, '*Jo enters and moves DSL* (downstage left)'.

Boater: a stiff, flat-topped straw hat with a ribbon band around its crown.

Bodice: the close-fitting upper part of a dress, from neck to waist.

Bowler: a black hat with a brim and a rounded top.

Box office: those who sell tickets.

Box set: a set with three complete walls, often used in naturalistic set designs, for example to create a believable room.

Bravado: the appearance of boldness or extreme confidence.

Breaking the fourth wall: breaking the imaginary wall between the actors and performers by speaking directly to the audience.

Breeches: knee-length trousers.

Call the cues: announce instructions, for example telling technicians when lighting or sound changes should occur.

Carpet bag: hand luggage made of a carpet-like material.

Chairography: choreographed movements involving chairs.

Characterisation: how the qualities of a character are shown, typically through description, dialogue and actions.

Chemise: a loose-fitting undergarment which resembles a long shirt.

Choral speaking: a group of people speaking together or sharing a speech.

Chronological: showing events in the order in which they occurred.

Clapboards: wooden boards used to cover the outside of buildings.

Clarion: a shrill medieval trumpet.

Comic relief: characters or interludes which provide light moments in contrast to more serious events.

Concept: a unifying idea about the production, such as when it is set or how it will be interpreted and performed.

Conflict: when two or more characters' desires are in opposition (external conflict) or when a character experiences opposing emotions (internal conflict).

Context: the circumstances of the setting of a play, such as the location, period of time or conventions.

Costumes: what the characters wear onstage.

Covering: learning the words and movements for a part that you do not usually perform.

Cross-cutting: alternating between two different scenes.

Cross-fade: fading lights out on one area of the stage while simultaneously bringing them up on another area.

Cues: instructions indicating when a change in lighting should occur.

Cyclorama: a large piece of stretched fabric upon which lights or images can be projected.

Describe: to write what you saw, heard or experienced.

Designer: person responsible for an aspect of the production, such as lighting, costumes, set, sound or puppets.

Devising: a way of creating drama that begins not with writers or a script but is based on the collaborative efforts of a group of people.

Diaphragm: the large muscle that stretches across the bottom of the rib-cage.

Diction: how clearly and precisely words are spoken.

Direct address: speaking directly to the audience.

Director: the person responsible for the overall production of a play including the performances and overseeing the designers.

Double-take: a reaction when a someone looks at something, looks away, then quickly looks at it again in realisation. In comedy, it is used to show that a character did not at first comprehend something, but suddenly does.

Doublet: a close-fitting padded jacket, which may or may not have sleeves.

Drapes: curtains or other hanging fabric.

Dynamic: energetic, forceful.

Dystopian: referring to an imagined world where society is presented in a highly negative light. Writers often create dystopian worlds in order to warn people about present dangers.

End on staging: a staging configuration in which the audience sits along one end of the stage, directly facing it.

Ensemble: an approach to acting involving everyone working together, rather than singling out 'star' performers. It also refers to a group of actors who play many roles in a play or a chorus.

Enunciate: to pronounce or articulate words.

Episodic: a series of loosely connected scenes.

Evaluate: to judge or form an opinion of something, such as explaining what effect was created and how successful it was.

Fade: in lighting, gradually getting lighter or darker.

Fade: in sound, gradually getting quieter or louder.

Fez: a flat-topped, round, brimless hat, worn in some middle-Eastern countries.

Filters: also sometimes called 'gels', sheets of plastic used to alter the colour of stage lighting.

Flat: a piece of scenery mounted on a frame, to represent a wall, for example.

Fly: raising and lowering scenery or other items onto the stage using a system of ropes and pulleys.

Fly space: area above the stage where scenery may be stored and lowered to the stage.

Footlights: lights placed at the front of the stage at the level of the actor's feet, with their light directed upwards.

Formica: a hard, durable plastic laminate used for worktops and cupboard doors.

Fourth wall: an imaginary wall between the audience and the actors giving the impression that the actors are unaware they are being observed.

Front of House: ushers and others who deal with the audience.

Fresnel: a common stage lantern which provides a soft-edged beam of light. It can be used to cover a large area of the stage creating a 'wash' of light'. They often have 'barn doors', which are metal flaps at the side to provide some control of the spillage of light. They are usually fitted with a colour slot in which colour filters can be inserted.

Frock coat: a formal knee-length coat.

Funeral pyre: a wooden structure which is set alight to cremate a body.

Furnishings: furniture on the set, such as chairs, cushions, tables.

Gamine: derived from the French word for 'waif' or 'urchin', the gamine look was popularised by Audrey Hepburn in the 1950s. It is associated with short hair, a slim figure and youthfulness.

Gels: coloured tranparencies used to create different-coloured lighting.

Genre: a category or type of music, art or literature, usually with distinctive features.

Girdle: stretchy undergarment which holds in and shapes the waist, stomach and hips.

Gobos: metal cut-outs that are used on lanterns to project patterns, such as leaves, stars, swirls or waves.

Ground plan: a bird's-eye view of the set showing the scale of the stage and set and where key elements of the design will be located.

Gymslip: a sleeveless knee length dress (pinafore dress), worn over a shirt.

Hills Hoist: a brand of rotary clothes line particularly popular in Australia.

Hose: a garment which tightly covers the legs (similar to thick tights or leggings).

Hot seat: one performer sits in a chair and, in character, answers questions.

House lights: lighting that makes the audience visible.

Iambic pentameter: a line of verse with ten syllables, where the stress falls on the second, fourth, sixth, eighth and tenth beats, forming a 'di-dum' rhythm.

Improvise: to act without a script.

Interpret: to make choices about a play. There may be many possible interpretations.

Interval: a break in a performance for both the performers and the audience. This often occurs between the first and second acts of plays. Some plays have more than one interval and some run without an interval.

Jerkin: a sleeveless jacket, often made of leather.

Kitchen sink drama: a type of realistic drama popular after the Second World War, which depicted the lives of working-class characters. They often showed the difficult domestic situations of the characters and explored important social issues.

Laban: a type of movement analysis created by Rudolf Laban (1879–1958) which influenced modern dance and actors' training.

Lanterns: the equipment used to produce light onstage, such as floods, fresnels or profiles.

LED lights: light-emitting diodes (LEDs) are light sources that have a high light output but use relatively little power.

Lighting plot: a guide to the lighting of a production, including the locations and types of various lighting instruments and a scene-by-scene list of lighting requirements.

Lighting rig: the structure that holds the lighting equipment in the theatre.

Lighting states: the settings and positioning of lighting to create certain lighting conditions, such as a bright afternoon or a moonlit scene.

Linoleum: an inexpensive, durable and easy-to-clean floor covering.

Machinations: plots, conspiracies or schemes.

Mackintosh: a long waterproof raincoat, sometimes with a short cape over the shoulders.

Mandilion: a decorative hip-length cloak, usually worn over one shoulder.

Minimalistic: simple; using few elements; stripped back.

Model box: a three-dimensional scale-model of the set that shows how the real set will look and work.

Morning coat: a single-breasted coat often worn as part of a suit.

Motif: a repeated image, idea or phrase of music.

Motivations: what a character wants or needs in a scene. For example, 'I need to escape' or 'I want you to admire me'. These are sometimes called 'objectives'.

Multimedia: film or other media technology used in a live theatre production.

Mutton chops: facial hair style where long thick sideburns cover the cheeks and may connect to a moustache.

Narration: providing the audience with background information or commentary on the action of the play.

National service: compulsory military training and duties. From 1947 to 1963, healthy men aged 18 or over were required to serve 18 months in the armed services.

Naturalistic: life-like, realistic, believable.

Non-naturalistic: stylised, not realistic.

Objective: what the character wants.

Offstage character: a character who is mentioned in a play, and often influences the action or characters, but is never seen by the audience.

Pea coat: a heavy woollen coat, usually navy blue and mid-thigh length, often worn by sailors.

Performance conventions: techniques used in a particular type of performance, such as soliloquies in Shakespeare or direct address in an epic play.

Petticoats: underskirts used to give fullness to a dress or skirt.

Physical theatre: theatre that emphasises physical movement, such as mime.

Pith helmet: a round, lightweight helmet worn in hot climates.

Playwright: responsible for the writing of the script of the play. This includes the dialogue and stage directions.

Pomade: a waxy, greasy or creamy substance used to style hair. It holds hair in place and adds shine.

Projection: a technique where moving or still images are projected to form a theatrical backdrop.

Promenade: to promenade means 'to walk' and promenade theatre is when the audience stands or follows the actors through the performance.

Prompt book: a master copy of the script, annotated with blocking and technical cues.

Props: small items that actors can carry onstage.

Proscenium arch: a stage configuration particularly popular for larger theatres or opera houses. The proscenium refers to the frame around the stage which emphasises that the whole audience is seeing the same stage picture.

Prose: text without rhythm or rhyme, usually set out in paragraphs.

Prosthetics: make-up that uses moulds and sculptural techniques to create special effects, such as scars or a false nose.

Proximity: the distance between people or objects; how near or far.

Received pronunciation (RP): a way of speaking which is considered the 'standard' form of English pronunciation. It is not specific to a certain location, but, instead, is associated with education and formal speaking.

Register: the vocal range of the voice (upper, middle or lower registers); the variety of tones of voice.

Repressing: holding back or restraining.

Resonance: the quality, strength and depth of sound.

Retrogression: going backwards, often to an earlier time or state.

Reverb: an echoing effect.

Revolve: a large turntable device that can be turned to reveal a different setting.

Rig: what the lights are positioned on (a lighting rig) or 'to rig the lights' is to set them in position.

Sari: an Indian garment of wrapped and draped fabric.

Satirical: a humourous way of criticising behaviour by mocking it.

Scribe: someone who writes documents.

Sets: items put onstage such as furniture or backdrops to create the world of the play; sometimes called scenery. There may also be props, which are objects used onstage.

Set dressings: items on the set not actually used as props, but that create detail and interest in it, such as vases or framed paintings on a wall.

Sightline: the audience's view of the stage.

Silhouette: the outline or shape created by a costume on a figure.

Site specific: a performance in a location, such as a warehouse or a park, which is not a conventional theatre. The space has often been adapted to suit the production.

Snap: quickly on or off.

Soliloquy: a speech when a character is alone onstage.

Sonnet: a 14-line poem with a formal rhyme scheme.

Sound plot: a list of the sound effects or music needed and sound equipment that will be used. This is usually organised scene-by-scene and contains information such as cues and volume.

Soundscape: a collection of sounds that create a setting or suggest a scene, or a drama technique where performers use their voices (and sometimes other items) to create sounds.

Special effects: lighting and sounds that are not 'usual' for the scene or production, such as lighting to recreate headlights or fires and the sounds of thunder or gunfire.

Spotlight: a lamp projecting a narrow intense beam of light directly onto a performer or area of the stage.

Stage business: the small movements an actor might do onstage, such as opening a book, brushing hair or straightening cushions. These may add to the naturalism of a scene or provide insight into the characters.

Stage manager: the person responsible for the backstage elements of the production, such as calling cues and checking props.

Staging configuration: the type of stage and audience arrangement.

Still image: a frozen moment showing the facial expressions and physical positions, including posture and gesture, of one or more characters.

Stimulus: a resource in drama used to start a creative process by providing context, inspiration or focus.

Stock characters: easily recognised, stereotypical characters.

Stock gestures: stereotypical gestures to signal certain emotions, such as shaking a fist to show anger.

Strobe: a lamp that produces rapid flashes of bright light.

Style: the way in which something is written or performed, such as the use of realistic dialogue or choreographed movement.

Stylised: non-realistic, done in a particular manner, perhaps emphasising one element.

Sub-plot: a secondary or less important plot in a story.

Subtext: the unspoken meaning, feelings and thoughts 'beneath' the lines, which may be shown in the characters' body language, tone of voice and facial expressions, for example, although not explicitly stated in the text.

Subliminally: so that it barely registers; the audience is affected without consciously being aware of what is affecting them.

Suttee: an ancient Hindu custom where a devoted wife was expected to kill herself when her husband died, usually by throwing herself on his funeral pyre.

Swing coat: a coat which is fitted at the shoulders but wide and flowing at the bottom.

Symbolic: using something that represents something else. Examples of symbolic design might be characters dressed in white to symbolise their purity or a set resembling a boxing ring to symbolise the conflict between the characters.

Technical rehearsal: a rehearsal which is used to make sure that all technical elements such as lighting, sound and set changes are operating correctly.

Tension: a sense of anticipation or anxiety.

Theatre in the round: a stage configuration when the audience is seated around all sides of the stage.

Theatrical metaphor: when comparisons and symbols are used to suggest meaning. For example, a set design which resembles a head might suggest that all the action is a characters' thoughts or dreams.

Thought-tracking: speaking aloud the thoughts of the character.

Thrust: a stage configuration in which the stage protrudes into the auditorium with the audience on three sides.

Top hat: a high crowned hat with a flat top, associated with formal wear.

Tragedy: a play involving the downfall of its lead character leading to an unhappy ending.

Transitions: moving from one lighting state to another, such as a fade to darkness or a sudden blackout.

Traverse: a stage configuration is when the acting takes place on a long central area with the audience seated on either side facing each other.

Trim: in sewing, this refers to any extra decoration such as ribbons, thread, lace, tassels, braid and cord.

Truck: a platform on wheels upon which scenery can be mounted and moved.

Valet: a gentleman's personal servant who is usually responsible for his clothes and grooming.

Verbatim: using exactly the same words as were used originally.

Verse: text arranged in lines, often with a regular rhythm.

Viol: a Renaissance stringed instrument, similar to a violin.

Visual: a cue that the technician must judge by watching the action onstage.

Ward: someone, usually a young person, who has a guardian or other legal authority responsible for them.

Waspies: corsets, shaped like a wide belt, worn from hip to under the bust, which cinch in the waist.

Whist: a card came for four players, popular in the 18th and 19th centuries.

Wing spaces: areas to the side of the stage. This is the area where actors, unseen by the audience, wait to enter and where props and set pieces may be stored.

INDEX